Spanish

Without the Fuss

Want to take your Spanish further?

Living Language® makes it easy with a wide range of programs that will suit your particular needs.

ADVANCED SPANISH

ISBN: 0-609-60487-2 • $29.95/C$42.00

The perfect follow-up to *Spanish Without the Fuss—Advanced Spanish* will help you master the art of Spanish conversation. The program teaches advanced vocabulary, idiomatic expressions, and grammar while introducing you to the finer points of Spanish culture. There are 20 lessons on four 60-minute cassettes, plus a 352-page coursebook.

Also available in French. Coursebooks are also sold separately for $6.95/C$9.50.

SKILL BUILDER: SPANISH VERBS

ISBN: 0-609-60444-9 • $29.95/C$42.00

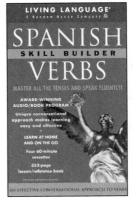

An award-winning program that will help you master verbs—the key to fluency. This is not just a book full of verb charts, but a program that teaches you how to <u>USE</u> verbs. There's also a handy grammar summary for easy reference. There are 40 lessons on four 60-minute cassettes, plus a 352-page coursebook.

Also available in French, Italian, and German.
Coursebooks are also sold separately for $6.95/C$9.50.

THE FEARLESS INTERNATIONAL FOODIE CONQUERS THE CUISINE OF FRANCE, ITALY, SPAIN & LATIN AMERICA

ISBN: 0-609-81113-4 • $11.00/C$17.00

The ultimate guide to help you conquer the fine art of international dining, whether abroad or in your own neighborhood! Each section begins with an overview of the cuisine followed by typical ingredients and dishes, from appetizers through desserts. There is an easy-to-follow pronunciation key, loads of fascinating culture notes, and a helpful glossary on spices, sauces, and more!

Also available: *The Fearless International Foodie Conquers Pan-Asian Cuisine*

AVAILABLE AT YOUR LOCAL BOOKSTORE OR BY CALLING 1-800-726-0600

For a complete list of Living Language titles, please visit our Web site at

www.livinglanguage.com

Spanish

Without the Fuss

BY

Pilar Munday, Ph.D.

EDITED BY Zvjezdana Vrzić, Ph.D.

LIVING LANGUAGE®
A Random House Company

Published by Living Language, A Random House Company, New York, New York.
Living Language is a member of the Random House Information Group.

Random House, Inc. New York, Toronto, London, Sydney, Auckland

www.livinglanguage.com

Manufactured in the United States of America.

Book design by Barbara M. Bachman

Illustrations by Norman Bendell

ISBN 0-609-81063-4

10 9 8 7 6 5 4 3 2 1

FIRST EDITION

PUBLISHER'S ACKNOWLEDGMENTS

Special thanks to the Living Language team:

Lisa Alpert, Elizabeth Bennett, Christopher Warnasch, Suzanne McQuade, Helen Tang,

Mary Lee, Denise DeGennaro, Linda Schmidt, Marina Padakis, Pat Ehresmann,

Lisa Abelman, Fernando Galeano, Sophie Chin, and Barbara M. Bachman.

Special thanks also to the reviewers, Marisa C. Cid and Juan J. Caicedo.

AUTHOR'S ACKNOWLEDGMENTS

Special thanks to: Jill Kovacs, Enriqueta Jiménez, Alfonso Sánchez,

Enriqueta Carrillo de Albornoz, and Naira Azpiri.

Also many thanks to Marisa Castro Cid, the reviewer, and to

Ana Stojanović for her help with the introduction.

Finally, I am indebted to my editor, Zvjezdana Vrzić,

for her advice and help with this project.

CONTENTS

WHAT'S GOING ON IN THE DIALOGUES	WHAT WORDS YOU'LL LEARN	WHAT STRUCTURES YOU'LL KNOW
Lesson 1: NOTHING IS IMPOSSIBLE • 15 (In Spain)		
Peter arrives in Madrid.	• **To the Hotel Princesa, please!:** Speaking Spanish after you land	• **Me, myself, and I:** Personal pronouns (*I, you, he, she, it,* etc.) • **To be or not to be:** The verb *ser* (to be) • **What's the difference?:** Cognates
Lesson 2: SHE IS • 27 (In Spain)		
Peter starts meeting people at the *pensión.*	• **Saying hello** • **How are you doing?** • **Hello, my name is . . . :** Introducing yourself and others • **Saying good-bye**	• **To be or not to be, Part II:** The verb *estar* (to be) • **(In)definitely so:** Definite and indefinite articles • **Let's talk about sex . . . and number:** Gender and number of nouns • **The countdown:** Counting from 0 to 19 • **There is this and there is that:** Using *there is* and *there are* in Spanish

WHAT'S GOING ON IN THE DIALOGUES	WHAT WORDS YOU'LL LEARN	WHAT STRUCTURES YOU'LL KNOW

viii

CONTENTS

WHAT'S GOING ON IN THE DIALOGUES	WHAT WORDS YOU'LL LEARN	WHAT STRUCTURES YOU'LL KNOW

WHAT'S GOING ON IN THE DIALOGUES	WHAT WORDS YOU'LL LEARN	WHAT STRUCTURES YOU'LL KNOW

WHAT'S GOING ON IN THE DIALOGUES	WHAT WORDS YOU'LL LEARN	WHAT STRUCTURES YOU'LL KNOW

WHAT'S GOING ON IN THE DIALOGUES	WHAT WORDS YOU'LL LEARN	WHAT STRUCTURES YOU'LL KNOW

WHAT'S GOING ON IN THE DIALOGUES	WHAT WORDS YOU'LL LEARN	WHAT STRUCTURES YOU'LL KNOW

Lesson 18: TELL ME THAT YOU LOVE ME • 267 (In Argentina)

Peter gets a taste of Buenos Aires nightlife and . . . meat.	• **What's on the menu?:** Learn some important food vocabulary • **Talk about fun:** Some vocabulary for a great evening	• **Listen!:** Giving orders • **Give it to me!:** Commands including pronouns • **I want you to do it!:** Saying what you want using *querer* (to want)

Lesson 19: I MISS YOU, I FORGET YOU, I LOVE YOU • 283 (In the United States)

Peter is back in New York looking for a place to live.	• **Home sweet home:** Rooms and things that make a home • **Same old, same old:** Daily activities and paying the bills	• **To whom it may concern:** Using *who, that, which,* etc., to connect nouns and sentences • **The good, the bad, and . . . the best:** Saying that something is the best or the worst • **Hold it for me, please:** Putting different pronouns together

Lesson 20: I WILL CONQUER YOU • 299 (In the United States)

Carmen visits Peter in New York, and this is just a beginning of a lasting relationship . . .	• **Let me suggest . . . :** Making suggestions using *vamos + a* • **Great idea!:** How to accept (or reject) suggestions • **Things change:** Talking about change using *ponerse* (to get; to turn), *hacerse* (to become), and *volverse* (to become)	• **Let's do it!:** Commands with *nosotros* (we; us) • **I scream, you scream . . . :** Verbs that change meaning in the preterite and imperfect tenses • **I've just done that:** Using *acabar* (to finish) to talk about what you've just done

Spanish

Without the Fuss

WELCOME!

So you want to learn some _español?_ But you don't want to do it by just memorizing long verb charts or ever-handy stock phrases like "Jeeves, please serve the mutton to the ambassador at eight." If that's the case, then you've come to the right place! _Bienvenidos!_ Welcome!

Spanish Without the Fuss will help you learn as quickly and easily as possible, and the best part is—you'll have fun along the way. You'll have a chance to hear real talk, the kind you might actually hear on the street and not just read in textbooks. And you won't need a crash course in grammar jargon before you start. We've made this book as accessible and user-friendly as possible. Of course, this doesn't mean you'll just wake up one morning fluent in Spanish. The bad news is: you **will** have to do some work, but the good news is: it **won't** be dry and boring. That, you can count on.

So, what's _Spanish Without the Fuss_ all about? Well, you'll start off with an introduction to the sounds and spelling of the language. Spanish is easy that way—what you see is pretty much what you get—so you should be able to start speaking and reading right off the bat. Then we really get down to business with 20 lessons, and an hour-long audio CD to give you plenty of listening and speaking practice. There are appendices, too, for quick reference if you get stuck, and a two-way glossary where you can look up any word in the book.

To make things easy, all the chapters have the same structure, and it's not just any structure—it's been specially designed to help you learn most effectively. Yes, we have the technology! Here's the basic layout of each chapter:

COMING UP ...
Get a quick overview of what you'll learn in the lesson.

LOOKING AHEAD
Get ready to listen to the chapter's dialogues and get some advance tips to help you follow along.

LET'S WARM UP
Think ahead about the topic of the dialogue and learn a few new words so you can get more out of it.

HEAR . . . SAY
Listen to a dialogue, try to understand as much as you can, then **read along** and **learn to speak** by repeating the phrases from the audio CD.

HOW'S THAT AGAIN?
Make sure you got the gist of the dialogue.

WORKSHOP
Discover the secrets of the Spanish language; learn about its words and structure.

THE NITTY-GRITTY
Overcome your fear of grammar with simple grammar explanations and plenty of practice.

WORDS TO LIVE BY
Stock up on new words and phrases and get to use them, too.

TAKE IT FOR A SPIN
Practice makes perfect! Try out all the good stuff you've just learned.

LET'S PUT IT IN WRITING
Read all about it! Texts help you learn to maneuver through the written word.

TAKE IT UP A NOTCH
Challenge yourself with additional practice that'll really make you think!

STRUT YOUR STUFF!
Put it all together and review what you've learned with more practice.

CRIB NOTES
Get answers to all your questions, and check the translations of the dialogues.

But that's not all! You'll also get loads of good stuff that will spice up your learning, teach you how best to learn a new language, what pitfalls to avoid, and tell you about the culture and habits of the place. All at no extra cost!

TAKE A TIP FROM ME!
Be smart and get the most out of your efforts—you'll get tips on how to study, short-cuts, and memory tricks.

HEADS UP!
Watch for the pitfalls and common mistakes typically made by new learners!

THE FINE PRINT
Get ambitious and learn more subtle details about grammar or vocabulary.

WORD ON THE STREET
Talk like a native Spanish speaker: learn common expressions, idioms, and even slang terms, so you won't sound like an out-of-date textbook.

DID YOU KNOW?

Get in the know by learning about Spanish-speaking countries, their culture and the everyday life of their people. That's a great way to start not just talking like a native speaker, but feeling like one, too. In case your geography is a bit rusty, we enclose the country maps so you can travel around while sitting at your desk.

That's it! You're ready to start. Good luck, or as we say in Spanish . . . *¡Buena suerte!*

GETTING STARTED IN SPANISH

BEFORE WE BEGIN . . .

So you **really** want to learn some *español?* *¡Qué bien!* How great! Are you are planning a trip to one of the many beautiful Spanish-speaking countries? Working with a Spanish-speaking colleague? Maybe you want to brush up on what you learned in high school? Or perhaps you simply want to exercise a different part of your brain? Whatever your motivations, *¡Felicitaciones!* Congratulations! I hope you'll enjoy studying with me. I know you're in for some fun.

Before we start our first lesson, let's talk a little about language learning in general. The first thing you need to know is: **you already know more than you think!** You don't believe me? Check out some of these words: *banana, idea, gala, hotel, taco, radio.* Okay. So, what's the big deal, right? You already know English! Well, as it turns out, this means that you also already know some Spanish. These words are exactly the same and have the same meaning in both languages. They're just pronounced a little differently. There are also many words that look slightly different, but that you should be able to recognize pretty easily. Take a look:

SPANISH	ENGLISH	SPANISH	ENGLISH
centro	center	*profesión*	profession
museo	museum	*profesor*	professor
difícil	difficult	*aire*	air
diferente	different	*agente*	agent
elegante	elegant	*idiota*	idiot
posible	possible	*inteligente*	inteligent

Many English words have Latin roots, and Spanish came from Latin. Yeah, so? Well, that's the reason you'll be able to recognize many Spanish words without really "learning" them. But Spanish and English don't have just word roots in common. They also share similar word endings. Take a look:

SOME WORD ENDINGS ENGLISH AND SPANISH HAVE IN COMMON		
SPANISH	ENGLISH	AS IN . . .
–ción	–tion	*conversación* = conversation
		información = information
–sión	–sion	*profesión* = profession
		pensión = pension

SPANISH	ENGLISH	AS IN . . .
–ente/–ante	*–ent/–ant*	*diferente* = different *elegante* = elegant *importante* = important
–al	*–al*	*general* = general *ideal* = ideal *normal* = normal
–able/–ible	*–ible*	*posible* = possible *responsable* = responsible
–dad	*–ty*	*realidad* = reality *universidad* = university *ciudad* = city

So, you get the idea. And if you're feeling confident now, just wait! There's a lot more to *comunicación* (communication, of course) than just words and grammar. It's amazing how much you can glean from a conversation just by watching facial expressions and body language. Try this sometime: Watch a movie or a sitcom and mute the sound. You'll be surprised by how much you'll be in tune with what's going on, even without hearing a single word.

And then there's *la cultura* (you guessed it!). Communication happens in context, and the more you know about the daily life and the rich history of Spanish-speaking countries the more easily you'll be able to read between the lines, get the point, and get your own message across. And don't worry, you're not on your own here—there'll be plenty of cultural tidbits and information to help you impress (or fool!) even the most discerning locals.

Okay, so now that your head is probably bigger than your doorway and you're wondering why you need to study Spanish in the first place, let's get serious for a moment. The truth is (you might want to sit down for this) that despite how much you already know, you still have to learn and study. That's the bad news . . . unless you're a little on the nerdy side, like I am, and you actually get excited when you hear words like *learn* and *study* (*estudiar* in Spanish, by the way, but you already know that!). The good news is that, as with everything else, I'll be there to help, not just by telling you **what** you need to know, but also by giving you some tips on **how** best to learn Spanish and how to make it easier.

Here comes my first tip: Pace yourself. Try to come up with a working schedule and set some goals. Ideally, you should spend a little bit of time on your Spanish every day—30 minutes a day will probably take you a lot farther than two hours in one sitting a couple of times a week. But if you can't manage to find time every day, don't despair, just try to work at it regularly, and grab a free moment here and there to remind yourself of what you've learned. Take advantage of your free time—maybe you can rent a movie in Spanish on movie night or pop in the latest Enrique Iglesias CD while you're cooking dinner. You should try to get as great and as varied an exposure to the language as possible. Words and expressions have a way of just creeping into your memory. And of course, the most important thing is to have fun.

¡Comencemos! Let's get started! Let's talk about Spanish pronunciation.

SOUNDING IT OUT IN SPANISH

When it comes to Spanish pronunciation, you're in luck, because what you see is pretty much what you get. What I mean is that, unlike English, with its seemingly endless pronunciation rules, which are forever being broken, Spanish pronunciation rules are simple and straightforward. Spanish words sound pretty much the way they look—their spelling is virtually phonetic. As long you remember a few simple rules, you should start sounding like a Spanish speaker in no time!

OOHS AND *AAHS*: SPANISH VOWELS

One of the easiest ways for a Spanish-speaking person to spot an American is by the way English-speaking people pronounce Spanish vowels. First, Spanish vowels are always pronounced—there's no such thing as a "silent *e*" in Spanish. Second, they're always pronounced the same way. An *a* always sounds like "ah" in *father*, *e* always sounds like "eh" in *get*, *i* is always pronounced "ee" as in *feet*, *o* is "oh" as in *ball*, and *u* is always "oo," as in, "Isn't this *cool*?" How simple is that? Finally—and this is where an American accent tends to show up the most—Spanish vowels are more crisp than English vowels. The Fonz is not cool in Spanish! Don't turn your "eh" into an "eh-eeeee." Short and sweet. That's the rule.

SPANISH VOWEL SOUNDS		
LETTER	SOUND	AS IN . . .
a	ah	*banco* (BAHN-koh), bank
e	eh	*elegante* (eh-leh-GAHN-teh), elegant
i	ee	*idea* (ee-DEH-ah), idea
o	oh	*doctor* (dohk-TOHR), doctor
u	oo	*tú* (too), you

Note that throughout the book, pronunciations will be placed in parentheses; the stressed syllable is in capital letters.

Take a Tip from Me!

When you first begin to speak, do some warm-up exercises to loosen up your mouth. Say all of the vowels in order (a-e-i-o-u), going from one vowel right into the next, and

Okay, so now that we have our *oos* and *ahs* in order, what happens when you have two vowels in a row? Sometimes, you get a diphthong. "Oy, vey! What's a diphthong?", you ask. Don't worry, it's not a strange disease; in fact, you just pronounced two of them: *ohy* and *vehy*. A diphthong is two vowels pronounced together as a single sound. While each vowel in a vowel combination is pronounced, they flow naturally into one another, forming a diphthong. Try your hand at these common combinations:

COMMON VOWEL COMBINATIONS

VOWEL COMBINATION	PRONOUNCED	AS IN . . .
ai/ay	*ahy*	*baile* (BAHY-leh), dance
au	*ow*	*auto* (OW-toh), car
ei	*ay*	*peine* (PAY-neh), comb
eu	*ehw*	*deuda* (DEHW-dah), debt
ia	*yah*	*gracias* (GRAH-syahs), thanks
ie	*yeh*	*siempre* (SYEHM-preh), always
io	*yoh*	*adiós* (ah-DYOHS), good-bye
iu	*yoo*	*ciudad* (syoo-DAHD), city
oi/oy	*oy*	*hoy* (OY), today
ua	*wah*	*cuando* (KWAHN-doh), when
ue	*weh*	*bueno* (BWEH-noh), good
ui/uy	*wee*	*muy* (mwee), very

Sometimes, you will find the *i* in an *ia* combination or and the *u* in an *au* combination accented, as in *ía* or *aú*, in which case each vowel is pronounced separately, as in *María* (mah-REE-ah) or *baúl* (bah-OOL), "trunk." In fact, there are vowel combinations where each vowel is **always** individually pronounced, as in *maestro* (mah-EH-stroh), "master," *poeta* (poh-EH-tah), "poet," or *leo* (LEH-oh), "I read."

    ¡Dios mío! (dyohs MEE-oh), Oh my goodness!, you say? There's more . . .

RRRRRRRRROLL THOSE *R*'S: SPANISH CONSONANTS

The good news with Spanish consonants is that most of them sound just like they do in English. A *p* is a "p," a *t* is a "t." No problem there! But here, too, there are a few important rules to remember. Let's review them.

We're on a Rrroll!

You've heard it. Those Spanish-speaking people sure can roll their *r*'s. How about you? Well, it does take some practice, but I know you can do it. In fact, you probably, at some time in your life, have made this sound. Did you ever play with cars when you were three or four? What sound did you pretend the cars made as you drove them? That's right! *Vrrrrrooom! Vrrrrrrrrooom!* It's a lot like that, but with more *r* than *v*. In other words, roll from the roof of your mouth instead of your lips. Well, that's what two *r*'s together sound like. By the way, this sound, spelled as double *rr*, is actually considered a separate letter of the alphabet. Different, huh? A single *r* at the beginning of a word or after the letter *n*, *s*, or *l* is pronounced just like the double *rr*. Here are some words to get you started:

carro (**KAH-rroh**)	car
perro (**PEH-rroh**)	dog
corro (**KOH-rroh**)	I run
radio (**RRAH-dyoh**)	radio
alrededor (**ahl-rreh-deh-DOHR**)	around
Enrique (**ehn-RREE-keh**)	Henry

But Don't Roll All of Them!

A single *r* within a Spanish word doesn't get rolled (except when at the beginning of a word or following *n*, *s*, or *l* as we saw in the previous section). It sounds softer and actually a lot like the American English *dd* in "udder," or *tt* in "butter." The difference between *r* and *rr* is important. Look at the examples below. These three words look almost like *carro*, *perro*, and *corro* you've seen above, except for the difference between *rr* and *r*, but check out their meanings. Pretty different, huh?

caro (**KAH-roh**)	expensive
pero (**PEH-roh**)	but
coro (**KOH-roh**)	choir

As Spanish as an Ñ (Ehnyeh)

This letter looks more difficult than the sound it represents. It is pronounced a lot like the sound you make when you say "onion," except that the the *n* and *i* combine without a pause to form one sound. Let's practice:

señor (seh-NYOHR)	Mr.
señora (seh-NYOH-rah)	Mrs.
señorita (seh-nyoh-REE-tah)	Miss
español (ehs-pah-NYOHL)	Spanish; Spaniard

More Spelling Tricks

A few letters are pronounced differently, depending on the letters that come after them. Similar to English, the letters *c* and *g* have both a "hard" and a "soft" pronunciation:

- *C* is pronounced "hard" like the *c* in *car*, unless it's followed by an *e* or *i*, in which case it's pronounced "soft" like the *c* in *cent* or *cinnamon*. (In Spain, *c* followed by *i* or *e* is pronounced like a *th* in *thick*.)
- *G* is pronounced "hard" like the *g* in *gold*, unless it's followed by an *e* or *i*, in which case it's pronounced "soft" like the *h* in *hello*.

Heads Up!

The combinations *qu* and *gu* are pronounced as hard "k" and "g" respectively, and the *u* isn't pronounced at all: e.g., *quince* (KEEN-seh), "fifteen," or *guerra* (GEH-rrah), "war." *U* is pronounced only if it has an umlaut over it, like this—*ü*: e.g., *güero* (GWEH-roh) "fair."

Let's practice:

cosa (KOH-sah)	thing
café (kah-FEH)	coffee
centro (SEHN-troh)	center
cine (SEE-neh)	cinema
qué (keh)	what

quién (kyehn)	who	
gorro (GOH-rroh)	hat	
gusto (GOOS-toh)	taste	
giro (HEE-roh)	tour	
geráneo (heh-RAH-neh-oh)	geranium	
guitarra (gee-TAH-rrah)	guitar	
guerra (GEH-rrah)	war	

- *Y* has two pronunciations. It will sound like an English *y* in *yes* if it is followed by a vowel, otherwise it sounds just like *ee*:

payaso (pah-YAH-soh)	clown
muy (mwee)	very

- The letter *h* is always silent in Spanish.

hotel (oh-TEHL)	hotel
hola (OH-lah)	hello

- The letter *v* is always pronounced just like a *b*.

vaca (BAH-kah)	cow
vino (BEE-noh)	wine

- The letter *j* is pronounced like "h" in *hello*.

José (hoh-SEH)	Joseph
rojo (RROH-hoh)	red

- The letters *ll* are pronounced like "y" in *yes*.

llover (yoh-BEHR)	to rain
calle (KAH-yeh)	street

- The letter *z* is pronounced like "s" in *send*.

zapato (sah-PAH-toh)   shoe

Okay, so we've talked about the individual sounds that make up the Spanish language, but now, let's tackle how those sounds are combined to form words.

The Fine Print

One final note about consonants. When the letters *b*, *d*, and *g* (when it is a "hard" *g*, as I described earlier) appear between vowels, their pronunciation is a bit softer than the corresponding American *b* and *d* and "hard" *g*. You can achieve this by pushing out extra air as you say the sounds. This rule is for extra-nerdy students, so take it or leave it, as you please!

CAN YOU HANDLE STRESS?

Word stress, that is. Of course you can . . . Spanish words are stressed on the second to last syllable, as in *fortuna* (fohr-TOO-nah), *idea* (ee-DEH-ah), *persona* (pehr-SOH-nah), except when they end in *d, l,* or *r*. In that case, the stress is on the last syllable, as in *normal* (nohr-MAHL), "regular; normal," *edad* (eh-DAHD), "age," or *favor* (fah-VOHR).

Some words do not follow either of these two rules. But don't worry, whenever that happens, the vowel of the stressed syllable will have an accent mark, as in *información* (een-fohr-mah-SYOHN), "information." It's really quite *fácil* (FAH-seel), "easy," don't you think? This is to say that you shouldn't worry about this too much. Even if you get the stress wrong, or mispronounce something, you'll probably be easily understood, and that should be your main goal in learning any language. I've said my piece and now we can move on and get down to business.

¡Adelante! Let's go! Lesson 1 awaits . . .

1.

NOTHING IS IMPOSSIBLE

Nada es imposible

Do you mind if I smoke?

COMING UP...

- *To the Hotel Princesa, please!:* Speaking Spanish after you land
- *Me, myself, and I:* Personal pronouns (*I, you, he, she, it,* etc.)
- *To be or not to be:* The verb *ser* (to be)
- *What's the difference?:* Cognates

¡Hola! ¿Qué tal? (Hi! What's up?) That's how people greet each other in Spanish-speaking countries. In this lesson, we are going to start our travels around the Spanish-speaking world together. *¿Estás preparado?* (Are you ready?) Let's go!

Peter Winthrop will be our guide through the Spanish-speaking world. He is a cool dude, or so he thinks. He majored in Spanish in college and spent a year in Spain, which has now helped him land a job as a photojournalist for *La Gente*, a Spanish-language magazine about famous people. But language skills alone are not enough. In order to communicate effectively, we need to get in the know—learn about the cultures and about how language is used from one Spanish-speaking country to another. Sometimes, Peter will discover this the hard way. He will learn that verb endings, object pronouns, and all that heavy-duty grammar stuff is useful up to a point. You, on the other hand, are lucky! You will learn about the language and the culture **at the same time**, while having fun all the way.

So, I'll say it again: *¿Estás preparado? ¿Sí?*, then, here we go!!

But . . . *¡¡Un momento, por favor!!* You say: Who is this person speaking? Yes, you already know about Peter, but you don't know anything about me. Well, I am your personal language coach and maybe, even a friend (*amiga*, by the way). In each lesson, I will jump in whenever I find it necessary to explain something. I will also tell you about the daily life of people like you in the Spanish-speaking countries we will be visiting. By doing so, you will feel like you are actually there, meeting real native speakers. I hope you have fun with the Spanish language and develop a lifelong interest in the Spanish-speaking world. Lofty goals, I know, but I like to aim high. And I have a feeling you do, too.

So, for the third time I ask: *¿Estás preparado? ¿Sí?*, then, here we go!!

Take a Tip from Me!

In the first dialogue, our friend Peter arrives in Madrid, Spain. The scene starts at the airport, where he grabs a cab to take him to the city.

This is the first dialogue you will hear. First, I recommend you listen to it a few times, without looking at the text, to see if you can already grasp some of the meaning. Remember, it is very important to learn how to listen to a foreign language *even if you don't understand much of what is being said* at first. Although this may sound strange, you need to learn how to listen to "gibberish" (because Spanish may sound like gibberish to you in the beginning) without disconnecting completely. Use your imagination constantly, and don't be afraid to guess. More often than you think, you will be right. And don't worry if it takes time for you to start speaking Spanish; it is natural for listening and understanding to come first.

So, listen to the dialogue two or three times. Use what you already know when trying to guess the meaning. In this case, you already know that Peter is taking a taxi to downtown Madrid. How do you know that? Because you have read the first sentence of this section. (Am I being tricky? I don't think so. Just keeping tabs on your progress.)

You also know that in a taxi, in any country, one of the first things said is the destination where the client wants to go.

If you wish, the last time you listen to the dialogue, you can also follow the text. It is important to always keep in mind that you do not need to understand every single word of a dialogue; just enough of them to get the gist of the story.

Take a Tip from Me!

HEAR ... SAY

Peter:	¡Taxi!
Taxista:	¿Sí?
Peter:	Al Hotel Princesa, por favor.
Taxista:	Muy bien, señor. ¿Es usted inglés?
Peter:	No. No soy inglés. Soy estadounidense.
Taxista:	¡Hombre! Un americano. ¿De dónde? ¿De Hollywood?
Peter:	*(chuckling)* No, no. Soy de Nueva York. Y usted ¿es de Madrid?
Taxista:	Sí. Soy de Madrid, pero mi familia es de Granada. ¿Quiere un cigarrillo?
Peter:	¿Un cigarrillo? ¡Yo no soy fumador!
Taxista:	Bueno, yo sí. ¿Le importa si fumo?
Peter:	*(not believing his ears)* ¿Aquí? ¿En el taxi? ¡Es increíble! ¡Qué horror!
Taxista:	Así es la vida en España, señor.

ACTIVITY 1:   **HOW'S THAT AGAIN?**

Let's see if you can now answer all these "where" questions! (In Spanish, *where?* is *¿dónde?*) For now, I'll let you answer in English:

1. Where is Peter going?
2. Where is Peter from?
3. Where is the taxi driver from?
4. Where is the taxi driver's family from?
5. What does the taxi driver ask that's so shocking to Peter?

You can now check your answers in the Crib Notes section at the end of the chapter. You can also read the translation of the dialogue, found in the same place. Remember, though, not to go crazy over every single word. If you were able to answer the previous questions (in English), then you got the gist of the story and that's more than enough for now. If you couldn't answer all of them, don't despair! Go back to the dialogue and, now that you've read the English translation, read it and listen to it again. This time, it will make more sense and you'll be able to answer the questions without a problem. Remember, the more you practice the better, and *poco a poco* (little by little), you'll speak as fast as the native speakers do.

Did You Know?

Although what happened to Peter in the cab is not really common, even in Spain, the truth is that smoking is still much more common in Spain (as in most of Europe) than in the United States. It is sometimes shocking for people from the United States that even in public spaces (such as a cab, a bus, or a train), smoking is not only allowed, but widely accepted. Most of the time, if you let Spaniards know politely that smoke bothers you, they (just like the taxicab driver in the dialogue) will not smoke in front of you. But don't be surprised if they tell you that one has to die of something, and they choose to die of cigarette smoke (which usually means "Mind your own business!").

Did You Know?

By the way, if you want to check out a really cool Spanish taxi driver, you can rent Pedro Almodóvar's movie *Mujeres al borde de un ataque de nervios* (*Women on the Verge of a Nervous Breakdown*). This guy has a cab that looks (and feels) more like a convenience store. Don't miss out on the cab interior! That's what I call classy! (*¡Qué estilazo!*)

WORKSHOP

THE NITTY-GRITTY

Now let's roll up the sleeves and work on the grammar that you are learning in this lesson. Yes, it's the g-word, but don't get scared away. I'll make it nice and simple for you.

ME, MYSELF, AND I: PERSONAL PRONOUNS (I, YOU, HE, SHE, IT, ETC.)

Sometimes you don't need to call people or things by their proper names, right? Well, that's when you can use personal pronouns, like *he*, *she*, *it*, or *they*. The subject pronouns are those pronouns that stand for a subject of a sentence, i.e., *he*, *she*, or *it* is performing the action. Here they are in Spanish:

SUBJECT PRONOUNS	
yo	I
tú	you (informal)
usted (Ud.)	you (formal)
él	he
ella	she
nosotros (masc.), *nosotras* (fem.)	we
vosotros (masc.), *vosotras* (fem.)	you all (informal)
ustedes (Uds.)	you all (formal)
ellos (masc.), *ellas* (fem.)	they

Let's now review the differences between Spanish and English with respect to the use of subject pronouns. These are:

• In *español*, there are two versions of the *you* form, both in the singular and the plural. You use the formal *usted* (you) and *ustedes* (you all) when you talk to people who are older than you (e.g., your friend Susan's great-grandmother), more powerful than you (e.g., your boss) or not familiar to you (e.g., a receptionist in a hotel, a taxicab driver, etc.). By the way, the abbreviations—*Ud.* and *Uds.*—are commonly used in writing for *usted* and *ustedes,* respectively. Notice also that these abbreviated forms are always capitalized. When I speak Spanish to you, I will be using *tú,* since I'm thinking of you as a friend.

   You use the informal *you,* (*tú* and *vosotros / vosotras*) for people of your own age or younger, and for family members and friends. This usage changes a little from country to country, and I'll warn you about it when necessary.

• In *español*, there are feminine and masculine subject pronouns not only in the singular (*él, ella*) but also in the plural (*nosotros, nosotras, vosotros, vosotras* and *ellos, ellas*). *Nosotros, vosotros,* and *ellos* are used for men, or groups including both men and women. *Nosotras, vosotras,* and *ellas* are used for women only. For example:

Nosotros no somos taxistas.   We are not taxi drivers.

Nosotras somos mujeres.   We are women.

Vosotros and *vosotras* are used only in Spain. These forms are very rare in Latin America where *ustedes* is used across the board, for both informal and formal address.

• Finally, *español* does not have the pronoun *it.* Don't look for it!

TO BE OR NOT TO BE: THE VERB *SER* (TO BE)

Let's now see how you can introduce yourself or talk about yourself using *ser.* First, here are its different forms:

PRESENT TENSE OF THE VERB *SER* (TO BE)	
yo soy	I am
tú eres	you (informal) are
usted es	you (formal) are
él / ella es	he / she is
nosotros / nosotras somos	we are
vosotros / vosotras sois	you all (informal) are
ustedes son	you all (formal) are
ellos / ellas son	they are

ACTIVITY 2:   TAKE IT FOR A SPIN

Let's go back to our dialogue. How many sentences include a form of the verb *ser*? Write them down. You can check in the Crib Notes section at the end of the chapter to see if you got them all.

Now, let's look at some of these sentences a little more carefully. We have five that include the *yo* form of the verb:

No <u>soy</u> inglés.	I am not English.
<u>Soy</u> estadounidense.	I am from the United States.
<u>Soy</u> de Nueva York.	I am from New York.
<u>Soy</u> de Madrid.	I am from Madrid.
No <u>soy</u> fumador.	I am not a smoker.

You can see that in Spanish **we don't need to use a personal pronoun** (*yo*) with the verb, as we do in English. The verb by itself is enough. Its different forms serve to show who's being talked about. This is true of all verbs in Spanish.

As for the subject pronouns, believe me, you'll be happy to know them when you want to emphasize who's doing what or to avoid confusion. Can it be any easier than that?

By the way, note that to say that something is not true in Spanish, all you need to do is place the word *no* (not) in front of the verb, as in *No soy fumador* (I'm not a smoker).

One more thing (I can't let you go yet!): The preposition *de* means "from," so when you want to talk about origin, yours or somebody else's, use *ser* and *de* together. *Yo soy de España.* And where are you from?

Your turn! Say three things about yourself using *ser*? (Hint: One of them can be your name! How do you say "I am Sebastian"?). Look for some examples in the Crib Notes section.

In the dialogue, we also have five sentences that use the *he / she* form of the verb *ser*.

¿Es usted inglés?	Are you English?
Y usted, ¿es de Madrid?	And you, are you from Madrid?
Mi familia es de Granada.	My family is from Granada.
¡Es increíble!	It's incredible!
Así es la vida en España.	This is what life is like in Spain.

The form *es* is used with *usted* (*you*, formal), as well as with other subjects, such as the pronouns *él* (he) and *ella* (she), or any subject that is singular and third person, such as *la vida* (life) or *mi familia* (my family).

WHAT'S THE DIFFERENCE?: COGNATES

You know already that many words in Spanish are quite similar to English words. Isn't that convenient? Words with similar roots in different languages are called cognates. They are here to make your life much easier. Here are some you have already seen and some others that are new. Can you guess their meaning?

increíble	diferente
interesante	difícil
importante	posible
necesario	imposible
perfecto	popular
horrible	probable

By just adding *es* you can create many sentences and sound just like a native speaker already!

¡Es increíble!	(that my taxi driver would smoke here)
¡Es necesario!	(that you study Spanish)
¡No es importante!	(that you make mistakes)
¡Es imposible!	(that you won't learn with this book)

The only tricky thing about Spanish cognates is their pronunciation, which can be quite different from English. Make sure you listen to the CD carefully or check the pronunciation in the glossary.

Heads Up!

You've noticed this weird thing already—Spanish has question and exclamation marks both at the beginning and at the end of a sentence. The one at the beginning of a sentence is upside down. Don't forget to include them!

Heads Up!

ACTIVITY 4:   **TAKE IT FOR A SPIN**

Now, read these sentences. I am sure you can understand them without a problem, but if you have doubts, you can always check at the end of the chapter!

1. Harvard es una universidad muy importante.
2. Peter es un fotógrafo increíble.
3. ¡¡El taxista es horrible!!
4. Brad Pitt es un actor muy romántico.
5. Los americanos son muy prácticos.
6. La gramática no es difícil.
7. ¿Eres inteligente?
8. Eres un estudiante muy serio y responsable.
9. Los españoles son religiosos.
10. Los turistas japoneses son numerosos.

WORDS TO LIVE BY

***TO THE HOTEL PRINCESA, PLEASE!*: SPEAKING SPANISH AFTER YOU LAND**

Here are the words used in this chapter, grouped according to their part of speech, with notes when necessary.

VERBS

Verbs will always be listed in their neutral "to" form (or the infinitive). I will note if they are regular or irregular and which kind of irregularity they have. The two verbs you'll learn in this chapter are irregular:

ser	to be
querer	to want

NOUNS

All nouns in Spanish, even those that stand for things, like *house* or *car*, are either masculine or feminine. When they are masculine, the article *el* precedes them. When they are feminine, *la* is used. When the same word is both feminine and masculine, I will list both articles, e.g., the word *el / la estudiante*.

People

el fotógrafo	photographer
el / la taxista	taxi driver
el / la turista	tourist
el fumador	smoker
el señor	sir
la señora	madam
la familia	family

Places

el taxi	taxi
el hotel	hotel

Things

el cigarrillo	cigarette
la vida	life
el horror	horror

ADJECTIVES

Adjectives also have a feminine and a masculine form, depending on the word they modify. Usually, feminine adjectives end in -*a*, while masculine adjectives end in -*o*. Sometimes, adjectives have only one form, used in all cases, e.g., *interesante* (interesting).

americano / a	American
estadounidense	from the United States, American

inglés / a	*English*
increíble	*incredible*

Did You Know?

Many Spanish-speaking people, particularly Spaniards, use the adjective *americano / a* to describe someone from the United States. But this can be a sensitive issue, because the word *americano / a* could apply to a lot of other people from the Americas (Mexicans, Argentineans, and Colombians, to name a few). That's why it is more accurate to use the adjective *estadounidense* when referring to people from the United States.

Did You Know?

USEFUL LITTLE WORDS

aquí	*here*
muy	*very*
bien	*well*
dentro	*inside*

Word on the Street

In this section, I will list commonly used expressions. Do not try to understand them word by word, just try to remember them as whole phrases.

Así es la vida.	*That's life.*
¿Le importa si . . . ?	*Do you mind if . . . ?*
¡Hombre!	*Lit.* man. In Spain, it is used to show surprise, as in* **¡Hombre, qué sorpresa!** *(Hey, what a surprise!).*

ACTIVITY 5:   **TAKE IT FOR A SPIN**

And you thought you were done! Time for another challenge! Let's review *ser* (to be) one more time.

Match pronouns and nouns on the left with a verb form on the right:

1.	nosotros	soy
2.	mi familia	eres
3.	yo	es
4.	ustedes	somos
5.	los mexicanos	son

**Lit.* stands for "Literally."

6. tú
7. usted
8. Brad Pitt
9. el fotógrafo
10. los estudiantes

CRIB NOTES

HEAR...SAY

Peter: Taxi!
Taxi driver: Yes?
Peter: To the Hotel Princesa, please.
Taxi driver: Very well, sir. Are you English?
Peter: No. I am not English. I am from the United States (American).
Taxi driver: Hey! An American! And where are you from in the U.S.? From Hollywood?
Peter: (chuckling) No, no! I am from New York. And you? Are you from Madrid?

Taxi driver: Yes. I am from Madrid, but my family is from Granada. Do you want a cigarette?
Peter: A cigarette? I am not a smoker!
Taxi driver: Well, I am. Do you mind if I smoke?
Peter: (not believing his ears) Here? Inside the taxi? That's incredible! How horrible!
Taxi driver: That's life in Spain, sir.

ANSWER KEY

ACTIVITY 1

1. to the Hotel Princesa
2. from New York
3. from Madrid
4. from Granada
5. if he can smoke inside the cab

ACTIVITY 2

The ten sentences are:
1. ¿Es usted inglés?
2. No soy inglés.
3. Soy estadounidense.
4. Soy de Nueva York.
5. ¿Es de Madrid?
6. Soy de Madrid.
7. Mi familia es de Granada.
8. No soy fumador.
9. ¡Es increíble!
10. Así es la vida en España.

ACTIVITY 3

1. Yo soy Pilar Munday.
2. Yo soy de España.
3. Yo soy de Granada.

ACTIVITY 4

1. Harvard is a very important university.
2. Peter is an incredible photographer.
3. The taxi driver is horrible!
4. Brad Pitt is a very romantic actor.
5. Americans are very practical.
6. Grammar is not difficult.
7. Are you intelligent?
8. You are a serious and responsible student.
9. Spaniards are very religious.
10. The Japanese tourists are numerous.

ACTIVITY 5

1. nosotros somos
2. mi familia es
3. yo soy
4. ustedes son
5. los mexicanos son
6. tú eres
7. usted es
8. brad Pitt es
9. el fotógrafo es
10. los estudiantes son

SHE IS

Ella es

Peter, Carmen doesn't have a boyfriend . . .

COMING UP. . .

- Saying hello
- How are you doing?
- *Hello, my name is . . . :* Introducing yourself and others
- Saying good-bye
- *To be or not to be, Part II:* The verb *estar* (to be)
- *(In)definitely so:* Definite and indefinite articles
- *Let's talk about sex . . . and number:* Gender and number of nouns
- *The countdown:* Counting from 0 to 19
- *There is this and there is that:* Using *there is* and *there are* in Spanish

¡Hola, amigo o amiga! Here we are in Lesson 2, a good sign. Peter arrived at the Hotel Princesa, found out it was too *caro* (expensive) and decided to settle in one of the *pensiones* near the Plaza Mayor. A *pensión* is a bit like a bed-and-breakfast, although not as nice. *Pensiones* are small hotels, usually run by families. They don't have many amenities, but they are affordable and pleasant for longer stays.

In the first dialogue, Peter is talking to the *pensión* owner, Don Miguel, who introduces him to another hotel guest.

ACTIVITY 1: **LET'S WARM UP**

Before you turn on your CD player, let's see what you remember about Peter. Tell me if these sentences are true or false.

1. Peter es inglés.
2. Peter es de Nueva York.
3. Peter es fumador.
4. Peter es un actor.
5. El Hotel Princesa es una pensión.

¡Excelente! Now you can check your answers in the Crib Notes section.

Take a Tip from Me!

When trying to guess the meaning of a dialogue in Spanish, first think of the things that you can rule out. For example, you already know that Peter will be greeting the *pensión*'s owner. If that's so, then you are not likely to hear anything related to, say, gardening in New England. You will probably hear things like: *Hi!* or *How are you?*

You already knew all this! Just making sure . . .

Now, just try to get the gist of the story.

Take a Tip from Me!

HEAR . . . SAY 1

Peter:	Buenas tardes. ¿Cómo está usted?
Dueño de la pensión:	Pues, aquí estamos. ¿Y usted? ¿Qué tal?
Peter:	¡Fantástico!
Dueño:	¿Fantástico? ¡Qué suerte! Y, ¿qué pasa?

Peter:	No mucho. Soy fotógrafo para una revista de Nueva York y estoy en Madrid para fotografiar la gira de Ricky Martin. Ahora tengo tiempo libre, pero no conozco a nadie.
Dueño:	Pues aquí en la pensión hay muchos jóvenes. Mire, aquí está Carmen, que es estudiante de arquitectura en la Universidad Complutense de Madrid.
Peter:	Hola, Carmen, ¿cómo estás? Me llamo Peter. Encantado.
Carmen:	Igualmente.
Peter:	¿De dónde eres?
Carmen:	Soy de Granada, pero ahora estoy en Madrid por mis estudios. ¿Y tú, de dónde eres?
Peter:	Soy de Nueva York. ¿Estás contenta en Madrid?
Carmen:	Sí. Mis padres no están muy contentos, porque todo es muy caro, pero yo sí. Aquí todo es muy interesante y divertido.
Dueño:	Peter, Carmen no tiene novio . . .
Carmen:	(*blushing*) ¡Pero, Don Miguel! (*thinking*: ¡Qué hombre más indiscreto!).

After listening to and reading the dialogue a few times, you can look at the English translation at the end of the lesson (if you need to).

ACTIVITY 2: HOW'S THAT AGAIN?

Try to answer the following questions in Spanish (although English is also fine for now). It's okay to answer with just one word, or just a *sí* or *no*.

1. ¿Dónde (*where*) está Peter?
2. ¿De dónde es Carmen?
3. ¿Qué (*what*) estudia Carmen?
4. ¿Dónde estudia Carmen?
5. ¿Tiene Carmen novio?

Did You Know?

If somebody asks a Spaniard "How are you?" (*¿Cómo estás?* / *¿Qué tal?*), he or she does not usually respond with a neutral "Fine, thanks" as Americans do. Spaniards are likely to say things like:

Pues, normal.	Well, okay.
Así, así.	So, so.
Pues, aquí estamos.	Here we are.

The translations provided are very approximate. What these expressions really mean is: "We are more or less OK, but let us not tempt our fate by provoking Somebody up there who may decide we are too arrogant if we say that we are doing very well."

In our dialogue, *el dueño de la pensión* (the owner of the *pensión*) shows surprise when Peter tells him he is doing fine. Do you remember?

Dueño de la pensión:	**¿Y usted? ¿Qué tal?**	And you? How are you?
Peter:	**Fantástico.**	Great.
Dueño:	**¿Fantástico? ¡Qué suerte!**	Great? How lucky!

Also, Spaniards often take the question seriously, so don't ask if you're not ready to listen! They might tell you about everything that is going on in their lives, mainly the bad things, such as, their car broke down, they have been diagnosed with a kidney stone and, on top of that, their mother-in-law just moved in . . . indefinitely.

Did You Know?

WORKSHOP 1

THE NITTY-GRITTY

TO BE OR NOT TO BE, PART II: THE VERB *ESTAR* (TO BE)

In Spanish there are two ways to express the English *to be*. One way is to use *ser*, the verb you learned in Lesson 1. The other way is to use the verb *estar*.

PRESENT TENSE OF *ESTAR* (TO BE)	
yo estoy	I am
tú estás	you (informal) are
usted está	you (formal) are
él / ella está	he / she is
nosotros / nosotras estamos	we are
vosotros / vosotras estáis	you all (informal) are
ustedes están	you all (formal) are
ellos / ellas están	they are

Go back to the dialogue and find sentences that include a form of the verb *estar*. (Hint: There are six of them.)

This time, you don't even have to look in the Crib Notes section. I have the answers right here for you:

Pues aquí _estamos_.

Here we are.

Soy fotógrafo para una agencia de Nueva York y _estoy_ en Madrid para fotografiar la gira de Ricky Martin.

I am a photographer from a New York agency and I am in Madrid to photograph Ricky Martin's tour.

Mire, aquí _está_ Carmen, que es estudiante de arquitectura en la Universidad Complutense de Madrid.

Look, here's Carmen, who is a student of architecture at the Universidad Complutense in Madrid.

Soy de Granada, pero ahora _estoy_ en Madrid por mis estudios.

I am from Granada, but I am now in Madrid because of my studies.

¿_Estás_ contenta en Madrid?

Are you happy in Madrid?

Mis padres no _están_ muy contentos, porque todo es muy caro, pero yo sí.

My parents are not very happy because everything is very expensive, but I am.

By looking at sentences 2 and 4, can you tell me which word follows *estar*? *Sí. Muy bien.* It's *en* (in). In sentences 1 and 3, *estar* appears with *aquí* (here). That's because one of the uses of *estar* (as opposed to *ser*) is to say where something or someone is located at a given moment.

Another use of *estar* is to describe states of being that are not a person's permanent characteristics, such as moods. See example sentences 5 and 6. So, if someone asks you *¿Cómo estás?*, possible answers are (in Spain, anyway!):

Estoy contenta / triste / deprimida / estresada / interesada.

I am happy / sad / depressed / stressed / interested.

(Change the *−a* at the end of your "mood" to *−o* if you're a guy!)

USES OF *SER* AND *ESTAR*

SER (TO BE)	*ESTAR* (TO BE)
— origin / nationality *Soy de España.* I'm from Spain.	— location *Estoy en Madrid.* I'm in Madrid.
— profession / occupation *Soy fotógrafo.* I'm a photographer.	

— inherent characteristics of a person
    or thing
Soy interesante.
I'm interesting.
Soy alta.
I'm tall.
	— temporary states of a person
	    or thing
	Estoy deprimida.
	I'm depressed.
	Estoy gordo.
	I'm fat.

ACTIVITY 4: TAKE IT FOR A SPIN

Fill in the blanks with the appropriate forms of the verb *estar*, as in this example:

La Mona Lisa _____ en París. → La Mona Lisa **está** en París.

1. Carmen y Don Miguel _____ en la pensión.
2. Peter _____ en España pero él es de Nueva York.
3. Probablemente, tú _____ en tu casa.
4. Yo _____ en la universidad.
5. Mis amigos y yo _____ muy contentos.

WORDS TO LIVE BY

SAYING HELLO

I'm sure you've already heard the most common greeting of all in Spanish:

¡Hola!   *Hi! or Hello!*

This greeting is used in every Spanish-speaking country in all types of situations, whether formal or informal.

Depending on the time of day, you may also use one of the following greetings:

¡Buenos días!	*Good morning!*
¡Buenas tardes!	*Good afternoon!*
¡Buenas noches!	*Good evening! or Good night!*

HOW ARE YOU DOING?

You can say:

¿Cómo estás?   *How are you?*

Or you can say:

¿Qué tal?   *What's up? / How are you?*

The latter is more common, at least in Spain, and often used together with *¡Hola!* just like English, Hi! How are you?

Qué, ¿cómo va la vida?   *How's life treating you?*

And the answers are:

Pues, bien. / Normal. / Así, así.   *Fine. / Okay. / So, so.*
Pues, aquí estamos.   *Here we are.*

For an even more casual approach, use:

¿Qué pasa?   *What's up? / What's going on?*
¿Qué hay?   *What's up?*

And answer:

Nada.   *Not much. (Lit. Nothing.)*
Pues, aquí andamos.   *Here we are. (Lit. Well, here we walk.)*

Usually, the next step is to ask about the other person's family, especially among older adults:

¿Y la familia, cómo está?   *What about your family?*
¿Y su esposa / esposo?   *And your wife/husband?*
¿Y sus niños?   *And your children?*
¿Qué tal andan todos?   *How are you all doing?*

By the way, if you're really, really doing fine, go ahead and say it. You can say:

Estoy muy bien / fenomenal / genial / fantástico.
(*Easy to figure out the meaning here*).

People will actually be very happy for you.

HELLO, MY NAME IS . . . : INTRODUCING YOURSELF AND OTHERS

When you meet someone for the first time, you can say:

Encantado (de conocerle).	*Pleased (to meet you).*
Mucho gusto (en conocerle).	*Very pleased (to meet you).*

And reply:

Igualmente.	*Likewise.*

You can continue with:

¿Cómo te llamas?	*What's your name (informal)?*
¿Cómo se llama Usted?	*What's your name (formal)?*
Me llamo Pilar Munday.	*My name is Pilar Munday. (Lit. I call myself . . .)*

Word on the Street

You've noticed already that the word **pues** pops up here and there in the dialogues. Remember:

Pues, aquí estamos.	*Well, here we are.*

Pues, like the English *well* is a filler, used to gain time in conversation but without a real meaning. So, if you want to sound like a native speaker, use it at the beginning of a sentence. People will be so *impresionados*.

ACTIVITY 5:	**TAKE IT FOR A SPIN**

Imagine you have just met Paco. Here are his replies. What are you asking?

You: _____

Paco: Me llamo Paco.

You: _____

Paco: Igualmente.

You: _____

Paco: Pues, nada. Aquí estamos.

HEAR . . . SAY 2

The conversation at Don Miguel's *pensión* continues . . .

Carmen: ¡Don Miguel, usted es muy indiscreto!

Don Miguel: Es cierto. Así soy yo. Bueno, jóvenes, es tarde. Es hora de trabajar un poco. ¡Hasta luego!

Carmen: ¡Hasta luego!

Peter: Adiós, Don Miguel. Carmen, ¿cuántas personas hay en tu familia? ¿Es una familia grande?

Carmen: No, es pequeña. En total, somos cinco. Todos están en Granada. Yo soy la única en Madrid. ¡Madrid es muy grande para ellos! ¿Y tu familia?

Peter: También es pequeña. Y todos están en Estados Unidos, claro.

Carmen: ¿Es difícil estar lejos de ellos?

Peter: Sí es difícil. Pero España es muy bonita y también es muy interesante. Es una buena oportunidad para mí.

Carmen: ¡Especialmente porque estás con Ricky Martin! ¡Es guapísimo!

Peter: Bueno, no estoy realmente con él. Estoy aquí, en esta pensión, ¿recuerdas?

(*Don Miguel returns after a while to find the pair still talking.*)

Don Miguel: ¡Peter y Carmen! ¡Qué sorpresa! ¿Están aún aquí?

Peter: Sí, aquí estamos.

Don Miguel: Pero si hoy es un día precioso. No es una buena idea estar aquí.

Carmen: (*looks at her watch*) ¡Díos mío! ¡Es super tarde! Adiós, Don Miguel. Hasta luego, Peter. (*She leaves.*)

Peter: Bueno, Don Miguel, y ahora ¿qué pasa?

ACTIVITY 6:   **HOW'S THAT AGAIN?**

Can you answer these questions? Remember, *sí* or *no*, or a single word is fine. (I give you full sentences in the Crib Notes section so you can learn more.)

1. ¿Es Peter muy indiscreto?
2. ¿La familia de Carmen es grande?
3. ¿Dónde está la familia de Peter?
4. ¿Está Ricky Martin en la pensión?

(IN)DEFINITELY SO: DEFINITE AND INDEFINITE ARTICLES

This is going to be simple . . . Like English, Spanish has useful little words that are placed in front of nouns. These words indicate whether we are talking about a person or a thing for the first time or if we have spoken about him, her, or it already. While English has only two of those words (a, the), Spanish has a whole variety of them. Here they are, in one simple table:

DEFINITE AND INDEFINITE ARTICLES					
	SINGULAR		PLURAL		
	MASCULINE	FEMININE	MASCULINE	FEMININE	
Definite articles	el	la	los	las	the
Indefinite articles	un	una	unos	unas	a / an / one / some

A look at these examples will make it all clear:

el **hombre**	the man	la **mujer**	the woman
los **hombres**	the men	las **mujeres**	the women
un **hombre**	a / one man	una **mujer**	a / one woman
unos **hombres**	(some) men	unas **mujeres**	(some) women

LET'S TALK ABOUT SEX . . . AND NUMBER: GENDER AND NUMBER OF NOUNS

In Spanish, a noun (e.g., *friend*) often has a different form depending on who or what it refers to. So, Peter is *un amigo*, but Carmen is *una amiga*, even though in English they're both just *a friend* to each other. When it comes to nouns that refer to people (who, we know, come in different sexes), things are pretty clear. Here's another example:

la novia	girlfriend	**el novio**	boyfriend

Things get less obvious with nouns that refer to things. In Spanish, even things are distinguished as either masculine (sort of like male) and feminine (sort of like female), even though nobody can really say why. Here are two examples you've already heard in the dialogues:

la agencia	the agency (feminine)
el taxi	the taxi or cab (masculine)

It helps to know that most nouns ending in *–o* are masculine and those ending in *–a* are feminine, just like in *amigo / amiga* or *novio / novia*. Most nouns that end in *–ión* and *–ad* are also feminine:

la pensión   the inn

la universidad   the university

When you don't see these endings, then you have to look at the article for help:

el actor   the actor (masculine)

la gente   the people (feminine)

Sometimes, a noun has only one form that can refer either to a man or a woman, such as *estudiante* (student). In that case, you still have to worry about the article, as it will be different depending on who you're talking about. So:

el estudiante   the (male) student

la estudiante   the (female) student

To distinguish "one" from "two or more" (i.e., singular from plural) in Spanish, follow these simple rules:

1. Add *–s* to a noun ending in a vowel:

    el hombre   →   **los hombres**

2. Add *–es* to a noun ending in a consonant:

    el actor   →   **los actores**

Heads Up!

If a noun ends in *–z* , its plural form ends in *–ces*:

la luz   →   **las luces**   the light, the lights

el lápiz   →   **los lápices**   the pencil, the pencils

Heads Up!

THE COUNTDOWN: COUNTING FROM 0 TO 19

I'm sure that you already know some numbers. (Don't tell me you don't know *uno*!) Here they are from 0 up to 19:

cero	0	*diez*	10
uno	1	*once*	11
dos	2	*doce*	12
tres	3	*trece*	13
cuatro	4	*catorce*	14
cinco	5	*quince*	15
seis	6	*dieciséis* or *diez y seis*	16
siete	7	*diecisiete* or *diez y siete*	17
ocho	8	*dieciocho* or *diez y ocho*	18
nueve	9	*diecinueve* or *diez y nueve*	19

ACTIVITY 7: TAKE IT FOR A SPIN

Don Miguel is counting the number of guests in the *pensión*:

- un hombre de Estados Unidos
- una mujer de Cuba
- catorce mujeres de España
- tres hombres de España

Help Don Miguel by doing the math.

1. How many guests are there right now?
2. How many women?
3. How many men?

WORDS TO LIVE BY

SAYING GOOD-BYE

"Sorry, but I must be going." Just kidding! But if you do have to go, here's what to say:

Adiós.	*Bye.*
Hasta luego.	*See you later. (Lit. Until later.)*

You can also say:

Hasta mañana.	*See you tomorrow.*
Hasta más tarde.	*See you later. (Like **hasta luego**, but a bit more specific. **Hasta luego** is more common, particularly in Spain.)*
Nos vemos.	*See you. (Lit. We see each other.)*

THERE IS THIS AND THERE IS THAT: USING *THERE IS* AND *THERE ARE* IN SPANISH

Only one word is used in Spanish for both *there is* and *there are: hay.*

Hay tres personas en mi familia.	There are three people in my family.
Hay un hombre en la pensión.	There is a man in the inn.

In the dialogue, you also heard Peter ask Carmen about her family, remember?

¿Cuántas personas hay en tu familia?	How many people are there in your family?

ACTIVITY 8:   **TAKE IT FOR A SPIN**

You are still talking to Paco (Remember Activity 5?). What are you saying to him?

You: _____

Paco: En mi familia hay diecinueve personas. Es una familia muy grande. Y en tu familia, ¿cuántas personas hay?

You: _____

Paco: ¡Muy interesante! ¡Dios mío! Es muy tarde. Tengo que irme (I have to go). ¡Hasta luego!.

You: _____

CRIB NOTES

HEAR...SAY 1

Peter:	Good afternoon. How are you?
Inn's owner:	OK. And you? How are you doing?
Peter:	Great!
Inn's owner:	Great? How fortunate! And, what's up?
Peter:	Not much. I am a photographer for a New York magazine and I am in Madrid to photograph Ricky Martin's tour. Right now I have some free time, but I don't know anyone.
Inn's owner:	Well, here in the inn, there are many young people. For example, here is Carmen, who is a student of architecture at the Complutense University in Madrid.
Peter:	Hi, Carmen. How are you? My name is Peter. Nice to meet you.
Carmen:	You, too.
Peter:	Where are you from?
Carmen:	I am from Granada, but right now I am staying in Madrid because of my studies. And you? Where are you from?
Peter:	I am from New York. Are you happy in Madrid?
Carmen:	Yes. My parents are not very happy, because everything is so expensive, but I am. Here, everything is interesting and fun.
Inn's owner:	Peter, Carmen does not have a boyfriend . . .
Carmen:	(*blushing*) But, Don Miguel! (*thinking: What an indiscreet guy!*)

Carmen:	Don Miguel, you are so indiscreet!
Don Miguel:	That's true. That's how I am. Well, my youths, it is late. It is time to work a little. See you later!
Carmen:	See you later!
Peter:	Bye, Don Miguel. Carmen, how many people are there in your family? Is it a big family?
Carmen:	No, it's small. In total, there are five of us. They are all in Granada. I am the only one in Madrid. Madrid is too big for them! What about your family?
Peter:	It is also small. And they are all in the United States, of course.
Carmen:	Is it difficult to be far away from them?

Peter:	Yes, it is difficult. But Spain is very beautiful and it's also quite interesting. It's a great opportunity for me.
Carmen:	Particularly because you are with Ricky Martin! He is so gorgeous!
Peter:	Well, I am not really with him. I am here in this inn, remember?
Don Miguel:	Peter and Carmen! What a surprise! You are still here?
Peter:	Yes, here we are.
Don Miguel:	But today is a gorgeous day. It's not a good idea to be here.
Carmen:	My goodness! It's very late! Bye, Don Miguel! See you, Peter!
Peter:	Well, Don Miguel, what's happening?

ANSWER KEY

ACTIVITY 1

1. Peter is English. False
2. Peter is from New York. True
3. Peter is a smoker. False
4. Peter is an actor. False
5. The Hotel Princesa is a pensión. True.

ACTIVITY 2

1. Está en España.
2. Carmen es de Granada.
3. Estudia arquitectura.
4. Carmen estudia en la Universidad Complutense de Madrid.
5. No, Carmen no tiene novio.

ACTIVITY 3

The answers are discussed in Workshop 1.

ACTIVITY 4

1. están; 2. está; 3. estás; 4. estoy; 5. estamos

ACTIVITY 5

¿Cómo se llama? *or* ¿Cómo te llamas?
Encantado. *or* Mucho gusto.
¿Qué pasa? *or* ¿Qué hay? *or* ¿Qué tal?

ACTIVITY 6

1. No, Peter no es muy indiscreto. Don Miguel es muy indiscreto.
2. No, la familia de Carmen no es grande.
3. La familia de Peter está en Estados Unidos.
4. No. Ricky Martin no está en la pensión.

ACTIVITY 7

1. Diecinueve personas en total.
2. Cuatro hombres.
3. Quince mujeres.

ACTIVITY 8

You:	¿Cuántas personas hay en tu familia?
You:	Hay _____ (number of people in your family) personas.
You:	Hasta luego. *or* Adiós.

3.

YOU ARE LIKE AIR

Eres como el aire

What about you? Do you listen to American music?

COMING UP...

- *All about me:* **Describing yourself and others**
- *Fun things to do . . .*
- *Make it all match:* **Using modifiers in Spanish**
- *To have and have not:* **The present tense of the verb** *tener* **(to have)**
- *Is that so?:* **Asking simple questions**
- *Living in the moment:* **The present tense of** *–ar* **verbs**
- *The countdown:* **Counting from 20 to 39**

Hola, ¿qué tal?¿Así, así? ¡Estupendo! Are you ready for the third lesson? *¡Magnífico! Pues, ¡a empezar!* (Let's start!)

Peter is sitting at an outdoor café in the Plaza Mayor in the center of Madrid. Using his laptop, he is surfing the Internet, trying to find young people for his new assignment. He's looking for young people (*gente joven*) who are fans of Ricky Martin.

As we speak, Peter is chatting with *una persona misteriosa* in an on-line chat room. They're just starting to get to know each other. As it turns out, the mysterious person is, indeed (*de verdad*), quite nosy.

ACTIVITY 1: LET'S WARM UP

How would you describe yourself with words you learned in the last two lessons? Try to write at least three sentences. Here's what I can tell you about myself:

Me llamo Pilar Munday. Soy una mujer española pero estoy en los Estados Unidos ahora (now). *Soy profesora de español en una universidad. Soy curiosa y también idealista.*

HEAR . . . SAY 1

Peter:	(*typing on his laptop*) Soy americano. Tengo veintiocho años. Trabajo en Nueva York y ahora estoy en Madrid para tomar fotos y escribir un artículo para *La Gente*.
Persona misteriosa:	¡Qué interesante!
Peter:	Quiero hablar con gente joven y conocer Madrid para mi artículo.
Persona misteriosa:	Hola, hombre. Yo soy joven. Tengo veintidos años y también estoy en Madrid ahora.
Peter:	¿Cómo te llamas?
Persona misteriosa:	¡Ah! Eso es un misterio . . . Oye, ¿eres atractivo o feo?
Peter:	Eres muy curioso (o ¿eres curiosa?). No sé si eres un hombre o una mujer.
Persona misteriosa:	Soy una mujer. Sí, soy muy curiosa. ¿Cómo eres físicamente?
Peter:	Soy alto. No soy delgado, pero no soy gordo. No soy atractivo, pero no soy feo.
Persona misteriosa:	O sea, muy normal.
Peter:	Exacto. Y tú, ¿cómo eres?

Persona misteriosa:	No soy alta, pero no soy baja. No soy guapa, pero no soy fea. Soy morena con ojos grandes y negros.
Peter:	O sea, también muy normal. Oye, ¿estudias o trabajas?
Persona misteriosa:	Estudio.
Peter:	¿Qué estudias?
Persona misteriosa:	Estudio arquitectura. ¿Tienes novia?
Peter:	¡De verdad eres curiosa!

ACTIVITY 2: HOW'S THAT AGAIN?

Ummm, muy interesante . . . Are these two hitting on each other? (By the way, *to hit on somebody* is *ligar* in Spanish.)

But let's get serious. Are these statements true or false?

1. Peter es de Boston.
2. Peter es cubano.
3. La persona misteriosa es un hombre.
4. La persona misteriosa estudia matemáticas.
5. La persona misteriosa es muy curiosa.

Did You Know?

Peter certainly knows a thing or two. He said, *¿Estudias o trabajas?* (Are you a student or do you work?), which is a popular pickup line in Spain.

Did You Know?

WORKSHOP 1

THE NITTY-GRITTY

MAKE IT ALL MATCH: USING MODIFIERS IN SPANISH

When you want to describe somebody or something you use words called adjectives. Peter said he is ordinary or *normal*; he is not tall or *alto*, fat or *gordo*. In Spanish, adjectives must match, or agree with, the noun they modify. So, if a noun is feminine and singular, the adjective modifying the noun also has to be feminine and singular.

el hombre <u>bajo</u>	the short man
la mujer <u>baja</u>	the short woman
los amigos <u>eternos</u>	eternal friends
las amigas <u>eternas</u>	eternal (female) friends

By the way, notice that the position of adjectives in the previous examples in Spanish is very different from English. They come **after** the noun in Spanish.

In the dialogue we also saw:

Soy alt<u>o</u>.

I am tall. (Peter is speaking so the adjective is masculine.)

No soy alt<u>a</u>.

I am not tall. (This is *persona misteriosa* speaking, so the adjective is feminine.)

The basic rules for adjective matching or agreement are these:

1. Adjectives ending in *–o* change to *–a* to indicate feminine gender, and add an *–s* to indicate the plural:

hombre alto	tall man
hombres altos	tall men
mujer alta	tall woman
mujeres altas	tall women

2. Adjectives ending in *–e* and in a consonant have only one form, used with either masculine or feminine nouns. For the plural of adjectives that end in *–e*, add *–s*. For the plural of adjectives that end in a consonant, add *–es*. Look at the examples:

niño inteligente	intelligent boy
niña inteligente	intelligent girl
niños inteligentes	intelligent children
hombre cruel	cruel man
mujer cruel	cruel woman
personas crueles	cruel people

3. For most adjectives that denote nationality and end in a consonant, add an –*a* to get the feminine form. Add an –*es* to the masculine form and a –*s* to the feminine to get the plural form:

(masc. sing.)	(fem. sing.)	(masc. pl.)	(fem. pl.)		
español	**española**	**españoles**	**españolas**	Spanish	
francés	**francesa**	**franceses**	**francesas**	French	

The Fine Print

Most adjectives that end in –*dor, –án, –ón,* and –*ín* follow Rule 3 above:

(masc. sing.)	(fem. sing.)	(masc. pl.)	(fem. pl.)	
trabajador	**trabajadora**	**trabajadores**	**trabajadoras**	*hardworking*
juguetón	**juguetona**	**juguetones**	**juguetonas**	*playful*
pequeñín	**pequeñina**	**pequeñines**	**pequeñinas**	*small (little ones)*

ACTIVITY 3:   **TAKE IT FOR A SPIN**

Do you have an opinion about the following people? Here's your chance to share it.

Connect the adjectives with the nouns using the appropriate form of *ser*. Don't forget to change the form of the adjective to match the noun!

Example: *Los Beatles son populares.*

1.	Hitchcock		romántico
2.	el Papa (*the Pope*)		interesante
3.	Penélope Cruz	es	generoso
4.	Antonio Banderas		cruel
5.	Los Beatles	son	popular
6.	Rosie O'Donnell		loco
7.	Los Rolling Stones		guapo

TO HAVE AND HAVE NOT: THE PRESENT TENSE OF THE VERB *TENER* (TO HAVE)

You can't go very far without this verb. Here are its different forms—in the present tense.

PRESENT TENSE OF *TENER* (TO HAVE)	
yo tengo	I have
tú tienes	you (informal) have
usted tiene	you (formal) have
él / ella tiene	he / she has
nosotros / nosotras tenemos	we have
vosotros / vosotras tenéis	you all (informal) have
ustedes tienen	you all (formal) have
ellos / ellas tienen	they have

Tener is used to express possession, just like the English phrase *to have*:

Tengo una casa preciosa.

I have a beautiful house.

Tenemos una computadora muy rápida.

We have a very fast computer.

It is also used to tell a person's age (English uses *to be* instead):

Peter tiene veintiocho años.

Peter is 28. (*Lit.* Peter has 28 years.)

Carmen tiene veintidos años.

Carmen is 22. (*Lit.* Carmen has 22 years.)

This is how to ask about age:

¿Cuántos años tienes?

How old are you?

¿Cuántos años tiene Carmen?

How old is Carmen?

IS THAT SO?: ASKING SIMPLE QUESTIONS

Asking questions in Spanish is a piece of cake. Let's look at these examples from the dialogue:

¿Eres curiosa?	Are you curious?
¿Estudias o trabajas?	Do you study or work?
¿Tienes novia?	Do you have a girlfriend?

As you can see, the verb always comes first in questions in Spanish. In addition, pronouns like *I, he, she*, etc. often don't show up in Spanish questions. That's why you don't see them in the questions above. However, if you wanted to use the pronouns for special emphasis, the same sentences would sound as follows:

¿Eres <u>tú</u> curiosa?

¿Estudias <u>tú</u> o trabajas?

¿Tienes <u>tú</u> novia?

Again, you'll note that the verb comes first, as it does in the following examples where the subject of the sentence is a noun:

¿Es <u>Carmen</u> curiosa?

Is Carmen curious?

¿Estudia <u>Peter</u> francés?

Does Peter study French?

WORDS TO LIVE BY

Things you can do to keep busy . . .

tomar fotos	to take pictures
escribir un artículo	to write an article
estudiar	to study
trabajar	to work
hablar	to speak

ALL ABOUT ME: DESCRIBING YOURSELF AND OTHERS

¿Cómo es? (What is he / she like?)

Here are some words to describe what you see . . .

alto / a	tall	**bajo / a**	short
guapo / a	beautiful, handsome	**feo / a**	ugly
delgado / a	thin	**gordo / a**	fat
joven	young	**viejo / a**	old
grande	big	**pequeño / a**	small
simpático / a	nice	**antipático / a**	grouchy

To describe hair color, use . . .

moreno / a	*brown / brunette*
rubio / a	*blond / -e*
castaño / a	*light brown-haired*
pelirrojo	*red-haired*

If you're really excited about the person, you can put *muy* (very) next to the adjective:

Eres muy guapa.	You are very beautiful.

Eres muy guapo.	You are very handsome.

Or you can add *qué* to form an exclamation:

¡Qué interesante!	How interesting!

Notice that many of the adjectives you heard in the dialogue are very similar to English, such as: *atractivo / a* (attractive); *normal* (ordinary; normal); *misterioso / a* (mysterious); *curioso / a* (curious); *interesante* (interesting).

Word on the Street

A couple of useful expressions:

de verdad	really, truthfully. Also used to mean "I mean it."
o sea	in other words; that is; so. This expression is very similar to **pues**, as it is often used as a conversation filler, particularly in Spain.

ACTIVITY 4: **TAKE IT FOR A SPIN**

How much do you know about these people? Answer these questions:

1. Don Miguel, ¿es viejo o joven?
2. Peter, ¿es alto o bajo?
3. Carmen, ¿es rubia o morena?
4. Yo, ¿soy hombre o mujer?
5. Y tú, ¿cómo eres? (Remember, use adjectives ending in *–o* if you're a man, or those ending in *–a* if you're a woman.)

Persona misteriosa:	Bueno, ¿tienes novia o no?
Peter:	No, no tengo novia. Y tú, ¿tienes novio?
Persona misteriosa:	¡Ah! Eso es otro secreto . . . hablas español muy bien.
Peter:	Bueno, ahora no hablo, ahora escribo. Pero hablo español porque visito muchos países donde hablan español.
Persona misteriosa:	¿Y también escuchas música española en Estados Unidos?
Peter:	¡Claro! Enrique Iglesias canta muy bien. Y es muy simpático.
Persona misteriosa:	¡Qué interesante! ¿Eres su amigo?
Peter:	No exactamente. Esa es otra historia . . . Y tú, ¿escuchas música americana?
Persona misteriosa:	Sí, claro, y también escucho música inglesa. Oye, tengo dos entradas para el concierto de Sting en la Plaza de Toros de Las Ventas.
Peter:	¿Sting en la Plaza de Toros? ¿Con toros?
Persona misteriosa:	¡No, hombre, no! Sting tiene un concierto allí. No hay toros.
Peter:	Bueno, si no hay toros, pues, ¡vamos!
Persona misteriosa:	Vale. ¿Dónde estás ahora?
Peter:	En la Plaza Mayor. ¿Y tú?
Persona misteriosa:	¡Qué coincidencia! Yo también estoy en la Plaza Mayor.
Peter:	(*He looks up and sees Carmen typing on her laptop.*) ¡Carmen! ¡Eres tú! ¡Eres como el aire, estás en todas partes!
Carmen:	¡Peter! ¡Ay, Dios mío, qué vergüenza!

ACTIVITY 5:   HOW'S THAT AGAIN?

Once more, tell me if these statements are true or false:

1. La persona misteriosa tiene entradas para el concierto de Enrique Iglesias.
2. Peter no habla español muy bien.
3. La persona misteriosa está en la pensión.
4. Peter es amigo de Enrique Iglesias.
5. La persona misteriosa es Carmen.

Did You Know?

The Plaza Mayor is a large and very beautiful square, lined with stores and outdoor cafés, in the old part of Madrid. In Spain, it is more common to meet with your friends in a café or a bar than to go to their homes. Bars and cafés are nice, cheap, and friendly establishments where truly everyone is welcome, from grandparents to babies.

One note about paying the bill: If you're out with a group of people, it is expected that everyone contribute an equal amount to the *mocho*, a sum of money used to pay for the bill, rather than have each person pay separately.

If you go out with only one or two people, somebody will usually offer to pay for everything. Everybody is expected to offer to do this at some point. Sometimes, you'll even see people argue over who will pay.

Did You Know?

WORKSHOP 2

THE NITTY-GRITTY

LIVING IN THE MOMENT: THE PRESENT TENSE OF –AR VERBS

The three verbs you have studied so far, *ser*, *estar*, and *tener*, are considered irregular; that is, their forms don't follow a regular pattern. Luckily, most verbs in Spanish are regular, so once you know one verb, you can pretty much say you know all the others that belong to the same group. All you need to do is add the right endings. Spanish verbs are divided into three types:

- –*ar* verbs (e.g., *habl**ar*** [to speak])
- –*er* verbs (e.g., *com**er*** [to eat])
- –*ir* verbs (e.g., *escrib**ir*** [to write])

To find out which type a verb falls into, look it up in the dictionary (the form you'll find there is called an infinitive). For instance, *hablar* (to speak) is *habl + ar*.

Here are the endings for the present tense of –*ar* verbs using *hablar* (to speak) as example:

PRESENT TENSE OF –*AR* VERBS	
ENDINGS	*HABLAR* (TO SPEAK)
–o	*yo hablo (habl + o)*
–as	*tú hablas (habl + as)*
–a	*el / ella / usted habla (habl + a)*

–amos	nosotros / nosotras hablamos (habl + amos)
–áis	vosotros / vosotras habláis (habl + áis)
–an	ellos / ellas / ustedes hablan (habl + an)

As you can see, it's quite simple: You take the root of the verb and add the appropriate endings.

There are many other verbs like *hablar*. For example:

estudiar **Tú estudias español, ¿no?**
You study Spanish, right? (I am assuming you do!)

trabajar **¿Estudias o trabajas?**
Do you study or do you work? (Our pick up line, remember?)

practicar **Nosotros practicamos mucho.**
We practice a lot. (Yeah, right!)

protestar **Ustedes protestan.**
You (formal, plural) complain. (Of course, you don't!)

ACTIVITY 6:   TAKE IT FOR A SPIN

Match the answers with their questions:

1. Sí, uso mucho el internet.
2. Hablan español.
3. Estudia arquitectura.

4. Sí, tengo una cámara Polaroid.
5. Trabaja en Nueva York.

a. ¿Tomas fotos?
b. ¿Qué estudia Carmen?
c. ¿Qué idioma hablan Carmen y Don Miguel?
d. ¿Dónde trabaja Peter?
e. ¿Usas mucho tu computadora?

THE COUNTDOWN: COUNTING FROM 20 TO 39

Let's continue . . .

veintiuno	21	**treinta y uno**	31
veintidós	22	**treinta y dos**	32
veintitrés	23	**treinta y tres**	33
veinticuatro	24	**treinta y cuatro**	34
veinticinco	25	**treinta y cinco**	35
veintiséis	26	**treinta y seis**	36
veintisiete	27	**treinta y siete**	37
veintiocho	28	**treinta y ocho**	38
veintinueve	29	**treinta y nueve**	39
treinta	30		

Can you figure out what number comes next?

1. uno, dos, tres, cuatro . . .
2. cinco, diez, quince . . .
3. veintitrés, veintiséis, veintinueve . . .
4. treinta y dos, treinta y cuatro, treinta y seis . . .

WORDS TO LIVE BY

FUN THINGS TO DO . . .

Here are some more ideas for fun things to do for people of any age. Which do you prefer?

visitar países	to visit countries
escuchar música	to listen to music
ir a un concierto	to go to a concert
escribir mensajes electrónicos	to write e-mail messages
cantar	to sing
tener novio / a	to have a boyfriend / girlfriend

Did You Know?

In Spain, large rock concerts are often held in the local bull ring, which is similar to using a stadium in the United States. And did you notice the word for bull ring? Yes, it is *plaza de toros*. (Remember that the word *plaza* can also mean "square.") The most famous *plaza de toros* in Spain is Las Ventas, in Madrid.

Word on the Street

More useful expressions:

¡Oye!	Hey! (Lit. Listen!)
¡Qué vergüenza!	How embarrassing!
¡Ay, Dios mío!	Oh, my God!
en todas partes	everywhere (Lit. in all places)

Now, I'd like to introduce a new section called **Let's Put It in Writing**, where you will find fun examples of written texts. The first example is just a paragraph. Let's read it. But before that, please take note of a small piece of advice:

Take a Tip from Me!

Reading paragraphs should be no different than listening to the dialogues. Try to get the gist of the story. Just think of what you do when you read in English. Do you stop and puzzle over every word that you don't know? Probably not, because the context usually helps you guess the meaning. Do the same in Spanish!

Take a Tip from Me!

LET'S PUT IT IN WRITING

We already know a few things about Carmen. Let's find out some more:

Carmen es una estudiante de arquitectura en la Universidad Complutense de Madrid. Ella y su familia son de Granada, pero Granada no tiene escuela de arquitectura. El arquitecto favorito de Carmen es Antonio Gaudí. Barcelona (donde están la mayoría de las obras de Gaudí) es su ciudad favorita. Ahora también le gusta (she likes) Frank Gehry y el Museo Guggenheim de Bilbao. ¡¡Es un museo impresionante!!

Carmen es muy tímida (shy) pero en el internet habla con otras personas sin (without) problemas.

ACTIVITY 8: TAKE IT FOR A SPIN

Pues, ahora, ¡tú trabajas! Let's see what you know about Carmen:

1. ¿De dónde son Carmen y su familia?
2. ¿Qué estudia Carmen?
3. Cómo es Carmen, ¿tímida o extrovertida?
4. ¿Cómo se llama el arquitecto favorito de Carmen?

Did You Know?

Antonio Gaudí (1852–1926) is Spain's most famous architect, well-known for the imagination and fantasy of his designs. His most famous works, including the Expiatory Church of the Holy Family (El Templo Expiatorio de La Sagrada Familia) can be found in Barcelona. Did you know that the white soldiers' uniforms from *Star Wars* (you know, the bad guys) were inspired by one of Gaudí's designs, a house called *La Pedrera*?

Did You Know?

Did You Know?

A Guggenheim Museum in a Spanish city? Yes, that's right. The famous Guggenheim Museum in New York has a branch in Bilbao, an industrial town in northern Spain. It's been incredibly popular, partially due to its impressive size. It was designed by the American architect Frank Gehry.

Did You Know?

ACTIVITY 9: TAKE IT UP A NOTCH

Here's your opportunity to shine! I am a bit nosy and would like to know a few things about you. Can you answer these questions for me?

1. ¿Tienes novio / a (or esposo / a)?
2. ¿Cuántos años tienes?
3. ¿Escuchas música española?
4. ¿Eres rubio / a o moreno / a?
5. ¿Eres simpático / a?

CRIB NOTES

HEAR...SAY 1

Peter:	I am American. I am 28 years old. I work in New York and I am now in Madrid to take photos and write an article for *La Gente*.
Mysterious person:	How interesting!
Peter:	I want to talk to young people and get to know Madrid for my article.
Mysterious person:	Hi, there. I am young. I am 22 and I am also in Madrid at the moment.
Peter:	What's your name?
Mysterious person:	Ah! That's a mystery . . . hey, are you handsome or ugly?
Peter:	You are very curious. I don't know if you are a man or a woman.
Mysterious person:	I am a woman. And yes, I am very curious. What are you like physically?

Peter:	I am tall. I am not thin but I am not fat. I am not handsome, but I am not ugly.
Mysterious person:	In other words, (you're) very ordinary.
Peter:	That's right. And you? What are you like?
Mysterious person:	I am not tall, but I am not short. I am not pretty, but I am not ugly. I have dark hair and I have big, black eyes.
Peter:	So, (you're) also ordinary. By the way, are you a student or are you employed?
Mysterious person:	I study.
Peter:	What do you study?
Mysterious person:	I study architecture. Do you have a girlfriend?
Peter:	You really are curious!

Mysterious person:	Well, do you have a girlfriend or not?	Mysterious person:	Yes, of course, and I also listen to British music. By the way, I have two tickets to Sting's concert in Madrid's bull ring, Las Ventas.
Peter:	No, I don't have a girlfriend. And you? Do you have a boyfriend?		
Mysterious person:	Ah! That's another secret . . . you speak Spanish very well.	Peter:	Sting, in a bull ring? With bulls?
Peter:	Well, right now I am not speaking, I am writing. But I do speak Spanish because I visit many countries where Spanish is spoken.	Mysterious person:	No, of course not! Sting will give a concert there.There are no bulls!
		Peter:	Well, if there are no bulls, then, let's go!
		Mysterious person:	Okay! Where are you now?
Mysterious person:	And do you also listen to Spanish music in the United States?	Peter:	I am in the Plaza Mayor. What about you?
Peter:	Of course! Enrique Iglesias sings very well. And he's a very nice guy.	Mysterious person:	What a coincidence! I am also in the Plaza Mayor.
Mysterious person:	How interesting! Are you his friend?	Peter:	Carmen! Is that you? You are like air! You are everywhere!
Peter:	Well, not exactly. That's another story . . . What about you? Do you listen to American music?	Carmen:	Oh, my God, Peter, this is so embarrassing!

ANSWER KEY

ACTIVITY 2

1. Peter is from Boston. False.
2. Peter is Cuban. False.
3. The mysterious person is a man. False.
4. The mysterious person studies math. False.
5. The mysterious person is very curious. True.

ACTIVITY 3

There are many possibilities. Here are some:
1. Hitchcock es interesante.
2. El Papa es generoso.
3. Penélope Cruz es guapa.
4. Antonio Banderas es guapo.
5. Los Beatles son románticos.
6. Rosie O'Donnell es generosa.
7. Los Rolling Stones son locos.

ACTIVITY 4

1. Don Miguel es viejo. (We assume he is not young.)
2. Peter es alto.

3. Carmen es morena.
4. Tú eres mujer.
5. Yo soy _____. (Have a ball! Fill in the blank with your favorite adjectives: guapo / a, alto / a, delgado / a . . . make yourself gorgeous!)

ACTIVITY 5

1. The mysterious person has tickets for an Enrique Iglesias concert. False.
2. Peter does not speak Spanish very well. False.
3. The mysterious person is in the inn. False.
4. Peter is a friend of Enrique Iglesias. False.
5. The mysterious person is Carmen. True.

ACTIVITY 6

a – 4; b – 3; c – 2; d – 5; e – 1.

ACTIVITY 7

1. cinco; 2. veinte; 3. treinta y dos; 4. treinta y ocho

ACTIVITY 8

1. Carmen y su familia son de Granada.
2. Carmen estudia arquitectura.
3. Carmen es tímida.
4. El arquitecto favorito de Carmen se llama Antonio Gaudí.

ACTIVITY 9

Possible answers:
1. No tengo novio / a.
2. Tengo _____ años.
3. Sí, escucho música española.
4. Soy rubio / a.
5. Sí, soy simpático.

THAT'S LIFE

Así es la vida

But is he your uncle or not?

COMING UP. . .

- *All in the family:* Words for family members
- *Tell me why:* Asking *why* and saying *because*
- *What's the difference?:* More cognates
- *How do you feel?:* More expressions with *estar* (to be)
- *The house of John:* Using *de* (of) to say what belongs to whom
- *More on human feelings:* Expressions with *tener* (to have)
- *Add up your possessions:* Saying *my, your, his, her,* etc., in Spanish

¡Hola! ¿Qué tal? Bueno, aquí estamos otra vez (here we are again). In this lesson, we are going to meet (*conocer*) more new people. As we saw before, a *pensión* is like an inn here in the United States. Often, it is run by a family who also lives there, so it has the atmosphere of a home. In the scene that's coming up, Peter is meeting Don Miguel's family (Remember: Don Miguel is the owner, or *el dueño*, of the *pensión*) and also some other people, who are *muy interesantes* . . .

ACTIVITY 1: LET'S WARM UP

Here are several words that describe family members:

hermano, madre, tío, primo, abuela, hermana, padre, tía, abuelo, prima

1. Can you make a wild guess and find the words for *father* and *mother*?
2. Of the four words: *tío, abuelo, hermana,* and *primo*, which one means "sister"?
3. Of the four words: *prima, abuelo, tía,* and *hermana*, which one means "grandfather"?

Muy bien, excelente. This time I'll be nice (*simpática*) and give you the answers right away, so you don't even have to flip to the end of the chapter.

For Question 1, the answers are *padre* and *madre*. You know that because these words are similar to their English counterparts.

You also know the answers to questions 2 and 3, *¿verdad? ¡Claro que sí!* (Right? Of course!). For Question 2, the answer is *hermana* and for Question 3, it is *abuelo*.

Although these words do not really sound like words in English, you picked a word that has the right ending: *–a* for a female family member and *–o* for a male family member.

HEAR . . . SAY 1

Peter is talking to Juan, Don Miguel's son. Today Juan is helping at the *pensión*'s desk.

Peter: Hombre, Juan, ¿qué pasa? ¿Por qué estás aquí hoy?

Juan: Pues, porque mi padre está muy ocupado. Está con mi abuelo en el hospital. Mi abuelo está regular.

Peter: Hombre, lo siento. ¿Y dónde trabajas normalmente?

Juan: Trabajo con mi tío Luis en su taller de automóviles. Hoy mi tío no está muy contento porque yo estoy aquí. Pero mi padre me necesita más. Y así es la vida. Un día aquí, otro allí.

Peter:	Vaya. Parece que la familia es muy importante aquí en España.
Juan:	Pues sí. En el taller de mi tío también trabajan sus hijos, mis primos, Arturo y Santiago. Es un negocio familiar. Pero a veces es un rollo, porque hay mucho control.
Peter:	Oye, y a tu abuelo, ¿qué le pasa?
Juan:	Pues que está un poco mal del estómago. Pero no estamos preocupados. No es nada serio.
Peter:	Bueno, menos mal.

ACTIVITY 2: HOW'S THAT AGAIN?

1. Listen one more time to the dialogue and write down all the words that refer to family members.
2. Now, answer these questions:

   a. ¿Dónde está Don Miguel (el padre de Juan)?
   b. ¿Dónde trabaja normalmente Juan?
   c. ¿Quién (*who*) trabaja en el taller del tío?
   d. ¿Qué problema tiene el abuelo de Juan?

Did You Know?

It is common in Spain and in other Spanish-speaking cultures to have family members help out when there is a need of any kind. Family needs always come before individual needs. This is great most of the time, but as Juan says in the dialogue, sometimes, it is a pain in the neck (*es un rollo*). Young people often try to escape the excessive control their families can have over their lives. Many young people in Spain achieve this by leaving their country. For example, it is very common, even fashionable, to study abroad.

Another huge (I mean *huge*) difference between Spanish and American families is that in Spain, you do not move out of your home unless you are getting married or you got a job in another town. Young people in Spain marry rather late (usually in the late twenties or even thirties) and getting a job in another town is uncommon. (Spaniards generally hate moving far from their hometowns.) Thus, it is quite common to find people in their thirties still living at home. So, in our *pensión*, Juan is probably helping out his *padre* because he still lives with his parents.

Did You Know?

HOW DO YOU FEEL?: MORE EXPRESSIONS WITH *ESTAR* (TO BE)

In the dialogue you heard *estar* (to be) several times, followed by different adjectives. Remember? Let me refresh your memory:

El padre de Juan está ocupado.	Juan's father is busy.
El abuelo está regular.	The grandfather is not (doing) so well.
El tío no está contento.	The uncle is not happy.
Ellos no están preocupados.	They are not worried.

Estar is used to describe how someone is feeling at a given moment. It is used with adjectives describing moods, which tend not to be permanent conditions:

Él está contento (ahora).	He is happy (now).

If an adjective describes a permanent characteristic, *ser* is used instead:

Él es alto (siempre).	He is tall (always).

One notable exception to this rule is the adjective *muerto* (dead), which is used with *estar* even though it describes a permanent state. (This just shows you how optimistic Spaniards are.)

In Spain *estar* is also used with adjectives describing someone's marital status:

Estar soltero / casado / divorciado / viudo.

To be single / married / divorced / widowed.

I guess nothing lasts forever, good or bad . . .

You already know that *estar* is used in the question *¿Cómo estás?* (How are you?). Of course, the possible answers always contain *estar*. Here are some other possibilities:

Estoy deprimido / confundido / interesado / nervioso / enojado.

I am depressed / confused / interested / nervous / annoyed.

You already knew all these adjectives, right? Maybe not *enojado*, which is a pretty useful one, *¿verdad?*

And finally, two more *estar* expressions you might need:

estar cansado	to be tired
estar enfermo	to be sick

Hey, *¿estás preparado?* Here are four sentences describing some less-than-uplifting human states. Replace the English term in italics with the Spanish translation.

1. Está *nervous* (female).
2. Está *depressed* (male).
3. Está *annoyed* (female).
4. Está muy *busy* (male).

Heads Up!

The following two sentences sound very similar but have very different meanings. Make sure you say what you really mean . . .

Estoy cansado / a.	I am tired.
Estoy casado / a.	I am married.

Heads Up!

What a difference can an *n* make, right? Hey, maybe you are **both**: tired of being married (*Estás cansado / a de estar casado / a.*).

Another tricky expression with *estar* is *estar embarazada*. No, it does not mean "to be embarrassed." There are "good" cognates and then there are some "bad" ones, better known as "false friends." The word *embarazada* is of the latter kind. While it sounds very much like *embarrassed*, it means "pregnant." Something to keep in mind . . .

Lastly, the adjective *regular* does not mean "regular," as you would reasonably expect. It has a slightly negative meaning, and could be translated as "just so-so."

¿Cómo está el café?	How's the coffee?
El café está regular.	The coffee is just so-so.

¡¡Ay, Díos mío, qué complicado es el español!! (I bet you understood this one!)

THE HOUSE OF JOHN: USING *DE* (OF) TO SAY WHAT BELONGS TO WHOM

When you want to say what belongs to whom in Spanish, you use the preposition *de* (of). Look at the examples:

El hijo de Don Miguel.

Don Miguel's son (*Lit.* The son of Don Miguel).

Los primos _de_ Juan.

Juan's cousins (_Lit._ The cousins of Juan).

El taller _de_ mi tío.

My uncle's workshop (_Lit._ The workshop of my uncle).

When _de_ is followed by the article _el_, it becomes _del_:

Es la casa _del_ tío.

It's the uncle's house.

To ask a question about somebody's ownership, use _¿de quién?_ (whose?).

¿De quién es el taller?

Whose workshop is it?

¿De quién es la pensión?

Whose _pensión_ is it?

Now, you tell me: _¿De quién es la Casa Blanca?_

WORDS TO LIVE BY

ALL IN THE FAMILY: WORDS FOR FAMILY MEMBERS

At the beginning of the lesson you learned several words for family members. Here they are, with some additions, in a handy table:

FEMALE FAMILY MEMBER		MALE FAMILY MEMBER	
abuela	grandmother	_abuelo_	grandfather
madre	mother	_padre_	father
hija	daughter	_hijo_	son
hermana	sister	_hermano_	brother
tía	aunt	_tío_	uncle
prima	cousin	_primo_	cousin

In the plural, the masculine form is used if a group contains both sexes:

padres   _parents_
abuelos   _grandparents_

| tíos | uncles; uncles and aunts |
| **hermanos** | brothers; brothers and sisters |

TELL ME WHY: ASKING *WHY* AND SAYING *BECAUSE*

To ask *why?*, say *¿por qué?* in Spanish. And to say *because*, use *porque* (this time as one word and without the accent on *que*):

¿Por qué estás aquí hoy?

Why are you here today?

Porque mi padre está muy ocupado.

Because my father is very busy.

We also saw how to ask what's the matter with somebody:

Y a tu abuelo, ¿qué le pasa?

And what's the matter with your grandfather? (*Lit.* And your grandfather, what is happening to him?)

But remember, *¿Qué pasa?*, without *le*, means "What's up / new?"

WHAT'S THE DIFFERENCE?: MORE COGNATES

Make note of the following cognates: *hospital* (hospital), *automóvil* (automobile, car), *control* (control), *estómago* (stomach), *preocupado / a* (preoccupied, worried), *serio / a* (serious).

Now let's look at some useful expressions you heard in the dialogue. Remember to learn them as fixed phrases, without thinking of their components.

Word on the Street

Lo siento.	I am sorry.
¡Vaya!	As an exclamation, **¡Vaya!** is close to the English **My goodness!** or **Oh, boy!** (Lit. Go!)
a veces	sometimes
ser un rollo	to be a pain in the neck. This expression is used only in Spain.
¡Menos mal!	Thank God! This is an interesting expression. Its actual meaning is very different from its literal meaning, "less bad."

HEAR . . . SAY 2

While Peter was talking to Juan, Carmen showed up. She was on her way to class. Here is a hint that will help you understand what Carmen and Peter are talking about: *estar liado* means the same thing as *estar ocupado*.

Peter: Hola Carmen, ¿qué tal?

Carmen: Pues, estoy muy liada. No tengo tiempo para nada. Tengo sueño y tengo hambre y tengo prisa siempre . . .

Peter: ¿Por qué?

Carmen: Pues, porque tengo una clase de arquitectura con un tío que es horrible, super duro.

Peter: ¿Con tu tío?

Carmen: No hombre, con un profesor.

Peter: No comprendo.

Carmen: Pues, que tengo un profe muy duro, muy difícil y tengo mucho miedo.

Peter: Pero, ¿es tu tío o no?

Carmen: Ay, Peter, ¡qué no te enteras! Un tío significa un hombre en lenguaje coloquial, ¿vale?

ACTIVITY 4:   **HOW'S THAT AGAIN?**

¿Qué tiene y qué no tiene Carmen? Now, go back to the dialogue and read it. Then, write what is happening with Carmen. I'll get you started by filling in the first two items.

1. Carmen no tiene tiempo.
2. Tiene sueño.
3.
4.
5.
6.
7.

Did You Know?

In Spain, after graduating from high school, students who choose to go to college have to make very specific, advance decisions about their courses of study. Basically, they need to choose a profession for which they wish to be prepared. Our friend Carmen is

studying *arquitectura*, which is a six-year college program. Medicine also takes six years (without the specialization which follows). Most other programs, though, take five years, including law, psychology, and the humanities.

Public universities are good and practically free. Because of this, there is overcrowding in most programs and the elimination process is very harsh. In many cases, only 15 percent of the class passes at the end of the year, especially in schools of engineering and architecture. Now you understand why Carmen is so worried!

Did You Know?

WORKSHOP 2

THE NITTY-GRITTY

MORE ON HUMAN FEELINGS: EXPRESSIONS WITH *TENER* (TO HAVE)

You already know that we use the verb *tener* to talk about age:

> *Tengo treinta y seis años.*

> I am 36.

Tener is also used to express certain states and feelings. Remember how Carmen was feeling?

> *Carmen tiene sueño.*

> Carmen is sleepy. (*Lit.* She has sleep.)

> *Tiene hambre.*

> She is hungry. (*Lit.* She has hunger.)

> *Tiene prisa.*

> She is in a hurry. (*Lit.* She has hurry.)

> *Tiene mucho miedo.*

> She is very scared. (*Lit.* She has much fear.)

Note that English uses *to be* in all such expressions.
Other similar expressions are:

tener sed	to be thirsty (*Lit.* to have thirst)
tener frío	to be cold (*Lit.* to have coldness)
tener calor	to be hot (*Lit.* to have heat)

And remember *to be embarrassed*? We use *tener* in this expression, too. And we do not use *embarazada* (pregnant) but *vergüenza* (shame).

tener vergüenza

to be embarrassed (*Lit.* to have shame)

TAKE IT FOR A SPIN

Now, tell me how you are feeling (by using *tengo* and one of the expressions described above) if:

1. . . . it is 101 degrees out.
2. . . . I am about to flunk you because you're not studying hard. (Just joking!)
3. . . . you are late for your meeting.
4. . . . you forgot to get dressed today!
5. . . . you haven't eaten in 10 hours.

ADD UP YOUR POSSESSIONS: SAYING *MY, YOUR, HIS, HER*, ETC., IN SPANISH

When you want to say what belongs to whom without using people's names, you use *my, your, his, her,* etc. These words are called possessive adjectives. Here they are in Spanish:

POSSESSIVE ADJECTIVES			
mi, mis	my	*nuestro / a, nuestros / as*	our
tu, tus	your	*vuestro / a, vuestros / as*	your
su, sus	your (formal), his, her	*su, sus*	your (formal), their

These adjectives act just like other adjectives in Spanish and agree with the noun they modify. Most have two forms, one for singular, one for plural. For example:

mi tío   my uncle

mis tíos   my uncles

But *nuestro* and *vuestro* each have four forms depending on whether the noun that follows is feminine or masculine and singular or plural:

nuestro padre   our father

nuestra madre   our mother

nuestros hermanos   our brothers; our siblings

nuestras hermanas   our sisters

Who are these people? Tell me who they are, following the model:

Son los padres de mis padres. → *Son mis abuelos.*

1. Son los hijos de nuestros abuelos.
2. Son las hijas de nuestros tíos.
3. Es la esposa de mi tío.
4. Es la madre de nuestra madre.
5. Son los abuelos de mis hijos.

WORDS TO LIVE BY

Let's review some of the words you heard in the dialogue related to education:

el profesor / a	*high school teacher, university professor*
	*The colloquial abbreviation is **profe**.*
la clase	*course, subject; classroom*
duro / a	*hard, difficult*

Word on the Street

Peter had some trouble understanding Carmen earlier. Let's see why, so it does not happen to you.

Tío and **tía** mean "uncle" and "aunt" respectively, but in Spain, they are also the slang terms for *man* or *woman*. It is a bit like *dude* in English. Also, the word **hombre** (man) is often used in conversations to address people directly, whether they are men or women. You saw that in the first dialogue of the lesson. More and more, the word **mujer** (woman) can be heard used in the same way, but among women only.

Enterarse is the slang form for *understand*. Remember what Carmen says? **¡Qué no te enteras!** (You just don't get it, do you?). People will ask you: **¿Te enteras?** (Do you get it? *or* Did you get that?). Just say: **Sí, me entero** (Yes, I get it) to really impress them.

LET'S PUT IT IN WRITING

Peter also met Rosario in the *pensión*. She is another of Don Miguel's (numerous) family members. Let's read about her:

Rosario es la hermana de Juan. Tiene veinticinco años. Trabaja en un bar en la Plaza Mayor. Su padre, Don Miguel, no está muy contento con ella. Está preocupado porque ella tiene un novio, Luis Miguel. Luis Miguel está casado, aunque (although) está separado de su esposa. Pero es un escándalo muy grande en la familia, claro.

Let's see what you learned about Rosario:

1. ¿Quién es Rosario?
2. ¿Quién es su novio?
3. ¿Qué piensa (*thinks*) Don Miguel de Rosario?
4. ¿Está soltero (*single*) Luis Miguel?
5. ¿Dónde trabaja Rosario?

ACTIVITY 8:   TAKE IT UP A NOTCH

Just when you thought you were done . . . Let's do one more activity to review the vocabulary you learned in this chapter. Here we have a paragraph with blanks and guess who gets to fill them! *Exacto. Tú trabajas.*

Juan es el _____ de Don Miguel. Su _____ es Rosario. Don Miguel está _____ con Rosario, porque su novio está aún (still) _____. Hoy Don Miguel está en el hospital con el _____ de Juan y Rosario. El padre de Don Miguel está _____ porque le duele el estómago (his stomach hurts).

And you? *¿Estás cansado? ¿Muy cansado?* Okay, then I'll let you rest now.

CRIB NOTES

HEAR...SAY 1

Peter: Hey, Juan, what's up? Why are you here today?
Juan: Because my dad is very busy. He is with my grandfather in the hospital. My grandfather is not doing so well.
Peter: Man, I am sorry. And where do you usually work?
Juan: I work with my uncle Luis, in his car shop. Today my uncle is not very happy because I am here. But my father needs me more. And that's life. One day here, the next, there.

Peter: Wow. It looks like family is very important here in Spain.
Juan: That's right. My cousins, and his sons, Arturo and Santiago, also work in my uncle's shop. It's a family business. But sometimes it is a pain, because there's a lot of control.
Peter: And, what's the matter with your grandfather?
Juan: His stomach is not well. But we are not worried. It is nothing serious.
Peter: Well, thank God.

Peter:	Hi Carmen, what's up?
Carmen:	I am super busy. I don't have time for anything. I am sleepy and I am hungry and I am always in a rush . . .
Peter:	Why?
Carmen:	Because I have an architecture class with a guy (*Lit.* uncle) who's horrible, very tough.
Peter:	With your uncle?

Carmen:	No, no, with a professor.
Peter:	I don't understand.
Carmen:	What happens is that I have a very tough, very difficult, professor and I am very scared.
Peter:	But, is he your uncle or not?
Carmen:	My goodness, Peter, you just don't get it. An "uncle" means a guy in colloquial Spanish, okay?

ANSWER KEY

ACTIVITY 2

1. padre, abuelo, tío, hijos, primos
2. a. Está en el hospital.
   b. Normalmente trabaja en el taller de automóviles de su tío.
   c. Los primos de Juan, los hijos de su tío, Arturo y Santiago.
   d. Está un poco mal del estómago.

ACTIVITY 3

1. Está nerviosa.
2. Está deprimido.
3. Está enojada.
4. Está ocupado.

ACTIVITY 4

1. Carmen no tiene tiempo.
2. Tiene sueño.
3. Tiene hambre.
4. Tiene prisa.
5. Tiene una clase de arquitectura.
6. Tiene un profesor muy duro.
7. Tiene mucho miedo.

ACTIVITY 5

1. Tengo calor.
2. Tengo miedo.
3. Tengo prisa.
4. Tengo vergüenza.
5. Tengo hambre.

ACTIVITY 6

1. Son nuestros padres.
2. Son nuestras primas.
3. Es mi tía.
4. Es nuestra abuela.
5. Son mis padres.

ACTIVITY 7

1. La hermana de Juan.
2. Luis Miguel.
3. Está preocupado.
4. No. Está casado pero separado de su esposa.
5. Ella trabaja en un bar.

ACTIVITY 8

1. hijo
2. hermana
3. preocupado
4. casado
5. abuelo
6. regular / enfermo

5.

SUGAR CANDY

Bombón de azúcar

You're in Spain now, and you should eat when Spaniards eat. Okay?

COMING UP...

- *Hello?:* **Making a phone call**
- *See you in the morning:* **Times of the day**
- *Enjoy your meal:* **Meals and mealtimes in Spain**
- *Never say never:* **Saying *nothing, nobody, never,* etc., in Spanish**
- *Time flies:* **Telling time**
- *The countdown:* **Counting from 40 to 100**
- *Living in the moment:* **The present tense of *–er* verbs**
- *Strut your stuff!*

Our *amigo americano*, Peter Winthrop, has been waiting for his new Spanish *amiga*, Carmen, at the Sevilla bar . She wants to introduce him to a group of her friends. He has been there for *treinta minutos* (30 minutes), wondering why Carmen isn't there yet. He takes out *su móvil* (his cell phone) and calls her in the *pensión*.

Now, relax, listen to your CD, and find out what happens. Remember, you do not need to understand every word to get the gist of the story. After you have heard the dialogue a couple of times, take a peek in the back of the lesson to see if you understood it correctly.

| ACTIVITY 1: | LET'S WARM UP |

Here is a list of things people say on the phone, in Spanish and in English. Try to match the two columns.

1. ¿Dígame?
2. ¿Está Carmen?
3. ¿Puede esperar un momento?
4. No, Carmen no está.
5. Hola, soy Peter.

a. Can you hold on a moment?
b. Hi, this is Peter.
c. No, Carmen is not here.
d. Is Carmen there?
e. Hello?

HEAR ... SAY 1

Peter: (*talking to himself while he dials Carmen's number and waits for an answer*) Pero, ¿dónde está Carmen? Este es el bar Sevilla. Son las once y media de la mañana. ¿Cuál es su número de teléfono? Nueve, catorce, veinte, treinta y dos, cuarenta y siete. . . .

Persona: Sí, dígame.

Peter: Hola, ¿está Carmen?

Persona: Sí. Aquí está. ¿De parte de quién?

Peter: Soy Peter Winthrop.

Persona: Un momento, por favor.

Peter: Muy bien, vale . . . espero.

(*Carmen answers the phone.*)

Carmen: ¿Sí? ¿Dígame?

Peter: Hola, Carmen, soy Peter.

Carmen: Peter, hombre, ¿qué pasa?

Peter: Oye, ¿dónde estás? Yo estoy en el bar Sevilla y ya son las doce menos veinticinco. Bueno, estoy en la calle, porque el bar está cerrado.

Carmen: Pero, ¿por qué estás ahí?

Peter:	¿Por qué? Pero, ¿no recuerdas? Hoy a las once esperamos a tus compañeros de clase, para comer tapas típicas.
Carmen:	Pero Peter, ¡es a las once de la noche! ¡Nadie come a las once de la mañana!
Peter:	En los Estados Unidos sí comemos a las once de la mañana. ¡Nunca comemos a las once de la noche!
Carmen:	¡Peter! Ahora estás en España y comes cuando los españoles comen. ¿Vale?

ACTIVITY 2: HOW'S THAT AGAIN?

Let's see if you can complete these sentences based on the Hear . . . Say section:

1. Peter está en el bar _____.
2. El número de teléfono de Carmen es el nueve, catorce, veinte, _____, cuarenta y siete.
3. Peter espera a los _____ de clase de Carmen.
4. Peter va a comer _____ típicas.
5. En los Estados Unidos nunca comen a las _____ de la noche.

Did You Know?

Tapas is the word used for small, tasty, and often spicy dishes or appetizers traditionally eaten at the counter in a bar. They are often accompanied by a glass of beer, wine, or *sangría* (a red wine punch). The word itself means "lid," and the legend goes that during the Spanish Civil War (1936–1939), bar patrons would ask the bartender to put a small plate over their drinks when they were being bombed to prevent ceiling debris from falling inside the glass. Then, they would ask the bartender to put food on the same plate (not to waste a clean plate, I guess). I'm not sure how true this story is, but I do know that while *tapas* are originally from Andalucía, their popularity has grown not only in Spain, but in the United States as well. You can find excellent *tapas* bars or restaurants in most major cities in the United States.

Did You Know?

WORKSHOP 1

THE NITTY-GRITTY

TIME FLIES: TELLING TIME

This is how you ask for the time in Spanish:

¿Qué hora es?   What time is it?

You answer using the construction *ser* + *la / las* + the hour:

Son las tres.	It's three o'clock.
Son las cinco y media.	It's five thirty.

With one o'clock (*la una*), in Spanish, use *es*, the singular form of the verb *ser*:

Es la una y cuarto.	It's one fifteen.

To express the time between the full hour and half past, add minutes to the hour with *y* (and):

Son las cuatro y veinte.	It's four twenty.
Es la una y cinco.	It's five past one.

To express the time after half past the hour, use *menos* (less), and subtract the minutes from the following hour:

Son las dos menos veinte.	It's twenty to two. (It's one forty.)
Es la una menos diez.	It's ten to one. (It's twelve fifty.)

To say a quarter of an hour, use *y cuarto* or *menos cuarto*:

Son las seis y cuarto.	It's a quarter past six. (It's six fifteen.)
Son las ocho menos cuarto.	It's a quarter to eight. (It's seven forty five.)

You can also say:

Son las seis y quince.	It's six fifteen.
Son las siete y cuarenta y cinco.	It's seven forty five.

Note that this way of telling time is not common in Spain. You'll still be understood everywhere, though.

For half an hour, use *y media*:

Son las cinco y media.	It's half past five. (It's five thirty).

To ask about times of events, use the question *¿A qué hora?*

¿A qué hora es la cena?	At what time is dinner?
La cena es a las diez. / A las diez.	Dinner is at ten o'clock. / At ten o'clock.

Look at the clocks! What time is it? *¿Qué hora es?*

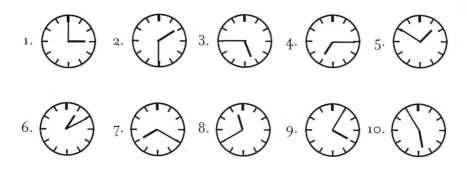

THE COUNTDOWN: COUNTING FROM 40 TO 100

You already know the numbers up to 39, *¿verdad?* Counting from 40 to 100 should be a piece of cake.

40	**cuarenta**	41	**cuarenta y uno**	42	**cuarenta y dos** . . .
50	**cincuenta**	51	**cincuenta y uno**	52	**cincuenta y dos** . . .
60	**sesenta**	61	**sesenta y uno**	62	**sesenta y dos** . . .
70	**setenta**	71	**setenta y uno**	72	**setenta y dos** . . .
80	**ochenta**	81	**ochenta y uno**	82	**ochenta y dos** . . .
90	**noventa**	91	**noventa y uno**	92	**noventa y dos** . . .
100	**cien**				

Hey, that wasn't hard at all!

WORDS TO LIVE BY

HELLO?: MAKING A PHONE CALL

While I don't suggest that you spend your life on the *teléfono* or on your *móvil* or *celular* when visiting Spain or other Spanish-speaking countries, these are some phrases you will need to know:

¿Dígame?

Hello? (Lit. Tell me.) In other Spanish speaking countries **¿Aló?** is used more commonly (Argentina, Venezuela, and Colombia). **¿Bueno?** is used as well, particularly in Mexico.

¿Está Carmen?

Is Carmen there? Note that in Spanish you don't need to say **there**.

No, no está.	No, he / she is not here. Again, there is no **here** in Spanish.
Sí, aquí está.	Yes, she is here. Here, the word **aquí** is actually used.
Sí, soy yo.	Yes, it's me. (Lit. Yes, I am.)
¿De parte de quién?	Who's calling? (Lit. On the part of whom?)
Un momento, por favor.	One moment, please.
¿Cuál es su número de teléfono?	What's your phone number?

Did You Know?

Note that, in Spain, phone numbers tend to be grouped in twos in speech, as most telephone numbers used to have six digits. Recently, they have been changed to include nine digits, but people still group them in twos, except for the first number, which is always nine. So:

Mi número es el nueve, catorce, treinta, cuarenta y dos, ochenta y tres.

My number is 9–14–30–42–83.

Did You Know?

SEE YOU IN THE MORNING: TIMES OF THE DAY

This is how the day is divided in Spanish. Notice that this is a bit different from English:

la mañana	morning; from daybreak until 1:00 PM
el mediodía	noon
la tarde	afternoon; from 1:00 until nightfall
la noche	evening, night; from nightfall until midnight
la madrugada	night; from midnight until daybreak

These are examples of times followed by the time of day:

las diez de la mañana	10:00 AM / in the morning
las dos de la tarde	2:00 PM / in the afternoon
las once de la noche	11:00 PM / in the evening
las tres de la madrugada	3:00 PM / in the morning

If you do not want to specify the time, use *por*:

por la mañana	in the morning
por la tarde	in the afternoon
por la noche	at night

Did You Know?

"AM" and "PM" are occasionally used in Latin America, but hardly ever in Spain. Instead, you say *de la mañana* (in the morning) or *de la tarde* (in the afternoon). Official schedules (trains, buses, airlines) and radio and television broadcasters in Spain and Latin America, however, use the 24-hour clock:

Son las dieciocho horas.   It's six PM. (*Lit.* It's eighteen hours.)

The play might then be at 21:00 or *a las veintiuna.* The quickest way to understand what the time is when using the 24-hour clock is to subtract 12 from the number given.

Did You Know?

Heads Up!

Be careful not to confuse *la mañana* (the morning) with *mañana* (tomorrow) and *la tarde* (the afternoon) with *tarde* (late). It's all a matter of the appearance of the article *la* before the word. So, you may say *mañana por la mañana* (tomorrow morning) or *tarde en la tarde* (late in the aftemoon).

Heads Up!

ACTIVITY 4:   TAKE IT FOR A SPIN

¿Cuál es tu / su número de teléfono? Can you write down the telephone numbers given in the answers below?

1. Mi número es el nueve, quince, veinticuatro, treinta seis, ochenta y ocho.
2. El número de los padres de Carmen es el nueve, cincuenta y ocho, veinte, veintidós, cero ocho.
3. El número de la pensión es el nueve, catorce, treinta y uno, ochenta y seis, noventa y cinco.
4. El número del taller es el nueve, quince, setenta y tres, sesenta y siete, cuarenta y cinco.
5. El número del radio-taxi es el nueve, catorce, cuarenta y seis, cincuenta y tres, setenta y seis.

HEAR ... SAY 2

Almost 12 hours later, Peter and Carmen finally get together to have drinks and *tapas*. While they wait for her friends from college, Carmen tries to explain to Peter the Spanish schedule for meals. While things may be a bit, well, different in Spain, Spaniards, too, start with *el desayuno*, or the breakfast.

Carmen:	Bueno, Peter, escucha bien. Esto es muy importante. El desayuno es a las ocho de la mañana. Normalmente, tomamos café con tostada mientras leemos el periódico.
Peter:	¿Sólamente? ¿No comen huevos o cereales?
Carmen:	No. Sólo el café y la tostada. El almuerzo es a las dos o las tres de la tarde, y todo el mundo ve las noticias de la televisión cuando comen.
Peter:	Un momento, un momento . . . ¿A las dos? ¡Es muy tarde!
Carmen:	Sí, a las dos. Además, el almuerzo es la comida principal. Comemos sopa o ensalada, un plato grande y postre.
Peter:	¡Muchísima comida!
Carmen:	Sí. Luego la merienda es a las seis. Los niños beben chocolate y comen pan con nocilla. Los adultos beben café.
Peter:	Para nosotros, las seis de la tarde es la hora de la cena.
Carmen:	Pues nosotros cenamos a las nueve o a las diez de la noche.
Peter:	¡Eso es tardísimo!
Carmen:	Yo creo que es una hora normal. Después ves a tus amigos en algún bar y tomas una copa.
Peter:	¿Y a las once de la mañana nunca comen tapas?
Carmen:	No, nunca. ¿Vale? ¿Te enteras ya o no?
Peter:	No estoy seguro. ¡Qué complicado es todo en España!

ACTIVITY 5: HOW'S THAT AGAIN?

Wow! That's a lot of meals! Do you remember what Spaniards eat or drink according to Carmen? Let's see:

1. Por la mañana toman café y _____.
2. A las dos de la tarde toman sopa o _____.
3. Por la tarde, los niños toman _____ con nocilla.
4. Por la noche, toman una _____ con sus amigos.

WORKSHOP 2

THE NITTY-GRITTY

LIVING IN THE MOMENT: THE PRESENT TENSE OF –ER VERBS

You have already learned the present tense of regular verbs ending in –ar. It's time for more verbs, those ending in –er. Here's an important verb that relates to our topic of food, *beber* (to drink):

PRESENT TENSE OF –ER VERBS	
ENDINGS	BEBER (TO DRINK)
–o	yo bebo (beb + o)
–es	tú bebes (beb + es)
–e	usted, él / ella bebe (beb + e)
–emos	nosotros / nosotras bebemos (beb + emos)
-éis	vosotros / vosotras bebéis (beb + éis)
-en	ustedes, ellos / ellas beben (beb + en)

As you can see, these endings are very similar to those of the –ar verbs.

There are many more verbs that follow the same pattern. *Por ejemplo:*

comer	**Los españoles comen tapas.**
	Spaniards eat tapas. (And not only Spaniards, right?)
leer	**Yo leo el periódico por la mañana.**
	I read the newspaper in the morning. (You wish you had time for it, huh?)
ver	**Peter ve a los amigos de Carmen.**
	Peter sees Carmen's friends. (Where? In the bar?)
aprender	**Tú aprendes mucho español.**
	You are learning a lot of Spanish. (Definitely!)
comprender	**Peter no comprende España.**
	Peter doesn't understand Spain. (If only he could read this book!)

TAKE IT FOR A SPIN

Here are some questions with *cuándo* (when) regarding your daily routine. Remember to use the *yo* form of the verb when answering them. These are the times of the day you can use in your answers:

por la mañana / por la tarde / por la noche

1. ¿Cuándo bebes café?
2. ¿Cuándo ves la televisión?
3. ¿Cuándo lees un periódico?
4. ¿Cuándo comes?

WORDS TO LIVE BY

ENJOY YOUR MEAL: MEALS AND MEALTIMES IN SPAIN

Here's a schedule so you will know when to show up:

MEALS AND MEALTIMES IN SPAIN				
MEALS *COMIDAS*		**TIMES** *HORAS*	**WHAT?** *¿QUÉ?*	
desayuno	breakfast	*8:00 a 9:00 de la mañana*	*café* *tostada* *bollo*	coffee toast pastry
almuerzo	lunch	*2:00 a 3:00 de la tarde*	*sopa* *ensalada* *plato grande* *postre*	soup salad main dish dessert
merienda	snack	*6:00 de la tarde*	*pan* *chocolate* *café*	bread chocolate coffee
cena	dinner	*9:00 de la noche*	*bocadillo* *huevos* *fruta*	sandwich eggs fruit

Remember when Carmen says:

Después de la cena ves a tus amigos en algún bar y tomas una copa.

After dinner, you get together with (*Lit.* see) your friends in a bar and have a drink.

Tomar una copa means to have an alcoholic drink, such as rum and coke. A beer (*cerveza*) or wine (*vino*) are not really considered *copas*. (The word *copa* itself just means a type of glass.)

Everything I've mentioned so far is typical of Spain. When it comes to food, each Spanish-speaking country has its idiosyncrasies. The times at which people eat, the types of food, and even the names of food items can vary quite a bit.

In Spain, the main meal is *almuerzo*, often also called *la comida* (a word which also means "food" or "a meal" in general). If you hear:

¿A qué hora es la comida?

At what time is the meal?

know that what they are talking about is the large meal in the middle of the day.

One more thing: in Spanish, there is a verb associated with each meal:

desayunar to have breakfast
almorzar to have lunch
merendar to have the late afternoon snack
cenar to have dinner

NEVER SAY NEVER: NOTHING, NOBODY, NEVER, ETC., IN SPANISH

Although we're trying to be positive here, sometimes you just need to say no and use negative words, such as *never* or *nobody*. You heard these two words in Spanish in the dialogues:

nadie	nobody, no one
nunca	never

Other negative words that might be useful are:

nada	nothing
ningún, ninguno / a	none, not any
ni . . . ni	neither . . . nor

You should also know that, in Spanish, a sentence like *I don't want nothing* is perfectly correct and is, in fact, the only correct way to express the thought. In other words, if a verb is negative, all related words in the sentence must match and be negative, too.

Yo <u>no</u> quiero <u>nada</u>.

I don't want anything.

More Words You'll Need

tarde	late. Be careful not to confuse with la tarde (the afternoon).
tardísimo	very, very late

So if *mucha comida* means "a lot of food," what does *muchísima comida* mean? Yes, "an awful lot of food."

todo el mundo	everybody
todo	everything
yo creo	I think (Lit. I believe)

Word on the Street

At the beginning of a meal, it is customary to say *¡Qué aproveche!* or *¡Buen provecho!* (Enjoy!). And the most common toast is *¡Salud!* (To your health!).

TAKE IT FOR A SPIN

Let's see if you remember what the mealtimes in Spain are:

1. ¿A qué hora es el desayuno?
2. ¿A qué hora es la cena?
3. ¿A qué hora es el almuerzo?
4. ¿A qué hora es la merienda?

LET'S PUT IT IN WRITING

After some *tapas* and *copas*, Carmen, Peter, and friends decided to go to a club, but they needed to call a cab to take them there. This is a printout of a page from the *Páginas Amarillas Online* (Online Yellow Pages) that Carmen brought with her. Cabs are called *radio-taxis* in Spain, because all of them are hooked up with radios.

PÁGINAS AMARILLAS ONLINE (MADRID–CAPITAL)

RADIO-TAXIS:

MUTUA MADRILEÑA DE TAXIS
PLAZA CIEZA, 1
28034 – MADRID
Tlf: 913 782 097

FEDERACIÓN PROFESION-AL DEL TAXI DE MADRID
CALLE JOSÉ BERGAMÍN, 70
28030 – MADRID
Tlf: 913 712 131

TAXI RECAMBIOS SL
CALLE RAMÓN CALABUIG, 46 – 48
28053 – MADRID
Tlf: 914 784 362

SOCIEDAD COOPERATIVA LIMITADA INDEPENDIENTE DEL TAXI DE MADRID
CALLE SAN LAMBERTO, 7
28017 – MADRID
Tlf: 914 051 213

Notice that although the numbers are grouped in threes when they are written, most people tend to say them in twos, as I explained earlier.

TAKE IT FOR A SPIN

Let's see if you can answer these questions about Madrid's *radio-taxi* companies:

1. ¿Cuál es el número de teléfono de la Federación Profesional del Taxi?
2. ¿Cómo se llama el radio-taxi con el número de teléfono nueve, catorce, cero cinco, doce, trece?

3. ¿Cómo se llama el radio-taxi que está en la Plaza (*square*) Cieza, número 1?
4. ¿Qué radio-taxi está en el número cuarenta y seis o cuarenta y ocho de la calle Ramón Calabuig?

STRUT YOUR STUFF!

Y esto, ¿qué es? And this, you say, what is it? A new section? Yes, this is your opportunity to review and show off what you've learned so far. Let's see . . .

ACTIVITY 9:   TAKE IT FOR A SPIN

These are different statements about Peter and Carmen. Which phrase applies to which person?

1. Es de Nueva York.
2. Es de España.
3. Es una mujer tímida.
4. Tiene veintiocho años.
5. Es morena con ojos grandes y negros.
6. Su número de teléfono es el nueve, catorce, veinte, treinta y dos, cuarenta y siete.

ACTIVITY 10:   TAKE IT FOR A SPIN

And now, answer these questions about yourself.

1. ¿Eres americano / a o español / a?
2. ¿Eres de Nueva York?
3. ¿De dónde son tus padres?
4. ¿Tienes novio / a?
5. ¿Estudias o trabajas?
6. ¿Cuántos años tienes?
7. ¿Eres alto / a?
8. ¿Tienes miedo de la profesora de español?
9. ¿Estás contento?

I don't know the answers to these questions, of course. But you can find a translation of the questions in the Crib Notes section to make sure you understood everything.

So, for now, *¡hasta más tarde, amigo / amiga!*

CRIB NOTES

Peter: (*talking to himself while he dials Carmen's number and waits for an answer*) But, where is Carmen? This is the bar called Sevilla. It is eleven thirty AM. What's her number? Nine, fourteen, twenty, thirty two, forty seven . . .
Person: Hello?
Peter: Hi! Is Carmen there?
Person: Yes, here she is. Who is calling?
Peter: This is Peter Winthrop.
Person: Just a second, please.
Peter: Sure, I'll wait.
(*Carmen answers the phone.*)
Carmen: Hello?
Peter: Hi, Carmen! This is Peter!

Carmen: Peter, my friend, what's up?
Peter: Hey, where are you? I am at the Sevilla bar and it is already 11:35. Well, I am actually in the street, because the bar is closed.
Carmen: But, why are you there?
Peter: Why? But, don't you remember? We are supposed to meet your friends at 11:00 today to eat the typical *tapas*.
Carmen: But Peter, it's at 11:00 in the evening! Nobody eats at 11:00 in the morning!
Peter: In the United States, we do eat at 11:00 in the morning. We never eat at 11:00.
Carmen: But, Peter! You are in Spain now, and you should eat when Spaniards eat. Okay?

Carmen: Hey, Peter, listen up. This is very important. Breakfast is at 8:00 AM. Usually, it's coffee and toast while we read the newspaper.
Peter: That's all? You don't eat eggs or cereal?
Carmen: No. Only coffee and toast. Lunch is at 2:00 or 3:00 PM, and everybody watches the news on TV while they eat.
Peter: Hold on a second! 2:00 PM? That's so late!
Carmen: Yes, at 2:00. And also, lunch is our main meal. We have soup or salad, a main dish, and dessert.
Peter: That's a lot of food!
Carmen: Yes. Then we have a snack around 6:00. Children have chocolate milk and bread

with a chocolate spread. Adults have a cup of coffee.
Peter: For us, 6:00 is dinnertime.
Carmen: We, instead, have dinner at 9:00 or 10:00 PM.
Peter: But that's so late!
Carmen: I think it's a normal time. After that, you meet your friends somewhere and have a drink.
Peter: And, at 11:00 AM, you never have a snack?
Carmen: No, never. Is that clear now? Do you finally get it or not?
Peter: I'm not sure. Everything is so complicated in Spain!

ANSWER KEY

ACTIVITY 1

1. e; 2. d; 3. a; 4. c; 5. b

ACTIVITY 2

1. Sevilla
2. treinta y dos
3. compañeros
4. tapas
5. once

ACTIVITY 3

1. Son las tres.
2. Son las dos y media.
3. Son las seis menos cuarto.
4. Son las siete y cuarto.
5. Son las dos menos diez.
6. Es la una y diez.
7. Son las ocho y veinte.
8. Son las doce menos veinte.
9. Son las cuatro y cinco.
10. Son las seis menos cinco.

ACTIVITY 4

1. 915–24–36–88
2. 958–20–22–08
3. 914–31–86–95
4. 915–73–67–45
5. 914–46–53–76

ACTIVITY 5

1. tostada; 2. ensalada; 3. pan; 4. copa

ACTIVITY 6

Possible answers are:
1. Bebo café por la mañana.
2. Veo la televisión por la tarde.
3. Leo el periódico por la mañana.
4. Como por la mañana, por la tarde y por la noche.

ACTIVITY 7

1. A las ocho de la mañana.
2. A las nueve o a las diez de la noche.
3. A las dos o tres de la tarde.
4. A las seis de la tarde.

ACTIVITY 8

1. El nueve, trece, setenta y uno, veintiuno, treinta y uno.

2. Se llama Sociedad Cooperativa Limitada Independiente del Taxi. (What a name!)
3. Se llama Mutua Madrileña de Taxis.
4. Taxi Recambios SL.

ACTIVITY 9

1. Peter; 2. Carmen; 3. Carmen; 4. Peter; 5. Carmen; 6. Carmen o Peter (If that's the pensión's number it could be both).

ACTIVITY 10

1. Are you American or Spanish?
2. Are you from New York?
3. Where are your parents from?
4. Do you have a boyfriend / girlfriend?
5. Do you study or work?
6. How old are you?
7. Are you tall?
8. Are you scared of your Spanish teacher?
9. Are you happy?

6. LOST WITHOUT YOU

Perdido sin ti

Here we have a Gucci model.

COMING UP. . .

- *On a shopping spree:* Store names
- *It's a colorful world:* Words for colors
- *On a shopping spree, again:* Shopping vocabulary
- *Q&A:* Asking questions with *quién* (who), *qué* (what), etc.
- *Whether you like it or not:* The verb *gustar* (to like)
- *Talking about this and that:* Showing and pointing with *este* (this) and *ese* (that)
- *Whether you like it or not:* More about the verb *gustar* (to like)
- *Do you agree or disagree?:* Using *también* (too) and *tampoco* (neither, either)
- *The countdown:* Counting from 100 to 1,000

¡Hola! The parents of one of Carmen's classmates own an art gallery and today, there is an opening. Carmen wants to take Peter along, but he asked her to take him shopping first. Peter needs to get new shoes (*zapatos*), because his old ones are not *elegantes*. They are going to a couple of stores including El Corte Inglés, a big department store. There, Peter will encounter some *sorpresas. Vamos a ver qué pasa . . .* (Let's see what happens. . . .)

ACTIVITY 1:   LET'S WARM UP

What kind of questions do you ask in a store? Pick those questions that seem to make the most sense (even if you don't know what every word means). Then you can check the translations at the end of the chapter.

1. ¿Cuánto cuestan estos zapatos?
2. ¿Qué hay para beber?
3. ¿Cuántos años tienes?
4. ¿Cómo te llamas?
5. ¿Tienen otros modelos diferentes?
6. ¿Qué número tiene?
7. ¿Es usted muy grande?

And now, let's listen to the conversation taking place in the *zapatería* (shoe store).

HEAR ... SAY 1

Carmen:	Esta zapatería es muy buena y tiene zapatos muy elegantes.
Peter:	(*talking to the salesperson*) Buenas tardes, busco unos zapatos elegantes.
Empleado:	Muy bien, señor. Aquí tenemos unos modelos de la casa Gucci. ¿Qué número calza usted?
Peter:	En Estados Unidos calzo el número trece. Aquí en Europa, no sé. Me gusta ese modelo marrón.
Empleado:	Bueno, estos zapatos son muy grandes. Son del número cuarenta y seis.
Peter:	(*after trying them on*) No, lo siento, son pequeños. ¿Tienen el cuarenta y siete?
Empleado:	No sé. (*stops to think for a moment*) Sí, un momento.
Peter:	(*after trying again*) No. También son pequeños.
Carmen:	¡Qué barbaridad, Peter! ¡Tienes unos pies gigantes!
Empleado:	Lo siento, señor. No tenemos zapatos grandes en ese modelo. Pero tenemos estos zapatos blancos en su número.

Peter:	Muy bien. Me gustan esos zapatos blancos. ¿Te gustan los zapatos, Carmen?
Carmen:	(*whispering in his ear*) ¿Esos zapatos? ¡Pero si son espantosos! Son grandes, pero no son nada elegantes. ¡Zapatos blancos! ¡Pero, qué ocurrencia! ¡Es una galería importante!
Peter:	No sé cuál es el problema, Carmen. A mí sí me gustan. ¿Cuánto cuestan?
Empleado:	Son doscientos euros.
Peter:	Pero, ¡son muy caros! Bueno, al final a mí tampoco me gustan.

ACTIVITY 2: HOW'S THAT AGAIN?

So, Peter did not have luck finding shoes in Spain. Let's see if you got the fine details of his great misfortune. After listening to the dialogue one more time, circle the right numbers in response to a question:

1. What is Peter's original shoe size? 14, 11, or 13.
2. Which sizes does he try on? 42, 46, 49, 47, or 43.
3. How much do the white shoes cost? Cuatrocientos cincuenta, doscientos euros.

Did You Know?

In Spain, fashion matters. When you're out of the house, you must look your best, even if you're just crossing the street to buy *pan* (bread). People will judge you based on your looks more so than in the United States. Moreover, the concept of elegance is also different. You have to look your best, but that can be achieved by wearing cool designer jeans with a special T-shirt and a scarf, for example. And while we're on the topic of shopping for shoes, I have to tell you that in Spain, sneakers are used only for sports. When dressing informally, people in Spain (and most Spanish-speaking countries) simply wear more casual shoes.

WORKSHOP 1

THE NITTY-GRITTY

Q&A: ASKING QUESTIONS WITH *QUIÉN* (WHO), *QUÉ* (WHAT), ETC.

You already know most of the question words in Spanish, but it's always good to learn more and to review:

QUESTION WORD			AS IN...
qué	what	¿Qué hora es?	What time is it?
quién	who	¿Quién es tu amigo?	Who is your friend?
de quién	whose	¿De quién es el libro?	Whose is the book? / Who does this book belong to?
dónde	where	¿Dónde está Carmen?	Where is Carmen?
de dónde	where from	¿De dónde es Peter?	Where is Peter from?
cuándo	when	¿Cuándo es la cena?	When is dinner?
por qué	why	¿Por qué no estás aquí?	Why aren't you here?
cómo	how	¿Cómo estás?	How are you?
cuánto	how much	¿Cuánto cuesta?	How much does it cost?
cuál	which (one) / what (kind)	¿Cuál es tu número?	What's your number?

A little nitty-gritty point: Note that all question words have accent marks.

Heads Up!

Cuál and qué are similar but not interchangeable. For now, simply learn the specific questions that are used with each.

Heads Up!

ACTIVITY 3:   **TAKE IT FOR A SPIN**

Imagine you have just met Carmen. Here are her answers. What are your questions?

1. Me llamo Carmen Jiménez Cejudo.
2. Soy de Granada, en España.
3. Ahora estoy en Madrid.
4. Estudio arquitectura.
5. Mi número es el 958–20–22–08.

Did You Know?

The traditional Spanish currency was the *peseta*, but that changed in January 2002, when the *euro* replaced it. The euro is now the currency of 12 member states of the European Union. This has made travel around much of Europe even more convenient.

Did You Know?

WHETHER YOU LIKE IT OR NOT: THE VERB *GUSTAR* (TO LIKE)

Gustar (to like) is a frequently used verb in Spanish, and therefore important for you to learn.

We'll talk more about it in Lesson 15, but for now, let's look at an example from the dialogue:

Me gustan esos zapatos blancos.   I like the white shoes.

If what you like is singular, you use *me gusta*. If it is plural, you use *me gustan*.

To say *you like* use *te gusta* and *te gustan*, as in:

¿Te gustan los zapatos blancos?   Do you like those white shoes?

And if you ask me:

No, no me gustan.   I don't like them.

Now, time for practice.

ACTIVITY 4:   **TAKE IT FOR A SPIN**

Look at all the things that I like. Match the objects on the right side with the correct sentence beginning on the left:

a. Me gusta _____   1. . . . los museos.
b. Me gustan _____   2. . . . los automóviles.
                            3. . . . mi casa.
                            4. . . . el español.
                            5. . . . los zapatos blancos.

TALKING ABOUT THIS AND THAT: SHOWING AND POINTING WITH *ESTE* (THIS) AND *ESE* (THAT)

We use words like *this* and *that* to show or point to people, places, or things. Such words are also called demonstrative adjectives (think: "demonstrate"). Here's the complete list of the Spanish equivalents.

DEMONSTRATIVE ADJECTIVES			
	THIS, THESE	THAT, THOSE	THAT, THOSE (OVER THERE)
masculine singular	este	ese	aquel
feminine singular	esta	esa	aquella
masculine plural	estos	esos	aquellos
feminine plural	estas	esas	aquellas

Take a look at the example from the Hear . . . Say section:

esta zapatería	this shoe store
ese modelo	that model
estos zapatos	these shoes
esos zapatos blancos	those white shoes

As you can see, demonstrative adjectives have to agree in number and in gender with the following noun, just like all other adjectives in Spanish.

The Fine Print

When you use Spanish demonstrative adjectives by themselves (e.g., I like **those** but not **these**), you add an accent mark to the first vowel of the word:

Me gustan <u>ésos</u>.	I like those.
¿Te gusta <u>ésta</u>?	Do you like this one?

WORDS TO LIVE BY

ON A SHOPPING SPREE: STORE NAMES

La zapatería (shoe store) is the store where they sell . . . *¡zapatos!* (shoes). The words for other stores, or *tiendas*, often end in *–ería*. Here are some examples:

STORE		WHAT THEY SELL
frutería	fruit store	*fruta* (fruit)
panadería	bakery	*pan* (bread)
librería	bookstore	*libros* (books)
carnicería	butcher	*carne* (meat)
pescadería	fish market	*pescado* (fish)
pastelería	pastry shop	*pastel* (pastry)
heladería	ice-cream store	*helado* (ice cream)

But, be careful! A *ferretería* does not sell ferrets! It is a hardware store.

IT'S A COLORFUL WORLD: WORDS FOR COLORS

So you won't end up with only white *zapatos*, here is a list of words for other colors:

blanco / a	white
negro / a	black
rojo / a	red

marrón	brown (used in Spain). In other Spanish-speaking countries, **color café** is also used.
azul	blue
amarillo / a	yellow
verde	green
rosado / a	pink
anaranjado / a	orange

Notice that *azul* and *verde* have only one form, used with either masculine or feminine nouns.

TAKE IT FOR A SPIN

What's the color of these things? *¿Cuál es su color?*

1. el océano
2. una planta
3. una banana
4. los zapatos de Gucci de Peter

Did You Know?

Although supermarkets and big department stores (like El Corte Inglés, in Spain) are more and more common, small specialty stores are still a big part of everyday life in all Spanish-speaking countries. Customers know the store owners and shopping is just one more chance to socialize.

Did You Know?

ON A SHOPPING SPREE, AGAIN: MORE SHOPPING VOCABULARY

Here's some more important shopping vocabulary:

el número de pie	shoe size (Lit. foot number)
la talla	size (for everything other than shoes)
la ropa	clothes
pequeño / a	small
mediano / a	medium
grande	large

And more phrases you will want to know:

No sé.	I don't know.
Lo siento.	I'm sorry.
¿Qué numero de pie tiene usted?	What shoe size do you wear (Lit. have)?

The last question can be also:

¿Qué número calza usted?   *What shoe size do you wear?*

And the last two questions you'll need:

¿Qué talla tiene?   *What size do you wear (Lit. have)?*
¿Cuánto cuesta? / ¿Cuánto cuestan?   *How much does it cost? / How much do they cost?*

Here are size charts for clothes and some more vocabulary, so you can always look your best when traveling abroad!

WOMEN'S CLOTHING SIZES (*Tallas para la ropa de mujer*)

COATS, DRESSES, SKIRTS, SLACKS (*ABRIGOS, VESTIDOS, FALDAS, PANTALONES*)

U.S.	4	6	8	10	12	14	16
SPAIN & LATIN AMERICA	36	38	40	42	44	46	48

BLOUSES, SWEATERS (*BLUSAS, SUÉTERES*)

U.S.	32/6	34/8	36/10	38/12	40/14	42/16
SPAIN & LATIN AMERICA	38/2	40/3	42/4	44/5	46/6	48/7

SHOES (*ZAPATOS*)

U.S.	4	4½	5	5½	6	6½	7	7½	8	8½	9	9½	10	11
SPAIN & LATIN AMERICA	35	35	36	36	37	37	38	38	39	39	40	40	41	42

MEN'S CLOTHING SIZES (*Tallas para la ropa de hombre*)

SUITS, COATS (*TRAJES DE CHAQUETA, ABRIGOS*)

U.S.	34	36	38	40	42	44	46	48
SPAIN & LATIN AMERICA	44	46	48	50	52	54	56	58

SLACKS (*PANTALONES*)

U.S.	30	31	32	33	34	35	36	37	38	39
SPAIN & LATIN AMERICA	38	39-40	41	42	43	44-45	46	47	48-49	50

SHIRTS (*CAMISAS*)

U.S.	14	14½	15	15½	16	16½	17	17½	18
SPAIN & LATIN AMERICA	36	37	38	39	40	41	42	43	44

SWEATERS (*SUÉTERES*)

U.S.	XS/36	S/38	M/40	L/42	XL/44
SPAIN & LATIN AMERICA	42/2	44/3	46-48/4	50/5	52-54/6

SHOES (*ZAPATOS*)

U.S.	7	7½	8	8½	9	9½	10	10½	11	11½
SPAIN & LATIN AMERICA	39	40	41	42	43	43	44	44	45	46

HEAR . . . SAY 2

This time, Carmen takes Peter to a big department store, El Corte Inglés. Finally he is able to find shoes. He also finds a shirt (*camisa*) and a jacket (*chaqueta*). But now, he will have to deal with the cashier (*la cajera*) . . .

Peter: Mira. Estos zapatos negros son bonitos, son grandes y son baratos. ¿Te gustan?

Carmen: A mí, sí. Y son modernos y apropiados para la galería. Y la camisa y la chaqueta también están fenomenal de precio. Vamos a la caja a pagar.

Cajera: Buenas tardes. Los zapatos son noventa euros. La camisa es treinta y tres y la chaqueta está en oferta especial y cuesta ciento cincuenta. En total, son doscientos setenta y tres euros. ¿Paga en efectivo o con tarjeta de crédito?

Peter:	Con tarjeta Visa.
Cajera:	Muy bien. Necesito su firma aquí.
(Peter signs his name.)	
Cajera:	Lo siento, pero esta firma es diferente. No acepto esta tarjeta.
Peter:	Pero, ¡si es mi firma!
Cajera:	Necesito ver su pasaporte.
Peter:	No tengo mi pasaporte aquí.
Cajera:	¿Tiene dinero?
Peter:	No.
Cajera:	Pues, lo siento. Hasta luego, señor.
Peter:	Pero, pero . . .
Carmen:	Ay, Peter, pero que desastre de día. Anda, yo pago. Aquí tiene el dinero.
Peter:	*(feeling really embarassed)* Carmen, la verdad es que . . . ¡estoy perdido sin ti!

ACTIVITY 6: HOW'S THAT AGAIN?

Let's see what you can remember:

1. ¿Cómo son los zapatos?
2. ¿Qué tarjeta de crédito tiene Peter?
3. ¿Acepta la tarjeta la cajera?
4. ¿Tiene Peter su pasaporte?
5. ¿Quién paga al final (*in the end*)?

Did You Know?

Your shopping experience can be quite different in Spain from the one in the United States. In the U.S., the customer is king. Not so in Spain. The cashier in our story didn't want to take any risks and wanted to make sure that Peter's credit card was really his; her job would be on the line if there was a problem later on. Beware, as this has happened to many people I know! It's a good idea, therefore, to carry some additional identification with you, such as your passport. You should also know that many stores still do not accept credit cards, so be prepared to shell out cash!

Did You Know?

WORKSHOP 2

THE NITTY-GRITTY

WHETHER YOU LIKE IT OR NOT: MORE ABOUT THE VERB *GUSTAR* (TO LIKE)

Phrases *a mí* or *a ti* are sometimes used with the verb *gustar* (to like). Peter says:

A mí sí me gustan.	I like them. (*Lit.* To me, yes, they are pleasing).
A mí no me gustan.	I don't like them.

These phrases are also used in short responses:

¿Te gusta?	Do you like it?
A mí sí. / A mí no.	Yes. / No.

Or when you want to emphasize something:

A ti sí te gusta, ¿verdad?	You do like it, right?

DO YOU AGREE OR DISAGREE?: USING *TAMBIÉN* (TOO) AND *TAMPOCO* (NEITHER, EITHER)

To agree or disagree in English, you use *too* and *neither / either*. In Spanish, it is the same. The word for *too* is *también*. The word for *neither / either* is *tampoco*. This is how they are used with a verb like *gustar*:

Peter:	**¿Te gustan estos zapatos?**	Do you like these shoes?
Carmen:	**A mí sí.**	I do.
Juan:	**A mí también.**	I do, too.
Peter:	**¿Y esa camisa?**	What about this shirt?
Carmen:	**A mí no.**	I don't.
Juan:	**A mí tampoco.**	Neither do I.

And this is how they are used with any other verb:

Peter:	**Busco ropa para una fiesta.**	I am looking for clothes for a party.
Carmen:	**Yo también.**	I am, too.
Don Miguel:	**Yo no necesito buscar.**	I don't need to look (for anything).
Juan:	**Yo tampoco.**	I don't either.

THE COUNTDOWN: COUNTING FROM 100 TO 1,000

For big ticket items you will need big numbers, right? Here they are:

cien	100	seiscientos	600
doscientos	200	setecientos	700
trescientos	300	ochocientos	800
cuatrocientos	400	novecientos	900
quinientos	500	mil	1,000

Did You Know?

In Spain and Spanish-speaking countries, the period and comma are used very differently with numbers from how they're used in the United States. A period marks thousands, and a comma separates whole numbers from decimals.

| 4.000 | = | *cuatro mil* | = | 4,000 or four thousand. |
| 4,75 | = | *cuatro coma setenta y cinco* | = | 4.75 or four point seven five. |

Did You Know?

ACTIVITY 7:   **TAKE IT FOR A SPIN**

How much are the pieces of clothing Peter and Carmen have been shopping for? Let's review:

1. ¿Cuánto cuestan los zapatos blancos de Gucci?
2. ¿Cuánto cuestan los zapatos del Corte Inglés?
3. ¿Cuánto cuesta la camisa?
4. ¿Cuánto cuesta la chaqueta?

WORDS TO LIVE BY

ON A SHOPPING SPREE, AGAIN: SHOPPING VOCABULARY

Here are the people who work in stores:

| *el empleado / la empleada* | sales clerk |
| *el cajero / la cajera* | cashier |

And the things they say:

¿Qué desea?	What would you like?
¿En qué puedo servirle?	How may I help you?
¿Cómo desea pagar, en efectivo	How would you like to pay, with cash
o con tarjeta de crédito?	or a credit card?

Word on the Street

In the dialogue, you heard two very common colloquial expressions. The first one is **¡Qué barbaridad!** (*Lit.* What a barbarity!). Another one is **¡No me digas!** (*Lit.* Don't tell me!). They don't have exact English equivalents, but they can be used when you are surprised, either positively or negatively. Look at the examples:

Los zapatos cuestan dos mil euros.	The shoes cost 2,000 euros.
¡Qué barbaridad!	Wow!
La camisa es muy barata.	The shirt is very cheap.
Sólo cuesta doce euros.	It costs only 12 euros.
¡No me digas!	No way!

LET'S PUT IT IN WRITING

Here is the invitation to the gallery opening that Carmen and Peter are going to tonight:

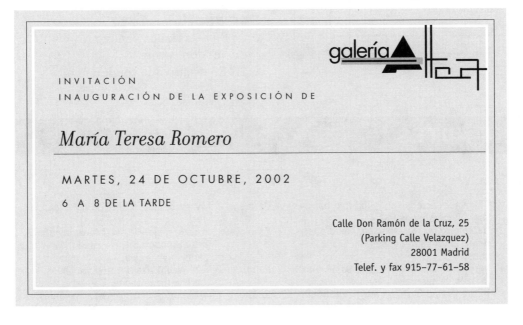

galería A

INVITACIÓN
INAUGURACIÓN DE LA EXPOSICIÓN DE

María Teresa Romero

MARTES, 24 DE OCTUBRE, 2002

6 A 8 DE LA TARDE

Calle Don Ramón de la Cruz, 25
(Parking Calle Velazquez)
28001 Madrid
Telef. y fax 915–77–61–58

ACTIVITY 8: HOW'S THAT AGAIN?

Can you answer these questions about it?

1. What's the name of the artist they are going to see?
2. How long does the opening last?

3. Where can you park your car?
4. What's the ZIP code?
5. Are the phone and fax numbers different?
6. What day of the week is the exhibition?

TAKE IT UP A NOTCH

Here's a crossword puzzle, which is your chance to practice some new vocabulary (consisting of mainly, but not exclusively, names for stores).

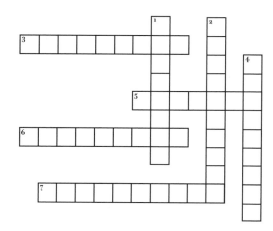

ACROSS:

3. Venden (*they sell*) helados.
5. Es similar a un hotel pero es más barato.
6. Venden zapatos.
7. Venden pescado.

DOWN:

1. En esta tienda venden libros.
2. Venden carne.
4. En esta tienda venden pan.

CRIB NOTES

HEAR...SAY 1

Carmen:	This shoe store is very good and has very elegant shoes.
Peter:	(*talking to the salesperson*) Good afternoon. I'm looking for some elegant shoes.
Employee:	Very well, sir. Here we have some Gucci models. What size shoe do you wear?
Peter:	In the United States, I am size thirteen. I don't know (my size) here in Europe. I like that brown pair.
Employee:	Well, these shoes are rather big. They are size 46.
Peter:	(*after trying them on*) No, I'm sorry, they are small. Do you have size 47?
Employee:	I don't know . . . yes, just a moment.
Peter:	(*after trying again*) No. They are also small.

Carmen:	My goodness, Peter! You have gigantic feet!
Employee:	I'm sorry, sir. We don't have big shoes in that model. But we have these white shoes in your size.
Peter:	Very well. I like these white shoes. Do you like these shoes, Carmen?
Carmen:	(*whispering in his ear*) Those shoes? But they are horrible! They are big, but they are not elegant at all. White shoes! What are you thinking? It's a very important gallery!
Peter:	I don't see the problem, Carmen. I do like them. How much are they?
Employee:	They are 200 euros.
Peter:	But, they are very expensive! Well, in the end, I don't really like them, either.

Peter: Look. These black shoes are nice, they are big and they are cheap. Do you like them?

Carmen: Yes, I do. And they are modern and appropriate for the gallery. The shirt and the jacket also have a great price. Let's go to the register to pay.

Cashier: Good afternoon. The shoes are 90 euros. The shirt is 33 and the jacket is on a special sale and it costs 150. The total is 273 euros. Are you paying in cash or with a credit card?

Peter: With a Visa card.

Cashier: Very well. I need your signature here. (Peter signs his name.)

Cashier: I am sorry, but this signature is different. I cannot accept this card.

Peter: But, this is my signature!

Cashier: I need to see your passport.

Peter: I don't have my passport here.

Cashier: Do you have cash?

Peter: No.

Cashier: Well, then, I am sorry. See you later, sir.

Peter: But, but . . .

Carmen: My goodness, Peter, what a disastrous day! Come on! Let me pay. Here's the money.

Peter: (feeling really embarrassed) Carmen, the truth is . . . I am lost without you!

ANSWER KEY

ACTIVITY 1

1. How much are these shoes?
2. What is there to drink?
3. How old are you?
4. What's your name?
5. Do you have different models?
6. What's your size?
7. Are you very big?

ACTIVITY 2

1. 13 (trece); 2. 46 (cuarenta y seis) and 47 (cuarenta y siete); 3. 200 (doscientos) euros

ACTIVITY 3

1. ¿Cómo te llamas?
2. ¿De dónde eres?
3. ¿Dónde estás ahora?
4. ¿Qué estudias? or ¿Qué haces? (What do you do?)
5. ¿Cuál es tu número de teléfono?

ACTIVITY 4

a. Me gusta + 3, 4
b. Me gustan + 1, 2, 5

ACTIVITY 5

1. azul; 2. verde; 3. amarilla; 4. blancos

ACTIVITY 6

1. Son negros, bonitos, grandes, baratos y modernos.
2. Tiene Visa.

3. No, no acepta la tarjeta.
4. No, no tiene su pasaporte.
5. Carmen paga.

ACTIVITY 7

1. Los zapatos blancos de Gucci cuestan doscientos euros.
2. Los zapatos del Corte Inglés cuestan noventa euros.
3. La camisa cuesta treinta y tres euros.
4. La chaqueta cuesta ciento cincuenta euros.

ACTIVITY 8

1. María Teresa Romero.
2. It lasts two hours, from 6:00 to 8:00 pm.
3. In Calle Velázquez.
4. It's 28001.
5. No, they are the same.
6. It's Tuesday.

ACTIVITY 9

Across:	Down:
3. heladería	1. librería
5. pensión	2. carnicería
6. zapatería	4. panadería
7. pescadería	

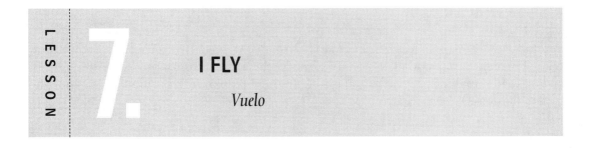

I FLY

Vuelo

He is asking for your plane ticket.

COMING UP. . .

- *Getting around:* Words for different means of transportation
- *All aboard!:* Some verbs you need to talk about travel
- *I have a reservation:* Checking into a hotel
- *Living in the moment:* The present tense of *–ir* verbs, plus a review of *–ar* and *–er* verbs
- *I scream, you scream . . . :* Stem-changing irregular verbs in the present tense
- More irregular verbs

Peter is leaving Spain to follow Ricky Martin's tour to Mexico. In our first *diálogo*, Carmen takes Peter to Barajas, Madrid's main airport where they are waiting for Peter's *avión* (plane). He is making sure he has all his belongings: *pasaporte* (passport), *billete* (ticket), *maleta* (suitcase) . . .

ACTIVITY 1:   **LET'S WARM UP**

Can you guess the meanings of the following words? Hint: they are all related to airports. Match up the two columns as well as you can. Remember that this is a guessing game, so don't worry if you don't get everything right.

a.	el avión	1.	passenger
b.	la línea aérea	2.	pilot
c.	la sala de espera	3.	waiting room
d.	piloto / a	4.	to check your luggage
e.	pasajero / a	5.	suitcase
f.	facturar el equipaje	6.	airplane
g.	la maleta	7.	airline

Take a Tip from Me!

Spanish is spoken in 22 different countries and on four different continents. Wow! That's a lot of countries, but you needn't worry. In general, everybody who speaks Spanish in one country can understand people from other Spanish-speaking countries. Of course, there are differences, some of which can cause misunderstandings. I will make sure to point out the most important ones as we go, so you will be well prepared to travel and speak on any continent. I want to assure you that Spanish is Spanish everywhere, and what you are learning here will be useful wherever you go.

HEAR . . . SAY 1

Peter and Carmen have just arrived at Madrid's Barajas airport. Peter is now checking his luggage at the Aeroméxico counter and Carmen is helping him.

Empleada: Su boleto, por favor.

Peter: ¿Puede repetir? No entiendo. ¿Boleto? ¿Qué es un boleto? Yo no tengo un boleto.

Carmen: Sí, Peter. El boleto es tu billete de avión. En México se llama boleto.

Peter: Ah, vale. Aquí está.

Empleada: Muchas gracias. Todo está correcto. El embarque es en la puerta número quince, a las tres menos cuarto.

(*Peter and Carmen move to the* sala de espera *and wait for boarding.*)

Peter: El avión sale a las cuatro. Tenemos tiempo para tomar un café.

Carmen: Vale. ¿Pido dos cafés con leche o quieres otra cosa?

Peter: No. Eso está bien. Si no tomo café, seguro que me duermo en el avión y necesito escribir un artículo durante el vuelo.

Carmen: ¿Escribes muchas horas al día normalmente?

Peter: Escribo unas dos horas al día, más o menos. Pero pienso escribir más en México. Aquí en España encuentro que no tengo tiempo para mucho.

(*Time goes by.* El tiempo pasa. Peter y Carmen dicen adiós.)

Carmen: Bueno, Peter, buen viaje.

Peter: Gracias. Carmen, sabes, podemos seguir en contacto por el Internet.

Carmen: Sí, claro. Oye, ¿piensas volver a España?

Peter: No sé. Pero si no vuelvo pronto, pues, te puedo ver en los Estados Unidos, ¿no?

Carmen: ¡El viaje cuesta mucho dinero! Pero, no sé, quizá . . . pero, ¿de verdad quieres que yo . . . ?

(*Final boarding for Peter's flight is announced. He has to run.*)

Peter: ¡Dios mío! ¡Qué pierdo mi vuelo! ¡Adiós, Carmen!

ACTIVITY 2: **HOW'S THAT AGAIN?**

Let's see if you can answer these questions about the dialogue:

1. ¿Qué es un boleto?
2. ¿A qué hora sale el avión?
3. ¿Qué toman Carmen y Peter?
4. ¿Qué necesita hacer Peter en el avión?
5. ¿Cuántas horas al día escribe Peter?

Did You Know?

The United Mexican States (Estados Unidos Mexicanos), or Mexico, is a confederation of 31 states (*estados*) and a federal district (*Distrito Federal*) encompassing Mexico's capital, Mexico City. Mexico City is one of the largest cities in the world, with 15 million in-

WORKSHOP 1

THE NITTY-GRITTY

LIVING IN THE MOMENT: THE PRESENT TENSE OF *–IR* VERBS, PLUS A REVIEW OF *–AR* AND *–ER* VERBS

You already know that Spanish verbs are divided into three groups according to their endings in the infinitive form. So, we have: *–ar* verbs like *hablar* (to speak), *–er* verbs like *comer* (to eat), and *–ir* verbs like *escribir* (to write).

Here's the table with the present tense endings attaching to *–ir* verbs for the present tense and the different forms of *escribir*, as an example:

PRESENT TENSE OF *–IR* VERBS	
ENDINGS	ESCRIBIR (TO WRITE)
–o	*yo escribo (escrib + o)*
–es	*tú escribes (escrib + es)*
–e	*usted, él / ella escribe (escrib + e)*
–imos	*nosotros / nosotras escribimos (escrib + imos)*
–ís	*vosotros / vosotras escribís (escrib + ís)*
–en	*ustedes, ellos / ellas escriben (escrib + en)*

Here are some examples from the dialogue:

¿Escribes muchas horas al día?   Do you write many hours a day?

Escribo dos horas al día.   I write two hours a day.

Another useful verb of this type is *vivir* (to live):

Peter vive en Nueva York.   Peter lives in New York.

Mis amigos viven en España.   My friends live in Spain.

Here's a chart with the three verb types put together, so you can review everything and see that they are really similar, particularly the –er verbs and the –ir verbs:

PRESENT TENSE OF ALL REGULAR VERBS		HABL+AR (TO SPEAK)	COM+ER (TO EAT)	ESCRIB+IR (TO WRITE)
Singular	yo	habl + o	com + o	escrib + o
	tú	habl + as	com + es	escrib + es
	él / ella, usted	habl + a	com + e	escrib + es
Plural	nosotros / nosotras	habl + amos	com + emos	escrib + imos
	vosotros / vosotras	habl + áis	com + éis	escrib + ís
	ellos / ellas, ustedes	habl + an	com + en	escrib + en

ACTIVITY 3: TAKE IT FOR A SPIN

Now, let's do a fill-in-the-blanks exercise, all about Peter. ¿Estás preparado? ¡Vamos!

Peter _____ (vivir) en Nueva York. _____ (trabajar) en una agencia de noticias, aunque también _____ (trabajar) para La Gente. Ahora _____ (estar) en México, en un hotel de la capital, el D.F. Sus padres _____ (vivir) en Ohio y sus hermanas _____ (vivir) allí también. Normalmente, Peter _____ (visitar) a su familia en las vacaciones. En Navidad (Christmas), toda la familia _____ (comer) una cena enorme y _____ (beber) champán.

I SCREAM, YOU SCREAM . . . : STEM-CHANGING IRREGULAR VERBS IN THE PRESENT TENSE

Alas, not all verbs follow a regular pattern. Those that don't are called irregular verbs. In Spanish there are two main groups of irregular verbs. Let's start with the so-called stem-changing verbs. These verbs take the same endings as the regular verbs (so far so good), but the root (or stem) changes slightly. (The root is the part of the verb that you add the endings to.) Stem-changing verbs are divided into three groups. The vowel in the root changes as follows (the symbol ">" means "becomes"):

1. e > ie   *querer* (to want), but *quiero* (I want)
2. o > ue   *poder* (can), but *puedo* (I can)
3. e > i   *pedir* (to ask), but *pido* (I ask)

Let's look at each group in more detail:

- e > ie group

As you see in the following table, *–ar* verbs (like *empezar*), *–er* verbs (like *querer*), or *–ir* verbs (like *preferir*) can be of this type. Note that their endings are exactly the same as those for any regular verb.

PRESENT TENSE OF STEM-CHANGING VERBS: *E > IE*					
EMPEZAR (TO START)		*QUERER* (TO WANT)		*PREFERIR* (TO PREFER)	
Singular	Plural	Singular	Plural	Singular	Plural
emp*ie*zo	empezamos	qu*ie*ro	queremos	pref*ie*ro	preferimos
emp*ie*zas	empezáis	qu*ie*res	queréis	pref*ie*res	preferís
emp*ie*za	emp*ie*zan	qu*ie*re	qu*ie*ren	pref*ie*re	pref*ie*ren

You can see that the stem vowels (which are boldfaced) change in singular (*yo, tú, usted, él,* and *ella*) forms and in the third person plural form (*ellos, ellas,* and *ustedes*) forms. The *nosotros* and *vosotros* forms remain unchanged. In order to remember which roots change, think of a shoe. Do you see the three "shoes" in the table? The forms inside the "shoe" are the ones that change.

Other verbs in this group include those you heard in the Hear . . . Say section:

entender (to understand)	→	**No entiendo.**	I don't understand.
pensar (to think)	→	**Pienso volver.**	I am thinking of coming back.
perder (to lose or to miss)	→	**Pierdo el avión.**	I am going to miss the plane.

- o > ue group

Again, any type of verb, *–ar, –er,* or *–ir,* can belong to this group:

PRESENT TENSE OF STEM-CHANGING VERBS: O > UE					
RECORDAR (TO REMEMBER)		*PODER* (CAN, TO BE ABLE TO)		*DORMIR* (TO SLEEP)	
Singular	Plural	Singular	Plural	Singular	Plural
rec*ue*rdo	recordamos	p*ue*do	podemos	d*ue*rmo	dormimos
rec*ue*rdas	recordáis	p*ue*des	podéis	d*ue*rmes	dormís
rec*ue*rda	rec*ue*rdan	p*ue*de	p*ue*den	d*ue*rme	d*ue*rmen

Other verbs in this group are:

volver (to return)	**Peter vuelve pronto.**
	Peter returns soon.
costar (to cost)	**El boleto de avión cuesta mucho.**
	The plane ticket costs a lot.

encontrar (to find)	**¡No encuentro mi billete!**
	I can't find my ticket!
recordar (to remember)	**¿Recuerdas dónde está el aeropuerto?**
	Do you remember where the airport is?
soñar con (to dream)	**Carmen sueña con viajar a Estados Unidos.**
	Carmen dreams about traveling to the U.S.
volar (to fly)	**Peter vuela a México, D.F.**
	Peter is flying to Mexico City.

The verb *jugar* (to play) also follows this pattern although its stem contains a "u" and not an "o". It's forms are *juego, juegas, juega, jugamos, jugáis, juegan*. It is the only verb of its kind:

Yo no juego al tenis. ¿Y tú? ¿Juegas al tenis?

I don't play tennis. And you? Do you play tennis?

- e > i group

Only *–ir* verbs undergo this type of change. Much easier, right?

PRESENT TENSE OF STEM-CHANGING VERBS: *E > I*	
PEDIR (TO ASK, TO REQUEST)	
Singular	Plural
pido	*pedimos*
pides	*pedís*
pide	*piden*

And other similar verbs that you've heard in the dialogue are:

repetir (to repeat)	→	**La empleada repite sus palabras.**
		The employee repeats her words.
seguir (to continue; to follow)	→	**Peter sigue en contacto con Carmen.**
		Peter remains in contact with Carmen. (*Lit.* Peter continues the contact with Carmen.)
servir (to serve)	→	**El hotel sirve el desayuno a las siete.**
		The hotel serves breakfast at 7:00.

The spelling of the *yo* form of *seguir* (to continue; to follow) is *(yo) sigo* (I continue). Notice that there is no "u" following "g" in this form. This has to do with some spelling and pronunciation rules you learned in the very first chapter of this book. If you're curious to know why this happens, you can go back and check there, or you can just remember this little detail as is. Here are two examples:

Peter sigue el programa.   Peter follows the program.

Yo no sigo el programa.   I don't follow the program.

Heads Up!

ACTIVITY 4:   TAKE IT FOR A SPIN

Wow. You've just learned a lot of verbs! And they are quite useful, too. Let's practice them some more, so you can use them *rápido*! Fill in the blanks with the right verb form. If you don't remember all the words, there's always the Crib Notes section.

1. Peter y Carmen _____ ser amigos.
2. Carmen _____ ir a Estados Unidos.
3. El café con leche _____ trescientas pesetas en la cafetería del aeropuerto.
4. Carmen y Peter _____ escribirse por el internet.
5. Don Miguel _____ trabajar en la pensión.

a. sueña con
b. prefiere
c. cuesta
d. quieren
e. pueden

WORDS TO LIVE BY

GETTING AROUND: WORDS FOR DIFFERENT MEANS OF TRANSPORTATION

el avión	*plane*
el tren	*train*
el automóvil	*car* (In Latin America: **el carro**; in Spain also: **el coche**)
el barco	*boat*
el autobús	*bus* (In México: **el camión**; in Central America also: **la guagua**)

ALL ABOARD!: SOME VERBS YOU NEED TO TALK ABOUT TRAVEL

WHEN YOU GO AWAY...		WHEN YOU REACH YOUR DESTINATION...	
salir	to go out	*llegar*	to arrive
despegar	to take off	*aterrizar*	to land

WHEN YOU GO AWAY...		WHEN YOU REACH YOUR DESTINATION...	
subir al autobús / al camión / a la guagua	to get on the bus	*bajar del autobús / del camión / de la guagua*	to get off the bus
embarcar	to board (a plane or a boat)	*desembarcar*	to get off (the plane or a boat
manejar	to drive (In Spain: *conducir*)		

Word on the Street

In the dialogue, we saw one word that is different in Mexico and Spain—the word for ticket. **Boleto** is used in Mexico and **billete** is used in Spain. There are other words in the dialogue that are also used differently according to the region. Thus, in Spain *vale* is used constantly, but not so in Latin America. **Claro** or **OK** are more common there. They drink coffee, **ellos toman café,** in Spain, but in Latin America, the verb **tomar** is most often used to mean "to drink alcohol." For example:

Ese hombre toma.   That man drinks.

But in Spain, you need an object, which can be alcoholic or not:

Ese hombre toma café / Coca-Cola / vino / cerveza.

That man drinks coffee / Coke / wine / beer.

Did You Know?

And speaking of *tomar,* or drinking . . . Mexico's most famous liquor, *el tequila*, is produced in the distilleries of the town of Tequila, in the Mexican state of Jalisco. The production of tequila is controlled by the Mexican government, and there are only a few other places outside Jalisco where tequila is made. This strong liquor is made by distilling the juice of the heart of the blue agave plant. You can visit the famous Sauza Distillery in the town of Tequila on your next visit to Mexico. And don't get regular tequila confused with *mezcal*. That's a similar type of liquor, but sometimes produced with a worm at the bottom of the bottle!

Did You Know?

Peter has arrived in Mexico City. He is checking in at Hotel Isabel, located in the Zócalo area.

Recepcionista: Buenas tardes. ¿Qué desea?

Peter: Buenas tardes. Tengo una reserva a nombre de Peter Winthrop.

Recepcionista: Vamos a ver . . . sí, aquí está. Una habitación doble, con cuarto de baño, aire acondicionado. Pero, un momento, la reserva es para mañana.

Peter: No es posible. Bueno, ¿puede darme otra habitación?

Recepcionista: Creo que no. Estamos completamente llenos, porque hay un congreso de traductores en estos momentos . . .

Peter: Por favor. ¿Qué hago ahora? Estoy muerto de cansancio. Vengo de España, de un vuelo de doce horas, con horario diferente . . .

Recepcionista: Mire, sí. Hay una cancelación de última hora. Es una habitación individual, con una cama de matrimonio y no tiene aire acondicionado . . .

Peter: De verdad que eso ahora no me importa. Muchísimas gracias. Sólo quiero dormir y dormir . . .

Recepcionista: Estupendo. El botones puede poner su equipaje en su habitación.

Peter: Muchas gracias. ¿A qué hora sirven el desayuno?

Recepcionista: Desde las seis y media hasta las nueve y media. Puedo llamar a su habitación por la mañana, si quiere.

Peter: No gracias. No es necesario. Creo que eso es todo. ¿Cuál es el número de mi habitación?

Recepcionista: ¿Es supersticioso? Es el trece . . .

ACTIVITY 5:   HOW'S THAT AGAIN?

Let's see what you can recall:

1. ¿Tiene Peter una reserva?
2. ¿Cuántas horas es el vuelo de Madrid a México?
3. ¿Qué quiere hacer Peter?
4. ¿A qué hora es el desayuno?
5. ¿Cuál es el número de su habitación?

Peter's hotel is located in a great area in *el D.F.,* the Zócalo, the heart and soul of the old downtown area. This old neighborhood contains monuments of Aztec origin, such as the Templo Mayor (Great Temple), as well as some colonial monuments, such as the Catedral Metropolitana and the eighteenth-century Capilla del Sagrario (Sagrario Chapel).

Did You Know?

WORKSHOP 2

THE NITTY-GRITTY

MORE IRREGULAR VERBS

Well, we need to look at some more irregular verbs. Unfortunately, most irregular verbs are also very useful and common verbs, so you do have to learn them.

The only peculiarity in the group of verbs given in the following table is their *yo* form, which is irregular. Notice that I have marked it in boldface:

		HACER (TO DO)	PONER (TO PUT, TO PLACE)	TRAER (TO BRING)	SALIR (TO GO OUT)	SABER (TO KNOW)
PRESENT TENSE OF VERBS WITH IRREGULAR FIRST PERSON SINGULAR						
Singular	yo	**hago**	**pongo**	**traigo**	**salgo**	**sé**
	tú	haces	pones	traes	sales	sabes
	él / ella, usted	hace	pone	trae	sale	sabe
Plural	nosotros / nosotras	hacemos	ponemos	traemos	salimos	sabemos
	vosotros / vosotras	hacéis	ponéis	traéis	salís	sabéis
	ellos / ellas, ustedes	hacen	ponen	traen	salen	saben

Except for *saber* (to know), all *yo* forms have a "g" in the middle.

Here's an example from the dialogue:

¿Qué hago ahora?

What do I do now?

Do you remember the verb *tener*, as in *Carmen tiene veintidós años*? Now that you're an expert, you can tell that *tener* really has two kinds of irregularities: a special *yo* form **and** a stem-changing vowel. There are two other very common verbs that are similar to *tener*. Here they are:

		TENER (TO HAVE)	VENIR (TO COME)	DECIR (TO SAY)
Singular	yo	**tengo**	**vengo**	**digo**
	tú	tienes	vienes	dices
	él / ella, usted	tiene	viene	dice
Plural	nosotros / nosotras	tenemos	venimos	decimos
	vosotros / vosotras	tenéis	venís	decís
	ellos / ellas, ustedes	tienen	vienen	dicen

PRESENT TENSE OF IRREGULAR VERBS
TENER (TO HAVE), VENIR (TO COME), DECIR (TO SAY)

ACTIVITY 6: TAKE IT FOR A SPIN

Can you figure out what these sentences mean? Write them down in English.

1. Peter dice, "Yo traigo mi computadora a México y puedo escribir a Carmen".
2. El avión de Peter sale a las cuatro.
3. El botones pone el equipaje de Peter en su habitación.
4. Yo sé que tú eres muy inteligente.
5. Yo digo, "El español no es difícil".
6. Peter dice, "Vuelvo pronto a España".

WORDS TO LIVE BY

I HAVE A RESERVATION . . . : CHECKING INTO A HOTEL

What do you normally find in a hotel? Here are some of the people or things you may encounter:

el botones	*bellboy*
la habitación individual	*single room*
la habitación doble	*double room*
la cama	*bed*
la cama supletoria	*extra bed*
la cama de matrimonio	*double bed (Lit. marriage bed. I know . . . very old-fashioned, but still common.)*
el cuarto de baño	*bathroom*
la toalla	*towel*

And a few useful phrases:

Tengo una reserva (in Spain) / **reservación a nombre de . . .**   *I have a reservation under the name of . . .*

¿Tiene una habitación con . . . ?   *Do you have a room with . . . ?*

Quisiera una habitación para . . . noche(s) or **semana(s).**   *I would like a room for . . . night(s) or week(s).*

Did You Know?

A note about bathrooms in Spanish-speaking countries: the "C" on the shower or sink faucet stands for *caliente* (hot), and the "F" is for *frío* (cold). An important thing to remember, don't you think?

Did You Know?

ACTIVITY 7:   TAKE IT FOR A SPIN

Cross out the word that does not belong:

1. hotel, reserva, novia, habitación
2. avión, hijo, tren, carro
3. despegar, aterrizar, embarcar, entender
4. cliente, botones, recepcionista, fotógrafo

LET'S PUT IT IN WRITING

Here's Peter's plane ticket from Madrid to Mexico City. Let's see if you can read it:

BILLETE DE PASAJE Y TALÓN DE EQUIPAJE

EMITIDO POR: <u>Aeroméxico</u>   FECHA DE EMISIÓN: <u>20NOV2002</u>

NOMBRE DEL PASAJERO: **PETER WINTHROP**

VÁLIDO PARA VIAJAR	VUELO	CLASE	FECHA	HORA	TARIFA
DE: MAD-Barajas	002	B	22NOV	1400	SKSXW7
A: MEX-Juárez Int.				1840	

Although you probably don't know every word printed on the ticket, I bet you can still answer these questions:

1. What airline company issued this ticket?
2. When was it issued?
3. What day is the flight?
4. At what time does it leave Barajas Airport?
5. What's the flight number?

Did You Know?

Dates in Spanish are given in a different order from the one normally used in the United States. The number of the day is followed by the number of the month. So, 18.10.2002 is October 18, 2002 (and not the 10th day of the 18th month of the year!!) Try to remember—because it will not always be this obvious! Also, note that names for days and months are not capitalized in Spanish.

Did You Know?

ACTIVITY 9:   TAKE IT UP A NOTCH

Time for a little challenge. Here is what Peter has been thinking lately. Can you put his thoughts in the right order?

1. Digo "No entiendo" a la mujer de Aeroméxico.
2. Duermo mucho en la habitación de mi hotel.
3. Escribo en el avión.
4. Pienso, "Quiero besar (to kiss) a Carmen".
5. Salgo para el aeropuerto con Carmen.
6. Hago la reserva para mi viaje a México.
7. Vuelo a México D.F.

HEAR...SAY 1

Employee:	Your ticket, please.
Peter:	Can you repeat? I don't understand. "Boleto?" What is a "boleto"? I don't have a "boleto."
Carmen:	Yes, Peter. The "boleto" is your plane ticket. In Mexico, it is called a "boleto".
Peter:	Oh, okay. Here it is.
E:	Thank you very much. Everything is okay. Boarding is at Gate 15, at a quarter to three.

(*Peter and Carmen move to the waiting area and wait for boarding.*)

Peter:	The plane leaves at four. We have time to have coffee.
Carmen:	Okay. Should I ask for two coffees with milk or do you want something different?
Peter:	No. That's fine. If I don't have coffee, I'm sure I'll fall asleep on the plane, and I need to write an article during the flight.
Carmen:	Do you usually write for many hours a day?
Peter:	I write for about two hours a day, more or less. But I am thinking about writing more in Mexico. Here in Spain, I find that I don't have time for anything.

(*Time goes by. Peter and Carmen say good-bye.*)

Carmen:	All right Peter, have a good trip.
Peter:	Thanks. Carmen. You know, we can keep in touch over Internet.
Carmen:	Yes, of course. Do you think you'll return to Spain?
Peter:	I don't know. But if I don't come back soon, well, I can see you in the U.S., right?
Carmen:	That trip costs a lot! But, I don't know, maybe . . . but, do you really want me to . . . ?

(*They announce final boarding for Peter's flight. He has to run.*)

Peter:	Darn! I am going to miss my flight! Bye, Carmen!

HEAR...SAY 2

Receptionist:	Good afternoon. How can I help you?
Peter:	Good afternoon. I have a reservation under the name of Peter Winthrop.
Receptionist:	Let me see . . . yes, here it is. A double room, with a bathroom and air-conditioning. But, just a moment, the reservation is for tomorrow.
Peter:	That's not possible. All right, could you give me another room?
Receptionist:	I don't think so. We are completely booked, because there is a translation conference (going on) at the moment . . .
Peter:	Please. What do I do now? I am exhausted. I came from Spain, on a 12-hour flight, from a different time zone . . .
Receptionist:	Let me see . . . yes. There is a last-minute cancellation. It's a single room with a double bed, and it doesn't have air-conditioning . . .
Peter:	The truth is that it doesn't even matter to me right now. Thank you so much. I only want to sleep and sleep . . .
Receptionist:	Great. The bellboy can put your luggage in your room.
Peter:	Thanks. What time is breakfast served?
Receptionist:	From half past six to half past nine. I can call your room in the morning, if you want.
Peter:	No thanks. It is not necessary. I think that's all. What's my room number?
Receptionist:	Are you superstitious? It's thirteen.

ANSWER KEY

ACTIVITY 1

a–6; b–7; c–3; d–2; e–1; f–4; g–5

ACTIVITY 2

1. Un boleto es un billete de avión en México.
2. Sale a las cuatro.
3. Toman dos cafés con leche.
4. Necesita escribir un artículo.
5. Normalmente escribe dos horas al día.

ACTIVITY 3

vive – trabaja – trabaja – está – viven – viven – visita – come – bebe

ACTIVITY 4

1. Peter y Carmen quieren ser amigos.
   Peter and Carmen want to be friends.
2. Carmen sueña con ir a Estados Unidos.
   Carmen dreams about going to the United States.
3. El café con leche cuesta dos euros.
   The coffee with milk costs two euros.
4. Carmen y Peter pueden escribir en el internet.
   Carmen and Peter can write on the Internet.
5. Don Miguel prefiere trabajar en la pensión.
   Don Miguel prefers to work in the inn.

ACTIVITY 5

1. Sí, tiene una reserva.
2. El vuelo es doce horas.
3. Peter quiere dormir.
4. Sirven el desayuno desde las seis y media hasta las nueve y media.
5. Su habitación es el número trece.

ACTIVITY 6

Here are the English translations:
1. Peter says, "I am bringing my computer to Mexico and can write to Carmen."
2. Peter's plane leaves at four.
3. The bellboy puts Peter's luggage in his room.
4. I know that you are very intelligent.
5. I say, "Spanish is not difficult."
6. Peter says, "I am coming back to Spain soon."

ACTIVITY 7

1. novia; 2. hijo; 3. entender; 4. fotógrafo

ACTIVITY 8

1. Aeroméxico; 2. Nov. 20, 2002; 3. Nov. 22; 4. At 2:00 PM; 5. Number 002

ACTIVITY 9

First, the translations:
1. I say: "I don't understand" to the woman at the Aeroméxico counter.
2. I sleep a lot in my hotel room.
3. I write in the plane.
4. I think, "I want to kiss Carmen."
5. I leave for the airport with Carmen.
6. I make my reservation for the trip to Mexico.
7. I fly to Mexico City.
And the order? 6, 5, 1, 4, 7, 3, and 2.

¿Cielito lindo?

A song for the sky?

COMING UP. . .

- *It's raining cats and dogs:* **Talking about the weather**
- *It's already Christmas:* **Talking about the seasons and the months**
- *What would you prefer?:* **Speaking your mind using** *preferir* **(to prefer)**
- *In the near future:* **Speaking about your immediate plans using** *ir a* **(to go to)**
- *As we speak:* **Talking about what you're doing right now**

Okay. So you have survived all those irregular verbs! *¡Estoy tan orgullosa de ti!* (I am so proud of you!) As a reward, I decided to give you a break in this lesson. (Well, not literally . . .)

Do you remember that Peter could not find a room because there was a conference on translation taking place in the hotel? Well, as it turns out, Carmen e-mailed Peter telling him that one of the people attending the conference is Professor Marcos Alvear, a friend of hers. Marcos and Peter meet, and Peter is taking the day off to do some sightseeing around Mexico City with Marcos. So, we are going to be *turistas típicos* with Peter. Let's go *visitar museos, caminar por las calles y plazas, tomar muchas fotos. . . .* Let's have fun in Mexico!

ACTIVITY 1:	LET'S WARM UP

¿Qué sabes de México? What do you know about Mexico? *Contesta en español.* Answer in Spanish. (Note that more than one answer may be right):

1. ¿Cuál es la capital de México?
   a. Madrid   b. México D.F.   c. Lima   d. Quito
2. ¿Qué idiomas hablan en México?
   a. español   b. francés   c. náhuatl   d. inglés
3. ¿Cómo se llama una comida famosa mexicana?
   a. paella   b. espaguetis   c. guacamole   d. quesadilla
4. ¿Cómo se llama un pintor mexicano famoso?
   a. Picasso   b. Renoir   c. Rivera   d. Dalí

Take a Tip from Me!

From now on, I am going to use Spanish to introduce the dialogues. While I will give you all kinds of hints and use Spanish you already know, I think you are ready for this next challenge. Remember, you only have to concentrate on getting the gist of what you read or what you hear, not on understanding every single word (that would make it really boring, don't you think?). Of course, after reading the introductions a couple of times, you can check the Crib Notes section to make sure you're getting it. *¡Vamos!*

Take a Tip from Me!

HEAR . . . SAY 1

Peter está en el vestíbulo del Hotel Isabel en el centro de Ciudad de México. En el hotel se celebra un congreso de traductores y uno de las participantes es el profesor Marcos Alvear, un amigo mexicano de Carmen. Peter decide tener el día libre para que Marcos le enseñe la ciudad.

Marcos: ¿Qué prefieres? ¿Visitar algún museo? ¿Andar por la ciudad?

Peter: Prefiero ir de paseo. Hoy hace un día estupendo para caminar.

Marcos: Magnífico, no estoy cansado y el tiempo no más es cuestión de suerte; hoy el día es bien lindo. No llueve y no hace frío. Además, el tránsito está muy mal y el estacionamiento aún peor. Manejar un carro en el D.F. es muy difícil.

Peter: ¿Dónde vamos primero?

Marcos: ¿Qué prefieres? ¿Un lugar tranquilo o turístico?

Peter: Prefiero ir a algún sitio muy turístico.

Marcos: ¡Pues ya estamos en uno! En el Zócalo vamos a visitar la Catedral y ver los frescos de Diego Rivera que están en el Palacio Nacional.

Peter: Muy interesante. ¿Y algo menos . . . cultural? Al terminar la visita al museo, claro.

Marcos: ¡Ay, Peter! ¡Ya veo que te gusta la diversión!

Peter: No es eso. Es que quiero probar un auténtico tequila mexicano.

Marcos: Pues por la noche podemos ir a la Plaza Garibaldi. Te va a gustar.

Peter: ¡Fantástico! En esa plaza cantan los mariachis, ¿verdad?

Marcos: Sí. Vamos a oír los mariachis. Aunque, sabes, yo prefiero a los Maná, un grupo rockero muy famoso aquí.

Peter: Bueno, Marcos, ¡veo que estoy en buenas manos!

ACTIVITY 2: **HOW'S THAT AGAIN?**

Marcos and Peter use a lot of verb forms that end in —*ar*, —*er*, or —*ir* in this dialogue. We'll be talking about these some more in this lesson. To get started on it, listen to the dialogue again and write them all down.

1. _____   2. _____   3. _____   4. _____

5. _____   6. _____   7. _____

Did You Know?

Mariachis are not found only in restaurants. The *conjuntos mariachis* are bands of famous, itinerant Mexican musicians that can often be seen singing in the streets in their traditional *charro* costumes—colorful cowboy-style suits and wide-brimmed Mexican hats. *Mariachis* are also hired by people to sing love songs at festive occasions, such as Mother's Day, birthdays, weddings, and *quinceañeras* (celebrations for girls who are turning 15). They can even be hired by a boyfriend who wants to show his love to his sweetheart. These sessions are called *serenatas* and the size and the quality of the *mariachi* band will depend on how many *pesos* you are worth.

By the way, the word *mariachi* is sometimes said to derive from the French word for wedding, *mariage*. Apparently, during Mexico's French occupation, which took place from 1864 to 1867, the French community used to hire these musicians to play at their weddings.

Did You Know?

While the *mariachis* are still very popular, younger audiences in Mexico prefer pop music. The *Manás* is a pop group famous everywhere in Latin America. Other well-known artists are heartthrob Luis Miguel, Lucero, and Ana Gabriel. Their melodies are mostly soft and very (oh, so very) romantic.

WORKSHOP 1

THE NITTY-GRITTY

WHAT WOULD YOU PREFER?: SPEAKING YOUR MIND USING *PREFERIR* (TO PREFER)

To express preferences, we can use the verb *preferir* (to prefer) followed by an infinitive. An infinitive is a neutral, "to" form of the verb (e.g., to prefer). In Spanish, it is the form which ends in *–ar*, *–er*, or *–ir*. Remember that *preferir* is a stem-changing verb (e > ie). Here are some examples from the dialogue:

¿Prefieres visitar algún museo?	Would (*Lit.* Do) you prefer to visit a museum?
¿Prefieres andar por la ciudad?	Would (*Lit.* Do) you prefer to walk in the city?

Prefiero ir de paseo.   I prefer to go for a walk.

Prefiero ir a algún sitio turístico.   I prefer to go to a tourist place.

Remember that to express desires, you can also use the verb *querer* [also stem-changing (e > ie) verb] followed by an infinitive:

Peter quiere ir de paseo.   Peter wants to go for a walk.

TAKE IT FOR A SPIN

Answer the following questions based on the dialogue or your own knowledge.

1. ¿Qué prefiere hacer Peter?
2. ¿Dónde quiere Marcos tomar un tequila?
3. ¿Qué prefieres hacer tú por las mañanas, estudiar español o desayunar?
4. ¿Cómo prefieres celebrar tu cumpleaños (*birthday*)? ¿Prefieres tener una fiesta en casa o en un restaurante?

Did You Know?

In Spain, birthday celebrations are quite different from those in other Spanish-speaking countries. Parties for children, similar to the ones in the United States, are common everywhere. But for adults, in Spain (as in many other parts of Europe), the person who is celebrating has to treat his or her friends, usually in a bar or a café. In Mexico and most other South and Central American countries, friends treat the birthday person. Maybe the people in Spain just have it backwards!

IN THE NEAR FUTURE: SPEAKING ABOUT YOUR IMMEDIATE PLANS USING IR A (TO GO TO)

While you might be the type of person who likes living in the moment, it's nice to have solid plans for the future. In English, you can talk about the future in two ways. You can say, "I will go on vacation in the future," or if you just can't wait that long, you can say, "I'm going to go on vacation soon." You can do the same thing in Spanish. The latter type of future tense is called, not surprisingly, the immediate future tense. In Spanish, it is formed by pairing the appropriate form of *ir* (to go) with the word *a* and then adding the infinitive form of the main verb. For example:

Vamos a tomar un tequila.

We're going to have (*Lit.* drink) tequila.

You have already encountered *vamos*, a form of the verb *ir*, so you can tell that it is an irregular verb. (Oh, no!, you say.) Let's look at all the other forms of *ir* you will need:

PRESENT TENSE OF *IR* (TO GO)		
Singular	yo	voy
	tú	vas
	él/ella, usted	va
Plural	nosotros / nosotras	vamos
	vosotros / vosotras	vais
	ellos / ellas, ustedes	van

As you can see, the endings are the same as for any regular *—ar* verb. So you may be wondering why *ir* is not really *var*? I have no idea! Just try and remember it as is!

So, now that you have all the bits and pieces, you can put it all together. Take a look at these examples from the lesson:

En el Zócalo vamos a visitar la catedral.

In the Zócalo, we're going to visit the cathedral.

Te va a gustar.

You're going to like it.

(Remember: this is the special verb *gustar* we talked about in Lesson 6.)

Vamos a oír a los mariachis.

We are going to listen to the mariachis.

ACTIVITY 4:   **TAKE IT FOR A SPIN**

Match the people with their actions:

1.	Marcos y Peter	a.	va a viajar a Estados Unidos.
2.	Peter	b.	van a tomar tequila.
3.	Carmen	c.	voy a visitar la catedral.
4.	Yo	d.	vamos a ser buenos amigos.
5.	Nosotros	e.	va a escribir un artículo.

IT'S RAINING CATS AND DOGS: TALKING ABOUT THE WEATHER

To talk about the weather in Spanish, use *hacer* (to make, to do). Specifically, use its form *hace*, followed by various expressions. Take a look:

Hace calor.	*It's hot.*
Hace frío.	*It's cold.*
Hace fresco.	*It's cool.*
Hace viento.	*It's windy.*
Hace sol.	*It's sunny.*
Hace buen / mal tiempo.	*The weather is good / bad.*

You can also use *hacer* to ask what the weather is like: *¿Qué tiempo hace?*

And if you're really surprised, you can make exclamations by changing the word order and using *qué*:

¡Qué calor hace!	*It's so hot! or What a hot day!*

Other weather expressions use the verb *hay* (there is / there are):

Hay nubes.	*There are clouds.*
Hay humedad.	*It's humid.*
Hay truenos y relámpagos.	*There is thunder and lightning.*

We haven't said anything about rain and snow yet, right? For those, you use these special stem-changing verbs:

llover (o > ue)	*to rain*
Llueve mucho.	*It rains a lot.*
nevar (e > ie)	*to snow*
En el D.F. nunca nieva.	*In Mexico City, it never snows.*

And, finally, a really nice weather verb:

refrescar	*to cool down*
Por las tardes refresca mucho.	*In the evenings, it cools down a lot.*

IT'S ALREADY CHRISTMAS: TALKING ABOUT SEASONS AND MONTHS

Here's the year at a glance. (I don't think you'll need too much help with this, but pay attention to pronunciation.)

2002

ENERO	FEBRERO	MARZO	ABRIL
1 2 3 4 5	1 2	1 2	1 2 3 4 5 6
6 7 8 9 10 11 12	3 4 5 6 7 8 9	3 4 5 6 7 8 9	7 8 9 10 11 12 13
13 14 15 16 17 18 19	10 11 12 13 14 15 16	10 11 12 13 14 15 16	14 15 16 17 18 19 20
20 21 22 23 24 25 26	17 18 19 20 21 22 23	17 18 19 20 21 22 23	21 22 23 24 25 26 27
27 28 29 30 31	24 25 26 27 28	24 25 26 27 28 29 30	28 29 30
		31	

MAYO	JUNIO	JULIO	AGOSTO
1 2 3 4	1	1 2 3 4 5 6	1 2 3
5 6 7 8 9 10 11	2 3 4 5 6 7 8	7 8 9 10 11 12 13	4 5 6 7 8 9 10
12 13 14 15 16 17 18	9 10 11 12 13 14 15	14 15 16 17 18 19 20	11 12 13 14 15 16 17
19 20 21 22 23 24 25	16 17 18 19 20 21 22	21 22 23 24 25 26 27	18 19 20 21 22 23 24
26 27 28 29 30 31	23 24 25 26 27 28 29	28 29 30 31	25 26 27 28 29 30 31
	30		

SEPTIEMBRE	OCTUBRE	NOVIEMBRE	DICIEMBRE
1 2 3 4 5 6 7	1 2 3 4 5	1 2	1 2 3 4 5 6 7
8 9 10 11 12 13 14	6 7 8 9 10 11 12	3 4 5 6 7 8 9	8 9 10 11 12 13 14
15 16 17 18 19 20 21	13 14 15 16 17 18 19	10 11 12 13 14 15 16	15 16 17 18 19 20 21
22 23 24 25 26 27 28	20 21 22 23 24 25 26	17 18 19 20 21 22 23	22 23 24 25 26 27 28
29 30	27 28 29 30 31	24 25 26 27 28 29 30	29 30 31

And now look at the seasons:

abril, mayo, junio	→	**la primavera**	(spring)
julio, agosto, septiembre	→	**el verano**	(summer)
octubre, noviembre, diciembre	→	**el otoño**	(fall / autumn)
enero, febrero, marzo	→	**el invierno**	(winter)

Note that in Spanish, the names for months and seasons are not capitalized.

ACTIVITY 5: TAKE IT FOR A SPIN

Let's review the new vocabulary. Answer the following questions as completely as possible. Remember that you don't need to answer only with *hace*. Try using other weather expressions as well:

1. ¿Qué tiempo hace en primavera?
2. ¿Qué tiempo hace en verano?
3. ¿Qué tiempo hace en otoño?
4. ¿Qué tiempo hace en invierno?

Did You Know?

Diego Rivera (1886–1957) is one of Mexico's most famous and recognized muralist painters of the twentieth century. In the National Palace (Palacio Nacional), located in the Zócalo, you can see several of his murals. He is known for his political and social themes and his precise, realistic, and colorful style. Rivera was married to another famous painter, Frida Kahlo. And why am I talking about this here? Because Peter was just admiring some of Rivera's murals. . . .

Did You Know?

HEAR . . . SAY 2

Peter toma el día libre y Marcos, el amigo mexicano de Carmen, le enseña los principales monumentos y lugares de interés de Ciudad de México, incluyendo los murales de Diego Rivera. Por la noche, Peter y Marcos están cenando al aire libre en la Plaza Garibaldi. Hay grupos de mariachis que animan la noche con sus canciones.

Marcos: ¿Qué hora es?

Peter: Son las diez y media. ¡Qué tiempo más bueno hace! ¡Qué noche tan bonita con esa luna llena!

Marcos: Ahorita parece que refrescó un poco pero estamos bien.

(*Tequila after tequila, time goes by rather quickly for the two men. They are happily enjoying the music.*)

Peter: ¿Qué canción están cantando?

Marcos: Se llama *Cielito lindo*. Es una de las canciones mexicanas más famosas.

Peter: ¿Una canción al cielo?

Marcos: ¡No! "Cielito" es una expresión cariñosa que dicen las parejas.

Peter: Muy romántico . . . el cielo, la luna. . . .

Marcos: Las nubes . . .

Peter: ¿Las nubes?

Marcos: Pienso que tienes el corazón entre las nubes. ¿No hay alguna persona en España que ahora estás recordando quizá?

Peter: Yo . . . esto . . .

Marco: Nada, nada, hombre. ¡Híjole! Son las doce de la noche y creo que estoy tomando demasiado tequila.

Peter: Sí, aunque lo estoy pasando muy bien, creo que es hora de salir.

Marcos: ¿Prefieres ir en taxi o en metro?

Peter:	Prefiero ir en taxi. Me gustan mucho los taxis aquí. Todos son Volkswagen "Escarabajo", ¿no?
Marcos:	Sí, es el carro más popular acá. ¿Qué tal si vienes mañana a casa a almorzar? Así puedes conocer a mi esposa Laura.
Peter:	¡Qué buena idea! Muchas gracias, Marcos.

HOW'S THAT AGAIN?

Take a moment to answer some questions about the dialogue you've just heard.

1. ¿Qué hora es?
2. ¿Cómo se llama una canción típica de México?
3. ¿Qué prefiere Peter, ir en taxi o en metro?
4. ¿Quién quiere conocer a Peter?

Did You Know?

The Volkswagen Beetle (the old kind, still being manufactured in Mexico), or *Escarabajo* in Spanish, is the most popular car in Mexico. Most taxis in *el D.F.* are green-and-white Beetles.

But Beetles aren't the only cars on the streets of Mexico. The traffic is so bad, a program called *Hoy no circula* (Lit. Today, it does not circulate) has been created to reduce the pollution caused by car emissions. Every registered vehicle is banned from being driven one day a week, and there is a police force division, run by *mujeres policías* (policewomen) in green patrol cars, that makes sure drivers do not "over-circulate."

WORKSHOP 2

THE NITTY-GRITTY

AS WE SPEAK: TALKING ABOUT WHAT YOU'RE DOING RIGHT NOW

When you want to talk about what is happening as you speak, use the present progressive. This tense describes an action that is in progress at the time the statement is made. For example: "I am writing this book right now." In Spanish, the present progressive is formed by pairing the verb *estar* and a form of the main verb. These are a couple of examples we heard in the dialogue:

Peter y Marcos están cenando al aire libre en la Plaza Garibaldi.

Peter and Marcos are having dinner in an outdoor café on the Plaza Garibaldi.

¿Qué canción están cantando?

What song are they singing?

Now, let's look at the different forms of the verb *hablar* (to speak) as an example:

PRESENT PROGRESSIVE OF *HABLAR* (TO SPEAK)			
	ESTAR HABLANDO (TO BE SPEAKING)		
Singular	yo	estoy	hablando
	tú	estás	hablando
	él / ella, usted	está	hablando
Plural	nosotros / nosotras	estamos	hablando
	vosotros / vosotras	estáis	hablando
	ellos / ellas, ustedes	están	hablando

As you may have noticed, the only thing that changes is the verb *estar*. And how is the —*ando* form, or the present participle, made?

For —*ar* verbs, add —*ando* to the stem:

habl-ar (to speak)　→　**habl-ando** (speaking)

For most —*er* and —*ir* verbs, add —*iendo*:

com-er (to eat)　→　**com-iendo** (eating)
escrib-ir (to write)　→　**escrib-iendo** (writing)

Of course, things can not always be so predictable. There are some irregular present participles, but you'll learn them as we stumble upon them in the upcoming lessons. I'll show you only three such irregular forms right now:

leer (to read)　→　**leyendo** (reading)
decir (to say)　→　**diciendo** (saying)
dormir (to sleep)　→　**durmiendo** (sleeping)

ACTIVITY 7:　TAKE IT FOR A SPIN

It's 11:00 in the morning. Could the activities in the sentences below logically be taking place now?

1. Peter está escribiendo un artículo.
2. Marcos y Laura están bebiendo tequila.
3. Yo estoy haciendo guacamole.
4. Carmen está durmiendo.
5. Don Miguel y su hijo están trabajando en el taller.

And what are you doing just now? Write it down!

6. _____
7. _____
8. _____

WORDS TO LIVE BY

The *mariachis* were singing *Cielito lindo*. The word *cielito* comes from *el cielo*, which means both "sky" and "heaven." As Marcos explained, it is also used as the equivalent of the English endearment term *honey*, when talking to a loved one. Look at the example:

¿Cómo estás hoy, cielo?

How are you today, honey?

Another such word in Spanish is *corazón* (heart).

Word on the Street

Here's a sampling of some typical Mexican expressions:

bien	really, e.g., **bien lindo** "really beautiful"
ahorita	right now, this minute. Look at how the ending **–ito / a** can be added to words like **ahora** (now). We also saw it with **cielo** and **cielito**. The ending, roughly meaning "little," makes the word more endearing. It doesn't really change its meaning, and it is very Mexican!
¡Híjole!	My goodness!

LET'S PUT IT IN WRITING

Peter is checking the five-day forecast on the Web because he will be doing so much sightseeing in Mexico. (Whatever happened to all the work he was planning to do?) Let's check the forecast with him:

EL TIEMPO—CIUDAD DE MÉXICO				
HOY	**24 DE NOV.**	**25 DE NOV.**	**26 DE NOV.**	**27 DE NOV.**
Lluvia	Parcialmente nublado	Sol	Nubes	Parcialmente despejado
máx. 28 mín. 8	máx. 25 mín. 8	máx. 24 mín. 9	máx. 19 mín. 6	máx. 19 mín. 10

Oh, my! It sure is cold in Mexico in November! But is it, really? No, of course not. The temperatures here are given in degrees Celsius, not Fahrenheit. Here's a conversion table to help you figure it all out:

To Convert Centigrade/Celsius to Fahrenheit	**To Convert Fahrenheit to Centigrade/Celsius**
$(^9/_5) C° + 32 = F°$	$(F° - 32) ^5/_9 = C°$
Divide by 5 Multiply by 9 Add 32	Subtract 32 Divide by 9 Multiply by 5

Centigrade / Celsius	−17.8	0	10	15.6	23.9	30	37	100
Fahrenheit	0	32	50	60	75	86	98.6	212

Pretty balmy weather, don't you think? Now that everything is perfectly clear, can you answer the following questions about the weather?

ACTIVITY 8: HOW'S THAT AGAIN?

1. ¿Cuál es la temperatura máxima hoy?
2. ¿Cuál es la temperatura mínima el veintiséis de noviembre?
3. ¿Qué tiempo va a hacer el veinticinco de noviembre?
4. ¿Qué día hay nubes?
5. ¿Cuándo va a llover?

One more thing, and you'll be done! You have been talking to a new Spanish-speaking friend and these are his answers. What are your questions?

Tú: _____

Tu amigo: Este verano voy a viajar a México.

Tú: _____

Tu amigo: Pues, prefiero ir en carro. Hace buen tiempo y el viaje es bonito. Además, el avión es muy caro.

Tú: _____

Tu amigo: En invierno voy a estudiar en la universidad.

Tú: _____

Tu amigo: Voy a estudiar inglés. Oye, ¡ya basta de preguntas! (Enough questions already!) ¡Vamos a tomar un café!

CRIB NOTES

HEAR...SAY 1

Peter is in the lobby of the Hotel Isabel in the center of Mexico City. A conference on translation is taking place in the hotel and one of the participants is Professor Marcos Alvear, a Mexican friend of Carmen's. Peter decides to take a day off so Marcos can show him the city.

Marcos: What do you prefer to do? Visit a museum? Walk around the city?

Peter: I prefer to take a walk. Today is a great day to walk.

Marcos: Great, I am not tired and we are lucky with today's weather. It's a beautiful day. It's not raining and it's not cold. Besides, the traffic is very bad and parking is worse. To drive a car in Mexico City is very difficult.

Peter: Where are we going first?

Marcos: What do you prefer? A quiet place or a tourist spot?

Peter: I prefer to go to a tourist spot.

Marcos: Well, we already are in one! In the Zócalo, we're going to visit the Cathedral and see the murals by Diego Rivera in the National Palace.

Peter: Very interesting . . . and something less . . . cultural? I mean, when we are done in the museum, of course.

Marcos: Ah, Peter! I can see you like having fun!

Peter: It's not that. It's just that I want to try an authentic Mexican tequila.

Marcos: Well, in the evening we can go to Garibaldi Square. You're going to like it.

Peter: Great! The mariachis sing on that square, right?

Marcos: Yes. We're going to hear the mariachis. Although, you know, I personally prefer Maná, a very famous rock band here.

Peter: Wow, Marcos! I can see I'm in very good hands!

HEAR...SAY 2

Peter takes a day off and Marcos, Carmen's Mexican friend, shows him the important monuments and places of interest in Mexico City, including Diego Rivera's murals. In the evening, Peter and Marcos are having dinner in an outdoor café (*Lit.* in the open air) in Garibaldi Square. The *mari-* *achis* are there enlivening the night with their songs.

Marcos: What time is it?

Peter: It is 10:30. We are having such nice weather! It's such a pretty night with that full moon!

Marcos: It seems like it cooled down a bit, but we're still fine.

(Tequila after tequila, time goes by rather quickly for the two men. They are happily enjoying the music.)

Peter: What song are they singing?

Marcos: It is called *Cielito lindo* (*Beautiful Sky*), it is one of the most famous Mexican songs.

Peter: A song for the sky?

Marcos: No! *Cielito* is a loving expression that couples use.

Peter: Very romantic . . . the sky, the moon . . .

Marcos: The clouds . . .

Peter: The clouds?

Marcos: I believe you're on cloud nine. (*Lit.* You have your heart in the clouds.) Isn't there a person, maybe in Spain, that you might be thinking of right now?

Peter: I . . . well . . .

Marcos: Hey, Peter, it's cool! My goodness! It's already midnight, and I think I'm drinking too much tequila.

Peter: Unfortunately, although I am having a great time, I think it is time to leave.

Marcos: Do you prefer to go by taxi or subway?

Peter: I prefer a taxi. I love taxis here. They are all Volkswagen Beetles, right?

Marcos: Yes, it is the most popular car here. How about coming to our house tomorrow for lunch? That way you can meet my wife Laura.

Peter: That sounds terrific! Thanks a lot, Marcos.

ANSWER KEY

ACTIVITY 1

1. México D.F.
2. Spanish and Náhuatl
3. Guacamole and quesadillas
4. Rivera

ACTIVITY 2

1. visitar; 2. andar; 3. ir; 4. manejar; 5. ver; 6. tomar; 7. gustar

ACTIVITY 3

1. Prefiere ir de paseo.
2. Quiere ir a la Plaza Garibaldi.
3. Prefiero estudiar español, claro. (*Of course you do!*)
4. Prefiero tener una fiesta en casa.

ACTIVITY 4

1. b; 2. e *or* a; 3. a; 4. c; 5. d

ACTIVITY 5

1. Hace fresco. Hace sol. Hay nubes. Llueve.
2. Hace calor. Hace sol.
3. Hace fresco. Llueve. Hay truenos y relámpagos.
4. Hace frío. Nieva.

ACTIVITY 6

1. Son las diez y media.
2. Se llama *Cielito lindo*.
3. Prefiere ir en taxi.
4. Laura, la esposa de Marcos, quiere conocer a Peter.

ACTIVITY 7

All of them could be taking place, except 2 (at least, I think so . . .).

ACTIVITY 8

1. La temperatura máxima hoy es veintiocho grados.
2. La temperatura mínima es seis grados.
3. Va a hacer sol.
4. El 26 (veintiséis) de noviembre hay nubes.
5. Hoy va a llover.

ACTIVITY 9

1. ¿Qué vas a hacer este verano?
2. ¿Prefieres ir en carro o en avión?
3. ¿Qué vas a hacer este invierno?
4. ¿Qué vas a estudiar?

9.

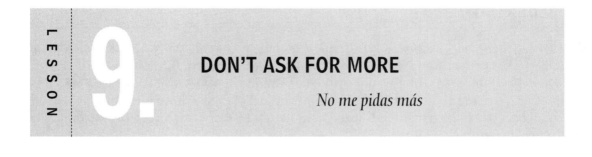

DON'T ASK FOR MORE

No me pidas más

That's not true! Only my girlfriends call me!

COMING UP. . .

- *Have a good meal!:* **Talking about food, recipes, and cooking**
- *I'd like to order, please:* **At the restaurant**
- *He likes me, he likes me not:* **Personal pronouns as direct objects (*me, you, him, her, it,* etc.)**
- *Give it to me!:* **Personal pronouns as indirect objects (*to me, to you, to him, to her,* etc.)**
- *I did it to myself:* **Reflexive verbs and pronouns (*myself, yourself, himself, herself,* etc.)**
- *As one might expect:* **Talking about actions without clear subjects**

Bueno, aquí estamos en México D.F. Vamos a continuar visitando sitios turísticos y comiendo con Peter y sus nuevos amigos mexicanos. Para el almuerzo (lunch), *Peter va a visitar la casa de sus amigos.* We're still hanging out with Peter and his new Mexican friends, doing some more sightseeing and of course, some more eating. We'll also find out that Marcos and Laura have a teenage daughter, Gabriela, who will join everybody later in a restaurant for dinner (*la cena*).

ACTIVITY 1:   LET'S WARM UP

In this lesson, there'll be some talk about food—Mexican food (*la comida mexicana*). To prepare you for it, I'm giving you a list of words in Spanish. Only three are **not** related to food or eating and drinking. Can you find them?

comer – tamales – chiles – arquitecto – receta – aguacate – cebolla – limón – restaurante – mesero – beber – fotógrafo – almuerzo – cena – nopal – dieta – ensalada – actor – sal – tequila – guacamole

Great! For more details on this exciting topic, you'll just have to keep reading . . .

Take a Tip from Me!

How did you do? Now that we're using more and more Spanish, it is important to remember that it is not necessary to understand every single word all the time. Most of the words in Activity 1 were new to you (and all will be used in the dialogues), but many are similar to words used in English, and therefore you were still able to find the words that did not belong. Good job!

Take a Tip from Me!

HEAR . . . SAY 1

Peter está en casa de Marcos y su esposa Laura. Laura prepara un almuerzo típicamente mexicano. Peter está maravillado.

Peter:	¿Cómo se llama este plato? ¡Está buenísimo!
Laura:	Este platillo se llama guacamole.
Peter:	Quiero la receta. ¿Cómo se prepara?
Laura:	Muy fácil. Se corta muy fino un aguacate y una cebolla. Se muele todo junto y se le agregan unas gotitas de limón.
Peter:	Voy a escribirlo porque me gusta mucho.

Laura:	No te preocupes, luego te doy la receta. ¿Sabes cocinar?
Peter:	No, como fuera o bien todo lo compro ya preparado.
Marcos:	¿No te comes estos tamales tan sabrosos?
Peter:	Ya no puedo más. Estoy lleno.
Marcos:	¡Pues además tenemos el postre que está requetebueno!
Laura:	Esta mañana hablé con Carmen por teléfono.
Marcos:	¿Le dijiste que Peter no la olvida?
Laura:	¡Oh Marcos, qué indiscreto!
Peter:	¿Cuál es el plan para esta tarde?
Marcos:	Después de la siesta podemos ir a ver el Museo de Antropología. Está en Chapultepec, un parque precioso en el centro de la ciudad.

ACTIVITY 2: HOW'S THAT AGAIN?

Listed below are the words from Activity 1. Listen to the dialogue (without looking at the text) and circle the ones you hear:

comer – tamales – chiles – arquitecto – receta – aguacate – cebolla – limón – restaurante – mesero – beber – fotógrafo – almuerzo – cena – nopal – dieta – ensalada – actor – sal – tequila – guacamole

Did You Know?

The Mexican Museo Nacional de Antropología (National Museum of Anthropology) is one of the best in the world. It is located in the beautiful Parque Chapultepec and contains numerous exhibits related to the indigenous cultures of Mexico. Its most famous piece is the Piedra del Sol (Sun Stone), the Aztec calendar that weighs 24 tons.

Did You Know?

WORKSHOP 1

THE NITTY-GRITTY

HE LIKES ME, HE LIKES ME NOT: PERSONAL PRONOUNS AS DIRECT OBJECTS (*ME, YOU, HIM, HER, IT,* ETC.)

Let's brush up a bit on some grammar terms. We know that a noun is the direct object of a sentence if it answers the question "whom?" or "what?".

Peter come un taco.	Peter eats a taco.
¿Qué come Peter?	What does Peter eat?
Un taco.	A taco.

Un taco is the direct object. A direct object pronoun can be used in place of the object noun, so we don't sound too repetitive:

> ***Peter come un taco. <u>Lo</u> come con carne.***
>
> Peter eats a taco. He eats **it** with meat.

Notice that in Spanish, the object pronoun comes **before** the verb. Only if the verb comes in its *–ar / –er / –ir* (infinitive) form is the pronoun placed after the verb, and is, then, written together with it:

> ***Peter dice, "Me gusta comer<u>lo</u> con carne".***
>
> Peter says, "I like to eat **it** with meat."

Here is a complete list of personal pronouns that can replace nouns that are objects of a sentence:

PERSONAL PRONOUNS REPLACING DIRECT OBJECTS			
SINGULAR		**PLURAL**	
me	me	*nos*	us
te	you	*os*	you
lo	him / it; you (formal)	*los*	them; you (formal)
la	her / it; you (formal)	*las*	them; you (formal)

Now, take a look at the examples from the lesson:

Voy a escribir<u>lo</u>.	I'm going to write **it**.
Peter no <u>la</u> olvida.	Peter does not forget **her**. (Carmen, of course!)

So you're ready when the time comes, look at the following examples that you will hear in the next dialogue.

> ***Los chavos no paran de llamar<u>la</u> a casa.***
>
> Guys don't stop calling her at home.

> ***Sólo <u>me</u> llaman mis amigas.***
>
> Only my friends call me.

> ***Acá <u>los</u> preparan sin espinas.***
>
> Here they prepare them without thorns.

Voy a comer<u>los</u>.

I am going to eat them.

TAKE IT FOR A SPIN

Let's say we're organizing a party (*fiesta*). I want to bring (*traer*) a lot of things, but you are a nice student who wants to please your teacher, so you offer to bring instead of me:

1. Model: *Yo traigo los platos.*   *No, yo **los** traigo.*

                     I'm bringing the plates.   No, I'm bringing **them**.

(We have substituted *los platos*, the direct object, with *los*, the direct object pronoun.) Now, you try it:

1. Yo traigo **el tequila**.   No, yo _____ traigo.
2. Yo traigo **la música**.   No, yo _____ traigo.
3. Yo traigo **el guacamole**.   No, yo _____ traigo.
4. Yo traigo **amigos**.   No, yo _____ traigo.
5. Bueno, pues yo traigo **amigas**.   No, yo _____ traigo.

GIVE IT TO ME!: PERSONAL PRONOUNS AS INDIRECT OBJECTS (*TO ME, TO YOU, TO HIM, TO HER,* ETC.)

Okay, time for the next set of pronouns. This time it's those that replace nouns that are indirect objects of a sentence. A noun is an indirect object of a sentence when it answers the questions "to whom?" or "for whom?". For example:

Laura da comida a Peter.   Laura gives food to Peter.

¿A quién da comida Laura?   To whom does she give food?

A Peter.   To Peter.

A Peter (to Peter) is the indirect object. If we want to replace *a Peter* with a pronoun we use *le* in Spanish and *to him / her* in English, as in:

Laura <u>le</u> da comida.   Laura gives food to him. (*or* Laura gives him food.)

The funny thing about Spanish is that you can use the indirect object pronouns not only when you want to replace a noun (so you don't repeat it), but also, and very frequently (about 99 percent of the time), **together** with it. So, in Spanish, you can say something like: *Laura gives him food, to Peter*. For example:

¿A quién <u>le</u> da comida Laura?   Laura <u>le</u> da comida <u>a Peter</u>.

Le stands for either *to him* or *to her* in Spanish. Here are the rest of the indirect pronouns.

PERSONAL PRONOUNS REPLACING INDIRECT OBJECTS

	SINGULAR		PLURAL
me	(to, for) me	*nos*	(to, for) us
te	(to, for) you	*os*	(to, for) you
le	(to, for) him / her / it; you (formal)	*les*	(to, for) them; you (formal)

Notice that the only indirect object pronouns in this table that are different from the direct object pronouns are those for *to him / her / it* and *to them*. Also, notice that *le* stands for both *to him* (masculine) and *to her* (feminine), another simplification. Aren't you lucky?

As with pronouns that replace direct objects, pronouns that replace indirect objects, can have two positions. They normally occur before the verb, but if the verb is in its *−ar / −er / −ir* (infinitive) form, they follow the verb and form one word with it.

Remember when Peter was buying shoes for the big night out with Carmen? Well, Carmen didn't really like his choice (the ugly white shoes, that is), so she said:

A mí no me gustan.

As for me, I don't like them. (Lit. To me, [they] are not pleasing to me.)

So, here you see the use of *me* (to me), the indirect object pronoun that you saw in the previous table. She also uses *a mí*, which could be translated as *as for me* and is used here mainly for emphasis.

All indirect object pronouns can be emphasized by using the following expressions: *a mí, a ti, a usted / él / ella, a nosotros / nosotras, a vosotros / vosotras, a ustedes / ellos / ellas.* Look at another example:

Marcos y Laura le hablan a él, no a usted.

Marcos and Laura talk to him, not to you.

Now let's look at the examples from the dialogue you've just heard:

Le agregas unas gotitas de limón.

You add a few drops of lemon juice to it.

Luego te doy la receta.

Later, I'll give the recipe to you.

¿Le dijiste que Peter no la olvida?

Did you tell her that Peter cannot forget her?

TAKE IT FOR A SPIN

Although we now have both the things and the people for our *fiesta*, there is still some work left to do. Complete the following sentences by adding the personal pronoun referring to the underlined nouns functioning as indirect objects:

1. _____ escribo una invitación **a Peter**.
2. _____ hablo directamente **a Carmen**.
3. _____ compro una piñata **a Marcos y Laura**.
4. _____ doy una fiesta **a todos**.
5. _____ preparo la comida **a todos**.

WORDS TO LIVE BY

HAVE A GOOD MEAL!: TALKING ABOUT FOOD, RECIPES, AND COOKING

Ready to whip up a great meal? Here are some words to describe the activities that take place in the kitchen:

cocinar	to cook	**Vamos a cocinar un platillo con Laura.**
		We are going to cook a dish with Laura.
cortar	to cut	**Cortamos el aguacate y la cebolla.**
		We cut the avocado and the onion.
moler	to grind	**Lo molemos.**
		We grind it.
agregar	to add	**Le agregamos sal.**
		We add salt (to it).
cocer	to boil	**¡No lo cocemos!**
		We don't boil it!
probar	to taste	**Pero sí lo probamos.**
		But we do taste it.

If the meal is good, you say, *¡Qué sabroso!* (How delicious!). If it's bad, don't say anything! (But you may think: *¡Qué horrible!*)

Did You Know?

In the Spanish-speaking world, refusing to eat a meal somebody prepared for you, or not complimenting the host(s) on it, is more than rude—it's taken as a personal offense. So, if you're invited to somebody's home for a meal, be prepared to swallow and

I'D LIKE TO ORDER, PLEASE: AT THE RESTAURANT

La mesa está puesta
The table is ready

el jarro de vins
carafe of wine

la copa de vino
glass of wine

el bajativo
after-dinner drink

el cuchillo
knife

el plato
plate

la taza de café
cup of coffee

la cuenta
check

el postre
dessert

el tenedor
fork

When you are in a *restaurante*, you order (*ordenar*) from the waiter or waitress (*el mesero* or *la mesera*). Here are a few handy phrases you might need:

¿Puede traer la carta?	*Can you bring the menu?*
¿Quisiera . . . ?	*Could I have . . . ?*
¿Me da la cuenta, por favor?	*May I have the check, please?*

Did You Know?

Mexico has given the world many common foods: potatoes, tomatoes, corn, and chocolate. Mexicans use these foods as the basis of most of their meals (*platillos*), which are all Aztec in origin: *enchiladas, tacos, quesadillas, mole poblano,* and many others.

Did You Know?

ACTIVITY 5: TAKE IT FOR A SPIN

Help me complete the following sentences. Pick the correct answer from the choices provided.

1. Cuando haces guacamole, es necesario _____ aguacates.
   - a. escribir
   - b. cortar
   - c. comprar
   - d. ir
2. En un restaurante, ordenamos a un _____.
   - a. mesero
   - b. actor
   - c. fotógrafo
   - d. amigo
3. Al finalizar la comida, comemos _____.
   - a. una cebolla
   - b. un limón
   - c. un postre
   - d. una ensalada
4. Peter bebe sus margaritas con _____.
   - a. pimienta
   - b. meseros
   - c. sal
   - d. cebolla

Word on the Street

- **requete–:**

When you wish to say "very, very much" in Mexico, use the word *requete*. You simply attach it to any adjective:

Está requetesabroso.	It is very, very flavorful.
Está requetebueno.	It's really good.

Requete– is very typical of Mexico and works like the English *super–*, as in *superhot*.

- **–ito, –ita or –illo, –illa:**

You add these endings to any noun to mean *little* or *smaller*, as in:

la gota (drop)	→	**la gotita** (little drop)
el plato (plate or dish)	→	**el platillo** (small plate or dish)

In Mexico, as in other Spanish-speaking countries, people also use these endings in everyday speech simply to make speaking more fun.

Peter, Marcos, Laura y su hija de dieciséis años, Gabriela, pasan toda la tarde en el Museo Nacional de Antropología de México. A la salida deciden ir a un restaurante.

Laura: Gabi, ¿vas a ordenar ya? Si no, el mesero te espera una hora.

Gabi: ¡Ay mamá, qué pesada! No me pidas más. No voy a comer nada; sólo voy a beber un refresco.

Laura: Gabi está a dieta, quiere lucir flaquita.

Marcos: Ahorita todas las muchachas están en los puros huesos. La opinión de los padres no sirve de nada. La televisión les dice cómo peinarse, vestirse y maquillarse.

Peter: ¿Por qué estás a dieta? (Gabriela se ruboriza.)

Laura: Está en la edad del llegue, los chavos no paran de llamarla a casa.

Gabi: Eso, ¡no es verdad! ¡Sólo me llaman mis amigas!

Marcos: Pues yo voy a comer unos chiles rellenos.

Laura: Yo quiero una ensalada de nopalitos.

Peter: A mí todavía me arde el estómago del almuerzo, pero bueno, voy a probar los nopalitos; ¿qué son?

Laura: Son las hojas del nopal. El nopal es como un cactus, sus hojas se pueden servir con espinas o sin espinas. Acá los preparan sin espinas. Se cuecen con sal y cebolla y se cortan en cuadraditos. Sirven para complementar muchos platillos. El nopal es una planta tan mexicana que hasta está en la bandera.

Peter: Voy a ser un patriota mexicano y voy a comerlos.

WORKSHOP 2

I DID IT TO MYSELF: REFLEXIVE VERBS AND PRONOUNS (MYSELF, YOURSELF, HIMSELF, HERSELF, ETC.)

When you get up in the morning, I know, you rush and don't have time to eat breakfast or read the paper. However, there are a few things you do for yourself that you cannot skip: you wash or shower, and then you dress. It is implied in the meaning of all these actions that you are doing them to yourself. In fact, if you wanted to insist, you could say:I wash or dress myself, although that is not what you normally do in English. In Spanish, things are different: whenever you talk about an action that you perform on, to, or for yourself, you actually have to spell that out. So, verbs that express such actions (called reflexive verbs— they sort of reflect back on you) are always followed by a reflexive pronoun, such as *my-*

self, yourself, himself, herself, etc. Let's look at a typical reflexive verb in Spanish—*bañarse* [to bathe (oneself)]:

THE REFLEXIVE VERB *BAÑARSE* (TO BATHE)			
SINGULAR		**PLURAL**	
yo me baño	I bathe (myself)	*nosotros / nosotras nos bañamos*	we bathe (ourselves)
tú te bañas	you bathe (yourself)	*vosotros / vosotras os bañáis*	you bathe (yourselves)
él / ella, usted se baña	he bathes (himself) she bathes (herself) you [formal] bathe (yourself)	*ellos / ellas, ustedes se bañan*	they bathe (themselves) you [formal] bathe (yourselves)

In Spanish, there are many reflexive verbs and more often than not, they do not correspond to reflexive verbs in English. You need to learn them as they are, because translating the pronoun into English, *myself*, *yourself*, etc., will not always help.

You have already learned another reflexive verb in Spanish: *llamarse* (to be called; *Lit.* to call oneself):

Me llamo Pilar Munday.

Te llamas _____ (write your name here).

Nuestro amigo se llama Peter Winthrop.

Nuestros amigos mexicanos se llaman Marcos y Laura.

In the dialogue, you heard:

La televisón les dice cómo peinarse, vestirse y maquillarse.

Television tells them how to comb their hair (*Lit.* comb themselves), to dress (*Lit.* to dress themselves), and to apply make-up (*Lit.* make themselves up).

Note that when the verb is in its infinitive form, as in the last example, we attach the reflexive pronoun to the end of it—*peinarse*, *vestirse*, and *maquillarse*.

The Fine Print

Some verbs change their meaning when used with a reflexive pronoun. One important example is *ir* (to go). When used with a reflexive pronoun, *ir* means "to leave" with the intention of departing:

Voy al gimnasio.	I'm going to the gym.
Me voy al gimnasio.	I'm leaving for the gym.

In everyday language, the reflexive form of *ir* is very commonly used and even preferred.

AS ONE MIGHT EXPECT: TALKING ABOUT ACTIONS WITHOUT CLEAR SUBJECTS

There are times when you want to talk about actions but do not want or do not need to make it clear who performed them. So, you can say: *It's been done* (in general, we do not know who has been doing the doing) or *As one might expect . . .* (in general, anybody might expect such a thing, we do not have anybody specific in mind).

In Spanish, you use (or should I say, one uses) reflexive verbs for the same purpose: to avoid making the subject of the action clear or specific. So, the reflexive pronoun *se* works just like English *one* in the following example:

Aquí se habla español.	Spanish is spoken here. (*Lit.* Here, one speaks Spanish.)

This construction is typically used in instructions, such as in manuals or in recipes. Remember, in this lesson, you learned how to make guacamole:

¿Cómo se prepara?	How is it made? (*Lit.* How does one make it?)
Se corta un aguacate muy fino.	An avocado is thinly cut. (*Lit.* One thinly cuts the avocado.)

WORDS TO LIVE BY

Now, let's look at today's selection of words.

pesado / a	*heavy. This word is also used for people that are insistent (but not in a good way), and people or things that are tedious, dull, plain, annoying, or boring.*

Marcos es un poco pesado. Siempre está mencionando a Carmen.

Marcos is a bit annoying. He's constantly talking about Carmen.

no parar de + –ar / –er / –ir form of verbs	*to not cease / stop doing something*
No para de hablar de Carmen.	He doesn't stop talking about Carmen.

(Ahem, ahem, who might I be talking about?)

estar a dieta	*(You know what that is!)*
La hija de Marcos y Laura está a dieta.	Marcos and Laura's daughter is on a diet.

Word on the Street

Here are more typical expressions used only in Mexico:

el llegue   flirting; **la edad del llegue**, the time when teenagers start thinking about flirting
el chavo   friend, pal
lucir   to look (*Lit.* to shine), as in **Luces muy bella** (You look very beautiful).

LET'S PUT IT IN WRITING

Laura is *una cocinera fantástica* (a fantastic cook) according to Peter. Would you like to taste one of her specialties? Here is a *receta* (recipe) for *flan*, a dessert that is enjoyed throughout the Spanish-speaking world. There are many different versions of it, but I'll give you one that is *fácil* (easy). Enjoy!

Receta para el flan

...

INGREDIENTES
1 lata de leche condensada
2 latas (de las de leche condensada) de leche normal
4 huevos
un poco de caramelo líquido

...

PREPARACIÓN

1. Se baten los huevos.
2. Se mezclan los huevos con la leche condensada y la leche normal.
3. Se pone el caramelo líquido en un recipiente grande.
4. Se pone la mezcla en el recipiente con el caramelo líquido.
5. Se calienta el horno.
6. Se pone el recipiente con la mezcla en el horno.
7. Se hornea una hora.

As you can see, a recipe in Spanish is full of the verbs used with *se*. Now, rewrite the sentences, using the *we* form instead. I'll do the first one for you:

1. *Batimos los huevos.* (We beat the eggs.)
2. _____
3. _____
4. _____
5. _____
6. _____

Let's end with something even more fun. What about a *sopa de letras* (alphabet soup)? That's the word used in Spanish for this game: a word search. Let's see if you can find these words in our *sopa*:

aguacate, sal, pimienta, ensalada, postre, cebolla

```
q  a  g  u  a  c  a  t  e  p  o  l  k  p  t
w  e  r  t  g  b  h  y  n  i  o  p  l  i  x
e  d  c  v  f  r  t  g  s  n  h  t  y  m  m
¡  p  o  s  t  r  e  l  a  a  ¡  g  f  i  s
w  e  r  t  y  u  i  o  l  g  l  d  s  e  x
p  o  i  u  y  t  r  e  a  q  l  k  ¡  n  g
c  e  b  o  l  l  a  v  d  n  m  q  a  t  w
s  x  e  d  c  v  f  r  a  g  b  n  h  a  u
```

CRIB NOTES

Peter is in Marco's and his wife Laura's house. Laura prepares a typical Mexican lunch. Peter is amazed.

Peter: What's the name of this dish? It's delicious.

Laura: This dish is called "guacamole."

Peter: I want the recipe. How is it prepared?

Laura: Very easy. You cut an avocado and an onion in very thin slices. You grind them together and then you add a few drops of lemon.

Peter: I have to write it down because I like it a lot.

Laura: Don't worry, I'll give you the recipe later. Do you know how to cook?

Peter: No, I eat out or buy everything already prepared.

Marcos: You don't want to eat those super-juicy tamales?

Peter: I can't [eat] any more. I am full.

Marcos: Well, we still have dessert, and it is extra good!

Laura: I spoke with Carmen on the telephone this morning.

Marcos: Did you tell her that Peter cannot forget her?

Laura: Oh, Marcos, you're so indiscreet!

Peter: What's the plan for this afternoon?

Marcos: After the nap, we can go to see the Anthropological Museum. It is in Chapultepec, a beautiful park in the middle of the city.

Peter, Marcos and Laura, and their 16-year-old daughter, Gabriela, have spent the afternoon in the National Museum of Anthropology of Mexico. On their way out, they decide to go to a restaurant.

Laura: Gabi, are you going to order already? If not, the waiter has to wait for you for an hour.

Gabi: Mom, you're so annoying! Don't ask me again. I am not going to eat anything. I am only going to drink a soda.

Laura: Gabi is on a diet. She wants to look skinny.

Marcos: Now, all girls are skin and bones. The parents' opinion doesn't count. The TV tells them how to comb, dress, and put on make-up.

Peter: Why are you on a diet? (*Gabi blushes.*)

Laura: She's at that age when they like boys. The guys don't stop calling her at home.

Gabi: That's not true! Only my girlfriends call me!

Marcos: I am going to have some stuffed chiles.

Laura: I want a nopalitos salad.

Peter: My stomach is still burning from lunch, but oh well, I am going to try the nopalitos. What are they?

Laura: They are the leaves of the nopal. Nopal is like a cactus, its leaves can be served with thorns or without thorns. Here, they prepare them without thorns. You boil them with salt and onion and cut them in cubes. They complement many dishes. Nopal is a plant that is so Mexican, it is even on the flag.

Peter: I am going to be a Mexican patriot and eat them.

ANSWER KEY

ACTIVITY 1

Arquitecto, fotógrafo y actor

ACTIVITY 2

Guacamole, receta, aguacate, cebolla, y limón

ACTIVITY 3

1. lo; 2. la; 3. lo; 4. los; 5. las

ACTIVITY 4

1. le; 2. le; 3. les; 4. les; 5. les

ACTIVITY 5

1. b *or* c; 2. a; 3. c; 4. c

ACTIVITY 6

1. Batimos los huevos. (*We beat the eggs.*)

2. Mezclamos los huevos con la leche conden-
sada y la leche normal. (*We mix the eggs with the condensed milk and the regular milk*.)
3. Ponemos el caramelo líquido en un recipiente. (*We put the caramel sauce in a container*.)
4. Ponemos la mezcla en el recipiente con el caramelo líquido. (*We put the mixture in the container with the caramel sauce.*)

5. Calentamos el horno. (*We turn on the oven*.)
6. Ponemos el recipiente con la mezcla en el horno. (*We put the container with the mixture in the oven*.)

ACTIVITY 7

q	**a**	**g**	**u**	**a**	**c**	**a**	**t**	**e**	p	o	l	k	**p**	t
w	e	r	t	g	b	h	y	**n**	i	o	p	l	**i**	x
e	d	c	v	f	r	t	g	**s**	n	h	t	y	**m**	m
¡	**p**	**o**	**s**	**t**	**r**	**e**	l	**a**	a	¡	g	f	**i**	s
w	e	r	t	y	u	i	o	**l**	g	**l**	d	s	**e**	x
p	o	i	u	y	t	r	e	**a**	q	l	k	¡	**n**	g
c	**e**	**b**	**o**	**l**	**l**	**a**	v	**d**	n	m	q	a	**t**	w
s	x	e	d	c	v	f	r	**a**	g	b	n	h	**a**	u

10. WHAT DAY IS IT TODAY?

¿Qué día es hoy?

A night of partying?

COMING UP. . .

- *The week at a glance:* The days of the week
- *Here, there, and everywhere:* Using words like *here, inside, near,* etc.
- *How are you feeling?:* Asking about other people
- *I'm so sorry:* Ways of apologizing in Spanish
- *You gotta do what you gotta do:* Talking about what you need or have to do using the verbs *deber* (must), *necesitar* (to need), and *tener que* (to have to)
- *I love Ricky:* Talking about people using the personal *a*

- *It's a pleasure to know you:* **Using the verbs** *conocer* **(to be acquainted with) and** *saber* **(to know)**
- *Strut your stuff!*

LOOKING AHEAD

All that *comida* (food) and *bebida* (drink) have been *estupendas,* but Peter finally has to start doing something related to his job. He hasn't reported to his office in New York since he arrived in Mexico. They must be wondering where *su hombre* is! So, it's time for him to get his act together. Tonight, Peter is going to *el concierto de* Ricky Martin, taking place in Foro Sol, one of the main concert halls in Mexico City. Hundreds of fans are awaiting for *su ídolo* (their idol) outside the hall. Peter is there, too, taking in the crowds of screaming teenagers.

ACTIVITY 1:   LET'S WARM UP

Here is Peter's To Do list. But, because he's been quite disorganized lately, he needs help figuring out which items on the list are related to doing work, and which are related to having fun. (As usual, if you're not sure what to do, use the Crib Notes section for help.)

COSAS QUE HACER

1. Comer en un restaurante típico
2. Enviar un correo electrónico a la oficina central
3. Escribir un informe
4. Sacar fotos de las fans
5. Pasar una noche de reventón, bebiendo y de fiesta
6. Usar la computadora portátil

HEAR . . . SAY 1

Tras una noche de diversión y fiesta con los Alvear, Peter decide que debe empezar a trabajar. A la mañana siguiente (*the following morning*) va a la redacción de su revista en México D.F. Allí ve a un viejo amigo—el periodista mexicano Enrique Rodríguez. Su amigo empieza a hacerle bromas (*starts teasing him*) sobre su mal aspecto.

Enrique: ¡Qué mala cara traes, amigo! ¿Noche de reventón?
Peter: No recuerdo nada. Tengo una resaca horrible. Bueno, necesito enviar un informe sobre mi trabajo a la redacción central de Nueva York

	pero tengo el portátil en el hotel. ¿Puedo utilizar tu correo electrónico?
Enrique:	¡Cómo no! ¡Con mucho gusto te presto mi computadora! ¿Y qué haces aquí en México?
Peter:	Desde que estoy en México no hago otra cosa que comer y beber. Tengo que trabajar más y divertirme menos.
Enrique:	¿Y qué vas a decirles en el informe?
Peter:	¡Dios mío! ¡Tienes razón! ¡Sí no tengo nada! ¡Debemos hacer algo! ¿Qué día es el concierto?
Enrique:	Es el viernes en el Foro Sol a las nueve de la noche. Hoy, por cierto, es jueves. Son las diez de la mañana y a las once tenemos que estar en el Hotel Marquis, que está en el Paseo de la Reforma. Ricky da una rueda de prensa. Conozco a un amigo que trabaja de mozo allí. Me dice que los granaderos a caballo patrullan fuera del hotel.
Peter:	¿El ejército a caballo? ¿Qué pasa?
Enrique:	¡Calma, Peter, calma! Los granaderos son de la policía. Son las fans. Miles de muchachas tienen el día libre y no van a ir a clase. ¡Los papás se van a enojar al ver a sus hijitas gritando en los noticieros!
Peter:	¡Venga! ¿Dónde tienes el coche? ¡Tenemos que irnos!
Enrique:	No se me alborote, gringo. Hoy no podemos ir en mi carro por la contaminación, tenemos que ir en bicicleta.
Peter:	¿En bicicleta?
Enrique:	Sí. Aquí en la oficina tenemos dos. Pero debemos rezarle a la Virgen de Guadalupe. La bicicleta es muy vieja y no funciona bien, pero la Virgen es muy milagrosa.
Peter:	¡Qué barbaridad!

ACTIVITY 2:   HOW'S THAT AGAIN?

Let's test your memory once more:

1. ¿Quién es Enrique?
2. ¿Qué hace Peter en México?
3. ¿Tiene Peter algo (*something*) para su informe?
4. ¿Qué día es hoy (*today*)?
5. ¿Qué hora es?
6. ¿Cómo van a ir al hotel, en carro o en bicicleta? (Extra credit: Do you know why?)

Did You Know?

The story of the Virgin of Guadalupe dates back to Dec. 12, 1531, when a poor Native American named Juan Diego was seeking water for his uncle in a desolate area in northern Mexico City. Suddenly, he saw a vision of a beautiful woman, who told him how to find fresh water. Some days later, he saw the image again and, this time, the Virgin told him to go to Mexico City to tell church officials to build a church in her name on that site. But the officials did not believe Juan Diego who, after all, was just a poor Indian. Juan Diego then returned to the hillside and asked the Virgin for a sign. Beautiful roses appeared in front of him, even though roses do not bloom in that area in December.

He gathered them into his rough Indian blanket and took them to Mexico City. When he opened the blanket in front of the church officials, they too saw the image of the Virgin of Guadalupe, exactly as Juan Diego had described her. Today, on the site of the apparition, sits a huge basilica. The poor man's blanket with the image of the Virgin of Guadalupe is displayed there, and thousands of devout Catholic pilgrims journey to the site each year.

Did You Know?

WORKSHOP 1

THE NITTY-GRITTY

***YOU GOTTA DO WHAT YOU GOTTA DO*: TALKING ABOUT WHAT YOU NEED OR HAVE TO DO USING THE VERBS *DEBER* (MUST), *NECESITAR* (TO NEED), AND *TENER QUE* (TO HAVE TO)**

The following verbs are followed by an infinitive (the *–ar, –er,* or *–ir* form of the verb) to indicate obligation or duty:

deber	must		
necesitar	to need	+	**infinitive**
tener que	to have to		

Let's look at the examples from the Hear . . . Say section, so you can see how this works:

> **Necesito enviar un informe sobre mi trabajo a la oficina central de Nueva York.**
>
> I need to send a report about my work to the central office in New York.
>
> **Tengo que trabajar más y divertirme menos.**
>
> I have to work more and enjoy myself less.
>
> **Debemos hacer algo.**
>
> We must do something.

A las once tenemos que estar en el Hotel Marquis.

At eleven we have to be at the Hotel Marquis.

¡Tenemos que irnos!

We have to go!

This is a piece of cake, right?

TAKE IT FOR A SPIN

Which of these things do you need to do in order to learn Spanish?

1. Tienes que leer las aventuras de Peter.
2. Necesitas estudiar el vocabulario.
3. Debes beber mucha tequila.
4. Tienes que hacer las actividades.
5. Necesitas hablar con la gente.

WORDS TO LIVE BY

THE WEEK AT A GLANCE: THE DAYS OF THE WEEK

Here are the days of the week (*los días de la semana*):

el lunes	*Monday*
el martes	*Tuesday*
el miércoles	*Wednesday*
el jueves	*Thursday*
el viernes	*Friday*
el sábado	*Saturday*
el domingo	*Sunday*

Note that, in Spanish, the week starts on *lunes* and ends on *domingo*. Also, unlike in English, names for the days are not capitalized. Let's look at how they are used:

Trabajo los lunes, martes y jueves.

I work on Mondays, Tuesdays, and Thursdays.

Mi día favorito de la semana es el sábado.

My favorite day of the week is Saturday.

Notice that preposition *on* is not used before the day of the week (as in the first example), and the article is always required.

Let's look at Peter's weekly planner:

LUNES	MARTES	MIÉRCOLES	JUEVES	VIERNES	SÁBADO	DOMINGO
Llego a México		*Rueda de Concierto*		*prensa*	*Llego a Yucatán*	

Now, answer the following questions:

1. ¿Qué día de la semana llega Peter a Yucatán?
2. ¿Qué día tiene la rueda de prensa?
3. ¿Qué días no tiene nada específico?
4. ¿Cuándo es el concierto?
5. ¿Desde cuándo (*since when*) está Peter en México?

HERE, THERE, AND EVERYWHERE: USING WORDS LIKE *HERE, INSIDE, NEAR,* ETC.

Here are some words and phrases that indicate location. You already know some of these, but it's always good to review:

aquí, acá	*here*
ahí	*there*
allí, allá	*there (farther away)*
todos lados	*everywhere*
a / en ninguna parte	*nowhere*
cerca	*near*
lejos	*far*
fuera	*out or outside*
dentro	*inside*

Note there is no difference in meaning between *aquí* and *acá* or *allí* and *allá*.

Now that you know these words, it will be no problem to figure out how the following verbs work. Check them out:

acercarse	→	(*a*-**cerca**-r-*se*)	→	*to go near*
alejarse	→	(*a*-**leja**-r-*se*)	→	*to go farther*
adentrarse	→	(*a*-**dentra**-r-*se*)	→	*to go in farther*

Word on the Street

Did You Know?

One of the most popular sports in Mexico is a type of wrestling called *catch* **(in Spanish pronounced as** *kahch*)**. The wrestlers are wildly popular, inside and outside the ring. One example is Superbarrio, who even became a political leader in México D.F. In most cases, however, the politicians are the ones that fight to get the wrestlers to support them publicly. As you can see, it's not just in the United States that celebrities can become political leaders.**

Did You Know?

HEAR . . . SAY 2

Llega el gran momento. Es viernes y son las nueve de la noche. Peter y Enrique Rodríguez están en el Foro Sol esperando la actuación de Ricky Martin. Peter está tomando fotos y entrevistando a las enloquecidas muchachas que esperan a su ídolo.

Peter: Debo tomar muchas fotos de las fans para ilustrar mi reportaje.

Enrique: Es fácil, estamos rodeados y todas están llorando. Conozco a una muchachita que lleva tres días en cola para tener buen sitio. ¡Imagínate ahí fuera desde el miércoles!

Peter: ¡Es increíble! ¡Qué cosas hacen las chicas de hoy para ver a un cantante famoso! Voy a acercarme a alguna. Hola, ¿cómo te llamas?

Marina: Marina Velasco. ¿Puede darme su tarjeta de identificación de prensa?

Peter: Pero, ¿estás loca? ¿Para qué la quieres?

Marina: ¡Necesito verlo! ¡Tengo que verlo! Quiero un autógrafo. Sé que con la tarjeta voy a poder llegar hasta su camerino. Luego se la regreso.

Peter: Lo siento, no puedo darte la tarjeta. Pero conozco a una persona que puede solucionar tu problema.

Marina:	¿A quién? Estoy desesperada, llevo desde el lunes sin dormir. Es mi única oportunidad, sé que sale para Colombia mañana, sábado.
Peter:	Tranquila, sé que va a estar en México más días. Mañana puedo darte tu autógrafo. Yo le pido a mi amigo tu autógrafo, no te preocupes Marina.
Marina:	¿Y quién es su amigo?
Peter:	Ricky Martín. ¿Qué te pasa? ¿Te encuentras bien? ¡Enrique, ayúdame que esta chica se desmayó!
Enrique:	¿Pero qué pasa? Desde luego no te puedo dejar solo, Peter. Tengo que ir contigo a todos lados.

ACTIVITY 5: HOW'S THAT AGAIN?

Are these statements true or false?

1. Las fans están comiendo.
2. La chica que habla con Peter se llama Marina.
3. La chica quiere hablar con Enrique Iglesias.
4. Peter le dice que es amigo de Ricky Martin.
5. Ricky sale para Argentina mañana sábado.

WORKSHOP 2

THE NITTY-GRITTY

I LOVE RICKY: TALKING ABOUT PEOPLE USING THE PERSONAL A

When the object of a verb is a person, you need to put the preposition *a* (also known as the "personal *a*") in front of it. This *a* has no real meaning and is not translated. Check out these sentences:

Quiero esta película.	I want this movie.
Quiero a Ricky.	I love Ricky.

Note that in Spanish, the verb *querer* means both "to want" and "to love."

Because *Ricky* (the object of the verb) is a person, you need to use the personal *a* in front of it.

Here's an example from Lesson 9 (that you may have been wondering about earlier):

Siempre está mencionando a Carmen.

He is always mentioning Carmen.

(We know who, right?)

When you form a question, you also need the *a*, so use *¿a quién?*:

¿A quién quieres?

Who do you love?

IT'S A PLEASURE TO KNOW YOU: USING THE VERBS *CONOCER* (TO BE ACQUAINTED WITH) AND *SABER* (TO KNOW)

The verb *to know* has two different equivalents in Spanish, depending on what exactly you mean: *Conocer* is used when we talk about knowing people or places. It is similar to the English phrase *to be acquainted with*. *Saber* is used in the general meaning of "knowing something." As you can see below, the *yo* forms of both verbs are irregular, but everything else is what you would expect of any *–er* verb:

PRESENT TENSE OF *CONOCER* AND *SABER*			
		CONOCER (TO BE ACQUAINTED WITH)	SABER (TO KNOW)
Singular	*yo*	conozco	sé
	tú	conoces	sabes
	él / ella, usted	conoce	sabe
Plural	*nosotros / nosotras*	conocemos	sabemos
	vosotros / vosotras	conocéis	sabéis
	ellos / ellas, ustedes	conocen	saben

Let's look at some examples:

Peter conoce a Enrique Rodríguez.

Peter knows Enrique Rodriguez.

Enrique conoce a un mozo del hotel.

Enrique knows a bellboy in the hotel.

Peter no conoce México bien.

Peter doesn't know Mexico well.

Peter sabe hablar español bien.

Peter knows how to speak Spanish well.

Marina sabe que Ricky va a Colombia.

Marina knows that Ricky is going to Colombia.

Heads Up!

Heads Up!

Don't forget to add the personal *a* when you are talking about knowing people! Review the examples I just gave you. The first two sentences have the personal *a*. The next two don't.

ACTIVITY 6:   TAKE IT FOR A SPIN

Should you use *saber* or *conocer* to say you know the following things and people?

1. Madrid
2. México
3. escribir en el correo electrónico
4. usar la computadora
5. la oficina de la agencia central en Nueva York

WORDS TO LIVE BY

HOW ARE YOU FEELING?: ASKING ABOUT OTHER PEOPLE

Besides using *¿Cómo estás?* (How are you?), you can also use the following:

¿Cómo te encuentras?
How are you feeling? (Lit. How do you find yourself?)

These are some possible answers:

No me encuentro bien.	*I don't feel well.*
Me encuentro estupendamente.	*I feel great. (That's a mouthful!)*
Me encuentro fatal. Tengo una resaca horrible.	*I feel awful. I have a horrible hangover.*

I'M SO SORRY: WAYS OF APOLOGIZING IN SPANISH

Here are some useful sentences when you have to say no or apologize:

Lo siento.	*I am sorry.*
Lo siento mucho.	*I am so / really sorry.*
Perdón.	*Sorry or Excuse me.*
¡Mil perdones!	*I'm extremely sorry.*
	(Lit. A thousand pardons.)
Perdóneme, pero no puedo ir.	*Forgive me, but I cannot go.*

Word on the Street

The basic meaning of the Spanish word **gringo / gringa** is "a foreigner" or "a non-Hispanic person." Most likely, it is a version of the word *griego* or "Greek." So, *gringo / gringa* is akin to the English phrase "It's Greek to me." In Latin America, *gringo / gringa* is mostly used to refer to a person from the United States, and it is often used disparagingly. However, it can be used in a humorous way among friends, as in our dialogue.

Did You Know?

Speaking of *gringos* . . . maybe you have heard of the novel *The Old Gringo* (*Gringo viejo*, 1985) which was made into a movie starring Jane Fonda. The novel was written by the Mexican writer Carlos Fuentes (b. 1928), one of the most important figures of Latin American literature.

Another well-known Mexican author is Octavio Paz (1914–1998). He won the Nobel Prize for literature in 1990. He gained his greatest fame with his meditations on Mexican culture, *El laberinto de la soledad (The Labyrinth of Solitude)*. Paz, however, was primarily a poet, and also wrote the famous poem, *La piedra del sol (Sun Stone)*, inspired by the Aztec calendar you read about earlier.

Did You Know?

LET'S PUT IT IN WRITING

Peter has received the following e-mail from María Cristina Fernández de Córdoba, the president of the youth club of the popular newspaper *Las Noticias*. It is an invitation to participate in a conference. Read it and see if you can answer the questions in Activity 7:

DE: "María Cristina Fernández de Córdoba" fernandezmc@noticias.mx

PARA: "Peter Winthrop" winthropp@lagente.com

ENVIADO: Miércoles, 25 de noviembre, 2002 14:30

ASUNTO: Invitación a conferencia

ADJUNTAR: Prensa&juventud.doc

Estimado Sr. Winthrop:

El Club Noticias, parte de Las Noticias, está organizando una serie de conferencias, "Prensa y Juventud". Nos gustaría que usted participara en la conferencia del viernes, 27 de noviembre. Se llama "La música y el periodismo", y es una ocasión perfecta para que hable con nuestro público (en su mayoría estudiantes de periodismo) de su experiencia como reportero de La Gente.

La conferencia es a las cinco de la tarde en la Casa del Lago, Antiguo Bosque de Chapultepec.

Le saluda atentamente,
María Cristina Fernández de Córdoba
Jefa de la Sección Juvenil de Las Noticias

ACTIVITY 7: TAKE IT FOR A SPIN

1. ¿Quién escribe el mensaje?
2. ¿Cómo se llama la serie de conferencias?
3. ¿Quién es el público?
4. ¿Dónde está el Club Reforma?
5. ¿Cuándo es la conferencia "La música y el periodismo"?

STRUT YOUR STUFF!

Now it's time to show off what you've learned in the past lessons. You'll be reminded of all the things and places Peter has seen so far.

ACTIVITY 8: TAKE IT FOR A SPIN

Here are some fragments from Peter's diary. Some of the verbs are missing. Can you write them in the correct form?

LUNES,

A mi no me_____(gustar) ir a las zapaterías en España. _____(preferir) ir de compras en los Estados Unidos. ¡Estos zapatos blancos no son nada cómodos! ¡Y costaron tantísimo dinero! _____(pensar) que todo es más complicado en Madrid, aunque gracias a Carmen, la visita a España fue maravillosa.

Ahora también_____(deber) comprarme una chaqueta. ¡Hace fresco aquí por las noches!

MARTES,

No_____(volver) a Nueva York hasta el invierno. ¡Tanto tiempo fuera de casa!

MIÉRCOLES,

_____(necesitar) comprar el billete para Colombia. _____(salir) para allá el viernes. No_____(conocer) a muchas personas allí. Aquí sí _____(conocer) a algunas personas: Enrique_____(ser) muy simpático. Y los Alvear también_____(ser) encantadores . . . No_____(saber) si llamar a Carmen por teléfono o escribirle un mensaje electrónico . . . Siempre estoy _____(pensar) en Carmen . . .

CRIB NOTES

HEAR...SAY 1

After a night of fun and partying with the Alvear family, Peter decides that he must start working. The following morning, he goes to the office of his magazine in Mexico City. There he sees an old friend, the Mexican journalist Enrique Rodriguez. His friend starts teasing him about how bad he looks.

Enrique: You don't look that great, my friend! A night of partying?

Peter: I don't remember anything; I have a terrible hangover. Well, I need to send a report about my work to the central office in New York but my laptop is in the hotel. Can I use your e-mail?

Enrique: Of course! I'll be glad to let you use my computer. And what are you doing here in Mexico?

Peter: Since I arrived in Mexico, I haven't done anything else but eat and drink. I have to work more and party less.

Enrique: And what are you going to tell them in your report?

Peter: My goodness! You're right! I don't have anything! We must do something! What day is the concert?

Enrique: It is Friday in Foro Sol, at 9:00 PM. Today, by the way, is Thursday. It is 10:00 in the morning, and at 11:00 we have to be at the Marquis Hotel, which is on Reforma Avenue. Ricky is giving a press conference. I have a friend who works as a bellboy there. He tells me that there are *granaderos* on horses patrolling outside the hotel.

Peter: The army on horses? What's the matter?

Enrique: Calm down, Peter, calm down! The *granaderos* are from the police department. It is the fans . . . thousands of girls took the day off and are not going to classes. Their fathers are going to get really angry when they see their little daughters screaming on the news!

Peter: Let's do it! Where do you have the car? We've got to go.

Enrique: Don't get too excited, *gringo*. Today we cannot use my car due to pollution. We have to go by bike.

Peter: By bike?

Enrique: Yup. Here in the office, we've got two. But we should pray to the Virgin of Guadalupe. One bike is really old and it might not work well, but the Virgin is very miraculous.

Peter: I can't believe this!

The big moment arrives. It is Friday and it is 9:00 PM. Peter and Enrique Rodriguez are in the Foro Sol waiting for Ricky Martin's show. Peter is taking pictures and interviewing the crazed girls waiting for their idol.

Peter: I must take a lot of pictures of the fans to illustrate my report.

Enrique: It is easy. We are surrounded, and they are all crying. I know a girl that has been in line for three days to get a good seat. Imagine, out there since Wednesday!

Peter: It's incredible! The things girls do nowadays to see a famous singer! I am going to get close to one. Hi! What's your name?

Marina: Marina Velasco. Can you give me your press I.D.?

Peter: Are you crazy? What do you want it for?

Marina: I need to see him! I have to see him! I want an autograph. I know that with the I.D. card I will be able to get to his dressing room. I'll return it later.

Peter: I am sorry. I cannot give you my I.D. card. But I know a person who can solve your problem.

Marina: Who? I am desperate, I haven't slept since Monday. It is my only opportunity. I know he's leaving for Colombia tomorrow, Saturday.

Peter: Calm down. I know he will be in Mexico for a few more days. Tomorrow I can give you your autograph. Don't worry Marina, I'll ask my friend for the autograph.

Marina: And who is your friend?

Peter: Ricky Martin. What's the matter with you? Are you all right? Enrique, help me! This girl just fainted!

Enrique: But, what's the matter? It looks like I cannot leave you alone, Peter. I have to go with you everywhere.

ANSWER KEY

ACTIVITY 1

1. Eat in a typical restaurant: FUN
2. Send an e-mail to the central office: WORK
3. Write a report: WORK
4. Take pictures of fans: WORK
5. Spend a night partying and drinking: FUN
6. Use the laptop: WORK

ACTIVITY 2

1. Enrique es un periodista, amigo de Peter.
2. Peter come y bebe.
3. Peter no tiene nada.
4. Hoy es jueves.
5. Son las diez de la mañana.
6. Van a ir en bicicleta porque Enrique no puede usar hoy su carro por la contaminación.

ACTIVITY 3

1. Sí. You have to read Peter's adventures.
2. Sí. You have to study the vocabulary.
3. No. You must drink a lot of tequila.
4. Sí. You have to do the activities.
5. Sí. You have to speak with people.

ACTIVITY 4

1. Peter llega a Yucatán el domingo.
2. Tiene la rueda de prensa el jueves.
3. El lunes, el miércoles y el sábado no tiene nada específico.
4. El concierto es el viernes.
5. Peter está en México desde el martes.

ACTIVITY 5

1. FALSE: Las fans están llorando.
2. TRUE
3. FALSE: La chica quiere hablar con Ricky Martin.
4. TRUE
5. FALSE: Ricky Martin sale para Colombia.

ACTIVITY 6

1. conocer; 2. conocer; 3. saber; 4. saber; 5. conocer

ACTIVITY 7

1. María Cristina Fernández de Córdoba lo escribe.
2. La serie se llama Prensa y Juventud.
3. El público son los estudiantes de periodismo.
4. Está en el antiguo Bosque de Chapultepec.
5. La conferencia es el viernes, 5 de octubre, a las cinco de la tarde.

ACTIVITY 8

gusta – prefiero – pienso – debo – vuelvo – necesito – salgo – conozco – conozco – es – son – sé – pensando

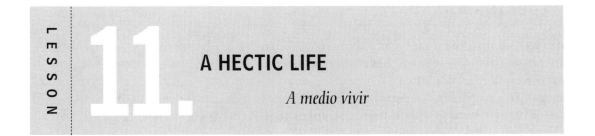

11.

A HECTIC LIFE

A medio vivir

He threw my shirt to the fans.

COMING UP...

- *It feels like yesterday:* Talking about the past—*yesterday, last year,* etc.
- *Don't be fooled:* Cognates and false cognates
- *A little* and *a lot* . . .
- *It's water under the bridge:* Talking about the past using the preterite tense
- *I'm slowly getting it:* Adding *–mente* to form adverbs

As you may imagine, Peter decides to accept the invitation he received from *Las Noticias*. In the next dialogue, you will hear him relating his stories (*contando historias*) to the journalism students from Mexico. Remember, as you listen, that he has been reporting on famous Latin singers in concerts in many countries (*países*). In the second dialogue, he will describe *una historia muy extraña* (strange) that involves the following items: two T-shirts, Enrique Iglesias, and the Chief of Police in Moscow! *Tienes que escuchar más* if you want to find out how these are connected.

ACTIVITY 1:	LET'S WARM UP

Can you match the places on the left with the phrases on the right? (There is some new vocabulary, but I am sure that by now you are a pro at the art of guessing, *¿verdad?*)

1. España
2. Japón
3. Los Estados Unidos
4. Rusia
5. Australia

a. Tiene un emperador.
b. Su capital es Moscú.
c. Tienen muchos canguros.
d. Es un país enorme.
e. Carmen está allí.

Take a Tip from Me!

In this lesson, we (or rather, Peter) will be talking about the past. Even though you don't know how to do that yet in Spanish, you'll still be able to understand most of the dialogues. Just focus on the story rather than on the verb endings. *¿Vale?*

Take a Tip from Me!

HEAR . . . SAY 1

Peter aceptó la invitación de María Cristina Fernández para participar en una conferencia sobre la prensa y la juventud. Tiene que hablar de sus experiencias como periodista.

Peter: Buenas tardes, estoy encantado de estar aquí con ustedes y de poder hablarles de mi experiencia profesional. Olvidé casi todo . . . pero, bueno, como tengo mucha imaginación, no hay ningún problema. Y como no sé por dónde empezar, pueden hacerme preguntas.

Persona 1: Señor Winthrop, ¿puede hablar de su trabajo más importante?

Peter: Sí, claro. El año pasado cubrí la gira de Gloria Estefan por todos los Estados Unidos, Europa, Japón y Australia. Es increíble la cantidad de cosas que vi, la cantidad de personas que conocí y la cantidad de dinero que gasté.

Persona 2: ¿Cómo es el público japonés en un concierto de una estrella latina?

Peter: ¡Oh! ¡Es increíble! Leí una vez que sólo en Tokio hay unas 500 (quinientas) escuelas de baile donde se enseñan los ritmos latinos. No lo creí pero cuando vi bailar salsa a 60.000 (sesenta mil) japoneses vi que es cierto.

Persona 3: ¿Cómo aprendió a hablar español así de bien?

Peter: Muchas gracias. Bueno, estudié español primero en mi escuela secundaria y luego en mi universidad, en los Estados Unidos. Pero es necesario practicar mucho.

Persona 4: ¿Cómo decidió ser periodista?

Peter: Bueno, siempre me gustó mucho escribir y tomar fotos. Y en una ocasión, trabajé un verano en el periódico *The New York News*. Entonces, decidí ser periodista.

Persona 5: ¿Y está contento con su decisión?

Peter: Pues, creo que sí, aunque a veces estoy a medio vivir con tanto viaje. Pero gracias a mi trabajo ahora estoy aquí en este bello país y también gracias a mi trabajo, en España conocí a una persona en particular muy interesante.

ACTIVITY 2: HOW'S THAT AGAIN?

Let's see how well you remember what you've just heard. Choose the right answer:

1. ¿Cuál es el trabajo más importante de Peter?
   a. Gloria Estefan   b. Marc Anthony   c. Enrique Iglesias
2. ¿Qué hacen los japoneses?
   a. Escriben cartas.   b. Leen el periódico.   c. Bailan salsa.
3. ¿Dónde trabajó Peter un verano?
   a. *The New York News*   b. *The Connecticut Daily*   c. *Las Noticias*
4. ¿Cómo es la persona que Peter conoció en España?
   a. horrible   b. increíble   c. interesante

Did You Know?

As you may remember, I mentioned that people in Spain usually don't like to say that they're fine when you ask them: *¿Cómo estás?* Well, in most countries in Latin America, people's response to that question is somewhere between the typical Spanish and the typical U.S. versions. They usually say *bien* or *muy bien* first. But, beware! Then, they tell you everything about their problems, too, just like the Spaniards . . .

Did You Know?

WORKSHOP 1

THE NITTY-GRITTY

IT'S WATER UNDER THE BRIDGE: TALKING ABOUT THE PAST USING THE PRETERITE TENSE

In Spanish there are two simple past tenses: the preterite and the imperfect. In this lesson, we'll talk about the preterite. The preterite is used to express a past action that has a definite beginning and end. Look at these examples and compare them with their English translation:

> **El año pasado cubrí la gira de Gloria Estefan.**

> Last year, I covered Gloria Estefan's tour.

> **Estudié español en la universidad.**

> I studied Spanish in college.

> **Peter escribió una novela.**

> Peter wrote a novel.

Notice that the Spanish preterite (e.g., *yo estudié*) always corresponds to the English simple past tense (e.g., *I studied*). Let's now see how the Spanish preterite is formed. The endings for *-er* and *-ir* verbs are the same. (Hey, finally less work in the grammar section!) Here we go—I studied, you studied . . . (or so I'd like to believe!).

PRETERITE TENSE OF REGULAR VERBS			
	ESTUDIAR (TO STUDY)	*COMER* (TO EAT)	*ESCRIBIR* (TO WRITE)
yo	estudi + é	com + í	escrib + í
tú	estudi + aste	com + iste	escrib + iste
él / ella, usted	estudi + ó	com + ió	escrib + ió

PRETERITE TENSE OF REGULAR VERBS			
	ESTUDIAR (TO STUDY)	COMER (TO EAT)	ESCRIBIR (TO WRITE)
nosotros / nosotras	estudi + amos	com + imos	escrib + imos
vosotros / vosotras	estudi + asteis	com + isteis	escrib + isteis
ellos / ellas, ustedes	estudi + aron	com + ieron	escrib + ieron

Some verbs require spelling changes in the *yo* form to keep the sound the same:

practicar → ***yo practiqué*** (prahk-tee-KEH)

"C" becomes "qu," because if not, it would be *practicé* (prahk-tee-SEH), a form that doesn't exist in Spanish.

pagar → ***yo pagué*** (pah-GEH)

"G" becomes "gu," because if not, the word would be *pagé* (pah-HEH), again, an unknown form.

ACTIVITY 3: TAKE IT FOR A SPIN

Go back to the Hear . . . Say section and find all the verbs in the preterite. Write them down in these two columns depending on whether they take *–ar* endings or *–er/–ir* endings:

–AR	–ER / –IR
Yo olvidé	Yo cubrí

WORDS TO LIVE BY

IT FEELS LIKE YESTERDAY: **TALKING ABOUT THE PAST—***YESTERDAY, LAST YEAR,* **ETC.**

When speaking about past events, you not only need verbs in the preterite tense, but some time expressions as well. Here are the most common ones:

el año pasado	last year
el mes pasado	last month
la semana pasada	last week
ayer	yesterday
anoche	last night

When telling a story, you can also use words such as:

luego	then
entonces	then
más tarde	later
después	later, afterwards
una vez	once

ACTIVITY 4: TAKE IT FOR A SPIN

Can you put these phrases in chronological order?

1. la semana pasada
2. ayer
3. el año pasado
4. el mes pasado

Did You Know?

The Spanish word for university or college is *la universidad*. The word *escuela* (school) is only used for primary and secondary schools. *El colegio* has the same meaning as *escuela*. It never refers to university-level education. In Spanish-speaking countries, students entering a university go directly to a specialized school of their choice. Thus, if you want to become a medical doctor, you start studying medicine as soon as you enter college. Usually, *la carrera* (course of study) lasts five or six years, and for some professions, like medicine, you have to study for at least three more years after that.

Did You Know?

HEAR . . . SAY 2

Peter continúa hablando de sus aventuras ante su público, en su mayoría estudiantes de periodismo.

Persona 1: Señor Winthrop, ¿cómo son las estrellas de la música? ¿Son tan excéntricas como dicen?

Peter: Te voy a contar una historia. El mes pasado una agencia me contrató para hablar con Enrique Iglesias. Viajé a Moscú rápidamente, vi su concierto y después caminé a su hotel. Cuando llegué al hotel vi a miles de chicas rusas gritando y chillando. Le pregunté al jefe de prensa del cantante qué pasó. "Quieren la camiseta que llevó en el concierto" me contestó. "¡Pero si está sucia!" exclamé yo. "Para ellas es igual" me contestó. Subí a su habitación y empezamos la entrevista. Poco después, llamaron a la puerta y entró ¡el jefe de policía de Moscú! Nos indicó que en la calle había ya veinte mil chicas pidiendo a gritos su camiseta. Enrique Iglesias le comentó que tiró la camiseta a la basura en el estadio. Entonces el jefe de policía de Moscú me miró y habló con sus ayudantes. Uno de ellos me abrió la chaqueta y ¡me quitó mi camiseta de Armani! Enrique Iglesias salió a la terraza y les tiró mi camiseta sucia a las fans. Después de esto, ¿ustedes piensan que las estrellas de la música pueden vivir normalmente? Y ¿puedo ir yo a algún concierto vistiendo ropa cara?

Persona 2: Sus anécdotas son muy divertidas. Y finalmente, ¿qué hace cuando no tiene que trabajar? ¿Escucha la música de los artistas como Ricky, Enrique o Gloria?

Peter: Pues, ¡por supuesto! (*ironically*) Y después de un gran concierto, normalmente salgo a comprar camisetas.

Persona 3: Por cierto, me encanta el sueter que tiene hoy.

Peter: ¡Pero bueno! ¡Eso sí que es cara dura!

ACTIVITY 5: HOW'S THAT AGAIN?

Answer the following questions about Peter's story. Try to use the preterite tense that you've just learned.

1. ¿Quién contrató a Peter para hablar con Enrique Iglesias?
2. ¿Hacia dónde caminó Peter?
3. ¿Qué vio Peter cuando llegó al hotel?
4. ¿Dónde tiró la camiseta Enrique Iglesias?
5. ¿Qué tipo de música escucha Peter en su tiempo libre?

Did You Know?

A popular activity in many Spanish-speaking countries is to watch *telenovelas* (soap operas). Mexican soap operas are the TV shows with the largest audience, not only in Mexico but also in all of Latin America. The story lines are long and winding, and that's why they are also called *culebrones* (from the word *culebra*—snake). One of the most famous soap operas ever, that was even seen in the Soviet Union, was *Los ricos también lloran* (*The Rich Also Cry*), with the well-known Mexican actress, Verónica Castro.

Did You Know?

WORKSHOP 2

THE NITTY-GRITTY

I'M SLOWLY GETTING IT: ADDING *–MENTE* TO FORM ADVERBS

Adverbs are words used to describe actions, such as *slowly*, *frequently*, or *freely*. In Spanish, many adverbs are formed by adding *–mente* to an adjective (a word used to describe a noun). If the adjective has both a masculine and a feminine form, you use the feminine form to add *–mente*:

rápido / rápida (fast): Take the feminine form, *rápida*, and add *–mente* to make *rapidamente*.

If the adjective has only one form, that's the one you use! (You've noticed this works just like in English, where we add *–ly* to adjectives to form adverbs.) Take a look at a few examples:

FORMING ADVERBS FROM ADJECTIVES

ADJECTIVE		ADVERB	
inmediata	immediate (feminine form of adjective *inmediato / a*)	*inmediata* + *mente*	immediately
frecuente	frequent (only one form)	*frecuente* + *mente*	frequently
libre	free (only one form)	*libre* + *mente*	freely

ACTIVITY 6: TAKE IT FOR A SPIN

Read Hear . . . Say 2 again. Write down the adverbs that end in *–mente* and their corresponding adjectives:

	Adverbs ending in *–mente*	Adjectives
1.		
2.		
3.		
4.		

WORDS TO LIVE BY

DON'T BE FOOLED: COGNATES AND FALSE COGNATES

You'll remember that cognates are those words that are so similar to English words that you can guess their meanings. In this chapter, we've seen many examples:

NOUNS: *la experiencia; la imaginación; la novela; el público; el ritmo; la universidad; el video; la agencia; la anécdota; el artista; el estadio; la terraza*
ADJECTIVES: *secundario / a; latino / a; profesional; excéntrico / a*
VERBS: *entrar; estudiar*

You have to be careful, however, because there are also "false cognates" or, as they are called in Spanish, *falsos amigos* (false friends). These are Spanish words that look just like English words but have (sometimes very) different meanings. We already saw one important example—*estar embarazada* (to be pregnant). Let's look at some more from this lesson:

contento / a	It means **happy**, not **content**.
aprender	It means **to learn**, not **to apprehend**.
contestar	It means **to answer**, not **to contest**.
contar (historias)	It means **to tell stories**, even though it looks a lot like **to count histories**. The word **la historia** is also a bit deceiving. It means not only "history" but also "story." And **la historieta** means "a comic strip."

A LITTLE AND A LOT

In Spanish, *poco* (a little) and *mucho* (a lot) are very handy words. They can be used with verbs, nouns, or adjectives. When you use them with actions (verbs), they don't change their form:

Me gusta poco.	I like it a little.
Escribo mucho.	I write a lot.

But *mucho* can also be used as an adjective to modify nouns. In that case, it changes its form according to the number and gender of the noun (*poco, –a, –os, –as; mucho, –a, –os, –as*). For example:

Hay muchas chicas.	There are a lot of girls. (*or* There are many girls.)
Hay pocos fotógrafos.	There are a few photographers.

This is a little story about Peter. Can you construct sentences with verbs in the preterite tense? (Also note how *mucho* and *poco* are used!) Let me get you started:

El año pasado / Peter / visitar / Japón.   El año pasado Peter visitó Japón.

Now you continue:

1. Ver / muchas cosas
2. Conocer / a muchas personas
3. Gastar / mucho dinero
4. Hablar / poco / japonés
5. También / bailar / mucho

Word on the Street

¡Pero, bueno!	What! or What do you mean! (It denotes surprise, usually not positive.)
¡Por supuesto!	Of course! (Lit. It is understood.)
estar a medio vivir	to be crazed; to have a hectic life (Lit. half living). It means that your life is hectic or falling apart, usually because of love- or work-related troubles.
igual	same
tener cara (dura)	to be shameless (Lit. to have a hard face)

The expression *tener cara (dura)* is especially common in Spain (where Peter picked it up) and means that one has no shame. It comes from the idea that when one is embarrassed, one tends to look down, but if you have no shame, you look up, defiant. Then, it is said that your face is so hard it cannot "look" down, like a statue. It is extremely common to hear, **¡Pero, que cara!**

LET'S PUT IT IN WRITING

Before moving on to his next assignment in Colombia, Peter has decided to take a vacation. He will spend a couple of days in Cancún, on the Yucatán Peninsula. Take a look at the hotel reservation form he found on the Internet. *¿Muy fácil, no?* What kind of information are they looking for? Here's some vocabulary to help you out (I am confident you can figure out the rest):

enviar	to send
apellido	last name

RESERVACIONES EN LÍNEA

CIUDAD: CANCÚN   ESTADO: QUINTANA ROO

HOTEL: CAMINO REAL

INFORMACIÓN PERSONAL

Apellido: ——————————————————————

Nombre: ——————————————————————

Teléfono ——————————————————————

E-mail ——————————————————————

País ——————————————————————

Ciudad ——————————————————————

DETALLES DE LA RESERVACIÓN

Fecha de llegada: Día/Mes/Año ————————————

Fecha de salida: Día/Mes/Año ————————————

Hora de llegada: Mañana/Tarde/Noche ————————

HABITACIONES

Habitación sencilla : Normal/Superior/Lujo ——————

Habitación doble : Normal/Superior/Lujo ——————

Habitación triple : Normal/Superior/Lujo ——————

Favor de indicar aquí sus peticiones especiales al hotel: ————

Enviar reservación

ACTIVITY 8:   TAKE IT FOR A SPIN

Here is some of Peter's information. Can you find the right place for it?

1. Habitación sencilla normal
2. Winthrop

3. Diez de la mañana
4. No fumador
5. Estados Unidos

And here's the last activity. I promise.

TAKE IT UP A NOTCH

This time I would like to know a bit about your past. Answer *sí* or *no* to these questions about yourself (you can check their translations in the Crib Notes section):

1. ¿Estudiaste en la universidad?
2. ¿Viajaste a México?
3. ¿Viviste en Nueva York?
4. ¿Subiste al Empire State?
5. ¿Lloraste cuando viste *Gone with the Wind*?
6. ¿Hablaste por teléfono ayer con tu madre?
7. ¿Trabajaste mucho la semana pasada?

CRIB NOTES

HEAR...SAY 1

Peter accepted María Cristina Fernández's invitation to participate in a panel discussion about the media and youth. He has to speak about his experiences as a journalist.

Peter: Good afternoon, I am pleased to be here with you and to be able to speak about my professional experience. I forgot almost everything I was going to say . . . but, well, as I have a lot of imagination, there is no problem. And as I don't know where to start, you can ask me some questions.

Person 1: Mr. Winthrop, could you speak about your most important job?

Peter: Yes, of course. Last year I covered Gloria Estefan's tour around the U.S., Europe, Japan, and Australia. It is incredible how many things I saw, how many people I met, and the amount of money I spent.

Person 2: What's the Japanese public like at a concert of a Latin star?

Peter: Oh! They're incredible! I read that in Tokyo alone, there are around 500 dance schools where Latin rhythms are taught. I didn't believe it, but when I saw 60,000 Japanese people salsa dancing, I saw it was true.

Person 3: How did you learn to speak Spanish so well?

Peter: Thank you very much. Well, I studied Spanish first in high school and then at my university in the United States. But it is necessary to practice a lot.

Person 4: How did you decide to be a journalist?

Peter: Well, I always really liked writing and taking pictures. I worked for The New York News for a summer. So I decided to be a journalist.

Person 5: And are you happy with your decision?

Peter: Well, I think so, although sometimes my life feels out of control with so much traveling. But thanks to my job, I am here in this beautiful country, and also, thanks to my job, I met a really special person in Spain.

Peter continues speaking about his adventures to his audience, many of whom are journalism students.

Person 1: Mr. Winthrop, what are music stars like? Are they as eccentric as they say?

Peter: I am going to tell you a story. Last month an agency hired me to speak with Enrique Iglesias. I traveled to Moscow right away, I saw his concert, and afterwards, I walked to his hotel. When I arrived at the hotel, I saw thousands of Russian girls screaming and shouting. I asked the singer's press manager what happened. "They want the T-shirt that he wore in the concert," he answered. "But, it's dirty!" I said. "For them it doesn't matter," he answered. I went up to his room and we started the interview. A bit later, there was a knock on the door and the Moscow chief of police walked in! He told us that in the street, there were already 20,000 screaming girls asking for his T-shirt. Enrique mentioned that he had thrown the T-shirt in the trash in the stadium. Then the Moscow chief of police looked at me and spoke to his officers. One of them opened my jacket and took off my Armani T-shirt! Enrique Iglesias went out to the balcony and threw my dirty T-shirt to the fans. After this, do you think that the music stars can have a normal life? And, can I go to any concert wearing expensive clothes?

Person 2: Your stories are very funny. So, finally, what do you do when you don't have to work? Do you listen to the music of artists like Ricky, Enrique, or Gloria?

Peter: But, of course! (*ironically*) And after big concerts, I usually go shopping for T-shirts.

Person 3: By the way, I love the sweater you're wearing today.

Peter: Well!! That's what I call shameless!

ANSWER KEY

ACTIVITY 1

1. España: Carmen está allí. (Spain: Carmen is there.)
2. Japón: Tiene un emperador. (Japan: It has an emperor.)
3. Los Estados Unidos: Es un país enorme. (The United States: It is a huge country.)
4. Rusia: Su capital es Moscú. (Russia: Its capital is Moscow.)
5. Australia: Tienen muchos canguros. (Australia: They have a lot of kangaroos.)

ACTIVITY 2

1. A; 2. C; 3. A; 4. C

ACTIVITY 3

–ar	–er, –ir
Yo olvidé	Yo cubrí
Yo gasté	Yo vi
Yo trabajé	Yo conocí
Ellos llevaron	Yo leí
Me gustó	Yo creí
Peter aceptó	Yo decidí
Yo estudié	Yo escribí
	Él aprendió
	Él decidió

ACTIVITY 4

2, 1, 4, 3

ACTIVITY 5

1. Una agencia contrató a Peter.
2. Caminó al hotel.
3. Vio a muchas chicas gritando y chillando.
4. La tiró a la basura.
5. Escucha música latina.

ACTIVITY 6

Adverbs	Adjectives
1. rápidamente	rápido / a
2. normalmente	normal
3. finalmente	final
4. usualmente	usual

ACTIVITY 7

El año pasado Peter visitó Japón. Vio muchas cosas. Conoció a muchas personas. Gastó mucho dinero. Habló poco japonés. También bailó mucho.
(Last year, Peter visited Japan. He saw a lot of things. He met a lot of people. He spent a lot of money. He spoke a little Japanese. He danced a lot.)

ACTIVITY 8

1. Habitación sencilla: normal (Single room: regular)
2. Apellido (Last name)

3.   Hora de llegada (Time of arrival): mañana (morning)
4.   Favor de indicar aquí sus peticiones especiales al hotel. (Please indicate your special requests for the hotel.)
5.   País (Country)

ACTIVITY 9

1.   Did you study at a university?
2.   Did you travel to Mexico?
3.   Did you live in New York?
4.   Did you go up the Empire State Building?
5.   Did you cry when you saw *Gone with the Wind*?
6.   Did you speak on the phone with your mother yesterday?
7.   Did you work a lot last week?

12. UP AND DOWN

Por arriba y por abajo

Now they are in Chichén Itzá.

COMING UP . . .

- *A long time ago:* Using *hace* to say how long ago you've done something
- *On the go:* Some travel vocabulary
- *So much* and *so many*
- *It's water under the bridge:* The preterite of some irregular verbs
- *I scream, you scream . . . :* The preterite of more irregular verbs
- *It's nobody's fault:* No-fault *se*

Bueno, aquí estamos otra vez (again). I am really glad you are still around. Although it might seem to you that the lessons are getting harder, just look back at Lessons 1 or 2 and see what a long way you've come. *¡Excelente!*

Pues, back to our story and your work. Peter is trying to get some rest before moving on to his next assignment. Here we find him in Cancún, but the place is swarming with tourists. So, he decides to go camping instead *(ir de camping)*. He has befriended a group of students at the conference, so he decides to go with them. Imagine: *una noche tranquila, el silencio, un grupo de amigos están contando historias . . .* what can go wrong? *Ya verás . . .* (You'll see . . .)

ACTIVITY 1:	LET'S WARM UP

How else to fill an evening when one goes camping if not with stories about past travel *(viajes)*. Peter and his friends are sitting around and doing just that. What trips could they be talking about? Select from the list below those that you'd like to hear about:

1. Un viaje en auto con los abuelos a Disneylandia
2. Un viaje de mochilazo *(backpacking trip)* a Oaxaca con la novia
3. Un viaje a las Vegas para jugar *(to gamble)*
4. Una excursión a Yucatán con los papás
5. Un viaje a Madrid para ver el Museo del Prado

HEAR . . . SAY 1

Peter viajó a Cancún para descansar pero hay demasiados turistas. Afortunadamente, conoció a un grupo de estudiantes mexicanos que van a viajar a Yucatán caminando y durmiendo al aire libre. Peter decide viajar con ellos. Ahora están en Chichén Itzá.

Peter: Este lugar es maravilloso. ¿Vinieron aquí antes?

Luisa: Yo sí. Hace mucho tiempo vine con mis papás. Hicimos muchas excursiones, pero en auto. Aunque ir de mochilazo es diferente. ¡Es padrísimo!

David: Yo también. Mi novia y yo vinimos hace dos años; viajamos como reyes, pero este año me quedé sin novia y sin plata y por eso vine con estos pelados.

Peter: Siempre supe que algún día vendría aquí. Esto es como un sueño para mí.

Dora: Pues yo en cambio desde niña quise ir al Cañón del Colorado. ¿Fuiste allá alguna vez, Peter?

Peter: Fui allí con mis abuelos una vez. Hace tanto tiempo que casi no lo recuerdo. Pero sí recuerdo que dimos muchas vueltas. Fuimos por arriba y por abajo y no vimos nada porque siempre hizo mal tiempo. Lo único que vi fueron nubes.

Dora:	¡Ah compadre! ¡Qué mala suerte tuviste!
Luisa:	Mala suerte la mía. Estuve un año ahorrando para pasar mis vacaciones en Oaxaca, y cuando llegué allá, me dieron unas fiebres horribles y me puse malísima. Estuve en la cama del hotel todo el tiempo.
Peter:	Bueno chicos, ¿dónde vamos a dormir esta noche? Porque parece que va a llover.
David:	Hace un mes que no llueve por acá, mano.
Peter:	¡Por si acaso le voy a rezar al Dios Tlaloc!
Todos:	¡No, Peter, por favor! ¡Tlaloc es el dios de la lluvia!

ACTIVITY 2: HOW'S THAT AGAIN?

You know the drill. Answer the questions, *por favor*:

1. ¿Cómo es el lugar?
2. ¿Con quién viajó Luisa, con sus padres o con sus hermanos?
3. ¿Cómo viajó Luisa, en motocicleta o en auto?
4. ¿Viajó Peter alguna vez al Cañón del Colorado?
5. ¿Quién estuvo en la cama del hotel todo el tiempo?

Did You Know?

The Aztec gods were primarily associated with various aspects of nature, such as rain, wind, and corn. The most powerful ones included Quetzalcoatl (the god of learning and the arts), Tlaloc (the god of rain), and Huitzilipochtli (the god of war). One legend says that it was Huitzilipochtli who led the Aztecs from the northwest part of Mexico to where Mexico City is today. They wandered around until a prophecy told them that they could stay where they find an eagle holding a snake in its mouth, perched on a cactus. This eagle is now a symbol of Mexico, and it is still part of the Mexican flag. Huitzilipochtli, according to the legend, also gave the Aztecs a new name—Mexica.

WORKSHOP 1

THE NITTY-GRITTY

IT'S WATER UNDER THE BRIDGE: THE PRETERITE OF SOME IRREGULAR VERBS

Just in case you doubted it, there are irregular preterites, too. I'm giving you some very important ones here. As usual with irregular verbs, the root or stem of the verb undergoes slight variations in form—the vowel in the root is different in the preterite form. Also note that there are no accents on the endings.

PRETERITE TENSE OF IRREGULAR VERBS HACER, VENIR, AND DAR			
	HACER (TO DO)	VENIR (TO COME)	DAR (TO GIVE)
yo	hice	vine	di
tú	hiciste	viniste	diste
él / ella, usted	hizo	vino	dio
nosotros / nosotras	hicimos	vinimos	dimos
vosotros / vosotras	hicisteis	vinisteis	disteis
ellos / ellas, ustedes	hicieron	vinieron	dieron

The verbs *ir* (to go) and *ser* (to be) share a single set of forms in the preterite:

PRETERITE TENSE OF IRREGULAR VERBS IR (TO GO) AND SER (TO BE)		
yo	fui	I was *or* I went
tú	fuiste	you were *or* you went
él / ella, usted	fue	he / she, you (formal) was / were *or* went
nosotros, nosotras	fuimos	we were *or* went
vosotros, vosotras	fuisteis	you were *or* went
ellos / ellas, ustedes	fueron	they, you (formal) were *or* went

Don't worry. The context always clarifies which one is being used. For example:

Benito Juárez fue una persona muy interesante. (*ser* is used here)

Benito Juárez was a very interesting person.

Fuimos a Nueva York el año pasado. (*ir* is used here)

We went to New York last year.

ACTIVITY 3: TAKE IT FOR A SPIN

These are some sentences from the dialogue. The verbs are in the *nosotros* form. Change them to the *ellos / ellas* form as in the model:

Vinimos con mis papás.　　　→　　　Ellos vinieron con sus papás.

1. Hicimos muchas excursiones.
2. Vinimos hace dos años.
3. Viajamos como reyes.

4. Dimos muchas vueltas.
5. Fuimos a Oaxaca con mis abuelos.

WORDS TO LIVE BY

A LONG TIME AGO: USING *HACE* TO SAY HOW LONG AGO YOU'VE DONE SOMETHING

To say *ago* in Spanish, you have to use the word *hace*. *Hace* is used at the beginning of the time phrase, not at the end as in English, so be careful.

Hace tres años fui a Cancún.	Three years ago, I went to Cancún.
Hace mucho tiempo hice una excursión.	A long time ago, I went on an excursion.

Here are a few more examples that were used in the dialogue:

hace dos años	two years ago
hace tanto tiempo	such a long time ago
hace un mes	a month ago

Heads Up!

An *hace* phrase can also be used with a verb in the present tense, but with a slightly different meaning.

No llueve hace un mes.	It hasn't rained in a month.
No veo a mis padres hace un año.	I haven't seen my parents in a year.

ON THE GO: SOME TRAVELING VOCABULARY

Our friends talk about the *excursiones* (short trips) they took during their *vacaciones*. Here are some verbs to help you talk about yours:

venir	to come
hacer una excursión / ir de excursión	to go on a day trip
hacer camping / ir de camping	to go camping
ir de mochilazo	to go backpacking (more colloquial, especially in Mexico)
dar vueltas	to go around

You won't get very far without *la plata* (silver), a word used in many countries to mean *money*. And now that we are at it, other words used for money are: *dinero, lana* (*Lit.* wool; used in Mexico), *papita* (*Lit.* potato; used in Colombia), and *pasta* (Spain).

Word on the Street

ACTIVITY 4:   **TAKE IT FOR A SPIN**

Here is a fragment of a story about a trip. Match the underlined phrases on the left with the correct English translations on the right:

1.	Hace tres años, hicimos <u>una excursión</u>.	a.	up and down
2.	Fuimos <u>por arriba</u> y <u>por abajo</u>.	b.	just in case
3.	<u>Dimos muchas vueltas</u>.	c.	day trip
4.	No <u>llegamos</u> hasta la noche.	d.	(we) arrived
5.	<u>Por si acaso</u>, llevamos mucha plata.	e.	(we) went around

HEAR . . . SAY 2

Peter y sus nuevos amigos están pasando la noche de camping en los alrededores de Chichén Itzá, cerca de un pueblo llamado Piste. De repente, estalla una tormenta (*storm*).

Peter: ¡Está entrando agua! ¿Quién puso la tienda de campaña?

Luisa: Yo lo hice. La puse lo mejor que pude.

David: Pues que mal te quedó. ¡Y eso que estuviste una hora!

Dora: ¡No pusiste el doble techo! ¡Esto parece el *Titanic*!

Luisa: Es que no lo traje, se me olvidó.

Dora: Además, no vimos dónde la pusimos, ya hacía un rato que el sol se fue. Voy a salir con la linterna a ver qué pasa . . . ¡Frijoles! ¡Acampamos en un cenote!

David: Lo dije. Debimos ir a la posada del pueblo que era muy barata, lo leí en la guía. No sé cómo me dejé engañar por esta bola de tacaños. ¡Estoy empapado!

Luisa:	¿Trajiste tu celular, Peter?
Peter:	Por supuesto. Lo llevo siempre cuando estoy de viaje. Nunca voy a ningún lado sin él. Es muy útil.
David:	Podemos telefonear a la posada de Piste, se llama Novelo, y reservar una habitación. Ahorita mismo te doy el número, lo escribí en mi agenda. ¿Qué te pasa, Peter? ¡Qué pálido estás, compadre!
Peter:	Lo siento muchachos, el móvil se quedó sin batería y no lo puedo cargar.
David:	No te preocupes, tampoco pude encontrar la agenda, creo que se me perdió en Cancún.
Dora:	¡Qué desastre! ¡No se lo van a creer! ¡Se me cayó la linterna al agua y ahora no funciona!
Todos:	¡Genial!

ACTIVITY 5: HOW'S THAT AGAIN?

Hey! *¿Qué pasó?* Somebody scrambled the following sentences related to the dialogue. Can you put them back in the right order?

1. La linterna no funciona.
2. Los chicos van a telefonear a la posada de Piste.
3. Un estudiante va a salir con la linterna.
4. El teléfono celular no tiene batería.
5. Está entrando el agua en la tienda de campaña.

Did You Know?

The Maya culture is one of the two indigenous Mexican cultures (the other is the Aztec culture). The Maya lived in the south of Mexico and in Central America from the year 300 BC until 1450 AD. The ruins in the Yucatán Peninsula, like Chichén Itzá and Uxmal, where our friends from the dialogue are camping, date back to the golden period of the Maya (called the period Maya-Tolteca) in the eighth and ninth centuries.

The Maya are called the "Greeks of the Americas" because they developed a very advanced urban civilization. Their cities, built in natural valleys called *cenotes*, were governed by priests whose achievements in astronomy, architecture, and mathematics are still impressive today.

By the way, the Maya invented soccer as well. Two teams would play the game in the main squares of their cities with a ball made of rugs.

Did You Know?

THE NITTY-GRITTY

I SCREAM, YOU SCREAM: THE PRETERITE OF MORE IRREGULAR VERBS

Like the verbs you saw earlier, these verbs do not have accents on their endings and have a different vowel in the stems. All the verbs in this group include the vowel *u* in the stem.

	PONER (TO PUT)	SABER (TO KNOW)	ESTAR (TO BE)	TENER (TO HAVE)
PRETERITE TENSE OF IRREGULAR VERBS *PONER, SABER, ESTAR,* **AND** *TENER*				
yo	puse	supe	estuve	tuve
tú	pusiste	supiste	estuviste	tuviste
él / ella, usted	puso	supo	estuvo	tuvo
nosotros / nosotras	pusimos	supimos	estuvimos	tuvimos
vosotros / vosotras	pusisteis	supisteis	estuvisteis	tuviste
ellos / ellas, ustedes	pusieron	supieron	estuvieron	tuvieron

Verbs that include the word *tener* are also irregular (e.g., *mantener* [to keep] or *contener* [to contain]):

> **Mantuvimos la amistad.**
>
> We kept our friendship.

The past tense of *hay* (there is / are) is *hubo.* (It takes the same *u* in the stem, as the verbs listed above.)

> **No hubo mucho tiempo.**
>
> There wasn't much time.

> **No hubo muchos problemas.**
>
> There weren't many problems.

The following two verbs include a *j* in their stem when they are used in the preterite tense:

	DECIR (TO SAY)	TRAER (TO BRING)
PRETERITE TENSE OF IRREGULAR VERBS *DECIR* **AND** *TRAER*		
yo	dije	traje
tú	dijiste	trajiste

PRETERITE TENSE OF IRREGULAR VERBS *DECIR* AND *TRAER*		
	DECIR (TO SAY)	*TRAER* (TO BRING)
él / ella, usted	*dijo*	*trajo*
nosotros, nosotras	*dijimos*	*trajimos*
vosotros, vosotras	*dijisteis*	*trajisteis*
ellos / ellas, ustedes	*dijeron*	*trajeron*

ACTIVITY 6: TAKE IT FOR A SPIN

Go back to Hear . . . Say 2 and write down all the verbs (both regular and irregular) that are in the preterite tense. Then write their infinitive form next to them. There are nineteen such forms in the dialogue.

IT'S NOBODY'S FAULT: NO-FAULT *SE*

Look at these sentences:

Perdí la agenda.   I lost my address book.

Se me perdió la agenda.   My address book got lost.

In Sentence 1, I am responsible for the action. In Sentence 2, I am the "victim" of the action.

In Spanish, you can use both constructions, but the second one is much more common, probably because it implies that you are not really responsible for your actions, but a victim of circumstances (isn't that convenient!). Here is how you form it:

se + indirect object pronoun + verb + subject

Here are some more examples:

Se me olvidó la agenda.

I forgot my address book. (*Lit.* My address book got forgotten.)

Se nos olvidaron las llaves.

We forgot our keys. (*Lit.* Our keys got forgotten.)

Se le olvidó el celular.

He / she forgot his / her cellular. (*Lit.* His / her cell phone got forgotten.)

There are other verbs used similarly, especially in the preterite. You saw some in the dialogues:

Se me rompió.	It broke.
Se me cayó.	I dropped it *or* It fell.

Take a Tip from Me!

These are very common expressions that include some complicated grammar. I recommend that you learn them as fixed expressions, especially *se me olvidó* (I forgot), because they are so useful.

Take a Tip from Me!

WORDS TO LIVE BY

SO MUCH AND SO MANY

Let's see how the concepts of "much" and "many" are expressed in Spanish. Now you can finally tell your Spanish-speaking friends how much you are really studying.

Tanto (so much, so many) can modify a verb. In this case, it does not change its form:

¡Viajas tanto!

You travel so much!

But *tanto* can also modify a noun, and then, like any adjective, it needs to agree with that noun in gender and in number:

¡Gastamos tanta plata!

We spent so much money!

¡Vimos a tantos amigos!

We saw so many friends!

When *tanto* is used with *hace* and a time phrase, the meaning changes slightly:

¡Fue hace tanto tiempo!

It was such a long time ago! (*Lit.* so much time ago)

Word on the Street

If you want to sound Mexican, here are some words you can use:

la posada	hostel
¡Frijoles!	My goodness! (Lit. beans)
¡Padrísimo!	Great!, Cool! (Used a lot in Mexico. Also, **¡Qué padre!**)
bola de tacaños	bunch of cheapskates

And there are many ways to call your friends. Here are some Mexican terms:

los pelados	It comes from the word **pelado, –a** (Lit. peeled). In the dialogue it means "friend," but it can also be insulting.
Esa pelada no me gusta nada.	I don't like that idiot one bit.
compadre	Originally used to address the godfather of your child or the father of your godchild. This term is now commonly used to mean "pal." It is used in other Spanish-speaking countries as well.
mano	This one comes from **hermano** (brother); it's just like **bro** in English.

Did You Know?

Another word for good friend in Mexico is *cuate* and it has an interesting story behind it. It is believed to come from Náhuatl, the language of the Aztecs. It was the word used to refer to Quetzalcóatl, the Aztec God, because he was depicted as a feathered serpent (in Náhuatl, *coatl*). Because this god had a twin brother, Xolotl, it also came to mean "twin." With time and use, it was transformed into *cuate*. Today, it simply means "very good friend" or "pal."

Did You Know?

LET'S PUT IT IN WRITING

While Peter was having *su aventura* with his new friends, this article came out in *Las Noticias*. It describes the concert. First, look at the questions in Activity 7. Then, read the article. Remember, you just need to look for the answers to the questions. There's no need to understand every word.

¡QUÉ DÍA MÁS LOCO, RICKY!

Por Enrique Rodríguez

CIUDAD DE MÉXICO. Miles de fans y decenas de reporteros vivieron un día realmente loco tratando (*trying*) de descubrir dónde estaba el famoso cantante Ricky Martin. La disquera Sony Music mantuvo la incógnita incluso en el Aeropuerto Internacional "Adolfo López Mateos". Más tarde, Sony anunció que el cantante estaba alojado en una suite del Hotel Marquis desde dos días antes. ¡La locura!

Las fans enloquecidas fueron inmediatamente al hotel, y los granaderos intentaron mantener el orden como pudieron.

Por la noche Ricky dio un gran concierto en el Foro Sol. Las fans gritaron tanto que la música del cantante fue difícil de escuchar. Después del concierto los autos de los reporteros fueron detrás del famoso puertorriqueño hasta el restaurante donde la estrella comió. ¡No hubo un accidente por un milagro! ¡Qué día más loco!

ACTIVITY 7: HOW'S THAT AGAIN?

Here are the questions:

1. ¿Quién escribió el artículo?
2. ¿Dónde ocurre? (*Where does it take place?*)
3. ¿De qué cantante famoso habla el artículo?
4. ¿Cómo se llama el aeropuerto de México D.F.?
5. ¿Cómo fue el día, según el reportero?

ACTIVITY 8: TAKE IT UP A NOTCH

In the two dialogues in this lesson, you heard a lot of pronouns. Let's review them a bit. They may be small words, but they are very important!

These sentences are too long. Replace the underlined phrases with pronouns. Here is an example:

Compré <u>frijoles</u>. → <u>**Los**</u> **compré.**
I bought **beans**.   I bought **them**.

1. No recuerdo <u>el viaje que hice hace dos años</u>.
2. No traje <u>la tienda de campaña</u>.

3. Puse <u>la linterna</u> ahí.
4. Podemos visitar <u>las posadas</u>.
5. No pude encontrar <u>los teléfonos celulares</u>.

CRIB NOTES

HEAR...SAY 1

Peter traveled to Cancún to rest but there were too many tourists. Fortunately, he had met a group of Mexican students who were going to travel to the Yucatán, hiking and sleeping outdoors. Peter decides to travel with them. Now they are in Chichén Itzá.

Peter: This place is great! Have you come here before?

Luisa: I did. A long time ago, I came here with my parents. We took many short trips, but by car. Camping out like this is so different. It's awesome!

David: Me, too. My girlfriend and I came here two years ago. We traveled like kings, but this year I lost my girlfriend and my money, and that's why I came with these guys.

Peter: I always knew that someday I would come here. This is like a dream for me.

Dora: I, on the other hand, always wanted to go to the Grand Canyon, ever since I was a little girl. Did you ever go there, Peter?

Peter: I went there with my grandparents once. It was such a long time ago that I almost don't remember. But I do remember that we went around a lot. We went up and down, up and down, and we didn't see anything because the weather was always bad. The only things I saw were the clouds.

Dora: Poor guy! You had such bad luck!

Luisa: I am the one that has bad luck! I spent a year saving to spend my vacation in Oaxaca, and when I arrived there, I had a high fever and became really sick. I was in bed at the hotel the whole time.

Peter: Hey, guys, where are we going to sleep tonight? Because it seems like it's going to rain.

David: It hasn't rained here for a month, bro.

Peter: Just in case, I am going to pray to the god Tlaloc.

All: No, Peter, please! Tlaloc is the god of rain!

HEAR...SAY 2

Peter and his new friends are spending the night camping on the outskirts of Chichén Itzá, near a town called Piste. Suddenly, a storm starts.

Peter: Water is coming in! Who put up the tent?

Luisa: I did. I put it up as best I could.

David: Well, you did it really badly. And it took you an hour!

Dora: You didn't put in the reinforcement! This looks like the *Titanic*!

Luisa: I didn't bring it. I forgot it.

Dora: And on top of that, we didn't see where we were putting it, since the sun had already gone down. I am going to go out with the flashlight to see what's happening. . . . My goodness! We camped in a swamp!

David: I told you. We should have gone to the hostel in the town. It was very cheap. I read it in the guide. I don't know how I let myself get fooled by a bunch of cheapskates. I'm soaking wet!

Luisa: Did you bring your cell phone, Peter?

Peter: Of course! I always carry it with me when I'm traveling. I never go anywhere without it. It is very useful.

David: We can call Piste's hostel—it is called Novelo—and reserve a room. I'll give you the number right now. I wrote it in my address book. What's the matter, Peter? You look so pale, my friend!

Peter: I'm sorry, guys. My cell phone battery is dead and I can't recharge it.

David: Don't worry, I can't find my address book either. I think I lost it in Cancun.

Dora: What a disaster! You're not going to believe it! I dropped the flashlight in the water and now it doesn't work!

All: Great!

ACTIVITY 1

To make sure you made the correct choice, here are the translations:
1. A trip by car with your grandparents to Disneyland
2. A backpacking trip to Oaxaca with your girlfriend
3. A trip to Las Vegas to gamble
4. An excursion to Yucatán with your parents
5. A trip to Madrid to see the Museo del Prado

ACTIVITY 2

1. El lugar es maravilloso.
2. Luisa viajó con sus padres (sus papás).
3. Luisa viajó en auto.
4. Sí. Peter viajó con sus abuelos.
5. Luisa estuvo en la cama todo el tiempo.

ACTIVITY 3

1. Hicieron muchas excursiones.
2. Vinieron hace dos años.
3. Viajaron como reyes.
3. Dieron muchas vueltas.
5. Fueron con sus abuelos.

ACTIVITY 4

1. c; 2. a; 3. e; 4. d; 5. b

ACTIVITY 5

1. Está entrando el agua en la tienda de campaña.
2. Un estudiante va a salir con la linterna.

3. Los chicos van a telefonear a la posada de Piste.
4. El teléfono celular no tiene batería.
5. La linterna no funciona.

ACTIVITY 6

1. puso: poner; 2. hice: hacer; 3. pude: poder; 4. quedó: quedar; 5. estuviste: estar; 6. pusiste: poner; 7. traje: traer; 8. olvidó: olvidar(se); 9. pusimos: poner; 10. acampamos: acampar; 11. dije: decir; 12. debimos: deber; 13. leí: leer; 14. dejé: dejar; 15. trajiste: traer; 16. escribí: escribir; 17. quedó: quedar; 18. perdí: perder; 19. cayó: caer

ACTIVITY 7

1. Enrique Rodríguez escribió el artículo.
2. Ocurre en México D.F.
3. Habla de Ricky Martin.
4. Se llama Adolfo López Mateos.
5. Fue un día loco.

ACTIVITY 8

1. No lo recuerdo.
2. No la traje.
3. La puse ahí.
4. Podemos visitarlas.
5. No pude encontrarlos.

13. FIRE AT NIGHT, SNOW DURING THE DAY

Fuego de noche, nieve de día

One day, I hired a group of mariachis, and we went to the crater to sing her a serenade in the snow.

COMING UP. . .

- *Sweet memories:* **Talking about your childhood**
- *Sweetie:* **Making words sound small and sweet**
- *How far is it?:* **Getting from kilometers to miles (and back)**
- *Love matters:* **A word or two about your love life**
- *Remember when we used to . . . :* **Talking about the past using the imperfect**
- *They really love each other:* **Saying** *each other* **in Spanish**
- *More or less:* **Making comparisons**
- *The way we were:* **Differentiating between the imperfect and the preterite**

Hola, ¿qué tal? ¿Estás preparado / a? Peter has decided to go back to Mexico City by bus to check out the landscape (*paisaje*) and save some *dinero*. The guy sitting next to him is chatty, so Peter (and you!) will get an earful of stories about his past. What do they talk about? *Infancia* (childhood), *familia, trabajo,* and, of course, *amor.* They also talk about what they see. Mexican geography is full of surprises: *montañas* (mountains), *valles* (valleys), *ríos* (rivers), and even *volcanes* (volcanos)!

ACTIVITY 1:	LET'S WARM UP

On page 196, I enclose a map of Mexico. Can you tell me through which states Peter will travel in order to go from Merida (in Yucatán) to Mexico City (D.F.)?

Take a Tip from Me!

You may have noticed that the vocabulary introduced in each lesson is growing fast. Of course, you don't need to memorize every single new word that you encounter (although I would definitely be highly impressed if you did). But you do need to have a basic stock of words on which you can build. For now, focus on things that interest you and that you think you will want to use. In this lesson, you will find some words related to geography. If this is your thing, go ahead and study them conscientiously. If not, just make sure you can recognize them in the future.

One great way to build your vocabulary is to read about things that you like. Thanks to the Internet, this is now something easy to do. So, after you're done with this lesson, go to the Web and search for a reading in Spanish on a topic that interests you. If you stick with the same topic, you'll be happy to see that the same vocabulary keeps coming up, over and over.

Take a Tip from Me!

HEAR . . . SAY 1

Peter quiere ver el paisaje mexicano y decide volver desde Mérida (Yucatán) a la Ciudad de México por carretera (*road*). Ahora, Peter está hablando con un señor que está sentado a su lado. En Villahermosa, una de las paradas, se sube al camión un grupo de chicos.

Señor Carrillo:	Ay estos chamaquitos de hoy en día! Cuando yo era niño mi mamá se enojaba conmigo si hacía ruido en público. Eran otros tiempos.
Peter:	¡Qué interesante!
Señor Carrillo:	Sí, eran otros tiempos. ¿Y su infancia?
Peter:	Pues mis padres se enojaban conmigo si hacía ruido dentro de casa. Mis hermanos y yo siempre jugábamos fuera. Teníamos un jardín pequeño en la parte de atrás y allí nos peleábamos mucho.
Señor Carrillo:	Yo era el único hombre; tenía seis hermanas y yo era el más pequeño. En mi casa sólo había muñequitas y ni una sola pelota. Cuando era un bebé, yo era el juguetito de todas; me peinaban, me vestían, me paseaban.
Peter:	Yo tengo una hermana y un hermano. Pero mi hermana nos ganaba a los dos en todo. Corría más que nosotros, tenía más fuerza que nosotros y en baloncesto encestaba más que nosotros.
Señor Carrillo:	¿Y qué hace ahora su hermana?
Peter:	Está en la marina, por supuesto. (*Looking out the window*) ¡Caramba, hay muchos árboles!
Señor Carrillo:	¡Qué suerte que vino en autobús! Las montañas, los ríos y los valles se ven mucho mejor así. En avión sólo se ven nubes. A mí me dan pánico los aviones.
Peter:	Pues yo no tenía dinero. ¿Cómo se llama esta región?
Señor Carrillo:	El Istmo de Tehuantepec, es la parte más estrechita de México; los dos océanos, el Pacífico y el Atlántico están muy cerquita el uno del otro.
Peter:	Usted sabe mucho. ¿Es maestro de geografía?
Señor Carrillo:	Qué va! Tengo una tienda de ropa para señoras. Necesito hacer este viaje cuatro veces al año. ¡Ya lo sé todo de memoria!

ACTIVITY 2:   **HOW'S THAT AGAIN?**

Who's saying what? Look at the following statements and decide whether they refer to Peter or Señor Carrillo:

1. Tiene seis hermanas.
2. Su hermana trabaja en la marina.
3. Tiene pánico a los aviones.
4. Es reportero.
5. No tiene dinero para el avión.
6. Sabe mucho de la geografía de México.
7. Trabaja en una tienda de ropa para señoras.

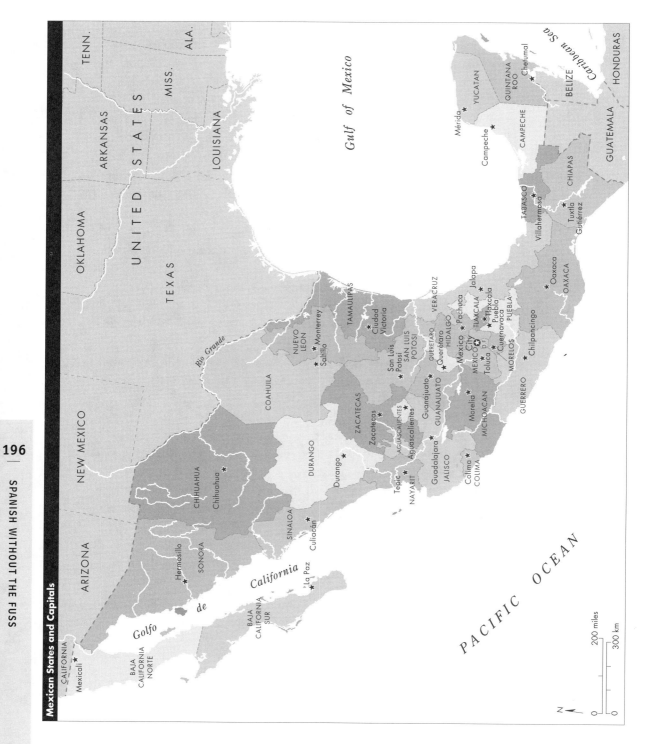

Did You Know?

Throughout Latin America and Spain, it is very common to talk to the people sitting next to you on a train or a bus, especially during long trips. And, if you are going to eat there, you better offer your co-passengers some food, too. They will probably not accept your offer, but it is considered somewhat rude not to try to share. Hey, can you imagine offering whatever you're eating to a perfect stranger on your commuter train? That's what people in Spanish-speaking countries commonly do. (Nice, don't you think?)

Did You Know?

WORKSHOP 1

THE NITTY-GRITTY

REMEMBER WHEN WE USED TO . . . : TALKING ABOUT THE PAST USING THE IMPERFECT

You have already learned one way of talking about the past in Spanish—the preterite tense. In this dialogue, you heard many examples of another past tense—the imperfect. Look at an example before we go on:

> ***Cuando yo <u>era</u> niño mi mamá se <u>enojaba</u> conmigo si <u>hacía</u> ruido en público.***
>
> When I was a kid my mom used to get angry with me if I made any noise in public.

The imperfect tense can be a bit tricky. Let's first see how it is formed, and then, discuss its different uses.

Here are the forms for regular verbs. As with the preterite, there are only two sets of endings: those for –*ar* verbs and those used for both –*er* and –*ir* verbs. (I know you like that!) Therefore, in the table below I give the forms for two verbs, *trabajar* and *correr*. An –*ir* verb, like *partir*, would then be formed just like *correr*.

IMPERFECT TENSE OF REGULAR –*AR* AND –*ER* / –*IR* VERBS

		TRABAJAR (TO WORK)	*CORRER* (TO RUN)
Singular	*yo*	*trabaj* + *aba*	*corr* + *ía*
	tú	*trabaj* + *abas*	*corr* + *ías*
	él / ella, usted	*trabaj* + *aba*	*corr* + *ía*
Plural	*nosotros / nosotras*	*trabaj* + *ábamos*	*corr* + *íamos*
	vosotros / vosotras	*trabaj* + *abais*	*corr* + *íais*
	ellos / ellas, ustedes	*trabaj* + *aban*	*corr* + *ían*

Believe it or not, there are only four irregular verbs in the imperfect: *ir* (to go), *ser* (to be), and *ver* (to see), all given in the table below. We'll talk about *hay* (there is / are) in a moment.

IMPERFECT TENSE OF IRREGULAR VERBS *IR*, *SER*, AND *VER*				
		IR (TO GO)	**SER** (TO BE)	**VER** (TO SEE)
Singular	*yo*	*iba*	*era*	*veía*
	tú	*ibas*	*eras*	*veías*
	él / ella, usted	*iba*	*era*	*veía*
Plural	*nosotros / nosotras*	*íbamos*	*éramos*	*veíamos*
	vosotros / vosotras	*ibais*	*erais*	*veíais*
	ellos / ellas, ustedes	*iban*	*eran*	*veían*

Hay (there is / are) has an irregular imperfect form, *había* (there was / were). For example:

Había un señor con Peter en el autobús.

There was a man with Peter on the bus.

Había tres personas en el autobús.

There were three people on the bus.

In English, the Spanish imperfect can be translated in several ways. Here are some examples of its possible meanings:

- *Used to, would:*

  La hermana de Peter corría más que él.

  Peter's sister used to run faster than he did.

  El señor Carrillo y sus hermanos siempre jugaban fuera.

  Mr. Carrillo and his siblings would always play outside.

- *Was doing:*

  Peter hablaba con el señor Carrillo mientras miraba por la ventana.

  Peter was talking to Mr. Carrillo while he was looking out the window.

- The imperfect is used to set the stage or the background of a story:

  Cuando yo era niño . . .

  When I was a boy . . .

  Era una noche tranquila . . .

  It was a quiet night. . . .

- When talking about the past, verbs like *ser* (to be), *tener* (to have), and *hay* (there is / are) are usually in the imperfect:

Tenía seis hermanas.	I had six sisters.
Era el único hombre.	I was the only man.
En mi casa sólo había muñequitas.	At my house, there were only dolls.

ACTIVITY 3: TAKE IT FOR A SPIN

What did you do when you were a kid? Indicate if these statements are true:

1. Cuando eras niño hablabas en un teléfono celular.
2. Cuando eras niño tenías una computadora.
3. Cuando tenías tres años leías a Shakespeare.
4. Cuando tenías cinco años eras el más fuerte de tu familia.
5. Cuando tenías siete años nunca te peleabas con tus hermanos.

THEY REALLY LOVE EACH OTHER: SAYING EACH OTHER IN SPANISH

In English, we use *each other* and *one another* to talk about actions that are reciprocal. In Spanish, this concept is expressed with the reflexive pronouns *se* and *nos:*

Mi hermana y yo <u>nos</u> hablamos mucho.

My sister and I talk to each other a lot.

Su hermano y él <u>se</u> peleaban mucho de niños.

He and his brother used to fight with each other a lot when they were kids.

Usted y sus padres <u>se</u> escriben mucho.

You and your parents write to each other a lot.

MORE OR LESS: MAKING COMPARISONS

Well, if you always thought that you were somehow better than others, now is your chance to express it even in Spanish. This is how it works. To make comparisons in Spanish, use *más* (more) or *menos* (less), followed by whatever adjective you need and *que* (than):

Mi hermana era más fuerte que yo.

My sister was stronger than me.

México es más grande que Costa Rica.

Mexico is bigger than Costa Rica.

To say that something or somebody cannot be topped, add an article and drop the *que*:

> **Mi hermana era la más fuerte.**

> My sister was the strongest.

So, Spanish can't be simpler here, except for the irregular adjectives:

IRREGULAR COMPARATIVES	
mejor (better)	*peor* (worse)
mayor (older)	*menor* (younger)

For a younger sibling, Spanish also uses the word *pequeño* (little):

> **Soy más pequeña que mi hermana.**

> I am younger than my sister.

> **Soy la más pequeña de la familia.**

> I am the youngest in my family.

WORDS TO LIVE BY

SWEET MEMORIES: TALKING ABOUT YOUR CHILDHOOD

What kind of games / sports did you play as a kid? Let's see:

De niño / a jugaba . . .	When I was a boy / girl I used to play . . .
. . . a la pelota	. . . ball
. . . al baloncesto	. . . basketball
. . . al fútbol	. . . soccer
. . . con muñecas	. . . with dolls
. . . en el jardín	. . . in the backyard

SWEETIE: MAKING WORDS SOUND SMALL AND SWEET

You may have noticed that some of the words that you learned earlier look a little different in this last dialogue:

> **Muñequita,** from **muñeca** (doll), is "a little doll."
> **Cerquita,** from **cerca** (near), is "very near."

The *–ito / a* ending, when used with nouns means "little," and when used with adverbs and adjectives, it means "very."

Although the diminutive forms are used around the Spanish-speaking world, the ending *–ito / a* is particularly common in Mexico. Sometimes, it just gives the word an endearing tone:

mis abuelitos	*my (dear) grandparents (<u>not</u> my little grandparents)*
mis amiguitos	*my (dear) friends (<u>not</u> my little friends)*

In other Spanish speaking countries, the suffix used may be *–illo / a* (typical of certain regions of Spain) or *–ico / a* (typical of Cuba):

mis amiguillos	*my (dear) friends*
mi maestrico	*my (dear) teacher*

Word on the Street

¡Caramba!	*My goodness!, Wow!*
¡Qué va!	*Not at all!, No way!*
hoy en día	*nowadays*
Eran otros tiempos.	*Those were the days.*
de memoria	*by heart*

Did You Know?

On November 2, Mexicans celebrate the Day of the Dead (*Día de los Muertos*). This festivity is a mixture of pre-Colombian and Catholic traditions. People flock to the cemeteries where they offer flowers and delicious dishes to the dead (the dishes, of course, are eaten right there by the living!). There is even a special candy that's eaten on that day. It is called *calaveritas* (little skulls). *¡Qué miedo!* (How scary!)

Another important date for Mexicans is September 16, when they celebrate Independence Day. On the eve of September 16, after *El Grito* (the cry, *¡Viva Mexico!*), the fireworks begin. There is dancing and music at thousands of parties throughout the country until the next day, when the patriotic acts begin. *El Grito* is reminiscent of the call to arms given in 1810 by the *cura* (priest) Hidalgo, who called on the people to rebel against the Spanish rule.

ACTIVITY 4:   TAKE IT FOR A SPIN

Here is a list of different childhood activities. Say which ones were favored by Mr. Carrillo, which ones by Peter, and which were done by both:

1. Corría en las montañas.
2. Él y sus hermanos se peleaban mucho.

3. Jugaba con muñecas.
4. Celebraba el cuatro de julio.
5. Comía calaveritas el dos de noviembre.
6. Jugaba en el jardín.

Did You Know?

Mexico is home to many volcanoes. The best known is Popocatépetl, or El Popo. It is the second-highest volcano (17,925 ft) in North America. Its name is the Aztec word for "smoking mountain." It is still active. On December 18, 2000, the largest eruption in 1,000 years took place. At least 50,000 people needed to be evacuated from their homes.

Did You Know?

HEAR . . . SAY 2

Peter continúa su largo viaje en autobús. Ya está cerca de (*close to*) Ciudad de México pero está entretenido. El paisaje es impresionante y no para de hablar con su compañero de asiento.

Peter:	¡Dios mío, qué viaje! ¡Selvas, ríos, valles, montañas y ahora . . . eso !
Señor Carrillo:	Es el volcán Popocatépetl. A cinco mil quinientos metros de altitud, tiene un cráter de un kilómetro de ancho y precisamente ahí me enamoré de mi mujer hace veinte años.
Peter:	¿En el volcán? ¡Qué increíble! ¿Y cómo fue?
Señor Carrillo:	Pues un día yo estaba en casa viendo la televisión cuando de repente apareció una linda geóloga, explicando algo sobre las cenizas del volcán. Fue un flechazo.
Peter:	¿Y qué hizo?
Señor Carrillo:	Al día siguiente fui allí. Tenía muchísimo miedo.
Peter:	¿Por la altitud?
Señor Carrillo:	No, porque la geóloga era aún más bella en persona que en la televisión.
Peter:	¿Y qué le dijo?
Señor Carrillo:	Nomás que la amaba. Estaba con un grupo de geólogos de la UNAM haciendo una investigación que iba a durar un año. Yo le platicaba cosas de amor mientras ella saltaba al interior del volcán con una cuerda. Allá nevaba pero a mí no me importaba.
Peter:	¿Y cómo ganó su amor?

Señor Carrillo:	Puse una tienda de ropa de montaña en Tlamacas, al pie del Popo, y todos los días iba a verla. Y llegó el gran momento. Un día contraté a unos mariachis y fuimos al cráter a cantarle una serenata en la nieve. Entonces ella me besó. ¡Y hasta hoy, mi cuate!

ACTIVITY 5: HOW'S THAT AGAIN?

Here are several sentences from Señor Carrillo's "love story," but they are mixed up. Put them in the correct order!

1. Contraté a unos mariachis.
2. Ella me besó.
3. Le dije que la amaba.
4. Vi a una linda geóloga.
5. Yo estaba en casa viendo la televisión.

Did You Know?

The most important educational institution in Mexico is UNAM (Universidad Nacional Autónoma de México), located in Mexico City. It's a huge institution with staggering numbers: close to 300,000 students, 30,000 professors, 30,000 administrators, and 25,000 graduates each year. Needless to say, it has an extremely important influence on Mexican society.

WORKSHOP 2

THE NITTY-GRITTY

THE WAY WE WERE: DIFFERENTIATING BETWEEN THE IMPERFECT AND THE PRETERITE

In the Hear . . . Say section we've seen examples of how the preterite and the imperfect tenses can be used together to talk about the past. Although they are both past tenses, they are used to describe different kinds of past actions. When relating a past story, the imperfect is used to set the background, talk about past habits, and mention actions that were in progress. In contrast, the preterite is used to talk about isolated past actions that were completed:

1. ***Un día yo veía la televisión.***   IMPERFECT
   One day, I was watching TV.

2. ***De repente, apareció una linda geóloga.***   PRETERITE
   Suddenly, there appeared a pretty geologist.

We will go over this again in future lessons but for now, every time you see a verb in the preterite or imperfect tense, make a mental note of it and try to understand how it is used.

TAKE IT FOR A SPIN

Which verbs are in the preterite and which are in imperfect?

1. Yo estaba en casa.
2. Trabajaba en mi computadora.
3. También escuchaba música en la radio.
4. De repente, una mujer dijo algo importante en la radio.
5. Decidí llamar por teléfono a mi madre.
6. Le dije que era muy importante.

WORDS TO LIVE BY

HOW FAR IS IT?: GETTING FROM KILOMETERS TO MILES (AND BACK)

When talking about El Popo's height, Mr. Carrillo uses kilometers. Remember that all Spanish-speaking countries use the metric system. Here is a chart, so you can see what he means:

MILES / KILOMETERS (millas / kilómetros)										
1 KILOMETER (KM) = 0.62 MILES					1 MILE = 1.61 KM (1,61 KM)					
KILOMETERS 1	5	8	10	15	20	50	75	100	150	200
MILES 0.62	3.1	5	6.2	9.3	12.4	31	46.5	62	93	124

LOVE MATTERS: A WORD OR TWO ABOUT YOUR LOVE LIFE

Quite a change in topic! Let's move to more romantic considerations. When Cupid hits you, you get a *flechazo* (*Lit.* arrow shot). Thus, love at first sight, is also called *un flechazo.*

And once you have been hit by a *flechazo,* this could also mean that you found your better half, which in Spanish is *tu media naranja* (*Lit.* your half orange). That means you must be *enamorado / a* (in love)!

Word on the Street

Here are some more words used in Mexico:

platicar	to speak, to chat
nomás	used as a filler, with no real meaning; from **no más** "no more"
chamacos or **chamaquitos**	kids
camión	bus; the more neutral Spanish term is autobús

LET'S PUT IT IN WRITING

Here is the online reservation service that Peter used to book his bus trip.

AUTOBUSES "UNO" DESTINOS Y RESERVACIONES

Información Turística	Compra previa con tarjeta de crédito
Servicios	Origen: Mérida Destino: México D.F.
Autobuses	Diario: Salida a las 7:00
Quejas y sugerencias	Precio: 1.600 pesos por boleto
Correo	Distancia: 1.525 kms
	Tiempo estimado de viaje: 24 hrs.

SELECCIONE LA FECHA EN LA QUE DESEA VIAJAR DE ACUERDO CON EL MENÚ DE ABAJO.

SÓLO ACEPTAMOS RESERVACIONES CON UN MÍNIMO DE 24 HORAS DE ANTICIPACIÓN.

Mes————————Día————————Número de Pasajeros————————

Nombre————————————————————

E-mail————————————————————

Teléfono————————————————————

RESERVAR

Based on the reservation, answer these questions:

1. ¿Dónde comienza el viaje?
2. ¿Dónde termina?
3. ¿Cuánto cuesta?
4. ¿Cómo puede pagar?
5. ¿Cuánto tiempo es el viaje?

ACTIVITY 8:   TAKE IT UP A NOTCH

Peter was quite impressed with Mr. Carrillo's childhood story. Here's an e-mail in which he tells Carmen about it. Fill in the blanks by using the imperfect form of the verbs in parentheses.

. . . Cuando el Señor Carrillo _____ (ser) niño, él _____ (vivir) en Mérida, en la Península de Yucatán. Él _____ (tener) muchas hermanas mayores. ¡Y ellas _____ (pensar) que él _____ (ser) su muñequita! Lo _____ (vestir), lo _____ (peinar). . . . Ahora él tiene una tienda de ropa para señoras. ¡No me extraña lo más mínimo! (It doesn't surprise me one bit!)

CRIB NOTES

HEAR...SAY 1

Peter wants to see the Mexican countryside and decides to go back from Yucatán to Mexico City by bus (*Lit.* by road). At the moment, Peter is talking with the man sitting next to him. At one of the stops, Villahermosa, a group of school children gets on the bus.

Señor Carrillo: Ah! These kids nowadays! When I was a kid my mom used to get angry with me if I made any noise in public. Those were different times.

Peter: How interesting!

Señor Carrillo: Yes, those were different times. What about your childhood?

Peter: Well, my parents got mad at me if we made noise inside the house. My siblings and I always played outside. We had a small backyard and we used to fight a lot with each other there.

Señor Carrillo: I was the only boy; I had six sisters and I was the youngest. In my house, the only toys we had were little dolls, not even a single ball! When I was a baby, I was my sisters' toy. They would comb my hair, dress me up, and take me for walks.

Peter: I have a brother and a sister. But my sister used to beat both of us in everything. She ran faster than us, she was stronger than we were, and in basketball, she would score more than us.

Señor Carrillo: And what does she do now?

Peter: She's in the marines, of course! (*looking out the window*) Wow, there are a lot of trees!

Señor Carrillo: It's great you took the bus! You can see the mountains, rivers, and valleys much better that way. On the plane, you only see the clouds. Anyway, I am terrified of planes.

Peter: I just didn't have money! What's the name of this region?

Señor Carrillo: It is the Tehuantepec Isthmus, the narrowest part of Mexico. The two

Peter:	oceans, the Pacific and the Atlantic, are very close to each other here. You know a lot. Are you a geography teacher?	Señor Carrillo:	Not at all! I have a clothing store for women. I need to make this trip four times a year. I already know it by heart!

HEAR...SAY 2

Peter continues his long trip by bus. He is now close to Mexico City, but he is still being entertained. The countryside is impressive and he hasn't stopped talking to the man sitting next to him.

Peter:	My goodness! What a trip! Jungles, rivers, valleys, mountains, and now . . . that!
Señor Carrillo:	It's the Popocatépetl volcano. It's 5,500 meters high, it has a crater one kilometer wide and precisely there I fell in love with my wife twenty years ago.
Peter:	In a volcano? That's amazing! How did it happen?
Señor Carrillo:	Well, one day I was at home watching television when suddenly a pretty geologist appeared, explaining something about the ashes of the volcano. It was love at first sight.
Peter:	And what did you do?
Señor Carrillo:	The next day, I went there. I was really scared.

Peter:	Because of the elevation?
Señor Carrillo:	No, because the geologist was even more beautiful in person than on TV.
Peter:	And what did you say to her?
Señor Carrillo:	That I loved her. She was with a group of geologists from UNAM doing a research project that was going to last a year. I would tell her sweet nothings while she would jump into the volcano with a rope. It was snowing, but I didn't mind.
Peter:	And how did you win her love?
Señor Carrillo:	I opened a mountain clothing store in Tlamacas, on the foot of El Popo, and I would go and see her every day. And the great moment arrived. One day, I hired a group of mariachis, and we went to the crater to sing her a serenade in the snow. Then she kissed me. Today we love each other just as much, my friend!

ANSWER KEY

ACTIVITY 1

He'll start in Yucatán, and go through Campeche, Tabasco, Veracruz, Oaxaca, Puebla, Morelos to Mexico D.F.

ACTIVITY 2

Peter:	2, 4, 5
Señor Carrillo:	1, 3, 6, 7

ACTIVITY 3

1. When you were a child you used to talk on a cell phone.
2. When you were a child you had a computer.
3. When you were three you used to read Shakespeare.
4. When you were five you were the strongest in your family.
5. When you were seven you never fought with your siblings.

ACTIVITY 4

Peter:	2, 4
Señor Carrillo:	3, 5
Both:	1, 6

ACTIVITY 5

5, 4, 3, 1, 2

ACTIVITY 6

Imperfect:	estaba, trabajaba, escuchaba, era
Preterite:	dijo, decidí, dije

ACTIVITY 7

1. El viaje comienza en Mérida.
2. El viaje finaliza en México D. F.
3. Cuesta mil seiscientos (1,600) pesos.
4. Se puede pagar con tarjeta de crédito.
5. El viaje es unas veinticuatro (24) horas.

ACTIVITY 8

era, vivía, tenía, pensaban, era, vestían, peinaban

14. REVOLUTION

Revolución

...Now, I'm really sleepy!

LOOKING AHEAD

Bueno, bueno, bueno. Peter has arrived in Bogotá, Colombia's capital, remember? But he does not have much to do, as Ricky Martin hasn't arrived yet. He is also *muy cansado* (very tired), and decides to try his *suerte* (luck) online with a Colombian chat room. Later on, he will also hear from his friend Carmen. He'll tell her about the beautiful things he has seen since he arrived in Bogotá. And, since we are in Colombia, I hope you have your cup of coffee ready and are listening to some *cumbias* on the radio, because *¡aquí estamos, amigos!* Welcome to Colombia! *¡Bienvenidos a Colombia!*

Did You Know?

Coffee is the authentic Colombian gold. Colombia is the second most important coffee exporter in the world. Coffee is the country's main industry. The culture that surrounds coffee is an integral part of Colombia, especially in the region of Antioquia. Here is a piece of advice: If you want an espresso, it is called *tinto*, and if you want it with just a touch of milk, order a *perico* or a *pintado*.

ACTIVITY 1: LET'S WARM UP

In our next dialogue, we are going to be in an online chat room, talking about computers and other technical things. You already know some of the vocabulary. Can you guess the rest?

1. la charla   a. technician
2. la sesión   b. world
3. el técnico   c. piece of advice
4. la explicación   d. chat / conversation
5. el consejo   e. explanation
6. el mundo   f. printer
7. la impresora   g. session

Take a Tip from Me!

Always remember that words contain a lot of information that can help you to guess their meanings. For example, in the activity that you've just finished (hopefully), you were probably able to guess some of the meanings because the Spanish words are similar to their English counterparts. *Charla* and *chat* have the first few letters in common. The same with *explicación* and *explanation*. And now that you have learned the word *charla,* can you tell me the meaning of the verb *charlar*? Yes, it's "to chat." What about the verb *explicar*? Yes, that's right, "to explain." Now I'll throw you a more difficult one. What about *aconsejar*? Did you guess "to advise"? Then you were right once again. Learning becomes much easier and more fun when you start associating words like that!

HEAR ... SAY 1

Peter ha llegado a Bogotá. Está muy cansado para salir y ha decidido quedarse esta noche en el hotel. Sin embargo no puede dormir y decide conectar su computadora portátil y buscar con quién charlar en Internet en los canales de charla colombianos. Su alias es Recién Llegado (*Just Arrived*).

Recién Llegado: Estoy en mi hotel muy cansado pero no me puedo dormir. ¿Puedo unirme a vosotros?

Super Ñ: Creo que sí, Recién Llegado, pero aquí el jefe es Ciberseñor. Aunque seguro que se duerme, porque esto es muy aburrido.

Ciberseñor: Ya he dicho antes que mis consejos son útiles para todo el mundo. Bienvenido a nuestra charla, Recién Llegado. Usted es de España, ¿no?

Recién Llegado: ¿Yo? ¡No! ¿Por qué piensa eso?

Ciberseñor: Pues, querido, está claro. Dijo "vosotros."

Recién Llegado: ¡Ah! ¡Por eso! No, no soy de España, pero estudié con un profesor de allí. Bueno, ¿cuál es el tema?

Ciberseñor: Bueno, ya hemos hablado de varias cosas importantes. Soy técnico de computadoras y he explicado ya cómo descargar archivos, cómo comprimirlos, cómo abrirlos y cómo guardarlos. Es muy útil, especialmente con los archivos de música. Mis consejos son muy interesantes.

Recién Llegado: Ya veo que Colombia se ha unido a la revolución tecnológica del Internet.

Ciberseñor: Pues, ¿qué se pensaba? Es usted algo ignorante.

Recién Legado: Usted perdone, no quise ofender . . .

Super Ñ: ¡Amigo, pasito con el invitado! No dijo nada malo. A veces, usted sí es bien estúpido . . .

Ciberseñor: ¿Yo? Usted sí que es . . . Ha estado interrumpiendo toda la sesión.

Super Ñ: ¿Cómo así? ¿Yo? ¿Interrumpiendo? Usted es el necio. Y además, ofende a los nuevos. Recién Llegado, ¿por qué nos visita?

Recién Llegado:	Tengo que escribir un artículo sobre los colombianos. Pero creo que me he equivocado con esta sala. ¡No me interesa mucho la informática!
Ciberseñor:	No pasa nada. Aquí somos expertos en todo. ¿Qué quiere saber? ¿Ha visitado ya nuestro maravilloso Museo del Oro?
Super Ñ:	¿Y cómo sabe que el invitado está en Bogotá? ¿No es acaso posible otra cosa? Recién Llegado, ¿dónde está?
Ciberseñor:	¡Qué difícil es hablar con algunas personas! ¿Por qué me ha interrumpido?
Super Ñ:	¡Pero, bueno! ¿Quién ha interrumpido a quién?
Recién Llegado:	Bueno, creo que es mejor decir adiós. . . . Muchas gracias por su interés sobre mi visita, pero parece que esta charla ha sido buena para dormirme porque ahora ya tengo mucho sueño.
Super Ñ:	Yo ya me dormí con ese bruto . . .
Ciberseñor:	¡Ignorante!

ACTIVITY 2: HOW'S THAT AGAIN?

Let's see what you know:

1. ¿Qué alias usan las tres personas del chat?
2. ¿Quién es el jefe?
3. ¿Quién es el técnico de computadoras?
4. ¿Qué hace Peter? ¿Participa en la discusión?
5. ¿Qué palabras negativas usan Ciberseñor y Super Ñ?

Did You Know?

The legend of El Dorado, a mythical country of gold, jewels, and many riches, has its origin in the descriptions of ritual ceremonies carried out by the Chibcha people. According to one of the many versions of the legend, Chibcha kings were anointed in a ceremony that took place at the lake of Guatavita in Colombia. The new ruler was completely covered in gold dust, and therefore, referred to as *el dorado* (the golden one) by Spaniards who told and retold the story. The dream about the country of El Dorado and its promise of gold motivated many vain searches in various parts of South America. For a long time, the bottom of the lake Guatavita was believed to be covered with gold, until, in this century, it was determined that it contains only mud.

WORKSHOP 1

***BEEN THERE, DONE THAT:* TALKING ABOUT THE PAST USING THE PRESENT PERFECT**

How to Form Past Participles

You might not have been aware of this, but when you say, *It's done* or *I've been there*, you're using past participles—*done* and *been*. A past participle is a form of the verb that works a bit like an adjective. For instance, when you say, "The door is closed," *closed* provides some useful information about the door. Past participles are used in the present perfect tense (e.g., I have <u>done</u> that) and with the verb *estar* (to be) to describe the state something is in (e.g., The door is <u>closed</u>).

Here is how you form past participles in Spanish:

–ar verbs**:**	**trabaj + ar**	→	**trabaj+ <u>ado</u>**
–er and **–ir** verbs**:**	**com + er**	→	**com + <u>ido</u>**
	sal + ir	→	**sal + <u>ido</u>**

Once again, verbs ending in *–er* and *–ir* share the same ending.

Now look at these sentences:

La oficina está cerrada.	The office is closed.
El hotel está cerrado.	The hotel is closed.
Las oficinas están cerradas.	The offices are closed.
Los hoteles están cerrados.	The hotels are closed.

As you can see, in these examples, the past participle is just like an adjective. When it describes temporary states (i.e., when used with the verb *estar*), it has to match in gender and number the noun it accompanies. *Oficinas* is feminine and plural and thus the participle *cerradas* is also feminine and plural. Peter's alias in the chat room was *Recién Llegado* (Just Arrived). *Llegado* is formed from *llegar* (to arrive). If Peter were a woman, the name would have been *Recién Llegada*.

I'm sure it comes as no surprise to you that there are some irregular participles. The ones you have seen in the Hear . . . Say section are the following:

decir	(to say)	→	**dicho**	(said)
hacer	(to do / to make)	→	**hecho**	(done)
abrir	(to open)	→	**abierto**	(opened)
romper	(to break)	→	**roto**	(broken)

How to Form the Present Perfect

The present perfect (e.g., *"I have done"*) is formed in Spanish the way it is in English, using the present tense of *haber* (to have) followed by the past participle of a verb. Let's look at an example:

PRESENT PERFECT OF *TRABAJAR* (TO WORK) AND *HABER* (TO HAVE)				
Singular	*yo*	*he*	*trabajado*	I have worked
	tú	*has*	*trabajado*	you have worked
	él / ella, usted	*ha*	*trabajado*	he / she / it has worked you (formal) have worked
Plural	*nosotros / nosotras*	*hemos*	*trabajado*	we have worked
	vosotros / vosotras	*habéis*	*trabajado*	you have worked
	ellos / ellas, ustedes	*han*	*trabajado*	they have worked you (formal) have worked

Here are several sentences you heard in the Hear . . . Say section using this tense:

Peter ha llegado a Bogotá.

Peter has arrived in Bogotá.

Ya hemos hablado de eso.

We have already talked about that.

¿Por qué me ha interrumpido?

Why have you interrupted me?

Me he equivocado con esta sala.

I have made a mistake entering this chat room.

ACTIVITY 3: TAKE IT FOR A SPIN

¿Qué ha hecho Peter últimamente? (What has Peter done lately?) Decide what you know about these sentences:

	TRUE	FALSE	DON'T KNOW
1. Peter ha participado en un chat colombiano.			
2. Peter ha reparado su computadora.			
3. Peter ha hablado con Carmen por teléfono.			
4. Peter y su familia han comido juntos.			
5. Peter y unos amigos han estado de camping en Yucatán.			

LET'S GET TECHNICAL: USEFUL E-MAIL AND INTERNET TERMS

Guess what? Due to the pioneering role that the United States has played in the development of computer technology, English has become a dominant influence on Internet-related vocabulary in Spanish. I bet you'll recognize many of these terms!

el buscador	search engine. The term comes from **buscar** (to search, to look for).
el correo electrónico	e-mail (only e-mail in general, not specific messages)
el mensaje electrónico	e-mail message. Sometimes people simply use the English word **e-mail** as in:

Voy a enviarte un e-mail.   I'm going to send you an e-mail.

(In Spain, an e-mail message is also jokingly called *un emilio*. Emilio is a guy's name that happens to sound a bit like the Spanish pronounciation of *e-mail* [eh-MAH-eel].)

la red	Internet, the Web (Lit. net). Both terms, **el internet** and **la red**, are used interchangeably.

For *chat room*, different terms are used. All of these are possible:

la sala de chat
la sala de charla
el salón de chat
el chatroom
el canal de charla

And what do you do when you are in a *sala de charla* or *chat*? The verbs used are *charlar*, an actual verb that means "to chat," or *chatear*, a verb coined from English for the information age (*la era de la tecnología*).

Lastly, *el foro* is the word for "discussion board" or "forum."

Just for fun, I want you to check out this ad from a Colombian newspaper. I bet you won't have a problem understanding it!

> ## COMPUTER ASSOCIATES:
> ---
> *El software para el eBusiness*

Now that you can listen to any music on *la red mundial* (the World Wide Web), why not look for some Colombian music?

Did You Know?

The Caribbean region of Colombia is the heart of the country's best-known folk music: the *cumbias*. It originates from the African dance *cumbe* (6 percent of Colombia's population is of African origin) mixed with Spanish and indigenous music. *Vallenatos* are the other type of typically Colombian music. Carlos Vives is a very popular Colombian singer throughout South America as well as the United States. He has taken old *valle-natos* and brought them back to life.

Did You Know?

HEAR ... SAY 2

Aunque tiene amigos en Bogotá, Peter ha pasado su primer día solo. Ha estado haciendo turismo y está muy cansado. Ahora es de noche y está en la habitación de su hotel. Decide escribirle un mensaje electrónico a Carmen.

Peter: *(writing on his laptop)* Hola Carmencilla. Ya estoy en Santa Fe de Bogotá. He pasado todo el día andando por esta maravillosa ciudad. He estado en el Cerro de Monserrate y he visto al Señor Caído, el de los milagros, pero lo que más me ha gustado ha sido la zona de La Candelaria, que es una zona antigua colonial. ¿Y tú? ¿Qué has hecho hoy? (ENVIAR)

(While he is checking other things, he hears, "You've got mail." Es Carmen, claro.)

Carmen: Hola Peter. ¡Qué bien! ¡Los dos estamos conectados a la vez! Pues, la verdad es que no he hecho mucho hoy. He estado en la universidad y ya está. Me he puesto a estudiar cuando he vuelto a casa porque tengo un examen muy difícil. (ENVIAR)

Peter: Bueno, buena suerte para mañana. Yo, en cambio, voy a continuar visitando Bogotá. No tengo que escribir nada hasta el martes. (ENVIAR)

Carmen: ¡Qué vida más dura la de un reportero! ¡Todo el día trabajando! (ENVIAR)

Peter: Oye, oye, ¡que sí estoy trabajando! Tengo que investigar bien el país donde Ricky canta para luego poder escribir artículos convincentes. (ENVIAR)

Carmen: ¿Sí? ¿Y qué has hecho hoy de "trabajo"? (ENVIAR)

Peter: Pues, he tomado muchas fotos y además he ido a nuestra oficina en Bogotá.

Carmen: Y allí seguro que te has matado trabajando . . . (ENVIAR)

Peter: Bueno, es que hoy es "viernes cultural" y cuando llegué ya estaba la oficina cerrada. (ENVIAR)

Carmen: Pero qué cuento tienes . . . viernes cultural . . . sí, seguro . . . (ENVIAR)

Some of these sentences are incorrect. Can you find the mistakes and fix them? (Hint: Two sentences are correct.)

1. Peter ha pasado todo el día andando en Madrid.
2. También ha visitado la zona de la Candelaria.
3. Carmen ha ido a la universidad.
4. Peter no necesita escribir hasta el sábado.
5. Carmen ha tomado muchas fotos.
6. Peter ha visitado su oficina.

Did You Know?

Colombians have something called *viernes cultural*. It is a bit like the idea behind "casual Fridays" here in the United States, only they extend beyond working hours. If you hear, *mañana, viernes cultural* on a Thursday, it means that the office will probably close a bit early and the employees will go out together to engage in "cultural" (and not so "cultural") activities: movies, concerts, or just socializing and having drinks together. Great idea, right? By the way, the preferred expression for partying in Colombia is *ir de rumba* or *rumbear*. A popular place in Santa Fe de Bogotá to do just that is *la zona rosa* (the pink area), a section of the city that is full of restaurants, cafés, and bars.

WORKSHOP 2

THE NITTY-GRITTY

MORE IRREGULAR PAST PARTICIPLES

Here are a few additional useful verbs and their past participles:

ver (to see) → **visto** (seen)

poner (to put) → **puesto** (put)

morir (to die) → **muerto** (died / dead)

The Fine Print

TIME AFTER TIME: TIME PHRASES USED WITH THE PRESENT PERFECT

The present perfect is frequently used with some of the following time expressions:

nunca (never)

alguna vez (sometime, ever)

varias veces (several times)

últimamente (lately)

recientemente (recently)

ya (already)

todavía (yet)

For example:

Has visto alguna vez algo así?   Have you ever seen anything like that?

Ellos nunca han reparado una impresora.   They have never repaired a printer.

Heads Up!

Watch the word order in Spanish! It is different from English. The time phrases *never* come in between the helping verb *haber* and the past participle, as they do in English. They always either precede or follow the *haber* + past participle block. For example:

I have **never** done that.   →   **Nunca he hecho esto.**

Have you **ever** seen anything like that?   →   **Has visto alguna vez algo así?**

Heads Up!

ACTIVITY 5:   TAKE IT FOR A SPIN

Make sentences using the present perfect and the following expressions of time:
nunca, varias veces, últimamente, todavía.

Model: estudiar español   →   He estudiado mucho español últimamente.

1. hablar por la computadora
2. escribir un mensaje electrónico

3. usar un buscador como Yahoo.es
4. comprimir un archivo
5. descargar música en el Internet

WORDS TO LIVE BY

Some new words and expressions worth remembering are:

antiguo / a	old, but only for things; former; for people, use **viejo** or **mayor**. Note that **viejo** can also have a negative connotation. Sometimes, to refer to older people, the expression **la tercera edad** (the third age) is used.
matarse	to kill oneself. You heard the expression **Me he matado trabajando** (I have killed myself working) in the dialogue.
tener cuento	to tell a made up story (Lit. to have a story). You can say, **¡Qué cuento tienes!** (You're just making that up! / You're giving me crap!).

Word on the Street

If you want to sound like a Colombian, use some of these:

¡Qué oso!	How embarrassing! (Lit. **oso** means "bear")
¡Pasito!	Be careful!, Go slow! [probably from **despacito** (slowly)]
querido / a	dear; used especially when saying hello to friends, as in:
¿Cómo le va, querida?	How are you doing, dear?
¿Cómo así?	How come? (used frequently to express doubt)

And don't forget *ir de rumba* (to go out to party). *Es muy importante.*

LET'S PUT IT IN WRITING

This is the Web page (*la página web*, by the way) Peter used to enter the Colombian chat room in our first dialogue. After you sign in, you have to decide which chat room you want to join. Take a look at the page and then answer the questions in Activity 6.

CÓMO ENTRAR EN NUESTRO CHAT

NOMBRE : _____

Introduzca su nombre o alias para acceder al canal de charla. Intente mantener un ambiente agradable y divertido. Pregunte lo que no sepa, todos le ayudaremos. Participe en la charla, nos gustaría conocerlo.

Seleccione un canal:

COLOMBIA: Lista de canales: Cachacos / Paisas / Vallunos / Boyacenses / Costeños / Llaneros / Colombianos en el Exterior / Extranjeros en Colombia

GENTE: Lista de canales: Mayores de 15 / Jóvenes / Mayores de 30 / Gente Seria

ENTRETENIMIENTO: Lista de canales: Cine / Música / Sitios de Rumba / Restaurantes / Arte

TECNOLOGÍA: Lista de canales: Internet / Juegos / Tecnología

ACTIVITY 6: HOW'S THAT AGAIN?

Answer these questions (in English):

1. How many general chat areas are there?
2. Within *TECNOLOGÍA*, how many possibilities can you choose from?
3. In *GENTE* (people), what are the relevant groups?
4. In *ENTRETENIMIENTO*, what could *sitios de rumba* be?

ACTIVITY 7: TAKE IT UP A NOTCH

Participles are very important. Some of the adjectives you already know are really past participles, like *cerrado* (closed) from *cerrar*, *aburrido* (bored; boring) from *aburrir* (to bore), *cansado* (tired) from *cansar*. Let's see how many you can find in this *sopa de letras*.

p	t	h	j	h	m	k	t	f	s
u	k	e	c	v	b	n	v	a	a
e	h	c	o	m	i	d	o	e	l
s	s	h	s	d	d	g	y	t	i
t	r	o	x	c	o	r	t	u	d
o	f	b	g	k	l	p	d	q	o

CRIB NOTES

Peter has arrived in Bogotá. He's too tired to go out and has decided to stay in the hotel tonight. However, he cannot sleep and decides to connect his laptop and to look for people to chat with in the Colombian chat rooms on the Internet. His alias is "Just Arrived."

Just Arrived: I am in my hotel, very tired but I cannot sleep. Can I join you?

Super Ñ: I think so, Just Arrived, but here, the boss is Cyberlord. Although I am sure you will fall asleep, because this is very boring.

Cyberlord: I have said before that my advice is useful for everybody. Welcome to our chat room, Just Arrived. You must be from Spain, right?

Just Arrived: Me? No! What made you say that?

Cyberlord: Because, my friend, it's clear. You said, "vosotros."

Just Arrived: Ah! That's why! No, I'm not from Spain, but I studied with a professor from there. Well, what's the topic?

Cyberlord: Well, we have already talked about several important things. I am a computer technician, and I have already explained how to download files, how to compress them, how to open them, and how to save them. It's very useful, especially with music files. My advice is very interesting.

Just Arrived: I see that Colombia has joined the technological revolution of the Internet.

Cyberlord: Well, what did you expect? You sound rather ignorant.

Just Arrived: My apologies. I didn't mean to be offensive . . .

Super Ñ: My friend, take it easy with the guest! He didn't say anything bad. Sometimes, you sure are stupid.

Cyberlord: I am? You are the one . . . . You have been interrupting throughout the session.

Super Ñ: How can you say that? Me? Interrupting? You're the idiot . . . besides, you are offending the new guests. Just Arrived, why are you visiting us?

Just Arrived: I have to write an article about Colombians. But I think I might have made a mistake with this chat room. I'm really not that interested in technology!

Cyberlord: That's okay. We're experts on everything here. What would you like to know? Have you already visited our wonderful Gold Museum?

Super Ñ: And how do you know that the guest is in Bogotá? Isn't it possible that he is someplace else? Just Arrived, where are you?

Cyberlord: It is so difficult to talk to certain people! Why have you interrupted me?

Super Ñ: What are you talking about? Who has interrupted whom here?

Just Arrived: Well, I think it's better to say goodbye . . . . Thanks for your interest in my visit, but it looks as if this chat has been good for my sleep, because now, I'm really sleepy.

Super Ñ: I've already fallen asleep because of this jerk.

Cyberlord: Imbecile!

Even though he has friends in Bogotá, Peter has spent his first day alone. He has been sightseeing and is very tired. It's night now and he is in his hotel room. He decides to write an e-mail to Carmen.

Peter: (writing on his computer) Hi, my little Carmen. I am already in Bogotá. I have spent the whole day walking around this marvelous city. I have been to the Montserrate Hill and I have seen the Fallen Lord, the one that does miracles, but what I have liked the most is the area called La Candelaria, which is an old colonial area. And you? What have you done today? (SEND)

Carmen: Hi, Peter. How great! We are both connected at the same time! Well, the truth is I haven't done much today. I have been to school and that's it. I started studying when I got back home because I have a very difficult exam on Monday. (SEND)

Peter: Well, good luck tomorrow. I, on the other hand, am going to continue sightseeing in Bogotá. I don't have to write anything until Tuesday. (SEND)

Carmen:	A reporter's life is so hard! Working all day! (SEND)
Peter:	Hey, listen, I **am** working! I have to research well the country where Ricky is singing so I can write convincing articles later. (SEND)
Carmen:	Yeah? And what "work" have you done today? (SEND)
Peter:	Well, I have taken a lot of pictures and, besides, I have gone to our office in Bogotá.

Carmen:	And there, I'm sure, you have killed yourself working . . .
Peter:	Well, the thing is, today is "cultural Friday" and when I arrived, the office was already closed.
Carmen:	You are so full of crap . . . "cultural Friday" . . . Yeah, I'm sure . . .

ANSWER KEY

ACTIVITY 1

1. d; 2. g; 3. a; 4. e; 5. c; 6. b; 7. f

ACTIVITY 2

1. Los aliases usados son Recién Llegado, Ciberseñor y Super Ñ.
2. El jefe es Ciberseñor.
3. Ciberseñor es el técnico.
4. No hace nada. No participa.
5. Ignorante, estúpido, bruto y necio.

ACTIVITY 3

1. TRUE; 2. DON'T KNOW; 3. DON'T KNOW; 4. FALSE; 5. TRUE

ACTIVITY 4

1. No. Peter ha pasado todo el día andando en **Bogotá**.
2. Sí.
3. Sí.
4. No. Peter no necesita escribir hasta **el martes**.

5. No. **Peter** ha tomado muchas fotos.
6. Sí y no. Peter ha visitado su oficina pero estaba cerrada.

ACTIVITY 5

1. He hablado por la computadora muchas veces.
2. He escrito un mensaje electrónico muchas veces.
3. He usado un buscador como Yahoo.es algunas veces.
4. Nunca he comprimido un archivo.
5. Nunca he descargado música en el internet.

ACTIVITY 6

1. There are four: *COLOMBIA, GENTE, ENTRETENIMIENTO, TECNOLOGÍA*.
2. Three: *Internet, Juegos* (games), *Tecnología*.
3. Older than fifteen and older than thirty.
4. Places to hang out, such as bars, pubs, disco, etc.

ACTIVITY 7

p	t	h	j	h	m	k	t	f	s
u	k	e	c	v	b	n	v	a	a
e	h	c	o	m	i	d	o	e	l
s	s	h	s	d	d	g	y	t	i
t	r	o	x	c	o	r	t	u	d
o	f	b	g	k	l	p	d	q	o

15. THE DISTANCE DOESN'T MATTER

No importa la distancia

Be careful!

COMING UP...

- *Arts and leisure:* **Talking about art**
- *How do you feel about it?:* **More verbs like** *gustar* **(to like)—***importar* **(to matter),** *encantar* **(to love),** *interesar* **(to be interested in), etc.**
- *What's missing?:* **The verbs** *faltar* **(to lack) and** *quedar* **(to remain)**
- *How wonderful!:* **Using exclamations**
- *Whodunit?:* **Nobody, somebody, anybody, nothing, something, and anything in Spanish**

LOOKING AHEAD

Bueno, amigo o amiga. Peter continua su viaje por Colombia. Ahora está en Medellín. Recently, Fernando Botero, one of Colombia's most beloved artists, a sculptor and a painter, decided to open a permanent exhibit in Medellín, his hometown. Botero is very well-known around the world for his portraits of people that look somewhat, say, big and round. Peter decides to visit the museum and maybe use the information in one of his articles.

LET'S WARM UP

Here are some sentences that are missing a word. Can you complete the sentences using the following choices?

arte, colección, escultor, museo, exhibición, pintor

1. Peter va a visitar un ____ de arte moderno.
2. Peter no sabe mucho de ____ en general.
3. La ____ que va a ver se llama "El Legado Botero".
4. Botero es un ____ y ____ colombiano muy famoso.
5. Botero tiene una ____ de arte moderno enorme.

Did You Know?

You have already seen the word *Don* used with names. Remember *Don Miguel* from the *pensión* in Madrid? This time, we'll meet *Doña Ana*, the museum curator. *Don* (masculine) and *Doña* (feminine) are added to somebody's name to show respect. They are similar to the English *Mr.* or *Mrs.* Remember that *Don* and *Doña* are used only with a person's first name, or their first and last name together, as in *Doña Ana García*. They are particularly appropriate when addressing elders or people of a higher rank.

Did You Know?

HEAR ... SAY 1

Peter ha llegado a Medellín, otra ciudad importante de la región de Antioquia, Colombia. Decide visitar el Museo de Antioquia, y allí habla con Doña Ana García, la curadora. Parte del museo está en obras por reforma (*under renovation*) y hay muchas cajas (*boxes*) y cosas en todas partes.

Peter: (*while looking up*) ¡Qué bonito es todo!
(*Peter stumbles over a box.*)
Doña Ana: ¡Cuidado! ¿Se hizo daño?

Peter:	Un poco. Me duele el tobillo.
Doña Ana:	Es que con las obras todo está desordenado.
Peter:	No importa, no es nada.
Doña Ana:	No. Usted no me importa. Pero sí me importa el contenido de esa caja.
Peter:	¡Cuánto lo siento! ¿Qué hay dentro?
Doña Ana:	Creo que es una cerámica de Picasso de la colección particular de Don Fernando Botero. Menos mal. No está rota.
Peter:	Hay muchas estatuas de gordos. ¿Por qué?
Doña Ana:	¡Ay! Usted no sabe mucho. . . . Pues, a Don Fernando Botero le gustan mucho los gorditos. Aquí tenemos muchas obras suyas porque es de aquí, de Medellín. Y él nos dio todas estas obras para esta exhibición.
Peter:	Muy interesante. ¿Puedo sentarme aquí? Estoy muy cansado.
Doña Ana:	Pero por favor, ¡si eso es un móvil de Alexander Calder!
Peter:	Me falta sensibilidad para el arte. Mil perdones.
Doña Ana:	¡Ánimo! Sólo le queda una sala por visitar.
Peter:	Voy a hacer una foto de esa escultura. Increíble. Por fin he visto una escultura de Botero de una mujer delgada.
Doña Ana:	Ay querido, definitivamente lo suyo no es el arte moderno. Esa escultura es de Giacometti.

ACTIVITY 2: HOW'S THAT AGAIN?

These sentences are all false. Can you make them true?

1. Con las reformas, todo está muy ordenado.
2. Hay muchas estatuas de personas delgadas.
3. Peter sabe mucho de arte.
4. Peter está muy nervioso.
5. A Peter le falta sensibilidad para la comida.

Did You Know?

In certain regions of Colombia, it is very common to drop by a friend's house without calling first. This is so common that when Colombians cook, they always add food for two additional people, just in case. Which does not mean that you should drop by at mealtime, unless you know the people really well. The preferred time to visit is in the afternoon, when people have *un algo* (a snack) (*Lit.* something). *Un algo* consists of a cup of coffee and something to eat like an *arepa*, a type of thick corn tortilla eaten with cheese, meat, or just butter.

Did You Know?

**HOW DO YOU FEEL ABOUT IT?: MORE VERBS LIKE *GUSTAR* (TO LIKE)—
IMPORTAR (TO MATTER), *ENCANTAR* (TO LOVE), *INTERESAR* (TO BE INTERESTED IN), ETC.**

Remember the verb *gustar* (to like)? Let's look at an example:

> **Me gusta Colombia.**
>
> I like Colombia. (*Lit.* Colombia is pleasing to me.)
>
> **Nos gusta el arte.**
>
> We like art. (*Lit.* Art is pleasing to us.)

Me and *nos* are indirect object pronouns. They indicate to whom something is pleasing. Let's review the different pronouns and the verb forms used:

PRONOUNS WITH THE VERB *GUSTAR* (TO LIKE)	
me	
te	
le	
nos	gusta / gustan
os	
les	

The form of the verb *gustar* changes depending on whether you are talking about one thing or more than one thing:

> **Le gusta el arte moderno.**
>
> He likes modern art. (*Lit.* Modern art is pleasing to him.)
>
> **Le gustan las esculturas de Botero.**
>
> He likes Botero's sculptures. (*Lit.* Botero's sculptures are pleasing to him.)

To clarify or emphasize to whom something is pleasing, you need to specify the person or persons with *a* (to). You either name the person or use a pronoun with *a*:

> **<u>A Don Fernando</u> le gustan muchos los gorditos.**
>
> Don Fernando likes chubby people very much. (*Lit.* Chubby people are pleasing to him.)
>
> **<u>A mí</u> no me gustan las exhibiciones de esculturas.**
>
> I don't like sculpture exhibitions. (*Lit.* Sculpture exhibitions are not pleasing to me.)

The pronouns you can use after the preposition *a* to emphasize who likes something are: *a mí* (to me), *a tí* (to you), *a él / ella* (to him / her), *a usted* (to you, formal), *a nosotros / nosotras* (to us), *a vosotros / vosotras* (to you all), *a ellos / ellas* (to them), and *a ustedes* (to you all, formal).

There are many other verbs that behave like *gustar*. Here are some examples:

doler *(o > ue)*	to hurt
Me duele el tobillo.	My ankle hurts me.
encantar	to like a lot, to love
A nosotros nos encantan las arepas.	We love arepas.
fascinar	to love, to be fascinated by
A Peter le fascina el español.	Peter loves Spanish.
importar	to be important to, to mind, to matter
¿No te importa si vamos al museo?	Do you mind if we go to the museum?
interesar	to be interested in
Me interesa mucho Picasso.	I am very interested in Picasso.
parecer	to seem, to think
A sus padres les parece bien.	Her parents think that's fine. (*Lit* It seems fine to her parents.)
¿Cómo le parece?	What do you think? (*Lit.* How does it seem to you?)

WHAT'S MISSING?: THE VERBS *FALTAR* (TO LACK) AND *QUEDAR* (TO REMAIN)

Two other important verbs often follow the structure used with *gustar*. Their meaning is a bit tricky, as they, like *gustar*, do not correspond exactly to English verbs:

faltar	to lack, to be left to do, to be still needed
quedar	to remain, to be left over, to be remaining

Here are some examples to help you understand them better:

Le faltan tres pesos.	He is lacking three pesos.
Le quedan tres pesos.	He has three pesos left.

In the Hear . . . Say section, we heard:

Me falta sensibilidad para el arte.	I lack a sensibility for art.
Sólo le queda una sala por visitar.	You only have one room left to visit.

ACTIVITY 3: TAKE IT FOR A SPIN

Okay. Let's practice these verbs. Answer the following questions about yourself! Remember that you need to use either the singular or the plural form of the verbs depending on what's being talked about. For example:

¿Qué país de Latinoamérica te interesa más?

Which country in Latin America interests you the most?

Me interesa la Argentina.

Argentina interests me.

1. ¿Cuántas lecciones te faltan para terminar este libro?
2. ¿Qué te parecen las historias de Peter?
3. ¿Qué te importa más, el amor, el dinero o la salud (health)?
4. ¿Cuánto dinero te queda en el banco?
5. ¿Te fascina el arte moderno?
6. ¿Te encanta el español?
7. ¿Te duele el estómago cuando comes muchos tacos?

Heads Up!

The verb *quedar* can also mean "to stay" when it is used with a reflexive pronoun (*me, te, se, nos, os, se*). The context will be most helpful here:

Hoy me quedo en casa.   Today I'm staying at home.

Parece (to seem), on the other hand, means "to resemble, to look like" when used with a reflexive pronoun:

Carmen se parece a Rosalba.   Carmen looks like Rosalba.

Did You Know?

Bullfighting is very popular in Colombia. Not only do Colombians have regular bullfights, but also they particularly enjoy something called *encierros*, where they let the bull loose and run in front of it. *¡Qué locos!* In Bogotá, Cali, and Medellín there are big bullfighting rings where the most important bullfighters from Spain and Latin America perform. César Rincón is Colombia's most popular bullfighter.

WORDS TO LIVE BY

ARTS AND LEISURE: TALKING ABOUT ART

Many Spanish words related to the art world are cognates. Do you remember them? Here are some: *el arte, el arte moderno, la cerámica, la colección, el contenido, la escultura, la estatua, la exhibición,* and *el museo.*

Here are three words that may cause you difficulty:

la obra (de arte)	work of art. The word can also mean "repair," especially when in plural: **las obras**.
la sala	room; classroom; living room
la sensibilidad	sensibility, sensitivity. Note: **sensible** does not mean "sensible." It means "sensitive." It's one of those falsos amigos!

Word on the Street

por fin	finally
¡Ánimo!	Cheer up and go for it!
¡Ay!	Oh!, Gosh! (used as a filler)
¡Cuánto lo siento!	I'm so sorry!

ACTIVITY 4: TAKE IT FOR A SPIN

Tell me if these sentences make sense. (All are based on the vocabulary from the dialogue.)

1. En el museo hay tobillos.
2. La sala se sienta.
3. La caja está rota.
4. Me hice daño en los mil perdones.
5. Por fin has terminado todas las lecciones del libro.

HEAR . . . SAY 2

Peter continua hablando con Doña Ana García.

Peter: ¡Cuántos gordos hay aquí! Empiezo a tener hambre.

Doña Ana: Pero, ¡si no hay ninguno!

Peter: Quiero decir en las esculturas y en los cuadros.

Doña Ana: Pues, aquí al lado puede comer una arepa si quiere. Yo también tengo hambre, así que le acompaño.

Peter: Bueno, no sé que es una arepa, pero suena bien.

(They are having an arepa *in a kiosk next to the museum.)*

Peter: Esta arepa con queso está muy buena. Gracias por la sugerencia.

Doña Ana: De nada. Me parece que tiene un trabajo muy interesante ¿Le gusta Colombia?

Peter: Me encanta. Este trabajo es estupendo porque he viajado a muchos países y he conocido a mucha gente fascinante.

Doña Ana: ¿Sí? ¿Ha conocido a alguien famoso?

Peter:	Sí. He conocido a Ricky Martin, claro y también a otros cantantes. Pero también hay otra gente . . .
Doña Ana:	Una muchacha . . .
Peter:	Sí. Conocí a una chica muy especial en España.
Doña Ana:	¡Ah, el amor! ¿Y van a verse otra vez?
Peter:	No sé. Yo estoy viajando todo el tiempo y ella está estudiando y no sé si ella quiere verme más . . .
Doña Ana:	El amor es como el arte: bello pero difícil de entender. Pero si el amor es verdadero, la distancia no importa. ¡Ánimo Peter!
Peter:	Gracias Doña Ana. Me gustó mucho la visita al museo. Y también me gustó la arepa. Gracias por la sugerencia.
Doña Ana:	Bueno, hasta pronto y buena suerte con todo.

ACTIVITY 5: HOW'S THAT AGAIN?

Once again, there is something wrong with the sentences below. Can you please fix them?

1. Peter y Doña Ana tienen frío.
2. Doña Ana piensa que el trabajo de Peter es muy aburrido.
3. Peter ha conocido al presidente de Colombia.
4. Peter está durmiendo todo el tiempo.
5. Doña Ana dice que el amor es como un banco.

Did You Know?

Without a doubt, the most internationally renowned Colombian is the writer Gabriel García Márquez, born in Aracataca in 1928. He is considered one of the greatest novelists in the Spanish language of the twentieth century. In 1982, he received the Nobel Prize for Literature. His most famous novel is *One Hundred Years of Solitude* (*Cien años de soledad*), which is the best example of "magic realism." Colombians prefer to call Márquez "Gabo," an endearing term.

Did You Know?

WORKSHOP 2

THE NITTY-GRITTY

HOW WONDERFUL!: USING EXCLAMATIONS

You can form exclamations in Spanish using *qué* followed by an adjective:

| ¡Qué bonito es el museo! | How beautiful the museum is! |
| ¡Qué enorme es esa estatua! | What a huge statue! |

To express surprise about quantity, *cuánto* is used:

| ¡Cuántos gordos hay aquí! | There are so many chubby people here! |
| ¡Cuánto dinero tiene ese hombre! | That man has so much money! |

WHODUNIT?: NOBODY, SOMEBODY, ANYBODY, NOTHING, SOMETHING, AND ANYTHING IN SPANISH

Here are the Spanish counterparts of these words:

alguien	somebody / anybody	**nadie**	nobody / anybody
alguno/a	some / any	**ninguno/a**	none, no one / anyone
algún	some / any	**ningún**	none, no one / any one
algo	something / anything	**nada**	nothing / anything

Look at these examples from the dialogue:

No es nada.	It's nothing.
Pero, si no hay ninguno.	But there aren't any.
Ha conocido a alguien famoso?	Have you met anybody famous?

Note that a*lguno* and *ninguno* shorten to a*lgún* and *ningún* before masculine singular nouns:

| algunos cuadros | some / any paintings |
| algún cuadro | a / any painting |

Note that Spanish often uses multiple negatives in the same sentence:

| Aquí <u>no</u> hay <u>nadie</u>. | There is nobody here. / There isn't anybody here. |
| <u>No</u> tengo <u>nada</u>. | I don't have anything. / I have nothing. |

| ACTIVITY 6: | **TAKE IT FOR A SPIN** |

Match the exclamations on the left with the phrases they refer to on the right:

1. ¡Qué alto!
2. ¡Cuánto dinero tiene!
3. ¡Qué famoso es!
4. ¡Qué gordo!
5. ¡Cuántas estatuas hay aquí!

a. Algún museo
b. Alguna persona obesa
c. Alguien de la familia Rockefeller
d. Algún cantante de Colombia
e. Alguna persona de los Knicks

Take a look. These adjectives have two meanings:
bueno/a, used with the verb *estar*, means "to feel fine"

> **El chico está bueno.**   The boy is fine.

or, it can mean, "to taste good" if you are eating something:

> **La arepa está buena.**   The *arepa* tastes good.

malo/a is used in similar ways:

> **El chico está malo.**   The boy is sick. (He is not fine.)

> **La arepa está mala.**   The arepa tastes bad.

Peter saw this sign at the entrance to El Museo de Antioquia:

MUSEO DE ANTIOQUIA
Legado Botero

INGRESO ADULTOS: *3.000 pesos*

HORARIO: Martes a viernes entre las 9.30 de la mañana y las 5.30 de la tarde en jornada continua. Sábados de 9.00 de la mañana a 2.00 de la tarde

DIRECCIÓN: Carrera 52 A No. 51 A 29. MEDELLÍN

TELÉFONO: 251–36–36

E-MAIL: museodeant@epm.net.co

ACTIVITY 7:   HOW'S THAT AGAIN?

Can you answer some questions about it?

1. ¿Cómo se llama la exhibición?
2. ¿Cuánto cuesta entrar al museo?
3. ¿Dónde está el museo?
4. ¿Qué día de la semana está cerrado?

Now take a look at this menu:

BAR RESTAURANTE

"LA QUEBRADA DEL BOSQUE". MEDELLÍN. COMIDA TÍPICA

Los viernes espectáculos musicales (cumbias, boleros)

ESPECIALIDADES:

Arepas con todo:	*2.500 pesos*
Carne asada:	*12.000 pesos*
Chorizos:	*3.000 pesos*

BEBIDAS

Aguardiente (media botella):	*17.000 pesos*
Ron (media botella):	*19.000 pesos*
Whisky (media botella):	*43.000 pesos*

FORMA DE PAGO: TODAS LAS TARJETAS

HORARIO: LUNES A SÁBADOS DE 4 P.M. A 2 A.M.

DOMINGOS DE 11 A.M. A 9 P.M.,

ZONA: *El Poblado*

DIRECCIÓN: Carrera 25B N⁰. 18ª- 137

CÓMO LLEGAR: *Por la Transversal Superior hasta llegar a la Iglesia de San Lucas.*

ESTACIONAMIENTO DE AUTOMÓVIL EN ZONA
DE PARQUEO DEL RESTAURANTE.

Answer these questions about the menu:

1. ¿Qué tipo de comida tienen?
2. ¿Qué bebidas tienen?
3. ¿En qué zona está?
4. ¿Qué tarjetas aceptan?

STRUT YOUR STUFF!

Congratulations! You've learned so much in the past lessons! Here's Doña Ana's account of her day with Peter. I'm sure you will understand most of it:

> . . . *Esta mañana fui al museo y allí conocí a un joven reportero de Estados Unidos que se llama Peter Winthrop. Estaba muy interesado en el arte moderno, aunque no sabía casi nada. Después de hablar un poco, me dijo que tenía hambre y comimos unas arepas en un restaurante al lado del museo. Entonces me habló de una chica llamada Carmen que conoció en España. ¡Creo que se ha enamorado un poco de ella!* . . .

ACTIVITY 9:   **TAKE IT FOR A SPIN**

Read the text again and tell me which verbs are in the preterite, which are in the imperfect, and which are in the present perfect.

CRIB NOTES

HEAR...SAY 1

Peter has arrived in Medellín, another important city in the Antioquia region of Colombia. He decides to visit the Museum of Antioquia, and he talks to Doña Ana García, the curator. Part of the museum is under renovation and there are many boxes and things everywhere.

Peter: How beautiful everything is!

(*Peter stumbles over a box.*)

Doña Ana: Be careful! Did you hurt yourself?

Peter: A little. My ankle hurts.

Doña Ana: Because of the renovations, everything is lying around.

Peter: It doesn't matter, it's nothing.

Doña Ana: No. It's not you that I'm concerned about. What I'm worried about is the content of that box.

Peter: I'm so sorry! What's inside?

Doña Ana: I think it is a ceramic by Picasso, from the personal collection of Don Fernando Botero. Thank goodness. It is not broken.

Peter: There are many sculptures of chubby people. Why?

Doña Ana: Gosh! You don't know very much. Well, Don Fernando Botero likes chubby people. We have a lot of his work because he is from Medellín. And he gave us all these works of art for this exhibition.

Peter: Very interesting. May I sit here? I'm very tired.

Doña Ana: Of course not! This is a mobile by Alexander Calder!

Peter: I lack a sensibility for art. I'm sorry.

Doña Ana: Cheer up! You only have one room left to see.

Peter: I'm going to take a picture of that sculpture. Amazing. Finally I have seen a sculpture of a thin woman by Botero.

Doña Ana: My dear friend, modern art is definitely not your thing. That sculpture is by Giacometti.

HEAR...SAY 2

Peter continues talking to Doña Ana García.

Peter: There are so many chubby people here! I am starting to get hungry.

Doña Ana: But, there are none!

Peter: No, I mean the sculptures and paintings.

Doña Ana: Oh, I see. Well, you can have an *arepa* right next door, if you wish. I am also hungry, so I'll join you.

Peter: Well, I don't know what an *arepa* is, but it sounds good.

(*They are having an* arepa *in a kiosk next to the museum.*)

Peter: This *arepa* with cheese is delicious. Thanks for the suggestion.

Doña Ana: You're welcome. It seems to me that you have a very interesting job. Do you like Colombia?

Peter: I love it. This job is great because I have traveled to many countries, and I have met a lot of fascinating people.

Doña Ana: Yeah? Have you met anybody famous?

Peter: Yes. I've met Ricky Martin, of course, and also some other singers. But there are other people . . .

Doña Ana: A girl . . .

Peter: Yes. I met a very special girl in Spain.

Doña Ana: Ah, love! And are you going to see each other again?

Peter: I don't know. I am traveling all the time and she is studying. And I don't know if she wants to see me again . . .

Doña Ana: Love is like art: beautiful but difficult to understand. But if the love is true, the distance doesn't matter. Cheer up, Peter!

Peter: Thanks, Doña Ana. I really liked the visit to the museum. And I also liked the *arepa*. Thanks for the suggestion.

Doña Ana: Well, see you soon and good luck with everything.

ANSWER KEY

ACTIVITY 1

1. museo; 2. arte; 3. exhibición; 4. escultor; pintor; 5. colección

ACTIVITY 2

1. Con las obras, todo está *desordenado*.
2. Hay muchas estatuas de personas *gordas*.
3. Peter *no* sabe mucho de arte.
4. Peter está muy *cansado*.
5. A Peter le falta sensibilidad para *el arte*.

ACTIVITY 3

1. Me faltan cinco.
2. Me parecen interesantes (o aburridas, cómicas, horribles, estúpidas . . .).
3. Me importa todo: el amor, el dinero y la salud.
4. No me queda mucho. (¡Qué pregunta más indiscreta!)
5. ¡Claro! Me fascinan muchas cosas.
6. Por supuesto, me encanta el español.
7. No, no me duele el estómago cuando como tacos.

ACTIVITY 4

1. NO: In the museum there are ankles.
2. NO: The room sits down.
3. YES: The box is broken.
4. NO: I hurt myself in the thousand sorries.
5. YES: You have finally finished all the lessons in the book.

ACTIVITY 5

1. Peter y Doña Ana tienen hambre.
2. Doña Ana piensa que el trabajo de Peter es muy interesante.
3. Peter ha conocido a muchos cantantes famosos.
4. Peter está viajando todo el tiempo.
5. Doña Ana dice que el amor es como el arte.

ACTIVITY 6

1. e; 2. c; 3. d; 4. b; 5. a

ACTIVITY 7

1. La exhibición se llama Legado Botero.
2. Entrar al museo cuesta 3.000 pesos.
3. El museo está en la Carrera 52 A No. 51 A 29. MEDELLÍN
4. El lunes y el domingo está cerrado.

ACTIVITY 8

1. Tienen comida típica.
2. Tienen aguardiente, ron y whisky.
3. Está en la zona del Poblado.
4. Aceptan todas las tarjetas.

ACTIVITY 9

PRETERITE: fui, conocí, dijo, comimos, habló, conoció
IMPERFECT: estaba, sabía, tenía
PRESENT PERFECT: se ha enamorado

16.

THANKS FOR THINKING OF ME

Gracias por pensar en mí

INTERNACIONAL

...bobo...

You mean to say that you spoke to a total stranger?

COMING UP. . .

- *What to say when you've lost it:* **Dealing with emergencies**
- *I'm desperate . . . :* **Words starting with *des–* in Spanish**
- *I would if I could:* **Saying what you "would do" and sounding polite by using the conditional form**
- *I scream, you scream . . . :* **Irregular verbs in the conditional form**
- **Is it *por* or *para*?**

Peter is getting ready to fly to Argentina, but he has one more adventure in Colombia, at the *aeropuerto*. He cannot find his *mochila* (backpack), where he put his wallet and important documents. He'll have to visit the *comisaría de policía del aeropuerto* (the airport's police station), located at the end of the *pasillo* (hallway).

Did You Know?

When you go to Colombia, you must visit Cartagena de Indias, the "crown jewel" of the country's tourism trade. This city is an impressive showcase of Spanish colonial architecture infused with a strong Caribbean cultural influence. You can find everything there, from magnificent hotels and beaches in the Bocagrande area, to the Inquisition Palace, and many beautiful churches and squares. There are also several enormous colonial forts that were frequent targets of pirates.

Did You Know?

ACTIVITY 1: LET'S WARM UP

Imagine you have lost some important documents. What kind of questions do you think you may be asked by the police officer helping you? Select the five questions that you find most logical.

1. ¿Cuántos años tiene?
2. ¿Dónde vio sus documentos por última vez?
3. ¿Cómo se hace una arepa con queso?
4. ¿Ha hablado con alguien desconocido (*unknown*)?
5. ¿Dónde ha estado en las últimas dos horas?
6. ¿Cómo se llama la madre de Enrique Iglesias?
7. ¿Cuándo salió para el aeropuerto?
8. ¿Dónde está el museo más importante de Colombia?
9. ¿De qué color es el caballo blanco de Santiago?
10. ¿Cuánto cuesta una habitación doble?

Take a Tip from Me!

You can use many different techniques to learn new words. I'll suggest some here:

1. **Put words on flashcards:** This is a popular technique with many advantages. You can take the cards with you anywhere and review them whenever you have five minutes to spare. Don't just list new words. Leave some space so you can add words related to the original word. For example, if you are listing the word

alto / a (tall), you can also add *bajo / a* (short), or other words used to describe people: *gordo / a* (fat), *delgado / a* (thin), *moreno / a* (with dark hair), *rubio / a* (blond), etc.

2. <u>Learn words in context:</u> Try to learn new words in context. Just adding a sentence can provide enough context. For example, with the word *alto / a*, you can think of: *Michael Jordan es muy alto. No es bajo.*

3. <u>Use what's around you:</u> Look around you. Do you know the word for that coffee you're sipping? Yeah, *café.* What about the person sitting next to you in the subway? Is she *rubia*? Is she *alta*? Maybe a bit *gorda*?

Most important, have fun with Spanish! Don't allow yourself to start thinking of learning as a chore. Remember your initial motivation for studying Spanish. Let me tell you a secret: if you really want to learn it, you most definitely will.

Take a Tip from Me!

HEAR . . . SAY 1

Peter tiene que viajar una vez más. Ahora está en el aeropuerto de Medellín. Va a tener algunos problemas . . .

Peter: (*talking to himself*) Bueno, aquí estoy, tengo un poco de sed. Me gustaría beber algo, quizá una limonada. (*He walks to the cafeteria.*) ¿Podría darme una limonada bien fría?

Camarera: Sí, por supuesto, aquí tiene. Son doscientos pesos.

Peter: Muy bien. (*He looks around for his backpack, but cannot find it.*) A ver . . . a ver . . . Lo siento. No encuentro mi mochila. (*He looks in his pocket and finds some money there.*) Pero aquí tiene. ¿Sabría decirme dónde está la estación de policía del aeropuerto?

Camarera: Ahí, al final del pasillo.

(*Peter walks to the police station. He explains to a police officer he has lost his backpack with his wallet and all his documents, including his passport.*)

Policía: ¿Y no sabe dónde vio su mochila por última vez?

Peter: Pues, vamos a ver . . . pagué el hotel. Pagué el taxi. Llegué al aeropuerto. No, no sé.

Policía:	¿Ha hablado con alguien en el aeropuerto?
Peter:	Pues, sí. Hablé con un hombre joven. Habló sin parar. Me dijo que iría a los Estados Unidos pronto. Probablemente llegaría a Nueva York. Allí estaría unas semanas y luego volvería a Colombia. Necesitaba información sobre mi país.
Policía:	¡Um! Muy interesante . . . y ¿qué más le dijo?
Peter:	Nada más. Yo le di mi teléfono y me dijo que me llamaría en Nueva York.
Policía:	O sea, que habló con una persona totalmente desconocida.
Peter:	Err . . . sí.
Policía:	Y además le dio su número de teléfono.
Peter:	Pues, sí.
Policía:	Pero usted sí es un poco . . . bobo.
Peter:	Perdone, ¿le importaría decirme que significa la palabra "bobo"? No la entiendo.
Policía:	Mejor así . . .

ACTIVITY 2:   HOW'S THAT AGAIN?

You know the routine. Here are some questions about Peter; try to answer them.

1. ¿Qué bebe?
2. ¿Qué no encuentra?
3. ¿A dónde va?
4. ¿Cómo llegó al aeropuerto?
5. ¿Con quién habló?
6. ¿Qué le dijo el policía?

Did You Know?

In the Spanish-speaking world, kissing when you first meet a person is quite common, but there are variations from country to country. In Spain, people (mostly women with women, or women with men) kiss twice (on both cheeks). In Colombia and Mexico, kissing is only done between family members and among very close friends, and only once.

Did You Know?

WORKSHOP 1

THE NITTY-GRITTY

I WOULD IF I COULD: SAYING WHAT YOU "WOULD DO" AND SOUNDING POLITE BY USING THE CONDITIONAL FORM

The Spanish present conditional form corresponds to the English "would." Here are its typical uses in Spanish:

- The conditional describes what you "would do":

  Me gustaría beber algo, quizá una limonada.

  I would like to drink something, maybe a lemonade.

  Iría a China.

  I would go to China.

  Visitaría a mi familia.

  I would visit my family.

- The conditional is commonly used to signal courtesy or to ask for something politely:

  ¿Sabría decirme dónde está la estación de policía?

  Would you tell me where the airport police station is?

  ¿Podría darme una limonada bien fría?

  Could you bring me a very cold lemonade?

- In Spanish, the conditional is also used to express probability or doubt about an action in the past; the English equivalents are "I wonder," "I guess," "probably," etc.:

  ¿Dónde pondría yo el pasaporte?

  Where, I wonder, did I put the passport? / Where could I have put my passport?

Finally, we have come across a tense that uses the same forms for all three types of verbs (*–ar*, *–er*, and *–ir*). You simply add the endings directly to the *–ar*, *–er*, and *–ir* form of the verb. Here are the conditional forms of *trabajar* (to work):

THE CONDITIONAL TENSE OF REGULAR VERBS

		TRABAJAR (TO WORK)	
Singular	*yo*	*trabajar + ía*	I would work
	tú	*trabajar + ías*	you would work
	él / ella, usted	*trabajar + ía*	he / she, you (formal) would work
Plural	*nosotros / nosotras*	*trabajar + íamos*	we would work
	vosotros / vosotras	*trabajar + íais*	you (plural) would work
	ellos / ellas, ustedes	*trabajar + ían*	they, you (formal) would work

Just remember that verbs that end in *–er* and *–ir* take the same endings as *trabajar*. Note: don't forget to add these endings directly to the infinitive! This even applies to verbs like *ser* (*yo sería* "I would be") and *estar* (*yo estaría* "I would be").

TAKE IT FOR A SPIN

What was Peter thinking? Tell me what Peter was really thinking, following the model, and using the conditional form:

El español es difícil.   Spanish is difficult.

Pensaba que el español sería difícil.   He thought Spanish would be difficult.

1. El viaje a Argentina es muy caro. Pensaba que . . .
2. El hombre es honesto.
3. El policía pregunta mucho.
4. La dependienta prepara la limonada.
5. Carmen escribe un mensaje.
6. Ricky Martin canta en Barranquilla.

Heads Up!

The conditional tense is *not* used in Spanish to refer to an action that one used to perform in the past, as in English. In this context, the imperfect tense is used:

Cuando era pequeña, todos los veranos íbamos a la playa.

When I was a kid, we would go to the beach every summer.

Did You Know?

WORDS TO LIVE BY

WHAT TO SAY WHEN YOU'VE LOST IT: DEALING WITH EMERGENCIES

When Peter realized he'd lost his backpack with his passport in it, he said:

> **¿Sabría decirme dónde está la estación de policía del aeropuerto?**
>
> Could you tell me where the airport police station is?

I realize that you're much less absentminded than he is, but other emergencies may arise as you travel. So, just in case, here are some useful emergency expressions. First, the basic one: "Help!" There are three ways to ask for help in Spanish:

¡Ayuda!	
¡Socorro!	Help!
¡Auxilio!	

Here are some more specific emergency phrases:

¡Llame a la ambulancia!	Call the ambulance!
¿Hay algún doctor aquí?	Is there a doctor here?
¡Me han robado!	I've been pickpocketed.
¡Al ladrón!	Catch that thief!

I'M DESPERATE: WORDS STARTING WITH *DES*– IN SPANISH

As in English, there are some prefixes (bits of words that come before the root of a word) that occur frequently in Spanish. Here are some useful Spanish words using the very common prefix *des*– :

desconocido	**des + conocido**	*unknown*
desaparición	**des + aparición**	*disappearance*
deshelar	**des + helar**	*to defrost*
desinfectar	**des + infectar**	*disinfect*
desintoxicar	**des + intoxicar**	*detoxify*

So, *des-* means something like "not," or "the reverse of." What about the word *desayuno*? Well, *ayuno* means "fast," so *desayuno* means "undoing of the fast," "breaking of the fast," or "breakfast" (similar to English!).

Word on the Street

o sea	that is. This phrase is very commonly used at the beginning of a sentence.
a ver . . .	let me see
nada más	nothing else
bobo	dumb, stupid (used frequently in Colombia)

Did You Know?

Shakira, Arabic for "a woman full of grace," is the most famous pop singer in Colombia. She was born in 1977 in Barranquilla, in the Caribbean section of the country, and has become a national idol. Millions of young fans love her, let's say, unique way of singing. Her love life, as well as her idiosyncratic wardrobe, are always objects of public curiosity. Two of her most popular songs, which topped the charts throughout the Spanish-speaking world, are "Estoy aquí" (you know what that means) and "Ciega, sordomuda" ("Blind, deaf-mute").

Did You Know?

HEAR . . . SAY 2

Peter continúa hablando con el policía del aeropuerto.

Policía: ¿Y cómo era ese hombre?

Peter: Tendría unos treinta o cuarenta años. No era muy alto, de pelo oscuro, delgado.

Policía: O sea, sería como el ochenta por ciento de los colombianos. ¿Y por dónde salió?

Peter: Por aquella puerta. ¡Dios mío! Mi avión para Argentina sale en veinte minutos. ¿Qué puedo hacer?

Policía: Creo que usted no va a ninguna parte por ahora. Si quiere, puede ir para la cafetería. Si hay algo nuevo, lo busco allí.

(Peter leaves for the cafeteria and sits at a table.)

Peter:	(*talking to the waiter*) Buenas tardes, ¿podría darme una arepa con queso?
Mesero:	Muy bien. ¿Le gustaría beber algo con su arepa?
Peter:	Sí, un café con leche.

(*After ten minutes, the policeman comes to his table.*)

Policía:	Bueno, esto es para usted. (*He gives Peter his backpack.*)
Peter:	¿Cómo la encontró?
Policía:	Yo no la encontré. Ese hombre que habló con usted pasó por la comisaría. Me dijo que usted olvidó su mochila después de su conversación. Cuando él pasó otra vez por allí, la reconoció y me la trajo. Está todo dentro. No falta nada. Usted ha tenido mucha suerte con ese tipo.
Peter:	¿Ve? No soy tan bobo como creía . . .

ACTIVITY 4: HOW'S THAT AGAIN?

Answer the following questions:

1. ¿Cómo era el hombre que habló con Peter?
2. ¿Cuándo sale el avión de Peter para Argentina?
3. ¿Qué come Peter en la cafetería?
4. ¿Quién encontró la mochila?
5. ¿Falta algo?

WORKSHOP 2

THE NITTY-GRITTY

I SCREAM, YOU SCREAM . . . : IRREGULAR VERBS IN THE CONDITIONAL FORM

The following verbs have irregular conditional stems:

VERB		IRREGULAR STEM
decir (to say)	→	**dir–**
haber (there is/are)	→	**habr–**
hacer (to do)	→	**har–**
poder (to be able to)	→	**podr–**
poner (to put)	→	**pondr–**

querer (to want / love)	→	**querr–**
saber (to know)	→	**sabr–**
salir (to go out)	→	**saldr–**
tener (to have)	→	**tendr–**
venir (to come)	→	**vendr–**

You just have to add the endings you learned earlier to these irregular stems. Here are some examples:

Tendría unos treinta años.	He must have been around 30.
¿Podría darme una arepa?	Could you give me an *arepa*?
Querría ser presidente.	I would like to be president.

IS IT *POR* OR *PARA*?

You have already heard these two words many times in the dialogues. They are frequently translated with the English word *for*, but they do not mean exactly the same thing and are used in different contexts. For starters, think of *por* as meaning "through," "by means of," or "because of," and *para* as referring to "a goal," "a limit / destination."

ACTIVITY 5: **TAKE IT FOR A SPIN**

Help me out a little. Read Hear . . . Say 2 again and write down all the sentences that include *por* and *para*.

You're right—there are nine sentences. Here are several of them:

El hombre salió <u>por</u> esa puerta.

The man left through that door.

El hombre pasó <u>por</u> la comisaría.

The man stopped by the police station. (I.e., He went through it.)

Peter fue <u>para</u> la cafetería.

Peter went towards the cafeteria.

mi avión <u>para</u> Argentina

my plane to Argentina

Esto es <u>para</u> usted.

This is for you.

Word on the Street

There are many expressions that take *por* or *para*. Here are some with *por*:

por ahora	*for now*
por desgracia	*unfortunately*
por supuesto	*of course*

WORDS TO LIVE BY

The word *policía* in Spanish is a bit tricky. Take a look:

la policía	*police, in general*
el policía	*policeman*
la mujer policía	*policewoman*

Word on the Street

Here are some typical Colombian expressions:

¿Qué hubo?	*What's up? (Lit. What was there?) As a way to start a conversation, this phrase is only used by Colombians, so you'll know one when you hear it.*
¿Cómo le va?	*How is it going?*
¿Cómo le fue?	*How did it go?*
¿Cómo así?	*How come? (Lit. How that way?)*
tipo	*guy, dude (especially in Colombia)*
mijo / a	*dear, darling; from **mi hijo** / **mi hija** (my son / my daughter)*

You can combine expressions to sound completely authentic:

¿Cómo así, mijo? ¿Qué hubo, querido? ¿Cómo le fue con ese tipo tan bobo?

LET'S PUT IT IN WRITING

This is the form Peter had to fill out at the police station to file his complaint about a lost backpack.

```
COMISARÍA DE POLICIA DEL AEROPUERTO DE
MEDELLÍN REPORTE DE QUEJA
─────────────────────────────────────────────────────

FECHA:    13-DICIEMBRE-2002

NOMBRE: PETER   APELLIDO: WINTHROP

CAUSA DE LA QUEJA:    DESAPARICIÓN DE MOCHILA.

OCURRIÓ A  LAS 11 DE LA MAÑANA, EN LA SALA DE ESPERA

DEL AEROPUERTO.

_____

_____

OFICIAL DE SERVICIO:  SARGENTO MARTÍNEZ SUÁREZ

FIRMA:_____
```

ACTIVITY 6:   HOW'S THAT AGAIN?

Time for questions:

1. ¿Qué día estuvo Peter en el aeropuerto?
2. ¿A qué hora desapareció su mochila?
3. ¿Dónde desapareció?
4. ¿Cómo se llama el sargento que le ayudó?

ACTIVITY 7:   TAKE IT UP A NOTCH

What would happen if you were at the airport and started talking to a stranger in Spanish? What kinds of questions would you ask if you knew you were traveling to his / her country? Show off by writing at least five questions. Then, look at the examples in the Crib Sheet section.

CRIB NOTES

Peter has to travel one more time. Now he is at Medellín's airport. He is about to have some problems.

Peter: Well, here I am. I'm a bit thirsty. I would like to drink something, maybe a lemonade. (He walks to the cafeteria.) Could you give me a very cold lemonade?

Waitress: Yes, of course. Here you go. That's 200 pesos.

Peter: Very well. (He looks around for his backpack, but he cannot find it.) Let me see . . . let me see . . . I'm sorry, I cannot find my backpack. (He looks in his pocket and finds some money there.) But here you are. Could you tell me where the airport police station is?

Waitress: There, at the end of the hall.

(Peter walks there. He explains to a police officer that he has lost his backpack with his wallet and all of his documents, including his passport.)

Policeman: And you don't know where you saw your backpack last?

Peter: Well, let's see. I paid the hotel. I paid the taxi. I arrived at the airport. No, I don't know.

Policeman: Have you spoken with anyone inside the airport?

Peter: Well, yes. I talked to a young man. He talked nonstop. He told me that he would go to the United States soon. Most likely, he would arrive in New York. He would stay there for a few weeks and then he would return to Colombia. He needed information about my country.

Policeman: Hmmm! Very interesting . . . and what else did he tell you?

Peter: Nothing else. I gave him my phone number and he told me that he would call me when he was in New York.

Policeman: You mean to say that you spoke to a total stranger?

Peter: Umm . . . yeah.

Policeman: And, in addition, you gave him your phone number.

Peter: Well, yeah.

Policeman: You are definitely a bit . . . *bobo* (dumb).

Peter: Excuse me, would you mind telling me what the word *bobo* means? I don't understand it.

Policeman: It's better that way . . .

Peter continues talking to the policeman at the airport.

Policeman: And what did that man look like?

Peter: He was probably around 30 or 40. He was not too tall, had dark hair, and was thin.

Policeman: That is, he was like 80 percent of male Colombians. And where did he go?

Peter: Through that door. My goodness! My plane for Argentina leaves in 20 minutes. What can I do?

Policeman: I think that you are not going anywhere for now. If you want to, you may go to the cafeteria. If there is anything new, I'll look for you there.

(Peter leaves for the cafeteria and sits at a table.)

Peter: Good afternoon, could you bring me an *arepa* with cheese?

Waiter: Very good. Would you like something to drink with your *arepa*?

Peter: Yes, coffee with milk.

(After ten minutes, the policeman comes to his table.)

Policeman: Well, this is for you. (He gives Peter his backpack.)

Peter: How did you find it?

Policeman: I didn't find it. The man that talked to you came by the police station. He told me that you forgot your backpack after your conversation. When he passed by the same place again, he recognized it and brought it to me. Everything is inside. There is nothing missing. You were very lucky with that guy.

Peter: See? I am not as dumb as you thought.

ANSWER KEY

ACTIVITY 1

Here are the translations of the questions:

1. How old are you?
2. Where did you last see your documents?
3. How do you make an *arepa* with cheese?
4. Have you talked to any strangers?

5. Where have you been in the past two hours?
6. What's Enrique Iglesias's mother's name?
7. When did you leave for the airport?
8. Where is the most important museum in Colombia?
9. What's the color of Santiago's white horse?
10. How much does a double room cost?
Questions 1, 2, 4, 5, and 7 make sense.

ACTIVITY 2

1. Peter bebe una limonada.
2. No encuentra su mochila.
3. Va a la estación de policía.
4. Llegó al aeropuerto en taxi.
5. Habló con un hombre.
6. El policía le dijo que es un bobo.

ACTIVITY 3

1. Pensaba que el viaje a la Argentina sería muy caro.
2. Pensaba que el hombre sería honesto.
3. Pensaba que el policía preguntaría mucho.
4. Pensaba que la dependienta prepararía la limonada.
5. Pensaba que Carmen escribiría un mensaje.
6. Pensaba que Ricky Martin cantaría en Barranquilla.

ACTIVITY 4

1. Era moreno, no muy alto y delgado.
2. En veinte minutos.

3. Una arepa con carne.
4. El hombre que habló con Peter.
5. No. No falta nada.

ACTIVITY 5

1. Sería como el ochenta ocho por ciento de los colombianos.
2. ¿Por dónde salió?
3. Por aquella puerta.
4. Mi avión para Argentina sale en 20 minutos.
5. Creo que usted no va a ninguna parte por ahora.
6. Puede ir para la cafetería.
7. Esto es para usted.
8. Ese hombre que habló con usted pasó por la comisaría.
9. Cuando el pasó otra vez por allí . . .

ACTIVITY 6

1. el trece de diciembre
2. a las once de la mañana
3. en la sala de espera
4. Martínez Suárez

ACTIVITY 7

1. ¿Cómo se llama?
2. ¿De dónde es?
3. ¿Dónde trabaja?
4. ¿Por qué está aquí?
5. ¿A dónde va a viajar ahora?

17.

YOU WILL COME BACK

Volverás

He's really crazy about soccer.

COMING UP...

- *There's no sport like soccer:* Chatting about sports, especially soccer
- *First things first:* Ordinal numbers
- *What will tomorrow bring?:* Using the future tense
- *Each and every time:* Saying *each* and *every* in Spanish
- *Get with it:* Using pronouns after prepositions—*with him, on it,* etc.

We have arrived in Argentina (Psst . . . do you need to look it up on a map? It's that big country in South America, below Bolivia, Paraguay, and Brazil and next to Chile and Uruguay). It's a magnificent place, and Peter is quite excited about being there. His first encounter with Argentine culture, though, will be a bit of a shock. These people are absolutely crazy about *fútbol* (soccer)! *¿Y a ti? ¿Te gusta el fútbol? ¡Espero que sí!*

ACTIVITY 1:   **LET'S WARM UP**

This is a list of words that will come up in the dialogue, with their English counterparts. They are all related to soccer. Can you guess their meanings? (Hint: Many soccer terms in Spanish come directly from English, so only the spelling will differ.)

1.	gol	a.	referee
2.	penal	b.	stadium
3.	referí	c.	sports fan
4.	hincha	d.	penalty
5.	partido	e.	soccer
6.	equipo	f.	goal
7.	estadio	g.	game / match
8.	fútbol	h.	team

Take a Tip from Me!

We have talked about studying vocabulary. What about memorizing verb conjugations? In this lesson we are going to learn yet another tense. (Oh, no!) How can you remember all those endings? Well, here are some suggestions:

1. <u>Focus first on general understanding.</u> This means that you should do as much reading and listening as possible. Whenever you read a Spanish text, first guess its general meaning, but then, consciously focus on the verb forms that you encounter. Ask yourself: What is / was that ending? Preterite? Conditional? *¡Muy bien!*

2. <u>Don't be a perfectionist.</u> Once you feel comfortable recognizing the endings, start paying attention to your own correct usage, but don't worry too much if you make mistakes. We all do . . . Do you remember how Tarzan spoke? He didn't conjugate any verbs! (And Jane didn't mind . . .) Even if you sound like him in the beginning, that's okay. More often than not, people will understand you just fine.

Take a Tip from Me!

Did You Know?

Soccer is serious business in Argentina. The Argentinean players are among the best in the world, and the national team has won the world championship twice, in 1978 and 1986. The two most famous teams in the national league are River Plate and Boca Juniors. (Yep, just like that, in English.) When these two teams play against each other, the whole country watches.

Did You Know?

HEAR . . . SAY 1

Peter ha llegado a Buenos Aires. Ahora está en su redacción, hablando con su jefa en Argentina.

Peter:	¿Y cuándo será el concierto?
María Jesús:	Ricky cantará el día martes cuatro en el Luna Park y también saldrá en la televisión en el programa de Susana Jiménez el viernes siete. Tendrás que hacer un reportaje sobre esa entrevista también.
Peter:	Me parece una buena idea.
Voz:	¡¡¡Gooool!!! ¡Qué golazo!
María Jesús:	También tendrás que viajar a Bariloche.
Peter:	Ese es un sitio muy turístico, ¿no? ¿Y allí que haré?
Voz:	¡Penal, penal! ¡Eso fue un penal!
María Jesús:	Ricky irá allá la semana próxima para descansar. Probablemente navegará, buceará, nadará, tomará el sol, ya sabes. Queremos incluir también esa información en tu reportaje.
Voz:	¿Pero, estará ciego ese referí? ¡Será pelotudo!
Peter:	¿Quién grita?
María Jesús:	Oh, ese es José María. Es un hincha del River. No se pierde un partido.
Peter:	¿El River? ¿Un río?
María Jesús:	No, hombre, no. El River Plate es un equipo de fútbol, el deporte nacional.
Peter:	¿Y está viendo un partido en la oficina?
María Jesús:	Normalmente ve los partidos en el estadio Monumental, pero hoy no pudo ir. Es un buen tipo, muy trabajador. Este . . . pero el fútbol lo vuelve completamente loco.
Peter:	María Jesús, eres una jefa muy comprensiva.
María Jesús:	No, che, esto es la Argentina. ¡Acá no podemos vivir sin el fútbol!

These are the notes Peter took while he spoke with María Jesús, but some information is missing. Can you fill in the blanks? Look for the missing words in the dialogue.

Ricky cantará el día ____ cuatro. Saldrá en la televisión el ____ siete. También viajará a Bariloche la semana ____ para descansar. Los argentinos son muy simpáticos y les gusta mucho el fútbol. He conocido a un hombre que se llama José María. Es un ____ de un equipo que se llama el River Plate. Normalmente ve los partidos en el ____ Monumental pero hoy está viendo el partido en la ____.

Did You Know?

The name of the guy Peter met at the office is José María (Joseph Mary). Mary?? A guy's name? Yep. And Peter's boss's name is María Jesús, so while she is a woman, part of her name is Jesús. In the Spanish-speaking world, there are no real middle names, as in the United States. Some people have two first names, which are used together. The first one always determines the sex of the person—José María is one example, and the name works as a block, so it does not matter that the second part is a female name. For women, any compound name with María is very common: María Luisa, María Teresa, María Isabel, etc. I bet you know someone named María, too!

WORKSHOP 1

THE NITTY-GRITTY

WHAT WILL TOMORROW BRING?: USING THE FUTURE TENSE

In English, the future tense is expressed with *will* followed by a verb. In Spanish, the verb is formed, as usual, with a special set of endings. The future tense in Spanish is as easy to learn as the conditional because it, too, attaches the endings to the infinitive form of the verb.

For example:

Iré a Bariloche.   I will go to Bariloche.

Tomaré el sol en la playa.   I will lay out in the sun at the beach.

As with the conditional, all the regular verbs take the same set of future tense endings. Learn the forms of the verb *trabajar*, and apply them to all other verbs.

THE FUTURE TENSE OF REGULAR VERBS			
		TRABAJAR (TO WORK)	
Singular	*yo*	*trabajar + é*	I will work
	tú	*trabajar + ás*	you will work
	él / ella, usted	*trabajar + á*	he / she, you (formal) will work
Plural	*nosotros / nosotras*	*trabajar + emos*	we will work
	vosotros / vosotras	*trabajar + éis*	you will work
	ellos / ellas, ustedes	*trabajar + án*	they, you (formal) will work

Of course, there are verbs that have irregular stems but, luckily, they are the same as those you saw for the conditional. Let's review them:

VERB		IRREGULAR STEM
decir (to say)	→	**dir–**
haber (to have)	→	**habr–**
hacer (to do)	→	**har–**
poder (to be able to)	→	**podr–**
poner (to put)	→	**pondr–**
querer (to want / love)	→	**querr–**
saber (to know)	→	**sabr–**
salir (to go out)	→	**saldr–**
tener (to have)	→	**tendr–**
venir (to come)	→	**vendr–**

For example:

Sabrás español pronto.	You will speak / know Spanish soon.
Saldremos esta noche.	We will go out tonight.
No tendrás que estudiar mucho.	You will not have to study much.

In Spanish, the future tense is also used to express probability and doubt about an action in the present:

¿Dónde estará Peter ahora?	I wonder where Peter is.

Do you want to know your future? What about "choosing" it? Here are some things that could happen to anyone. Choose those that you would like to happen to you (If it only were so easy!), but, be careful, there are some horrendous ones, as well. (You can check the translations in the Crib Notes section, to make sure you do choose a rosy future for yourself!)

1. Hablarás español perfectamente.
2. Tendrás quince hijos.
3. Nunca irás a la Argentina.
4. Perderás mucho dinero en Wall Street.
5. Serás millonario / a.
6. No tendrás tiempo para nada.
7. Verás un huracán.

Heads Up!

You have just learned that the future tense is also used to express probability, but that was also one of the functions of the conditional. Confused? Don't be! The future tense is used to express probability in the present, while the conditional is used for probability in the past. (Now you're thinking: What is she talking about? I read minds.) Look at these examples for clarification:

Probability in the present (use future tense)

¿Dónde irá? I wonder where she's going.

Probability in the past (use conditional)

¿Dónde iría? I wonder where she went.

These forms, used in everyday language, also express a certain level of exasperation on the part of the speaker, so translations such as "Where the heck is she going?" or "Where the heck did she go?" would also be appropriate.

Heads Up!

Did You Know?

Buenos Aires has a reputation as a city with a large number of psychoanalysts. Argentineans are believed to be "crazy" about this very popular type of therapy. Thus, often, when someone wants to make fun of a Spanish-speaking psychoanalyst, almost inevitably, they will fake an Argentinean accent.

Did You Know?

THERE'S NO SPORT LIKE SOCCER: CHATTING ABOUT SPORTS, ESPECIALLY SOCCER

el deporte	sport
el equipo	team
el fútbol	soccer
el gol	goal
el hincha	sports fan. Notice that although the word ends in "a", it is not feminine, but rather invariable—**el hincha**, masculine; **la hincha**, feminine.
el partido	the match (for any sport)
el penal	a type of foul deserving a penalty (only used in Argentina). In other Spanish-speaking countries, they say **el penalti**.
el referí	referee (only in Argentina). In most other countries, **el árbitro** is used.
bucear	to scuba dive
nadar	to swim
navegar	to sail

And if you're a couch potato:

salir en la televisión	to be on TV
¿Qué sale esta noche en la tele?	What's on TV tonight?

The Fine Print

–azo	Add this ending to nouns to make them sound large or impressive:
gol	goal
golazo	great goal

Word on the Street

If you want to sound like an Argentinean:

pelotudo	jerk (more or less). Friends can say it to each other, but if somebody you don't like says it to you, you've just been insulted!
che	like "you" in "Hey, you!" (very colloquial)
este . . .	Used in Argentina in the middle of a sentence to gain time, with no real meaning, similar to English "umm."

Did You Know?

Buenos Aires, Argentina's capital, has more than 3 million inhabitants. It was modeled after Paris, Madrid, and London, so it looks and feels like a European capital. It has a very famous avenue, la Avenida de Mayo, which is said to be one of the widest streets in the world.

Did You Know?

HEAR . . . SAY 2

Peter aún está en la oficina. María Jesús le presenta a José María en el intermedio del partido.

María Jesús: Mira José María, éste es Peter Winthrop. Hará un reportaje sobre la visita a la Argentina de Ricky Martin.

José María: Encantado, Peter.

Peter: Mucho gusto. Oye, José María, parece que para ti el fútbol es muy importante, ¿no? ¿Por qué no eres reportero deportivo?

José María: El fútbol es mi pasión, no mi trabajo.

Peter: ¡Pero si estás viendo el partido en la oficina!

José María: Es que para mí, el fútbol es lo primero en importancia en mi vida; la Selección Argentina es lo segundo, lo tercero, el River y el trabajo, el laburo, será, como mucho, cuarto o quinto.

Peter: Ya veo. ¿Y la familia? ¿El amor? ¿Tampoco son importantes para ti?

José María: Hombre, claro. Mis viejitos son mucho para mí . . . pero, este . . . nada se compara a un gol de mi equipo. Oye, María Jesús, este pibe no entiende, ¿no?

María Jesús: No es su culpa. Es gringo y a ellos nos les gusta darle a la pelota con los pies. Y sabes, Peter, José María incluso viajó a Corea en el año 2002, aunque turo que vender hasta la camisa para obtener plata para el viaje.

Peter: ¿Qué pasó en Corea?

José María: ¡Pero, qué ignorancia! Pues, los mundiales de fútbol. Yo quise verlo con mis propios ojos.

María Jesús: Y si no va, sufriremos todos en la oficina, porque tendremos el mundial hasta en la sopa. Aunque seguro que nadie se perderá un partido. Un mundial es un mundial.

Peter: ¿Y cada cuántos años hay un mundial?

María Jesús: Cada cuatro años solamente, gracias a Dios, o si no, nadie trabajaría en este país.

Let's see if you understood the important stuff:

1. ¿Qué hará Peter en Argentina?
2. ¿Por qué no quiere José María ser reportero deportivo?
3. ¿Qué es muy importante para José María?
4. ¿Qué pasó en Corea en el año 2002?
5. ¿Cada cuántos años hay un mundial de fútbol?

WORKSHOP 2

THE NITTY-GRITTY

EACH AND EVERY TIME: SAYING *EACH* AND *EVERY* IN SPANISH

Were you in Korea for the *Mundial de fútbol*? Well, if you've missed this one, you now know that the soccer World Cup takes place *cada cuatro años*, or every four years, so you can plan for the next one.

Anyway, once in a while, you get a free ride (even) in Spanish, and now that you know how to say *every* using *cada*, you also know how to say *each*, because Spanish uses the same word for the latter, as well. Look at the examples:

cada uno	each one
cada año	every year

GET WITH IT: USING PRONOUNS AFTER PREPOSITIONS—*WITH HIM, ON IT,* ETC.

After a preposition like *para* (for), *por* (through), *en* (in), etc., you use the already famil-iar subject pronouns (*él / ella, usted, nosotros / nosotras, vosotros / vosotras, ellos / ellas, ust-edes*). Only *mí* (me) and *ti* (you) are new.

PREPOSITIONAL PRONOUNS	
mí	me
ti	you (singular)
él / ella	him / her
usted	you (formal, singular)
nosotros / nosotras	us
vosotros / vosotras	you (plural)
ellos / ellas	them
ustedes	you (formal, plural)

With the preposition *con* (with), there are two special forms: *conmigo* (with me) and *contigo* (with you).

Take a look at these examples:

Para mí, el fútbol es muy importante.

Soccer is very important to me.

Vendrás a Corea conmigo.

You will come to Korea with me.

Heads Up!

To differentiate between *me* and *my* in Spanish you have to remember to write the accent mark:

my house	→	*mi casa*
for me	→	*para mí*

WORDS TO LIVE BY

FIRST THINGS FIRST: ORDINAL NUMBERS

First, second, third, etc., in English are ordinal numbers. Here they are in Spanish from *first* to *tenth*. Now you can get your priorities straight.

primero / a	first
segundo / a	second
tercero / a	third
cuarto / a	fourth
quinto / a	fifth
sexto / a	sixth
séptimo / a	seventh
octavo / a	eighth
noveno / a	ninth
décimo / a	tenth

Note that these words, like other adjectives, have masculine and feminine forms, and must match the noun they modify.

Primero and *tercero* have an abbreviated masculine form that is used when they precede a noun, as in *mi primer amor* (my first love) and *El Tercer Mundo* (The Third World).

Let's do a little personality test. Put the following activities in order according to your own taste. (Let's see if you are any different from José María!)

1. primero   a. amor
2. segundo   b. dinero
3. tercero   c. trabajo
4. cuarto   d. familia
5. quinto   e. deportes
6. sexto   f. salud
7. séptimo   g. amigos

Word on the Street

Here are a couple of funny expressions with **hasta** (until; even):

hasta en la sopa	everywhere, all the time (Lit. even in the soup)
vender hasta la camisa	Similar to "It will cost you an arm and a leg."
	(Lit. "to sell even the shirt," meaning something is going to cost you so much, the bank is going to take from you everything you own, including the shirt on your back.)

And here are more words that will make you sound Argentinean:

la plata	money (slang). Also used in other Latin American countries. (Lit. silver)
pibe	kid, friend, pal (Argentinean slang)

LET'S PUT IT IN WRITING

Here is the sign posted outside the stadium for the team River Plate:

Información sobre venta anticipada de entradas para
el partido entre las selecciones de Argentina y Paraguay válido por la
7a fecha de la competición preliminar del XVII Copa del Mundo
de la FIFA Corea-Japón 2002

ESTADIO DEL CLUB A. RIVER PLATE
16/08/2000 21.00 HS
PRECIO DE LAS LOCALIDADES

PLATEAS LATERALES MEDIAS EN TRIBUNAS	$60	ENTRADA GENERAL INCLUIDA
San Martín y Belgrano		
Plateas laterales bajas en tribunas	$50	ENTRADA GENERAL INCLUIDA
San Martín y Belgrano		
Plateas laterales altas en tribunas	$35	ENTRADA GENERAL INCLUIDA
San Martín y Belgrano		
Plateas Cabeceras medias en tribuna alte.	$25	ENTRADA GENERAL INCLUIDA
Brown y Centenario		
Plateas cabeceras bajas en tribunas alte.	$20	ENTRADA GENERAL INCLUIDA
ENTRADA GENERAL	$10	
Entrada popular menor (hasta 11 años)	$5	

LAS LOCALIDADES DE PLATEA SE PONDRÁN A LA VENTA
A PARTIR DEL DÍA 09.08.00, EN
EL HORARIO DE 11.00 A 19.00 HORAS, EN LOS SIGUIENTES LUGARES:

ESTADIO DEL CLUB **A. River Plate**
ESTADIO DEL CLUB **A. Vélez Sarsfield**
ESTADIO **Luna Park**

Menores a partir de 3 años abonan PLATEA

Miércoles: (Día del partido)
La venta de PLATEAS exclusivamente en el
Luna Park de 10 a 20 hs.

ENTRADA GENERAL

LA VENTA DE ESTAS LOCALIDADES (ASIENTOS SIN NUMERAR EN TRIBUNAS ALTE.
BROWN Y CENTENARIO ALTAS) COMENZARÁ EL DÍA 11.08.00,
DE 10.00 A 20.00 HORAS, SOLAMENTE EN LOS SIGUIENTES LUGARES:
ESTADIO DEL CLUB **A. River Plate**
ESTADIO DEL CLUB **A. Vélez Sarsfield**

Los sectores para PARAGUAY, en RIVER Y VÉLEZ exclusivamente,
a partir del viernes 11/08 de 10 a 20 hs.

ACTIVITY 6: TAKE IT FOR A SPIN

Scan the text of the sign posted outside the stadium and find all the verbs that are in the future tense. Remember that you don't need to understand every word in order to do this. You are just looking for words that look like verbs, and then you check their endings.

ACTIVITY 7: TAKE IT UP A NOTCH

Take a look at the following scoreboard for the South American soccer teams that participate in the World Cup. Try to make sense of it. Let's see if you can answer these questions. I'll give you some help:

ganar	win
perder	lose
fuera	out

TABLA DE POSICIONES

Equipos	Jugados	Ganados	Empatados	Perdidos	Goles fuera: Goles casa	Puntos
Argentina	10	8	1	1	32:8	25
Brasil	10	6	2	2	21:9	20
Paraguay	10	6	2	2	18:9	20
Ecuador	10	5	1	4	12:14	16
Uruguay	10	4	3	3	12:7	15
Colombia	10	4	3	3	8:7	15

TABLA DE POSICIONES						
Equipos	Jugados	Ganados	Empatados	Perdidos	Goles fuera: Goles casa	Puntos
Chile	10	3	1	6	12:12	10
Bolivia	10	2	3	5	5:13	9
Perú	10	2	2	6	7:13	8
Venezuela	10	1	0	9	6:28	3

1. Which country has the most points?
2. Which has the least?
3. How many goals has Bolivia scored in a home game?
4. How many games has Chile tied?
5. Tell me, in Spanish, in which order are Paraguay, Uruguay, and Perú. (Example: *Brasil es segundo.*)

CRIB NOTES

HEAR...SAY 1

Peter has arrived in Buenos Aires. Now he is in his office, talking to his boss in Argentina.

Peter: And when will the concert take place?

María Jesús: Ricky will sing on Tuesday, the fourth, in the Luna Park Stadium, and he'll be on TV, on the Susana Jiménez show on Friday, the seventh. You'll have to write an article about that interview as well.

Peter: That sounds like a good idea.

Voice: Goal!! What a goal!!!

María Jesús: You will also have to travel to Bariloche.

Peter: That's a very touristy place, isn't it? What will I do there?

Voice: Penalty kick! That was a foul!

María Jesús: Ricky will also go there next week to rest. He will probably sail, dive, swim, lay out in the sun, you know, the usual. We want to include that information in your article, too.

Voice: But, what the heck is the matter with the referee! Is he blind? What an idiot!

Peter: Who's screaming?

María Jesús: Oh, that's José María. He is a fan of the River. He never misses a game.

Peter: The River? A river?

María Jesús: No, of course not. The River Plate is a soccer team. You know, soccer, our national sport.

Peter: And he's watching a game at work?

María Jesús: He usually goes to see the games in Monumental stadium, but today he couldn't go. He is a good guy, very hard working. But . . . but he's really crazy about soccer.

Peter: María Jesús, you are quite an understanding boss.

María Jesús: No, Peter, this is Argentina. Here we cannot live without soccer!

Peter is still in the office. María Jesús introduces him to José María during the game's halftime.

María Jesús: Hey, José María, this is Peter Winthrop. He will be doing an article about Ricky Martin's visit to Argentina.

José María: Nice to meet you, Peter.

Peter: Nice to meet you, too. Listen José María, it seems that soccer is really important to you, isn't it? Why don't you become a sports reporter?

José María: Soccer is my passion, not my job.

Peter: But you are watching a game right here in the office!

José María: Because for me, soccer is the most important thing in my life, the Argentinean National Team is the second, the third is the River, and work is only, at most, the fourth or fifth.

Peter: I see. And what about family? Love? Are they not important to you?

José María: Of course they are. My folks mean a lot to me but . . . nothing compares to seeing my team score. (Turning to María Jesús) Hey, María Jesús, this guy doesn't get it, does he?

María Jesús: It's not his fault. He is a *gringo* and they don't particularly like to kick a ball with their feet. And you know, Peter, José María even traveled to Korea in 2002, although he had to spend every last dime in order to go.

Peter: What happened in Korea in 2002?

José María: My goodness! What ignorance! We are talking about the soccer World Cup. I want to see it with my own eyes.

María Jesús: And if he doesn't go, we will all suffer here in the office, because it will be the Cup 24 hours a day. Although, the truth is, I am sure no one is really going to miss a thing. The World Cup is something quite special.

Peter: And how often does the World Cup happen?

María Jesús: Only every four years, thank God, or no one would ever do a thing in this country!

ANSWER KEY

ACTIVITY 1

1. f; 2. d; 3. a; 4. c; 5. g: 6. h; 7. b; 8. e

ACTIVITY 2

1. martes; 2. viernes; 3. próxima; 4. hincha; 5. estadio; 6. oficina

ACTIVITY 3

1. You will speak Spanish perfectly.
2. You will have 15 kids.
3. You will never go to Argentina.
4. You will lose a lot of money on Wall Street.
5. You will be a millionaire.
6. You will not have time for anything.
7. You will see a hurricane.

ACTIVITY 4

1. Peter hará un reportaje.
2. Porque el deporte es su pasión, no su trabajo.
3. el fútbol
4. Los mundiales de fútbol fueron en Corea.
5. cada cuatro años

ACTIVITY 5

Here are the translations:
a. love; b. money; c. work; d. family; e. sports; f. health; g. friends (I hope you didn't choose *deportes* as *primero*! Hey, if you did, that's great too!)

ACTIVITY 6

se pondrán; comenzarán; se venderán; retirarán; tendrán

ACTIVITY 7

1. Argentina
2. Venezuela
3. Thirteen
4. One
5. Paraguay es tercero; Uruguay es quinto; Perú es noveno.

Do you have your famous "devil's lamb" today?

COMING UP. . .

- *What's on the menu?:* **Learn some important food vocabulary**
- *Talk about fun:* **Some vocabulary for a great evening**
- *Listen!:* **Giving orders**
- *Give it to me!:* **Commands including pronouns**
- *I want you to do it!:* **Saying what you want using *querer* (to want)**

As it turns out, José María is a nice guy, and he has invited Peter out for a night on the town. He wants to give him a taste of Buenos Aires's nightlife, including *la cena* (dinner), *un espectáculo de tango* (a tango show), and *una discoteca* (you don't need me for that one!). There is nothing more Argentinean than grilled meat, so Peter will learn everything there is to know about *vaca* (beef), *cerdo* (pork), *cordero* (lamb), and *pollo* (chicken), before listening to some tango and trying to shake his *cuerpo* (body) at the city's hot club, La Morocha.

Did You Know?

Porteño is the word used to name an inhabitant of Buenos Aires. It comes from the word **puerto** (harbor), because most of the city's original dwellers were immigrants who came by boat from Europe and settled in the city's port area, La Boca.

Did You Know?

ACTIVITY 1:   LET'S WARM UP

Would you say these sentences to a waiter? Read them and decide which ones sound like they could be used in a restaurant. (You can check their translations in the Crib Notes section to make sure you don't sound crazy, as well as like a foreigner!):

1. Quiero pollo frito.
2. Me gustaría tomar un café con leche.
3. ¿Podría traerme un libro con salsa?
4. Quisiera cordero con carros.
5. ¿Tienen semanas con cerdo?

Take a Tip from Me!

Today I'm going to throw a suggestion your way that might make you look strange in front of other people, so do this when you're alone! Stand in front of a mirror and start saying what you already know in Spanish, pronouncing everything very clearly. Do this every day, starting just with *¡Hola! Me llamo _____*, and adding a few more sentences every day. You could pretend you are a Latino TV personality, for example. This exercise sounds silly, but it will give you confidence and prepare you for the time when you will speak with real people.

Take a Tip from Me!

José María invita a Peter a salir por la noche para descubrir una auténtica noche porteña. Primero, van a cenar a un restaurante típico, en una parrilla (*a restaurant that serves grilled meat*).

Peter: Oye, José María, gracias por invitarme a salir. Buenos Aires es una ciudad fascinante.

José María: Así es. Bueno, aquí estamos, en El Palacio de la Papa Frita. Aquí tienen un asado magnífico. (*He calls the waiter.*) ¡Mesero! Por favor, tráiganos un menú. ¿Tienen hoy su famoso "cordero del diablo"? ¿No? Bueno, entonces traiga un lomito.

Peter: ¿Lomito? ¿Eso es carne de res?

José María: Sí, exacto. Aquí lo hacen buenísimo. También ponga una brocheta de bife como aperitivo.

Peter: ¿Bife? ¿Cómo? ¿En inglés?

José María: Sí, eso es. Viene del inglés *beef*. (*to the waiter*) Y también añada un poco de cerdo asado.

Peter: Pero es que yo no . . .

José María: ¡No me digas que no te gusta el cerdo, Peter! Bueno. Aquí tienen un pollo muy rico. ¡Mesero! Quite ese cerdo y escriba pollo.

Peter: No. Es que el pollo . . .

José María: ¿Tampoco sos amigo del pollo? Peter, vos sos complicado, che. ¡Mesero! Denos cordero entonces.

Peter: (*his voice raised*) ¡José María! ¡No me dejas decir nada! ¡Déjame hablar!

José María: ¿Pero qué es este alboroto, Peter? Habla, habla.

Peter: José María, soy vegetariano! No como cerdo, vaca, cordero, ni siquiera pollo. El restaurante se llama El Palacio de la Papa Frita, ¿no?. Pues,¡ yo quiero papas fritas!

ACTIVITY 2:   HOW'S THAT AGAIN?

Did you get all that? Let's review:

1. ¿Cómo se llama el restaurante donde están comiendo?
2. ¿Tienen "cordero del diablo"?
3. ¿Qué quiere José María como aperitivo?
4. ¿A Peter le gusta el cerdo?
5. ¿Qué quiere comer Peter?

WORKSHOP 1

THE NITTY-GRITTY

LISTEN!: GIVING ORDERS

We use commands to give direct orders and instructions to others. In Spanish, commands are divided into formal and informal ones (each corresponding to the use of *usted* and *tú* forms).

To form formal commands, you have to follow these steps:

1. Start with the **yo** form of the present tense:

trabajar	→	*yo trabajo*
tener	→	*yo tengo*
vuelvo	→	*yo vuelvo*

2. Drop the "o":

trabajo	→	*trabaj–*
tengo	→	*teng–*
volver	→	*vuelv–*

3. Add these endings:

    –e or *–en* for *–ar* verbs

    –a or *–an* for *–er* and *–ir* verbs

Here are examples using the verbs *esperar* (wait) and *comer* (eat):

FORMAL COMMANDS WITH *USTED* AND *USTEDES*				
GIVING ORDERS TO	*ESPERAR* (TO HOPE)		*COMER* (TO EAT)	
usted	espere	Wait!	coma	Eat!
ustedes	esperen	Wait!	coman	Eat!

Of course, as usual, there are some irregular verbs:

saber	(to know)	→	**sepa, sepan**
ser	(to be)	→	**sea, sean**
ir	(to go)	→	**vaya, vayan**
dar	(to give)	→	**dé, den**
estar	(to be)	→	**esté, estén**

Informal commands (corresponding to the use of *tú*), take different endings depending on whether the command is positive or negative. For example:

¡Espera aquí!

Wait here!

¡No esperes aquí!

Don't wait here!

1. To form the positive informal commands, you start with the *él* form of the present. For example:

hablar	→	**él habla**
comer	→	**él come**

2. To form the negative informal commands, just follow the rules for formal commands that I gave earlier, except in step three; add these endings instead:

    –es for *–ar* verbs

    –as for *–er* and *–ir* verbs

You can see all this summarized in this chart:

INFORMAL COMMANDS WITH *TÚ*				
	ESPERAR		*COMER*	
Positive command	*espera*	Wait!	*come*	Eat!
Negative command	*no esperes*	Don't wait!	*no comas*	Don't eat!

Here you have some irregular *tú* commands for some of the more common irregular verbs. The forms in bold do not follow the previously outlined rules.

IRREGULAR COMMANDS WITH *TÚ*			
	POSITIVE COMMANDS	NEGATIVE COMMANDS	
decir	**di**	*no digas*	Say! / Don't say!
hacer	**haz**	*no hagas*	Do! / Don't do!
poner	**pon**	*no pongas*	Put! / Don't put!
salir	**sal**	*no salgas*	Go out! / Don't go out!
tener	**ten**	*no tengas*	Have! / Don't have!
venir	**ven**	*no vengas*	Come! / Don't come!
ir	**ve**	*no vayas*	Go! / Don't go!
ser	**sé**	*no seas*	Be! / Don't be!
saber	*sabe*	*no sepas*	Know! / Don't know!
dar	*da*	*no des*	Give! / Don't give!
estar	*está*	*no estés*	Be! / Don't be!

ACTIVITY 3: TAKE IT FOR A SPIN

Imagine that you and a friend are organizing a surprise birthday party, but you are the one with the ideas (of course!) and you have to tell your friend what to do. Look at the example and use informal positive commands:

Ve al supermercado.
Go to the supermarket.

1.	(comprar)	→	_____ champán.
2.	(traer)	→	_____ aperitivos.
3.	(poner)	→	_____ las cosas en la cocina (kitchen).
4.	(hacer)	→	_____ invitaciones para la fiesta.
5.	(decir)	→	_____: ¡Sorpresa!

How would you tell your friend **not** to do those things? Change the commands into their negative form as in the example:

No vayas al supermercado.   Don't go to the supermarket.

GIVE IT TO ME!: COMMANDS INCLUDING PRONOUNS

Look at these commands:

¡Espére_me_!

Wait for me!

¡No _me_ espere!

Don't wait for me!

Do you notice the difference? Pronouns such as *me*, *te*, *le*, *nos*, *os*, and *les* are attached to the end of a positive command. However, the pronouns are placed before the command if it is negative. Here are some more examples, some of which you heard in Hear . . . Say 1.

Traíga_nos_ un menú.

Bring us a menu.

No _nos_ traiga un menú.

Don't bring us a menu.

Di_me_.

Tell me.

¡No _me_ digas!

Don't tell me!

De_nos_ cordero.

Give us lamb.

No _nos_ dé cordero.

Don't give us lamb.

The Fine Print

You may have noticed that in Hear . . . Say 1, José María uses a verbal form and a pronoun that you haven't studied before:

<u>Vos sos complicado.</u>   You are complicated.

Vos means "you" and it is equivalent to *tú* in Argentinian Spanish. It is used in certain regions of South America, mainly in the South Cone. The pronoun also goes with older (archaic) verbal forms: *sos* instead of *eres* or *tenés* instead of *tienes*. You don't really need to study this, but it's useful to be familiar with these forms so you're ready for your trip to Argentina!

WHAT'S ON THE MENU?: LEARN SOME IMPORTANT FOOD VOCABULARY

What type of meat would you like?

el bife / la carne de res	beef (**bife** is used only in Argentina)
el cordero	lamb
el cerdo	pork; also, pig
el pollo	chicken (meat and the animal)

And how would you like it cooked?

asado / a	roasted
frito / a	fried
a la parrilla	grilled
en brocheta	shish kebab style
lomito	A cut of beef similar to filet mignon, often served thinly sliced in a sandwich.

What else would you like?

el aperitivo	appetizer
la papa	potato (in Spain, it is called **la patata**)
la ensalada	salad
las verduras	vegetables

ACTIVITY 4:   **TAKE IT FOR A SPIN**

Imagine you are at a restaurant. How do you order these things?

Mesero, yo quisiera . . .

1. appetizers
2. lamb shish kebab
3. roasted pork
4. french fries
5. coffee

Word on the Street

And remember how you tell someone to enjoy their meal? It is customary to say, *¡Qué aproveche!* or *¡Buen provecho!* before a meal, or if somebody else is eating. Don't forget to say it!

Después de la cena, José María lleva a Peter a ver un espectáculo de tango. Allí hablan sobre la noche.

Peter: ¡Qué sitio tan elegante! ¡La música es maravillosa! Gracias por decirme que venga aquí.

José María: De nada, che. Después de mi fracaso con la cena, quiero que veas algo sublime, y así es nuestro tango.

Peter: Gracias otra vez. Espero no dormirme. ¡Es tan tarde!

José María: ¡Ni hablar, Peter! ¡La noche es joven! Son sólo las doce de la noche. Y quiero que vivas una auténtica noche porteña. Después de aquí quiero que vayamos a La Morocha, una discoteca de moda.

Peter: Bueno, pediré un café. ¡Por favor, mesero! Tráigame un café bien fuerte.

José María: ¿Necesitas que te den un café? ¡Peter, no sabes vivir!

Peter: No me acostumbro a salir tan tarde. En España y en Colombia es igual. Nada comienza hasta las diez.

José María: Pues es necesario que te acostumbres. ¡Esto es lo mejor del día, sin contar el fútbol, por supuesto!

(*After the tango show, they take a taxi to La Morocha.*)

José María: Es necesario que tomemos un taxi, porque el subte cierra a las diez de la noche. Aunque luego es posible que lo tomemos a las cinco de la mañana, cuando lo abran.

Peter: ¿El subte es el metro?

José María: Sí, Peter. Esto no es España. Es necesario que ya aprendas el argentino.

(*When they arrive, the club is closed.*)

Peter: ¿Y este es el sitio de moda tan importante que teníamos que ver?

José María: ¡Ay, se me olvidó! ¡Estamos en enero y están de vacaciones de verano en Uruguay!

ACTIVITY 5:   HOW'S THAT AGAIN?

Can you finish José María's sentences from the dialogue?

1. Quiero que veas ____ ____.
2. Quiero que vivas ____ ____ ____ ____.
3. Quiero que vayamos a ____ ____.
4. ¿Necesitas que te den ____ ____?
5. Es necesario que ya aprendas ____ ____.

Did You Know?

Tango is a musical genre that originated at the beginning of the twentieth century on the outskirts (the poor and somewhat questionable areas) of Buenos Aires. It is also one of the most sensual dances in the world. The main instrument in tango is the *bandoneón*, an instrument of German origin. During the roaring 1920's, tango was brought to the United States and Europe, where it became immensely popular. In the 1930's, Carlos Gardel took it to the height of its popularity and, more recently, Astor Piazzola has mixed it with classical and jazz music.

Did You Know?

Argentina is in the Southern Hemisphere, meaning that summer there starts in January and lasts through March. The owners of the club that Peter and José María wanted to visit, like other similar businesses, move their operations to Uruguay during the summer. Uruguay is a fashionable place for fancy vacations.

WORKSHOP 2

THE NITTY-GRITTY

I WANT YOU TO DO IT!: SAYING WHAT YOU WANT USING *QUERER* (TO WANT)

So far, you have studied the so-called indicative tenses, such as the present, the preterite, and the imperfect. Indicative is just a fancy word that means it is used to **indicate** or communicate objective information. Think of it as being based on reality. The subjunctive tenses, on the other hand, are not based in reality. Think of them as being **subject to** the speaker's wishes, attitudes, hopes, and other emotional reactions to events and actions of others. This verbal form tends to be difficult for English speakers to master because the English language has retained very little of the subjunctive tense. It appears only occasionally in modern use. Look at this example of a case still used:

It's necessary that he **be** on time.   Here **be** is in the subjunctive.

To form the present subjunctive, you follow the first two steps that you used to form commands:

1.   Start with the **yo** form of the present indicative:

trabajar   →   *yo trabajo*

tener   →   *yo tengo*

2. Drop the "o":

trabajo → **trabaj–**

tengo → **teng–**

3. Add the endings that you see in the following chart:

		TRABAJAR (TO WORK)	TENGO (TO EAT)
PRESENT SUBJUNCTIVE TENSE OF REGULAR VERBS			
Singular	yo	trabaj + e	teng + a
	tú	trabaj + es	teng + as
	él / ella, usted	trabaj + e	teng + a
Plural	nosotros / nosotras	trabaj + emos	teng + amos
	vosotros / vosotras	trabaj + éis	teng + áis
	ellos / ellas, ustedes	trabaj + en	teng + an

Here are the typical situations when you will need to use the subjunctive:

• When you want to express that you **want** or **need** somebody else to do something:

Quiero que veas algo sublime.

I want you to see something awsome.

Necesitas que te den un café.

You need them to give you a coffee.

Veas and ***den*** are in the present subjunctive form.

• When you use expressions like *es necesario* (it is necessary) or *es posible* (it is possible):

Es necesario que tomemos un taxi.

It is necessary that we take a taxi / We need to get a taxi.

Es posible que vaya a visitarte.

It is possible that she go visit you.

The subjunctive is used here because one cannot be completely certain that the actions will be carried out. The subjunctive expresses that doubt.

The Fine Print

TAKE IT FOR A SPIN

What do you think a parent would say to a kid when sending him or her off to college? Start the sentences with:

Quiero que . . .	I want you to . . .
Es necesario que . . .	It is necessary that you . . .

Finish the sentences by selecting logical endings:

1. . . . bebas mucha cerveza.
2. . . . estudies mucho.
3. . . . algas con tus amigos todas las noches.
4. . . . aprendas mucho.
5. . . . tomes clases muy fáciles.
6. . . . vayas a todas las fiestas.

Heads Up!

When creating sentences with *querer*, remember that if the person "wanting" is the same as the person "doing," then you do not use *que* + subjunctive, but just the infinitive form of the verb:

Quiero <u>viajar</u> a Londres.   I want to travel to London.

Quiero que Peter <u>viaje</u> a Londres.   I want Peter to travel to London.

In Sentence 1, *I* want and *I* travel. In Sentence 2, *I* want, but *Peter* travels.

Did You Know?

WORDS TO LIVE BY

TALK ABOUT FUN: SOME VOCABULARY FOR A GREAT EVENING

What things might you do when you go out? *Puedo . . .* (I may . . .):

ver un espectáculo	*see a show*
bailar en la discoteca de moda	*dance in a fashionable club*

tomar una copa en un sitio de moda	*have a drink at the fashionable place*
cenar en un resturante elegante	*have dinner in an elegant restaurant*

Don't forget that *to be late* in Spanish is *llegar tarde* (to arrive late), and you sure can arrive late to all these places. (Well . . . maybe not to the first one!)

Word on the Street

Let's review some of the words you have heard that are only used in Argentina:

el subte	subway. It comes from the word **subterráneo** (underground). **Metro** is used in Spain.
la parrilla	A restaurant that prepares grilled meats. In other Spanish-speaking countries, it just means "grill."
che	pal
el laburo	work. It comes from the Italian word **lavorare**. Because there is a large Italian community in Argentina, many words of Italian origin are used in Argentine Spanish.

LET'S PUT IT IN WRITING

Here is the section of the newspaper where José María found the information on the nightly *espectáculos de tango*.

Nombre del espectáculo	Lugar	Dirección	Género	Protagonistas
Alejandra Verziera	*Los Arcanos*	*J. Newberry 3902*	*Recital*	*Alejandra Verziera*
Magia de Tango	*Café Tortoni*	*Avenida de Mayo 829*	*Baile*	*Claudia Montes*
Una noche de Tango	*Teatro Alvear*	*Avenida Corrientes 1659*	*Canto, baile*	*Compañía Tango x 2*
Tango y Milonga	*Buenos Aires Del*	*Pasaje Giufra 40*	*Baile, canto*	*Carlos Lagos y Carla Gabriel*

Can you answer these questions based on this newspaper clipping?

1. ¿Dónde está el Teatro Alvear?
2. ¿Cómo se llama la cantante (*singer*) del espectáculo Magia de Tango?
3. ¿En qué número de la Avenida de Mayo está el Café Tortoni?
4. ¿Qué hacen los miembros de la Compañía Tango en su espectáculo?
5. ¿Qué espectáculo hay esta noche en Los Arcanos?

ACTIVITY 8:   **TAKE IT UP A NOTCH**

This exercise has two parts. Imagine I forgot all my Spanish, and I need you to help me say the following things. Can you translate the sentences for me?

1. I want you to study a lot.
2. It is necessary that you speak a lot.
3. I want you to read a lot.
4. I want you to write a lot.
5. It is necessary that you think in Spanish.

And now that I have told you this (with your help), I am going to tell you again, but this time, it's an order:

1. Study!
2. Speak!
3. Read!
4. Write!
5. Think in Spanish!

You can check the Crib Notes section to see if you can be bossy in Spanish as well!

And about the lesson title? Tell me: Who is Peter thinking about?

CRIB NOTES

HEAR...SAY 1

Jose María invites Peter to go out for a night on the town, to experience an authentic *porteña* night. First, they are going to have dinner at a typical restaurant serving grilled meat.

Peter: Hey, José María, thanks for inviting me out. Buenos Aires is a fascinating city.

José María: That's right. Well, here we are in The French Fry Palace. They have great grilled meat here. *(He calls the waiter.)* Waiter! Please, bring us a menu. Do you have your famous "devil's lamb" today? You don't? OK, then bring us some *lomito*.

Peter: *Lomito?* Is that beef?

José María: Yeah, that's right. They serve a wonderful *lomito* here. (To the waiter) Also, please bring us some beef shish kebab as an appetizer.

Peter: *Bife?* Just like in English?

José María: Yes, that's it. It comes from the English *beef*. *(to the waiter)* And, also, please bring some roasted pork.

Peter: But, I don't . . .

José María: Don't tell me that you don't like pork, Peter! Oh, well . . . .Here they also have a delicious chicken. Waiter! Cancel that pork and bring us chicken instead!

Peter: No, chicken is also . . .

José María: You don't like chicken either? Peter, you are a bit difficult, my friend. Waiter! Bring us lamb then!

Peter: *(his voice raised)* José María! You're not letting me say a word! Let me speak!

José María: But, what is all this fuss about, Peter? Speak, speak.

Peter: José María, I'm a vegetarian! I don't eat pork, beef, lamb, or even chicken. Isn't this restaurant called The French Fry Palace, isn't it? Well, I want french fries!

HEAR...SAY 2

After dinner, José María takes Peter to see a tango show. There, they talk about the evening.

Peter: What an elegant place! The music is great! Thanks for telling me to come here.

José María: You're welcome, my friend! After my fiasco at dinner, I want you to see something awesome, and that's what our tango is.

Peter: Thanks again. I hope I don't fall asleep. It's so late!

José María: Oh, come on, the night's still young! It's only midnight! And I want you to experience a real Buenos Aires night. After this place, I want us to go to La Morocha, a very hip club.

Peter: All right, then. I'll order a coffee. Please, waiter! Bring me a very strong coffee.

José María: You need them to bring you a coffee? Peter, you don't know how to live!

Peter: I can't get used to going out so late. It's the same in Spain and in Colombia. Nothing starts until ten.

José María: Well, you have to get used to it! This is the best part of the day, if we don't count soccer time, of course!

(After the tango show, they take a taxi to "La Morocha.")

José María: We need to grab a cab, because the subway closes at ten PM. Although it would be possible for us to take it at five AM, when they open.

Peter: *Subte* means subway?

José María: Yes, Peter. This is not Spain. It's about time you start speaking Argentinean.

(When they arrive, the club is closed.)

Peter: And this is the hip place that we absolutely had to see?

José María: Shucks! I forgot! It is January and they have all gone on summer vacation to Uruguay!

Answer Key

ACTIVITY 1

1. I want fried chicken.
2. I would like to have a coffee with milk.
3. Could you bring me a book with sauce?
4. I would like lamb with cars.
5. Do you have weeks with pork?

ACTIVITY 2

1. Se llama El Palacio de la Papa Frita.
2. No, no tienen "cordero del diablo".
3. Quiere una brocheta de bife.
4. No, a Peter no le gusta el cerdo.
5. Peter quiere comer papas fritas.

ACTIVITY 3

Positive commands:
1. compra; 2. trae; 3. pon; 4. haz; 5. di
Negative commands: 1. no compres; 2. no traigas;
3. no pongas; 4. no hagas; 5. no digas

ACTIVITY 4

1. aperitivos; 2. cordero en brocheta; 3. cerdo
asado; 4. papas fritas; 5. café

ACTIVITY 5

1. algo sublime; 2. una auténtica noche porteña; 3.
la Morocha; 4. un café; 5. el argentino

ACTIVITY 6

1. . . . that you drink a lot of beer.
2. . . . that you study a lot.
3. . . . that you go out with your friends every
   night.
4. . . . that you learn a lot.
5. . . . that you take very easy classes.
6. . . . that you go to every party.

ACTIVITY 7

1. Está en la Avenida Corrientes, Número 1659
   (mil seiscientos cincuenta y nueve).
2. Se llama Claudia Montes.
3. En el número 829 (ochocientos veintinueve).
4. Cantan y bailan.
5. Hay un recital.

ACTIVITY 8

Part 1
1. Quiero que estudies mucho.
2. Es necesario que hables mucho.
3. Quiero que leas mucho.
4. Quiero que escribas mucho.
5. Es necesario que pienses en español.
Part 2
1. ¡Estudia! 2. ¡Habla! 3. ¡Lee! 4. ¡Escribe! 5.
¡Piensa en español!

19.

I MISS YOU, I FORGET YOU, I LOVE YOU

Te extraño, te olvido, te amo

And did you tell him how very cold it is at night?

COMING UP. . .

- *Home sweet home:* **Rooms and things that make a home**
- *Same old, same old:* **Daily activities and paying the bills**
- *To whom it may concern:* **Using *who, that, which,* etc., to connect nouns and sentences**
- *The good, the bad, and . . . the best:* **Saying that something is the best or the worst**
- *Hold it for me, please:* **Putting different pronouns together**

Take a Tip from Me!

Congratulations! You only have two more lessons to go! I am so proud of you! The last two lessons take place in the United States. Surprised? Well, while that may seem a bit strange at first, I wanted to draw your attention to what's around you—plenty of Spanish language. Just look at the names of many places in the United States, check your TV listings, or listen to the radio. No matter where you live, I am sure you'll be able to find Spanish speakers. Get to know where the people around you come from! Or, get to know your own history! And remember, don't be afraid to speak, because practice makes perfect.

Did You Know?

. . . that the first European language that was spoken in the United States was Spanish? That's right. On September 5, 1565, Spaniard Pedro Menéndez de Avilés founded the first permanent European settlement in St. Augustine, Florida.

LOOKING AHEAD

Peter is back in New York City. He has just learned that his traveling will slow down for a while, so he decides to find an *apartamento*. With prices having skyrocketed, he's considering getting a *cuarto* (a room) in an apartment, which he will share with two other people. It happens that the two people living in the apartment he's looking at today are Spanish speakers: Alberto is from the República Dominicana, and Isabel is from Puerto Rico.

ACTIVITY 1:　LET'S WARM UP

What kinds of things do you find in a home? Here is a list of things that Peter needs and doesn't need. Can you try to guess what they mean? Look for the right answers in the Crib Notes section, before moving on to the dialogue.

NECESITO . . .
un cuarto
un dormitorio
una mesa y una silla para escribir
compañeros de casa
practicar español

NO NECESITO . . .
un apartamento completo
una cama (ya tengo un sofá-cama)
un gran escritorio (*desk*)
estar solo (*to be alone*)
hablar inglés

Peter visita un apartamento. Habla con Isabel sobre el cuarto que Isabel y Alberto alquilan.

Isabel: Y éste sería tu dormitorio. Es el más soleado de la casa. No tiene muebles, sólo esa mesa y esa silla que puedes usar si quieres.

Peter: Sí. Es una buena idea. Yo tengo un sofá-cama que puedo traer. Me gusta el cuarto y la casa. Y lo que más me gusta de todo es que hablan español. Así puedo practicar.

Isabel: Bueno, tú sabes, aquí en Nueva York a veces lo que es difícil es oír el inglés, sobre todo en este barrio. Aquí hay muchos boricuas como yo y también muchos dominicanos como Alberto.

Peter: ¿Boricua? Pensaba que tú eras de Puerto Rico.

Isabel: Pues eso es boricua. Es otro nombre para la gente de Puerto Rico.

Peter: Ya veo que voy a aprender mucho en esta casa. . . . Y ¿cuánto cuesta el cuarto al mes?

Isabel: Yo de eso no sé nada. Ahora con quién tienes que hablar es Alberto. Él sabe lo que cuesta el alquiler. Creo que va a llegar en un minutito. ¿Te importa esperarlo?

Peter: No, nada. Lo espero.

Isabel: ¿Quieres un café? ¿Una soda? Podemos beber algo en la cocina.

Peter: Bueno, gracias. Un café estaría bien, porque tengo un sueño. . . . Por favor, dame el café más oscuro de por aquí.

Isabel: Entonces, lo que quieres es un café bien cargado. No te preocupes, que ésa es la especialidad de la casa.

ACTIVITY 2: HOW'S THAT AGAIN?

Please answer the following questions:

1. ¿De dónde es Isabel?
2. ¿De dónde es Alberto?
3. ¿Qué tiene Peter?
4. ¿Cuánto cuesta el cuarto?
5. ¿Qué va a beber Peter?

Did You Know?

According to the latest census, around 35 million U.S. citizens (or more than 12 percent of the total population) are of Hispanic descent. That is an increase of more than 50 percent since 1990. While the Spanish-speaking people in this country come from many different areas of Latin America, there are three main groups: Mexicans (around 20 million), who mostly live in California and Texas; Puerto Ricans (around 3.5 million), living in New York, Chicago, and Philadelphia; and Cubans (more than 1 million), mostly concentrated in south Florida.

Did You Know?

Do you recognize these names? Antonio Banderas, Salma Hayek, Benicio del Toro, Andy Garcia, Jennifer Lopez, Christina Aguilera, and Ricky Martin. . . . I bet you know most of them. They are the new superstars of Hispanic descent currently making it big in the United States. But did you know that many of these stars were already famous in the Spanish-speaking world before they achieved fame here? And they are not the first ones. I'm sure you have also heard of Anthony Quinn, Rita Moreno, Martin Sheen, Raúl Juliá, and Edward James Olmos.

WORKSHOP 1

THE NITTY-GRITTY

***TO WHOM IT MAY CONCERN*: USING *WHO, THAT, WHICH*, ETC., TO CONNECT NOUNS AND SENTENCES**

Relative pronouns are used to join a noun (e.g., the man) with the phrase that describes it (e.g., the man *who is standing in the corner*). In English, the four main relative pronouns are *that*, *which*, *who*, and *whom*. Let me now tell you about the three most common relative pronouns in Spanish:

1. *que*

Que can mean "that," "which," or "who." It can refer to a person, place, or thing. Examples are:

> **La mujer _que_ habla con Peter se llama Isabel.**

The woman **who** is talking to Peter is named Isabel.

Peter tiene un sofá-cama _que_ puede traer.

Peter has a sofa bed **that** he can bring.

2. *quien(es)*

Quien(es) can mean "who" or "whom," and is used after a preposition to refer to a person or persons. Examples are:

La persona _con quien_ hablé es dominicana.

The person (whom) I talked to is Dominican. (*or* The person **with whom** I talked is Dominican.)

Alberto es _a quien_ le di el dinero.

Alberto is the person (whom) I gave the money to. (*or* Alberto is (the person) **to whom** I gave the money.)

Peter y Carmen son _a quienes_ quiero ver juntos.

Peter and Carmen are the ones (whom) I want to see together. (*or* Peter and Carmen are (those) **who** I want to see together.)

3. *lo que*

Lo que can mean "what" or "that which." It is used to refer to abstract ideas, situations, actions, or concepts. Examples are:

Es muy interesante _lo que_ dices.

What you are saying is very interesting.

Lo que más me gusta es practicar español.

What I like best is to practice Spanish.

ACTIVITY 3: **TAKE IT FOR A SPIN**

What do these people need or want? Answer using *lo que*. Example:

Peter / apartamento   →   Lo que Peter necesita es un apartamento.

1. Isabel y Alberto / compañero de casa (*roommate*)
2. Tú / practicar el español
3. Nosotros / hablar en un foro
4. Tus amigos / comprar este libro
5. Carmen / visitar los Estados Unidos

You must have noticed already that in English, a relative pronoun can be omitted:

The house (that) we saw . . .

But in Spanish, it is <u>always</u> used: *La casa que vimos . . .*

Heads Up!

The Fine Print

In colloquial English, people tend to end a sentence with a preposition, such as *with* or *to*:

He is the man I spoke with.

This is never the case in Spanish:

Él es el hombre con quien hablé.

The preposition always stays with the noun or pronoun it modifies.

THE GOOD, THE BAD, AND . . . THE BEST: SAYING THAT SOMETHING IS THE BEST OR THE WORST

To say that something is the best or the worst, we use a superlative form of an adjective: the tallest, highest, fastest, etc. In Spanish, this is expressed using the following formula:

definite article <u>(el / la / los / las)</u> + (noun) + <u>más / menos</u> + adjective + <u>de</u>

Look at the examples:

el más alto de la clase	the tallest in the class
la más guapa de todas	the prettiest of all
el café más fuerte de por aquí	the strongest coffee around
el cuarto más soleado de la casa	the sunniest room in the house

And there are some irregular superlatives:

el mejor	the best
el peor	the worst
el mayor	the oldest
el menor	the youngest

HOME SWEET HOME: ROOMS AND THINGS THAT MAKE A HOME

These are the rooms in a house:

el cuarto, la habitación, **la pieza** (in Colombia)	room
el dormitorio, la alcoba, **la recámara** (in México)	bedroom, from **dormir** (to sleep)
la sala, el living (in Argentina), **el cuarto de estar** (in Spain)	living room
la sala de baño, el baño, el aseo, **el cuarto de baño, el lavabo**	bathroom
el comedor	dining room, from **comer** (to eat)
la cocina	kitchen, from **cocinar** (to cook)

And here is the furniture that goes in those rooms:

el mueble	piece of furniture
la cama	bed
la mesa	table
la silla	chair
el sofá	sofa

The hundred-dollar question: What does *el sofá-cama* mean?

ACTIVITY 4:   **TAKE IT FOR A SPIN**

This is a floor plan of the apartment that Peter is thinking of moving into. Can you name the rooms in it?

289

Word on the Street

The word *boricua* means "of Puerto Rican origin." It is derived from Borinquen, the Amerindian name for the island, which was inhabited by the Taino Indians when Columbus landed on it in 1493. It is a word used with pride, as it reflects the pre-colonial history of the island.

HEAR . . . SAY 2

Alberto llega a casa y los tres hablan del cuarto que alquilan.

Isabel: Alberto, éste es Peter Winthrop. Quiere alquilar el cuarto.

Alberto: Encantado. ¿Y ya le dijiste que el precio es muy elevado?

Isabel: No se lo dije porque no lo sabía. ¿De qué hablas?

Alberto: Pues eso, en el precio no entra la electricidad, la calefacción, el agua . . .

Peter: Eso es importante saberlo.

Alberto: Isabel, ¿le dijiste que tenemos unos vecinos que hacen mucho ruido, que siempre hay bembé?

Isabel: No, no se lo dije. Yo creo que no está tan mal. Son músicos de jazz y a mí me gusta cuando practican.

Alberto: ¿Y le dijiste que hace muchísimo frío por las noches?

Isabel: No, no se lo dije. Eso es sólo en enero y febrero y tenemos muchas frazadas.

Alberto: ¿Y le dijiste que yo me levanto a las tres de la mañana y me ducho a las tres y media y hago mucho ruido y uso toda el agua caliente?

Isabel: ¡Alberto! No, no se lo dije, porque no es verdad. ¿Podría hablar contigo a solas un minutito? (*They go to another room to talk undisturbed.*) Pero, bendito . . . ¿Qué te pasa? ¿Quieres alquilar el cuarto o no?

Alberto: Sí, pero, no sé si ese Peter me gusta.

Isabel: Parece serio, responsable y además habla español. Tú sabes, a mí me parece bien chévere.

Alberto: Pero, ¿no sería mejor una mujer?

Isabel: ¿Una mujer? ¡Ay nene, lo que tú tienes es celos!

ACTIVITY 5: HOW'S THAT AGAIN?

Which of these statements does Alberto make to try to discourage Peter from renting the room?

290

SPANISH WITHOUT THE FUSS

1. El cuarto cuesta mucho dinero.
2. Los vecinos hacen mucho ruido.
3. No puede usar la cocina.
4. Alberto se despierta a las tres de la mañana.
5. No hay calefacción por las noches.

Did You Know?

You surely have heard the terms *Hispanic* and *Latino / a*. Both are used to describe Americans of Latin American origin. Is there a difference?

Hispanic comes from the Latin words *hispanicus* (Spanish) and *Hispania* (Iberian Peninsula, Spain). Its usage in the United States is probably derived from the Spanish word *hispano*, short for *hispanoamericano / a* (*Lit.* Spanish-American). It was initially used to refer to Spanish-speaking people of the southwestern United States who had settled there before the annexation, mostly Mexicans.

Nowadays, the term *Latino* is preferred by many Americans of Latin-American descent because it seems to include in its meaning the strong African and indigenous elements so important in Latin America. Of course, there are also those who think that the term *Latino* refers back to the Romans (who spoke Latin) and the Roman Empire, and thus, it is really not representative of Latin America.

The truth is that many Spanish speakers just prefer to say the country they (or their ancestors) come from: Puerto Rico, Cuba, Mexico, etc. *¿Y tú? ¿Qué piensas de esta controversia?*

Did You Know?

WORKSHOP 2

THE NITTY-GRITTY

HOLD IT FOR ME, PLEASE: PUTTING DIFFERENT PRONOUNS TOGETHER

Take a look at these sentences:

Peter te envía un mensaje electrónico.	→	*Peter **te lo** envía.*
Peter sends you an e-mail.		Peter sends it to you.
Carmen me da una sorpresa.	→	*Carmen **me la** da.*
Carmen surprises me. (*Lit.* Carmen gives me a surprise.)		Carmen gives it to me.

When you use both indirect (e.g., *me* "to me") and direct object (e.g., *lo* "him; it") pronouns together, the indirect object pronoun comes before the direct object pronoun, e.g. *te lo* or *me la* in the examples above. All such pronouns always come before the verb.

When the verb is in its *–ar / –er / –ir* form, the pronouns must follow the verb and attach to it. For example:

Carmen quiere dár<u>mela</u>.   Carmen wants to give it to me.

Peter quiere enviár<u>telo</u>.   Peter wants to send it to you.

Heads Up!

When the indirect object pronouns *le* (to him / her) or *les* (to them) are followed by the direct object pronouns *lo* (him) or *la* (to her), the pronouns *le* or *les* change in form and become *se* (probably to facilitate pronunciation). So, if we start with the following sentence:

Peter le envía un mensaje a Carmen.   Peter sends a message to Carmen.

We can replace *un mensaje* and *a Carmen* with pronouns, but it would be incorrect to say *Peter le lo envía*. *Le* must be changed to *se*:

Peter <u>se lo</u> envía.   Peter sends it to her.

In the dialogue, you heard Isabel repeat several times the following:

No se lo dije.   I didn't tell him that.

Now you know why it sounded strange!

Heads Up!

ACTIVITY 6:   TAKE IT FOR A SPIN

Change the sentences by replacing the object nouns with the corresponding pronouns!

Le di un libro a María.   →   Se lo di.

1. Peter le compró a Carmen unos zapatos.
2. Carmen me trajo unos libros.
3. Alberto le dijo a Isabel que no le gustaba Peter.
4. Isabel le dio a Peter un café.
5. Isabel y Alberto le compraron una silla a su amigo Esteban.

Remember that with positive commands, pronouns come *after* the verb (just like with the infinitives) and attach to them:

| **Dímelo.** | (Di + me + lo) | Tell me (it). |
| **Tráiganoslo.** | (Traiga + nos + lo) | Bring it to us. |

Note that this is not the case with negative commands.

Heads Up!

WORDS TO LIVE BY

SAME OLD, SAME OLD: DAILY ACTIVITIES AND PAYING THE BILLS

Of course, everyone has bills to pay—you need to *pagar tus gastos* (*Lit.* pay your expenses), such as:

el alquiler	rent
la electricidad	electricity
la calefacción	heating

Here a few daily activities:

ducharse	to take a shower
levantarse	to get up
despertarse	to wake up

Note that all these verbs are "reflexive" in Spanish, i.e., must be used with a reflexive pronoun [e.g., *me* (myself), *te* (yourself), *se* (himself / herself), etc.].

And finally, what your neighbors like to do (but not you) is:

| **hacer ruido** | to make noise |

ACTIVITY 7: TAKE IT FOR A SPIN

Imagine you need to rent a room, too. Make up questions to these answers:

1. Tú: _____
   Casero (landlord): El cuarto cuesta doscientos pesos al mes.
2. Tú: _____
   Casero: Sí, el precio incluye el agua, la calefacción y la electricidad.

3. Tú: _____
   Casero: No. Los vecinos no hacen mucho ruido.
4. Tú:_____
   Casero: En casa, nos levantamos a las ocho de la mañana.

Word on the Street

These are expressions typical of Caribbean Spanish, in particular, Puerto Rico:

el bendito	Lit. blessed. Here, it just means "you."
el bembé	a loud and happy party
el nene / la nena	Lit. child. Here, it's used similar to **man, pal, babe.**
chévere	great (used in Puerto Rico, but also in Venezuela and Colombia)

Did You Know?

Santo Domingo, the capital of the Dominican Republic, a country situated on the Caribbean island of Hispaniola, is the oldest permanent city established by the Europeans in the Americas. It was founded in 1496 by Bartolomeo Columbus, brother of Christopher Columbus.

LET'S PUT IT IN WRITING

While Peter is looking for an apartment, Carmen sends him this e-mail:

PARA: Peter Winthrop
ASUNTO: Visita a EE.UU.

Hola Peter:

¡No te lo vas a creer! Tengo una amiga que está estudiando en Nueva York y me ha invitado a visitarla a su casa (tiene un dormitorio extra). He encontrado un billete de avión super barato y voy a pasar allí la Semana Santa. ¿Tienes planes para entonces? Hasta pronto,

Carmen

HOW'S THAT AGAIN?

What did Carmen say? Let's see . . .

1. ¿Qué hace la amiga de Carmen en Nueva York?
2. ¿Dónde va a estar Carmen?
3. ¿Qué es super barato?
4. ¿Cuándo va a viajar Carmen a Nueva York?
5. ¿Qué le pregunta Carmen a Peter?

Did You Know?

Did you notice the acronym Carmen uses in her e-mail—EE.UU.? It stands for *Estados Unidos* (United States). Each of the initial letters is doubled to denote that the word the acronym stands for is in the plural form.

ACTIVITY 9: **TAKE IT UP A NOTCH**

Let's talk about the different activities around the house again. What do you do in each of these rooms?

1. En la cocina lo que hago es . . . (In the kitchen what I do is . . .)
2. En el comedor lo que hago es . . .
3. En el dormitorio lo que hago es . . .
4. En el baño lo que hago es . . .
5. En la sala lo que hago es . . .

And the lesson title? What is that about? Are we talking about Peter and Carmen or about Isabel and Alberto? I think it describes Peter:

Te extraño → Peter está en Colombia y en Argentina y piensa en Carmen.

Te olvido → Peter está en Nueva York, muy ocupado (busy) buscando apartamento.

Te amo → Peter recibe el fax.

Y tú, ¿qué piensas?

By the way, I'll let you in on a secret. All of the lesson titles in this book come from songs by none other than . . . Ricky Martin! Yes! Check your local music store. I bet you will recognize many of the titles on his albums!

HEAR...SAY 1

Peter is looking at an apartment. He is talking to Isabel about the room that Isabel and Alberto are renting out.

Isabel: And this would be your bedroom. It is the sunniest room in the house. It does not have any furniture, except for that table and that chair that you may use if you want to.

Peter: Sure. That's a good idea. I've got a sofabed that I can bring. I like the room and the apartment. And what I like the best is that you speak Spanish. That way I can practice.

Isabel: Well, you know, here in New York, sometimes, what is difficult is to hear English, especially in this neighborhood. There are a lot of Boricuas here, like myself, and Dominicans, like Alberto.

Peter: Boricua? I thought you were from Puerto Rico.

Isabel: That's what Boricua means. It's another name for Puerto Ricans.

Peter: I can see that I am going to learn a lot in this place. How much is the room a month?

Isabel: I don't know a thing about that. You'll have to talk to Alberto. He knows how much the rent is. I believe he's going to arrive any minute. Would you mind waiting for him?

Peter: No, not at all. I'll wait.

Isabel: Would you like a cup of coffee? A soda? We can have something to drink in the kitchen.

Peter: Fine, thanks. A coffee sounds great, because I'm rather sleepy. . . . Please, give me the darkest coffee you can find.

Isabel: Then what you want is a strong espresso. Don't worry, this is the specialty of the house.

HEAR...SAY 2

Alberto comes home and the three people talk about the room for rent.

Isabel: Alberto, this is Peter Winthrop. He wants to rent the room.

Alberto: Nice to meet you. And did you tell him that the price is very high?

Isabel: I didn't tell him because I didn't know about that. What are you talking about?

Alberto: Just that, the price does not include the electricity, heat, water . . .

Peter: That's important to know.

Alberto: Isabel, did you tell him that we have very noisy neighbors, who are always partying?

Isabel: No, I didn't tell him. I don't think it's that bad. They are jazz musicans and I like it when they practice.

Alberto: And did you tell him how very cold it is at night?

Isabel: No, I didn't tell him. That's only in January and February and we have plenty of blankets.

Alberto: And did you tell him that I get up at three AM and take a shower at three thirty and I make a lot of noise and use up all the hot water?

Isabel: Alberto! No, I did not tell him, because it's not the truth! Could I talk to you alone for a second? *(They go to another room to talk undisturbed.)* My goodness, what is the matter with you? Do you want to rent the room out or not?

Alberto: Yeah, but I am not sure I like that Peter.

Isabel: He looks serious, responsible and, on top of that, he speaks Spanish. I think he is super.

Alberto: But, don't you think a woman would be better?

Isabel: A woman? My goodness! Your problem is that you're jealous!

ACTIVITY 1

I need . . .	I don't need . . .
a room	a whole apartment
a bedroom	a bed (I already have a sofabed)
a table and a chair to write on	a big desk
roommates	to be alone
to practice Spanish	to speak English

ACTIVITY 2

1. Isabel es de Puerto Rico.
2. Alberto es de la República Dominicana.
3. Peter tiene un sofá-cama.
4. No sabemos cuánto cuesta el cuarto.
5. Va a beber un café.

ACTIVITY 3

1. Lo que Isabel y Alberto necesitan es un compañero de casa.
2. Lo que yo necesito es practicar el español.
3. Lo que nosotros necesitamos es hablar en un chat.
4. Lo que mis amigos necesitan es comprar este libro.
5. Lo que Carmen necesita es visitar los Estados Unidos.

ACTIVITY 4

These are the rooms in the apartment:
1. el cuarto de estar
2. el dormitorio
3. la sala de baño
4. la cocina
5. el comedor

ACTIVITY 5

1. Yes: The room costs a lot of money.
2. Yes: The neighbors are very noisy.
3. No: He cannot use the kitchen.
4. Yes: Alberto wakes up at three AM.
5. Yes: There is no heating during the night.

ACTIVITY 6

1. Peter se los compró.
2. Carmen me los trajo.
3. Alberto se lo dijo.
4. Isabel se lo dio.
5. Isabel y Alberto se la compraron.

ACTIVITY 7

1. ¿Cuánto cuesta el cuarto?
2. ¿El precio incluye el agua, la calefacción y la electricidad?
3. ¿Hacen mucho ruido los vecinos?
4. ¿A qué hora se levantan?

ACTIVITY 8

1. Ella estudia en Nueva York
2. En la casa de su amiga.
3. El billete de avión.
4. En Semana Santa.
5. Le pregunta "¿Tienes planes?"

ACTIVITY 9

1. En la cocina lo que hago es cocinar. (In the kitchen what I do is cook.)
2. En el comedor lo que hago es comer. (In the dining room what I do is eat.)
3. En el dormitorio lo que hago es dormir. (In the bedroom what I do is sleep.)
4. En el baño lo que hago es ducharme. (In the bathroom what I do is take a shower.)
5. En la sala lo que hago es mirar la televisión. (In the living room what I do is watch TV.)

297

LESSON 19 • I MISS YOU, I FORGET YOU, I LOVE YOU

20.

I WILL CONQUER YOU

Te voy a conquistar

And that Cuban guy . . . who was he?

COMING UP. . .

- *Let me suggest . . . :* Making suggestions using *vamos + a*
- *Great idea!:* How to accept (or reject) suggestions
- *Things change:* Talking about change using *ponerse* (to get; to turn), *hacerse* (to become), and *volverse* (to become)
- *Let's do it!:* Commands with *nosotros* (we; us)
- *I scream, you scream . . . :* Verbs that change meaning in the preterite and imperfect tenses
- *I've just done that:* Using *acabar* (to finish) to talk about what you've just done

LOOKING AHEAD

Bueno, finalmente, Carmen y Peter están juntos (together). Oh, my! *¿Qué pasará?* (What will happen?) To start, they decide to go out on the town. But first, they have to plan what to do. They are thinking of going to *una obra de teatro* (a play) or *ver una película* (see a movie), or maybe *un concierto* (no doubt about this one).

Did You Know?

New York City has always been the preferred destination for Puerto Ricans moving to the mainland. The Puerto Rican community is so large and strong that they have a name for those from the island who live in New York or have been born here. They call themselves Nuyoricans.

ACTIVITY 1: **LET'S WARM UP**

Let's think about leisure activities. Can you match the Spanish terms on the left with their English equivalents on the right?

1. ver la televisión
2. asistir a una obra de teatro
3. ir a un concierto
4. pasear en la playa
5. ir de compras
6. oír un recital de poesía

a. walk on the beach
b. watch TV
c. go shopping
d. listen to a poetry reading
e. go to a play
f. go to a concert

HEAR . . . SAY 1

Carmen está en Estados Unidos, visitando a su amiga Maite Arcos. Ahora está en casa de Peter y están hablando de sus planes para la noche. Isabel está viendo la televisión.

Peter: Isabel, quiero presentarte a una persona. Ésta es mi amiga Carmen, de España.

Isabel: ¿Ésta es tu novia? (*Both Peter and Carmen blush.*) Ay, nene, pero no se pongan rojos, que era sólo una pregunta . . . .Mucho gusto, Carmen. Bueno, me

300

SPANISH WITHOUT THE FUSS

van a disculpar, pero va a empezar el capítulo de *Betty la fea* y no quiero perderme ni un minutito. Me vuelve loca esta Betty.

Peter: *(talking to Carmen) Betty la fea* es una telenovela colombiana que tiene muchísimo éxito aquí también.

Carmen: ¿Pero aquí hay televisión en español?

Peter: Por supuesto. Aquí en Nueva York tenemos al menos cuatro canales sólo en español.

Carmen: ¡Qué bien!

Peter: Bueno, y ¿qué quieres que hagamos esta noche?

Carmen: Bueno, como no sé hablar inglés no podemos ir ni a un teatro, ni al cine, ni casi nada, porque no voy a poder entender mucho.

Peter: ¡Ni hablar! Miremos el diario *La Prensa*. Seguro que hay un montón de actividades en español.

(They both look at the newspaper.)

Peter: Pues, veamos una obra de teatro en español, o un musical con canciones de Latinoamérica . . .

Carmen: ¡No, no! ¡Oigamos mejor este recital de poesía! Me encanta la poesía del cubano Nicolás Guillén.

Peter: Muy bien. Y después cenemos en un buen restaurante dominicano y bailemos salsa y merengue en Paladium, una discoteca que siempre tiene mucha música caribeña en directo.

Isabel: *(talking to herself in the other room, after having overheard the conversation)* Pues, si no es su novia hoy, seguro que lo será mañana . . . .

ACTIVITY 2: HOW'S THAT AGAIN?

Here are the people in our story (on the right) and a list of activities (on the left). Who wants to do what?

1. ver una telenovela
2. ver una obra de teatro
3. mirar el diario *La Prensa*
4. cenar en un restaurante dominicano
5. ir al cine
6. oír un recital de poesía
7. bailar salsa

a. Carmen
b. Peter
c. Isabel
d. ninguno (*no one*)

Did You Know?

The fastest-growing Spanish-language TV network in the United States is Univisión. Its headquarters are in Florida and among its most popular programs are Latin American *telenovelas,* or soap operas. *Betty la fea* (*Betty, the Ugly One*), a super-popular Colombian soap opera Isabel is crazy about, was showing on another Spanish-language channel, Telemundo. Can you view one of these channels in your town? It's a great and fun opportunity for additional exposure to Spanish that will do wonders for you!

Did You Know?

Nicolás Guillén (1902–1989) was a famous Cuban poet. He is well-known for his themes inspired by African mythology and the pronounced Afro-Cuban rhythms that mark his style. His poetry is an homage to the African cultures that greatly influenced Latin American and, in particular, the Caribbean societies.

WORKSHOP 1

THE NITTY-GRITTY

LET'S DO IT!: COMMANDS WITH *NOSOTROS* (WE; US)

This command is used when we want some activity to be done by **us** or in Spanish, *nosotros / nosotras*. It is the equivalent to *let's* in English, as in, for example, *Let's do the exercise!* Remember that you already know how to form commands with *tú* (you, informal), *usted* (you, formal), and *ustedes* (you, plural, formal):

> *La profesora dice: "Escriban una carta a un amigo".*

> The teacher says, "Write a letter to a friend."

> *Peter le dice a Carmen: "Ven a Nueva York".*

> Peter says to Carmen, "Come to New York."

To form *nosotros* commands, do the following:

1. Start with the **yo** form of the present indicative:

trabajar	→	*yo trabajo*
tener	→	*yo tengo*

2. Drop the o:

trabajo → **trabaj–**

tengo → **teng–**

3. Add these endings:

–emos for **–ar** verbs

–amos for **–er** and **–ir** verbs

Here are some example:

esperar (to wait) → **esperemos** (let's wait)

comer (to eat) → **comamos** (let's eat)

You already know the ones that are irregular because they are the same as those for *usted* commands. Let's review them:

saber (to know) → **sepamos** (let's know / learn)

ser (to be) → **seamos** (let's be)

ir (to go) → **vayamos / vamos** (let's go)

dar (to give) → **demos** (let's give)

estar (to be) → **estemos** (let's be)

Stem-changing verbs take the stem used in the *nosotros* form of the present tense:

volver (to return) → **volvamos** (let's return)

There are five sentences using *nosotros* commands in the Hear . . . Say 1. Can you find them before you look below?

And now, here they are:

Miremos el diario La Prensa.   Let's look at the daily *La Prensa*.

Veamos una obra de teatro en español.   Let's see a play in Spanish.

Oigamos este recital de poesía.   Let's listen to that poetry reading.

Cenemos en un buen restaurante.   Let's have dinner in a good restaurant.

Bailemos en la discoteca.   Let's dance in a club.

After all this practice, I have a question for you. Does this grammatical form look familiar to you? If you haven't noticed, let me remind you that this is also the *nosotros* form of the present subjunctive.

Imagine that you and a friend are planning a trip to various different Spanish-speaking countries. What kind of activities do you suggest the two of you should do? Look at the example:

Quieren comer tapas en España.   →   ¡Comamos tapas en España!

1. Quieren visitar las playas de la República Dominicana.
2. Quieren ver las esculturas de Botero en Colombia.
3. Quieren oír la música de Ricky Martin en Puerto Rico.
4. Quieren caminar por la pampa argentina.
5. Quieren bailar salsa en Venezuela.

The Fine Print

An alternative way to express *let's* in Spanish is by using *a* followed by an infinitive. For example:

¡A comer!   Let's eat.

This only works with positive commands. For negative commands you always have to use the standard *nosotros* form that you have just learned:

¡No comamos!   Let's not eat.

WORDS TO LIVE BY

LET ME SUGGEST . . . : MAKING SUGGESTIONS USING VAMOS + A

Instead of using a *nosotros* command, you can use the construction made of *vamos + a* followed by a verb in the infinitive from. Making your request this way will make it sound more like a suggestion:

Vamos a ver una obra de teatro.   Let's see a play.

Vamos a comer fuera.   Let's eat out.

You can also use *por qué no . . . ?* (why not?), just like in English:

¿Por qué no damos un paseo?   Why don't we go for a walk?

Or use *querer* (to want):

¿Quieres visitar el museo Guggenheim?

Do you want to visit the Guggenheim Museum?

GREAT IDEA!: **HOW TO ACCEPT (OR REJECT) SUGGESTIONS**

And this is what you can say:

ACEPTAR	NO ACEPTAR
¡Qué buena idea! What a good idea!	*¡Qué mala idea!* What a bad idea!
¡Claro que sí! Of course!	*¡Claro que no!* Of course not!
¡Estupendo!; ¡Magnífico! Great!	*Mejor no . . .* It's better if we don't . . .
¡Venga! ¡Vamos! Come on! / Let's do it! / Go for it!	*¡Ni hablar!* No way!

ACTIVITY 4: **TAKE IT FOR A SPIN**

Your friend wants you to do a lot of things today, but you just feel like staying home. How do you respond?

Tu amigo: Veamos una obra de teatro.

Tú: _____

Tu amigo: Pues, vamos a cenar en un restaurante italiano.

Tú: _____

Tu amigo: Entonces, mejor nos quedamos en casa y vemos la tele.

Tú: _____

HEAR ... SAY 2

Después de oír poesía, comer comida dominicana y bailar toda la noche, Peter y Carmen deciden dar un paseo en el Puente de Brooklyn, desde donde contemplan el amanecer (*sunrise*).

Carmen: ¡Qué noche más estupenda! De verdad, no sabía que Nueva York podía ofrecer tantas actividades en español. Una vez, conocí a un cubano que vivía aquí y me habló de todo esto, pero no quise creerle. Pensaba que exageraba . . .

Peter: Pues, así es. Y, ese cubano ¿quién era? ¿Algún novio?

Carmen: No, no. Lo conocí en clase. Vino a España a estudiar, pero no quiso quedarse porque quería hacerse millonario y pensó que allí no podía. Así que prefirió volver a los Estados Unidos . . . . Novios, novios, no tengo ninguno. Tengo algunos pretendientes.

Peter: ¿Y qué son "pretendientes"? ¿Qué "pretenden"?

Carmen: Ja, ja, no sabes tanto español como pensaba. . . . Un pretendiente es alguien que quiere ser tu novio, alguien que quiere "conquistarte". ¿Sabes lo que es "conquistar"?

Peter: Pues, puedo imaginarlo. . . . "Conquistar a una persona" es obtener su amor ¿no?

Carmen: Su amor y su vida. Exacto.

Peter: ¡Ah! ¿Y tienes muchos "pretendientes" o quieres ponerme celoso?

Carme : (*with a flirting tone*) ¿Y por qué vas a ponerte celoso?

Peter: ¿Es que no sabes que soy tu "pretendiente"?

Carmen: (*joking*) ¡Anda ya! ¡Pues acabo de enterarme!

Peter: Supe que eras especial desde el momento que te vi en la pensión de Don Miguel.

Carmen: (*lowering her voice*) Peter, no continúes, o voy a ponerme como un tomate. . . . (*looking at the view from the bridge*) ¡Qué bonito es esto!

ACTIVITY 5: HOW'S THAT AGAIN?

Wow! Wasn't that nice? I thought so, too. Let's review what this was all about:

1. ¿Dónde están Peter y Carmen?
2. ¿Quién es ese hombre cubano?
3. ¿Tiene Carmen novio?
4. ¿Qué es un "pretendiente"?
5. Piensa en el título de la lección. ¿Es apropiado?

Did You Know?

Pretendiente and *conquistar* are rather old-fashioned words still used, particularly in Spain, when talking about romance. They are reminiscent of a tradition of male initiative in love matters. There is really no female equivalent of *el pretendiente*; for a woman, the word used is *admiradora* (admirer). But don't think things are that simple. Although there are definitely some chauvinistic attitudes left in most Spanish-speaking countries, women have made huge strides in all levels of society. And now, women also *conquistan* their men. (Of course, they've always done it, but they can do it more publicly now!)

THE NITTY-GRITTY

I SCREAM, YOU SCREAM . . . : VERBS THAT CHANGE MEANING IN THE PRETERITE AND IMPERFECT TENSES

Most verbs describe actions: *go, jump, do, write,* etc., but some describe states, such as *want, know,* or *can.* In Spanish, when the past tense is used, most state verbs are in the imperfect because imperfect describes continuous past events, and states fall into that category:

No <u>sabía</u> eso.   I didn't know that.

No <u>quería</u> ir a la oficina.   I didn't want to go to the office.

But if these verbs are used in the preterite, they take on a special meaning. Here are some of them:

VERB	PRETERITE		IMPERFECT	
saber (to know)	*supe*	I found out	*sabía*	I knew
conocer (to be acquainted with)	*conocí*	I met; I got to know	*conocía*	I knew; I was acquainted with
querer (to want)	*quise*	I tried	*quería*	I wanted
no querer (to not want)	*no quise*	I refused	*no quería*	I didn't want
poder (can)	*pude*	I could (and did)	*podía*	I was able to
no poder (to not be able to)	*no pude*	I (tried and) couldn't; I failed	*no podía*	I wasn't able to

VERBS THAT CHANGE MEANING IN THE PRETERITE AND IMPERFECT TENSES

Here are some examples so you can see the contrast better:

Una vez, conocí a un cubano . . .

Once I met a Cuban . . .

Cuando era pequeño, Peter no conocía a sus vecinos.

When he was a kid, Peter didn't know his neighbors.

No supe eso hasta el final.

I didn't find out until the end.

No sabía que estabas aquí.

I didn't know you were here.

In general, though, remember that these verbs [and others like *ser*, *estar* (to be), or *tener* (to have)] are most frequently used in the imperfect when talking about the past, so when in doubt, go with the imperfect!

I'VE JUST DONE THAT: USING *ACABAR* (TO FINISH) TO TALK ABOUT WHAT YOU'VE JUST DONE

If you wish to say that you have **just** finished doing something in Spanish, you have to use the verb *acabar* (to finish) followed by the proposition *de* and the verb.

Here is acabar in the present tense:

ACABAR (TO FINISH)
yo acabo
tú acabas
él / ella, usted acaba
nosotros / nosotras acabamos
vosotros / vosotras acabáis
ellos / ellas, ustedes acaban

Here are some examples:

Acabo de enterarme.

I have just found out.

Acabamos de comer.

We have just finished eating.

Acabo de oír un poema muy bonito en la radio.

I have just heard a very beautiful poem on the radio.

Could you translate these sentences for me? Remember that the verbs used have something special about them.

1. I refused to go to the party.
2. We couldn't see the play.
3. You didn't know I was here.
4. Peter met Carmen in Madrid.
5. I have just drunk another cup of coffee.

Heads Up!

Do not confuse the expression *acabar de* with the present perfect:

<u>Acabo de</u> comer.   I have **just** eaten.

He comido.   I have eaten.

Heads Up!

WORDS TO LIVE BY

THINGS CHANGE: TALKING ABOUT CHANGE USING *PONERSE* (TO GET; TO TURN), *HACERSE* (TO BECOME), AND *VOLVERSE* (TO BECOME)

To talk about changes in some states of affairs, you can use several different verbs in Spanish. In English, we use *to become* or *to get*, as in, *I'm becoming a better person as I'm getting to know you*. Let's look at the Spanish counterparts of *to become* and *to get* (notice that all of the verbs are used with a reflexive pronoun):

- Use *ponerse* (to get; to turn) with most adjectives: *triste* (sad); *furioso / a* (furious); *contento / a* (happy): *enojado / a* (angry); *celoso / a* (jealous); *rojo / a* (red; blushed); and also, with some expressions: *de buen humor* (in a good mood); *de mal humor* (in a bad mood).

     Examples from the dialogues:

¡No se pongan rojos!

Don't blush! (*Lit.* Don't turn red!)

Voy a ponerme como un tomate.

I am going to look like a tomato! (*Fig.* I'm going to blush.)

- Use *hacerse* (to become) with *rico / a* (rich), *pobre* (poor), and with nouns of professions or religions: *abogado / a* (lawyer); *doctor / a* (doctor); *profesor / a* (professor or teacher); *católico / a* (Catholic); *budista* (Buddhist).

Quería hacerse rico.

He wanted to become rich.

Su hermano se hizo budista.

His brother became a Buddhist.

- Use *volverse* (to become) with *loco / a* (crazy). In Spanish, *to get / make crazy*, can have both a positive and a negative meaning:

Esta telenovela me vuelve loca.

I love this soap opera. (*Lit.* It makes me crazy.)

Se vuelve loca con ese hombre.

She goes nuts about that man. (This one can be good or bad.)

Word on the Street

And just for fun, here are some terms in "Spanglish," which is Spanish heavily influenced by English. I bet you can understand **these** words!

el rufo	roof	for **el techo, el tejado**
la yarda	backyard	for **el jardín, el patio**
la carpeta	the carpet	for **alfombra, moqueta**
vacumear	to vacuum	for **pasar la aspiradora**

LET'S PUT IT IN WRITING

Here is the list of activities Peter and Carmen found in the local Spanish-language newspaper *La Prensa*. As you can see, there are many events in Spanish in New York City, and they may be coming to a town near you!

TEATRO

El Guernica de Picasso
de Jerónimo López Mozo

Thalia Spanish Theater
41 – 17 Greenpoint Avenue
Sunnyside, Queens

*Ríase El Show de Julián Arango y
Antonio Sanint*
(Teatro Nacional de Bogotá)

Repertorio Español
138 East 27th St.
New York, NY 10016

MUSICALES

*Four guys named José … and
una mujer named María*
Producida por Enrique Iglesias

Blue Angel,
323 W. 44th St.

MÚSICA CLÁSICA

María de Buenos Aires
Opereta Argentina
de Astor Piazzola

Town Hall,
123 W. 43rd St.

POESÍA

*Recital de poesía de
Nicolás Guillén*
Organizado por el grupo
CUBA-LIBRE
Nuyorican Poets Café Inc.
236 E. 3rd St.
New York, NY 10009

ACTIVITY 7:   HOW'S THAT AGAIN?

1. ¿Cuántos teatros hay con obras en español?
2. ¿Dónde está el Nuyorican Poets Café?
3. ¿Qué obra ha producido Enrique Iglesias?
4. ¿Quién compuso *María de Buenos Aires*?
5. ¿A dónde van Peter y Carmen?

STRUT YOUR STUFF

TAKE IT FOR A SPIN

Hey, let's end on a good note. How about playing a game? Do you know about *¿Quién quiere ser millonario?* The Without the Fuss Edition? Well, now you will. . . .Here are 15 questions I'd like you to answer.

1. LA CAPITAL DE COLOMBIA ES:

a. Madrid
b. Nueva York
c. Buenos Aires
d. Santa Fe de Bogotá

2. EN ARGENTINA, EL BAILE TÍPICO ES:

a. la rumba
b. el flamenco
c. el tango
d. el merengue

3. IN SPANISH-SPEAKING COUNTRIES THEY___WHEN THEY MEET YOU:

a. give you a hard time
b. tell you you are a foreigner
c. kiss
c. pat you on the back

4. WE WOULD WORK SE DICE...

a. trabajaríamos
b. comeríamos
d. tendríamos
c. saldríamos

5. NO ENCUENTRO MI MOCHILA MEANS...

a. I got lost
b. I missed my train
c. Hey, you are no lady!
d. I can't find my backpack

6. I WOULD GO SE DICE...

a. iría
b. irán
c. voy
c. fui

7. EL DEPORTE MÁS POPULAR EN ARGENTINA ES:

a. el judo
b. el fútbol
c. el ciclismo
d. el boxeo

8. WITH ME *SE DICE*...

a. con me   b. conmigo

c. sinmigo   d. sin me

9. DON'T WAIT FOR ME *SE DICE*...

a. No me esperes   b. No esperesme

c. No esperarme   d. No me esperas

10. WHEN IS *BUEN PROVECHO* USED?

a. When talking to lawyers   b. When talking to people who are about to eat

c. When talking to a waiter   d. When talking to strangers

11. WHICH OF THESE ITEMS DOES NOT BELONG IN A HOUSE?

a. el dormitorio   b. el comedor

c. la cocina   d. el sicoanalista

12. *VIAJO A ESPAÑA PRONTO* IN THE FUTURE TENSE WOULD BE...

a. Viajaré a España pronto.   b. Viajamos a España pronto.

c. Viajaría a España pronto.   c. Viajé a España prontó.

13. YOU ARE THE BEST *SE DICE*...

a. Eres un desastre.   b. Eres estupendo.

c. Eres el mejor.   d. Eres el peor.

14. I GAVE IT TO HIM *SE DICE*...

a. Me lo dio.   b. Se lo di.

c. Se la dimos.   c. Te lo di.

15. *UNA PERSONA QUE ESTUDIA TODO ESTE LIBRO COMPLETO ES MUY...*

a. rara   b. extraña

c. inteligente   d. problemática

Well, this is it for your Spanish lessons. Or is it? I certainly hope not! I hope this is just the beginning of a long and lasting relationship with the Spanish language and Spanish-speaking cultures. Remember that regular and abundant exposure to the language is the best way to learn it. Because you live in the United States, you're truly in luck—opportunities for exposure are plentiful. So keep using what's around you—the TV, the radio, the Internet, and . . . your neighbors. *¡Los hispanohablantes te esperan, amigo o amiga!* I certainly hope to meet with you again. *¡Hasta la vista!*

CRIB NOTES

HEAR...SAY 1

Carmen is in the United States, visiting her friend Maite Arcos. Now she is in Peter's home and they are talking about their plans for the evening. Isabel is watching TV.

Peter: Isabel, I would like to introduce you to someone. This is my friend Carmen, from Spain.

Isabel: Is this your girlfriend? *(Both Peter and Carmen blush.)* Gee, guys, don't blush! It was just a question . . . .Nice to meet you Carmen. Well, excuse me, but *Yo soy Betty, la fea* is about to start and I don't want miss a second of it. I'm just crazy about Betty.

Peter: (talking to Carmen) *Betty la fea* is a Colombian soap opera that is wildly popular here as well.

Carmen: But, you get TV in Spanish here?

Peter: Of course. Here in New York we have at least four channels that broadcast only in Spanish.

Carmen: That's great!

Peter: Well, and what do you want us to do tonight?

Carmen: Since I don't speak English, we can't really go see a play, or a movie, or almost anything, because I'm not going to be able to understand much.

Peter: Not really! Let's look at *La Prensa*. I am sure there's a ton of activities in Spanish.

(They both look at the newspaper.)

Peter: Let's see a Spanish play or a music show with Latin American songs . . .

Carmen: No, even better! Let's go listen to this poetry reading! I love the poetry by the Cuban Nicolás Guillén.

Peter: Sounds good. And after that, let's have dinner at a good Dominican restaurant and let's dance salsa and merengue at the Palladium. It's a club that always has live Caribbean music.

Isabel: *(talking to herself in the other room after having overheard the conversation)* Well, if she is not his girlfriend today, I have a feeling she will be tomorrow . . . .

HEAR...SAY 2

After listening to poetry, eating Dominican food, and dancing all night, Peter and Carmen decide to take a walk on the Brooklyn Bridge, where they observe the sunrise.

Carmen: What a great night! I had no idea New York could offer so many events in Spanish. Once, I met a Cuban guy that lived here and he told me about all this, but I didn't want to believe him. I thought he was exaggerating . . .

Peter: It's really like that. And, that Cuban guy . . . who was he? Maybe a boyfriend?

Carmen: Oh, no. I met him in class. He went to Spain to study but he didn't want to stay because he wanted to become a millionaire, and he thought that he couldn't do

it there. Boyfriends, I don't have any . . . . I have some *pretendientes*.

Peter: What are they? What do they pretend?

Carmen: Ha, ha! I guess you don't know as much Spanish as I thought. A *pretendiente* is somebody who wants to be your boyfriend, someone who wants to "conquer" you. Do you know what *conquistar* means?

Peter: I can imagine. "To conquer a person" means to obtain their love. Right?

Carmen: Their love and their life. Exactly.

Peter: And, do you have many of those suitors or are you just trying to make me jealous?

Carmen: *(with a flirting tone)* And why would you get jealous?

Peter:	Don't you know that I am your *preten-diente*?
Carmen:	*(joking)* Oh, get out! I didn't know!
Peter:	I knew you were special from the moment I saw you in Don Miguel's *pensión*.

| Carmen: | *(lowering her voice)* Peter, stop right there, or I am going to turn completely red! *(looking at the view from the bridge)* This is so beautiful! |

ANSWER KEY

ACTIVITY 1

1. b; 2. e; 3. f; 4. a; 5. c; 6. d

ACTIVITY 2

Isabel: 1; Peter: 2, 3, 4, 7; Carmen: 6; ninguno: 5

ACTIVITY 3

1. ¡Visitemos las playas de la República Dominicana!
2. ¡Veamos las esculturas de Botero en Colombia!
3. ¡Oigamos la música de Ricky Martin en Puerto Rico!
4. ¡Caminemos por la pampa argentina!
5. ¡Bailemos salsa en Venezuela!

ACTIVITY 4

1. Ni hablar. Estoy muy cansado.
2. Mejor otro día.
3. ¡Estupendo! ¡Qué buena idea!

ACTIVITY 5

1. Peter y Carmen están en el puente de Brooklyn.
2. Ese hombre cubano es un amigo de Carmen.
3. No, no tiene novio.
4. Un pretendiente es una persona que quiere tu amor.
5. Yo pienso que sí.

ACTIVITY 6

1. No quise ir a la fiesta.
2. No pudimos ver la obra.
3. No sabías que estaba aquí.
4. Peter conoció a Carmen en Madrid.
5. Acabo de tomar otra taza de café.

ACTIVITY 7

1. Hay dos teatros.
2. Está en 236 E. 3rd St.
3. Ha producido *Four guys named José . . . and una mujer llamada María*
4. Astor Piazzola la compuso.
5. Al Nuyorican Poets Café.

ACTIVITY 8

1. d; 2. c; 3. c; 4. a; 5. d; 6. a; 7. b; 8. b; 9. a; 10. b; 11. d; 12. a; 13. c; 14. b; 15. c (It's you! You're really amazing! Congratulations!)

A SHORTCUT TO SPANISH GRAMMAR

PRONOUNS							
	SUBJECT PRONOUNS		DIRECT OBJECT PRONOUNS		INDIRECT OBJECT PRONOUNS		REFLEXIVE PRONOUNS
SINGULAR	*yo*	I	*me*	me	*me*	to me	*me*	myself
	tú	you	*te*	you	*te*	to you	*te*	yourself
	él, ella, usted	he, she, you (formal)	*lo, la*	him, her, it, you (formal)	*le*	to him, her, it, you (formal)	*se*	himself, herself, itself, yourself (formal)
PLURAL	*nosotros, nosotras*	we	*nos*	us	*nos*	to us	*nos*	ourselves
	vosotros, vosotras	you	*os*	you	*os*	to you	*os*	yourselves
	ellos, ellas, ustedes	they, you (formal)	*los, las*	them	*les*	to them, you (formal)	*se*	themselves, yourselves (formal)

- Subject pronouns are not obligatory: *Yo leo el libro.* = *Leo el libro.* (I read the book.)
- **Se** is used when the direct and indirect objects appear together and are both third person:

Le doy el libro a Simón. → **Se lo doy.** (I give the book to Simón. / I give it to him.)

	SINGULAR		PLURAL		
	Masculine	Feminine	Masculine	Feminine	
DEFINITE ARTICLES	*el*	*la*	*los*	*las*	the
INDEFINITE ARTICLES	*un*	*una*	*unos*	*unas*	a / some

CONTRACTIONS
DE + EL = DEL
A + EL = AL

POSSESSIVE ADJECTIVES

SINGULAR	PLURAL	
mi	*mis*	my
tu	*tus*	your
su	*sus*	his, her, your (formal)
nuestro, nuestra	*nuestros, nuestras*	our
vuestro, vuestra	*vuestros, vuestras*	your
su	*sus*	their, your (formal)

EMPHATIC POSSESSIVE ADJECTIVES

SINGULAR	PLURAL	
mío, mía	*míos, mías*	my, (of) mine
tuyo, tuya	*tuyos, tuyas*	your, (of) yours
suyo, suya	*suyos, suyas*	his, (of) his her, (of) hers your, (of) yours (formal)
nuestro, nuestra	*nuestros, nuestras*	our, (of) ours
vuestro, vuestra	*vuestros, vuestras*	your, (of) yours
suyo, suya	*suyos, suyas*	their, (of) theirs your, (of) yours (formal)

The emphatic possesive adjective must follow the noun:

Ese es el carro suyo.	That one is her car. / That one is the car of hers.
Esta casa es mía.	This house is mine.

POSSESSIVE PRONOUNS

With the addition of a definite article (*el, la, los, las*), the emphatic possessive adjectives become possessive pronouns:

Aquí tengo mi libro. ¿Tienes el tuyo?	Here I have my book. Do you have yours?

DEMONSTRATIVE ADJECTIVES

	MASCULINE	FEMININE	
SINGULAR	*este*	*esta*	this
	ese	*esa*	that
	aquel	*aquella*	that (farther removed)
PLURAL	*estos*	*estas*	these
	esos	*esas*	those
	aquellos	*aquellas*	those (farther removed)

DEMONSTRATIVE PRONOUNS				
	MASCULINE	FEMININE	NEUTER	
SINGULAR	éste	ésta	esto	this (one)
	ése	ésa	eso	that (one)
	aquél	aquélla	aquello	that (one) (farther removed)
PLURAL	éstos	éstas		these
	ésos	ésas		those
	aquéllos	aquéllas		those (farther removed)

QUESTION WORDS	
Qué	What
Quién, quiénes	Who
De quién	Whose
Dónde	Where
De dónde	Where from
Cuándo	When
Por qué	Why
Cómo	How
Cuánto, cuánta/cuántos, cuántas	How much/How many
Cúal	What/Which

- There are three alternative ways to form simple "yes / no" questions in Spanish:

   1. **¿Mark es de Estados Unidos?**

   2. **¿Es Mark de Estados Unidos?**   Is Mark from the United States?

   3. **¿Es de Estados Unidos Mark?**

The first type of question involves only a rising intonation. In the second type, the verb comes first and is immediately followed by the subject. In the third type, similar to the second, the verb comes first, and the subject appears at the very end of the sentence.

- Spanish does not need a helping verb to form questions, as does English:

   What does Mark eat?   →   **¿Qué come Mark?**

ADVERBS OF QUANTITY	
mucho	a lot
poco	a little

ADVERBS OF TIME	
nunca	never
siempre	always
a veces	sometimes
muchas veces, a menudo	often

WORD ORDER

- The subject of a sentence may appear after the verb or at the end of the sentence:

    Juan viaja mucho. = Viaja Juan mucho. = Viaja mucho Juan. → Juan travels a lot.

NEGATIVE SENTENCES

- In a negative sentence, at least one negative word comes before the verb. In Spanish (unlike in English) a negative sentence can have more than one negative word:

    No bebo café nunca. = Nunca bebo café. → I never drink coffee.

EXCEPTIONS THAT PROVE THE RULE

IRREGULAR VERBS*

INFINITIVE, PRESENT AND PAST PARTICIPLES	PRESENT INDICATIVE	PRESENT SUBJUNCTIVE	IMPERFECT	PRETERITE	FUTURE	CONDITIONAL	IMPERATIVE
andar to walk	ando	ande	andaba	anduve	andaré	andaría	anda
andando	andas	andes	andabas	anduviste	andarás	andarías	andad
andado	anda	ande	andaba	anduvo	andará	andaría	
	andamos	andemos	andábamos	anduvimos	andaremos	andaríamos	
	andáis	andéis	andabais	anduvisteis	andaréis	andaríais	
	andan	anden	andaban	anduvieron	andarán	andarían	
caber to fit,	quepo	quepa	cabía	cupe	cabré	cabría	cabe
to be	cabes	quepas	cabías	cupiste	cabrás	cabrías	cabed
contained in	cabe	quepa	cabía	cupo	cabrá	cabría	
cabiendo	cabemos	quepamos	cabíamos	cupimos	cabremos	cabríamos	
cabido	cabéis	quepáis	cabíais	cupisteis	cabréis	cabríais	
	caben	quepan	cabían	cupieron	cabrán	cabrían	
caer to fall	caigo	caiga	caía	caí	caeré	caería	cae
cayendo	caes	caigas	caías	caíste	caerás	caerías	caed
caído	cae	caiga	caía	cayó	caerá	caería	
	caemos	caigamos	caíamos	caímos	caeremos	caeríamos	
	caéis	caigáis	caíais	caísteis	caeréis	caeríais	
	caen	caigan	caían	cayeron	caerán	caerían	
conducir	conduzco	conduzca	conducía	conduje	conduciré	conduciría	conduce
to lead,	conduces	conduzcas	conducías	condujiste	conducirás	conducirías	conducid
to drive	conduce	conduzca	conducía	condujo	conducirá	conduciría	
conduciendo	conducimos	conduzcamos	conducíamos	condujimos	conduciremos	conduciríamos	
conducido	conducís	conduzcáis	conducíais	condujisteis	conduciréis	comínciríais	
	conducen	conduzcan	conducían	condujeron	conducirán	conducirían	

*To form compound tenses, use the appropriate form of *haber* together with the past participle of the irregular verb.

(continued)

INFINITIVE, PRESENT AND PAST PARTICIPLES	PRESENT INDICATIVE	PRESENT SUBJUNCTIVE	IMPERFECT	PRETERITE	FUTURE	CONDITIONAL	IMPERATIVE
dar to give *dando* *dado*	*doy* *das* *da* *damos* *dais* *dan*	*dé* *des* *dé* *demos* *deis* *den*	*daba* *dabas* *daba* *dábamos* *dabais* *daban*	*di* *diste* *dio* *dimos* *disteis* *dieron*	*daré* *darás* *dará* *daremos* *daréis* *darán*	*daría* *darías* *daría* *daríamos* *daríais* *darían*	*da* *dad*
decir to say, to tell *diciendo* *dicho*	*digo* *dices* *dice* *decimos* *decís* *dicen*	*diga* *digas* *diga* *digamos* *digáis* *digan*	*decía* *decías* *decía* *decíamos* *decíais* *decían*	*dije* *dijiste* *dijo* *dijimos* *dijisteis* *dijeron*	*diré* *dirás* *dirá* *diremos* *diréis* *dirán*	*diría* *dirías* *diría* *diríamos* *diríais* *dirían*	*di* *decid*
estar to be *estando* *estado*	*estoy* *estás* *está* *estamos* *estáis* *están*	*esté* *estés* *esté* *estemos* *estéis* *estén*	*estaba* *estabas* *estaba* *estábamos* *estabais* *estaban*	*estuve* *estuviste* *estuvo* *estuvimos* *estuvisteis* *estuvieron*	*estaré* *estarás* *estará* *estaremos* *estaréis* *estarán*	*estaría* *estarías* *estaría* *estaríamos* *estaríais* *estarían*	*está* *estad*
haber to have (auxiliary) *habiendo* *habido*	*he* *has* *ha* *hemos* *habéis* *han*	*haya* *hayas* *haya* *hayamos* *hayáis* *hayan*	*había* *habías* *había* *habíamos* *habíais* *habían*	*hube* *hubiste* *hubo* *hubimos* *hubisteis* *hubieron*	*habré* *habrás* *habrá* *habremos* *habréis* *habrán*	*habría* *habrías* *habría* *habríamos* *habríais* *habrían*	

(continued)

INFINITIVE, PRESENT AND PAST PARTICIPLES	PRESENT INDICATIVE	PRESENT SUBJUNCTIVE	IMPERFECT	PRETERITE	FUTURE	CONDITIONAL	IMPERATIVE
hacer to do to make *haciendo* *hecho*	*hago* *haces* *hace* *hacemos* *hacéis* *hacen*	*haga* *hagas* *haga* *hagamos* *hagáis* *hagan*	*hacía* *hacías* *hacía* *hacíamos* *hacíais* *hacían*	*hice* *hiciste* *hizo* *hicimos* *hicisteis* *hicieron*	*haré* *harás* *hará* *haremos* *haréis* *harán*	*haría* *harías* *haría* *haríamos* *haríais* *harían*	*haz* *haced*
ir to go *yendo* *ido*	*voy* *vas* *va* *vamos* *vais* *van*	*vaya* *vayas* *vaya* *vayamos* *voyáis* *vayan*	*iba* *ibas* *iba* *íbamos* *ibais* *iban*	*fui* *fuiste* *fue* *fuimos* *fuisteis* *fueron*	*iré* *irás* *irá* *iremos* *iréis* *irán*	*iría* *irías* *iría* *iríamos* *iríais* *irían*	*ve* *id*
oír to hear *oyendo* *oído*	*oigo* *oyes* *oye* *oímos* *ois* *oyen*	*oiga* *oigas* *oiga* *oigamos* *oigáis* *oigan*	*oía* *oías* *oía* *oíamos* *oíais* *oían*	*oí* *oíste* *oyó* *oímos* *oísteis* *oyeron*	*oiré* *oirás* *oirá* *oiremos* *oiréis* *oirán*	*oiría* *oirías* *oiría* *oiríamos* *oiríais* *oirían*	*oye* *oíd*
poder to be able, can *pudiendo* *podido*	*puedo* *puedes* *puede* *podemos* *podéis* *pueden*	*pueda* *puedas* *pueda* *podamos* *podáis* *puedan*	*podía* *podías* *podía* *podíamos* *podíais* *podían*	*pude* *pudiste* *pudo* *pudimos* *pudisteis* *pudieron*	*podré* *podrás* *podrá* *podremos* *podréis* *podrán*	*podría* *podrías* *podría* *podríamos* *podrías* *podrían*	*puede* *poded*
poner to put to place *poniendo* *puesto*	*pongo* *pones* *pone* *ponemos* *ponéis* *ponen*	*ponga* *pongas* *ponga* *pongamos* *pongáis* *pongan*	*ponía* *ponías* *ponía* *poníamos* *poníais* *ponían*	*puse* *pusiste* *puso* *pusimos* *pusisteis* *pusieron*	*pondré* *pondrás* *pondrá* *pondremos* *pondréis* *pondrán*	*pondría* *pondrías* *pondría* *pondríamos* *pondríais* *pondrían*	*pon* *poned*

INFINITIVE, PRESENT AND PAST PARTICIPLES	PRESENT INDICATIVE	PRESENT SUBJUNCTIVE	IMPERFECT	PRETERITE	FUTURE	CONDITIONAL	IMPERATIVE
querer to want to love *queriendo* *querido*	quiero quieres quiere queremos queréis quieren	quiera quieras quiera queramos queráis quieran	quería querías quería queríamos queríais querían	quise quisiste quiso quisimos quisisteis quisieron	querré querrás querrá querremos querréis querrán	querría querrías querría querríamos querríais querrían	quiere quered
reír to laugh *riendo* *reído*	río ríes ríe reímos reís ríen	ría rías ría riamos riáis rían	reía reías reía reíamos reíais reían	reí reíste rió reímos reísteis rieron	reiré reirás reirá reiremos reiréis reirán	reiría reirías reiría reiríamos reiríais reirían	ríe reíd
saber to know *sabiendo* *sabido*	sé sabes sabe sabemos sabéis saben	sepa sepas sepa sepamos sepáis sepan	sabía sabías sabía sabíamos sabíais sabían	supe supiste supo supimos supisteis supieron	sabré sabrás sabrá sabremos sabréis sabrán	sabría sabrías sabría sabríamos sabríais sabrían	sabe sabed
salir to go out, to leave *saliendo* *salido*	salgo sales sale salimos salís salen	salga salgas salga salgamos salgáis salgan	salía salías salía salíamos salíais salían	salí saliste salió salimos salisteis salieron	saldré saldrás saldrá saldremos saldréis saldrán	saldría saldrías saldría saldríamos saldríais saldrían	sal salid
ser to be *siendo* *sido*	soy eres es somos sois son	sea seas sea seamos seáis sean	era eras era éramos erais eran	same as preterite of *ir*.	seré serás será seremos seréis serán	sería serías sería seríamos seríais serían	sé sed

(continued)

INFINITIVE, PRESENT AND PAST PARTICIPLES	PRESENT INDICATIVE	PRESENT SUBJUNCTIVE	IMPERFECT	PRETERITE	FUTURE	CONDITIONAL	IMPERATIVE
tener to have teniendo tenido	tengo tienes tiene tenemos tenéis tienen	tenga tengas tenga tengamos tengáis tengan	tenía tenías tenía teníamos teníais tenían	tuve tuviste tuvo tuvimos tuvisteis tuvieron	tendré tendrás tendrá tendremos tendréis tendrán	tendría tendrías tendría tendríamos tendríais tendrían	ten tened
traer to bring trayendo traído	traigo traes trae traemos traéis traen	traiga traigas traiga traigamos traigáis traigan	traía traías traía traíamos traíais traían	traje trajiste trajo trajimos trajisteis trajeron	traeré traerás traerá traeremos traeréis traerán	traería traerías traería traeríamos traeríais traerían	trae traed
valer to be worth valiendo valido	valgo vales vale valemos valéis valen	valga valgas valga valgamos valgáis valgan	valía valías valía valíamos valíais valían	valí valiste valió valimos valisteis valieron	valdré valdrás valdrá valdremos valdréis valdrán	valdría valdrías valdría valdríamos valdríais valdrían	val valed
venir to come viniendo venido	vengo vienes viene venimos venís vienen	venga vengas venga vengamos vengáis vengan	venía venías venía veníamos veníais venían	vine viniste vino vinimos vinisteis vinieron	vendré vendrás vendrá vendremos vendréis vendrán	vendría vendrías vendría vendríamos vendríais vendrían	ven venid
ver to see viendo visto	veo ves ve vemos veis ven	vea veas vea veamos veáis vean	veía veías veía veíamos veíais veían	vi viste vio vimos visteis vieron	veré verás verá veremos veréis verán	vería verías vería veríamos veríais verían	ve ved

IRREGULAR ADJECTIVE AGREEMENT

- Adjectives ending in a consonant normally have only one form, e.g., *fácil*. Adjectives of nationality that end in a consonant have feminine forms ending in *–a*:

MASCULINE	FEMININE	
español	*española*	Spanish
francés	*francesa*	French
japonés	*japonesa*	Japanese

- Adjectives ending in *–or, –án, –ón,* or *–ín* have feminine forms ending in *–a*:

MASCULINE	FEMININE	
trabajador	*trabajadora*	hard-working
holgazán	*holgazana*	lazy
granduñón	*granduñona*	really big
pequeñín	*pequeñina*	really small

- Several adjectives ending in *–ista* have only one common form:

MASCULINE AND FEMININE	
idealista	idealistic
hombre idealista / mujer idealista	idealistic man / idealistic woman
pesimista	pessimistic
hombre pesimista / mujer pesimista	pessimistic man / pessimistic woman
optimista	optimistic
hombre optimista / mujer optimista	optimistic man / optimistic woman

IRREGULAR ADJECTIVE COMPARATIVES AND SUPERLATIVES

bueno / a,	good	*mejor*	better	*el / la / lo mejor* *los / las mejores*	the best
malo / a,	bad	*peor*	worse	*el / la / lo peor* *los / las peores*	the worst
grande	big	*mayor*	older	*el / la mayor* *los / las mayores*	the oldest
pequeño, -a	small	*menor*	younger	*el / la menor* *los / las menores*	the youngest

IRREGULAR PLURALS

- Nouns that end in *–z* change to *–ces* when forming the plural:

SINGULAR	PLURAL	
luz	*luces*	light / lights
lápiz	*lápices*	pencil / pencils

APPENDIX C

WHEN YOU'RE STUCK FOR WORDS . . .

TRAVELING

Here is my passport.	*Aquí está mi pasaporte.*
May I close my luggage?	*¿Puedo cerrar mi equipaje?*
Can I exchange my money here?	*¿Puede cambiarme el dinero?*
I would like a ticket for the 8:30 train.	*Desearía un billete para el tren de las 8.30.*
At what time does the train for . . . . leave?	*¿A qué hora sale el tren para . . . ?*
How much is a ticket for . . .?	*¿Cuánto cuesta un billete para . . . .?*
This seat is taken.	*Este asiento está ocupado.*
May I smoke?	*¿Puedo fumar?*
These are my suitcases.	*Éstas son mis maletas.*
At what time do we arrive?	*¿A qué hora llegamos a . . . ?*
Please, fill it up.	*Por favor, llene el depósito.*
My car broke down.	*Mi automóvil se ha averiado.*
How long will it take you to repair it?	*¿Cuánto tiempo tardará en repararlo?*
How far is . . .?	*¿A qué distancia está . . . ?*
Is this the road to . . .?	*¿Es ésta la carretera para . . . ?*
Can I exchange this traveler's check here?	*¿Puede cambiarme este cheque de viaje?*
What's the exchange rate for a dollar?	*¿Cuál es el cambio del dólar?*

IN A RESTAURANT

Can you recommend a good restaurant?	*¿Puede recomendarme un buen restaurante?*
How much do I owe you?	*¿Qué / cuánto le debo?*
How much is it?	*¿Cuánto es?*
At what time do you serve dinner / lunch?	*¿A qué hora se sirve la comida / la cena?*
Where can we sit?	*¿Dónde podemos sentarnos?*
Which wine do you recommend?	*¿Qué vino me recomienda?*
I am on a diet. I may only eat vegetables.	*Estoy a régimen. Sólo puedo comer verdura.*
I want my meat very well done.	*Quiero la carne muy hecha.*

IN A HOTEL

Have we arrived yet?	*¿Hemos llegado?*
I have a reservation under the name . . .	*Tengo reservada una habitación a nombre de . . .*
How much is it?	*¿Cuánto cuesta?*
Are there any messages, any call for me?	*¿Hay algún mensaje, alguna llamada para mí?*
Do you have a city map?	*¿Tiene usted un plano / un mapa de la ciudad?*

PHRASES FOR THE TOURIST

I want to develop this film.	*Quiero revelar este carrete de fotos.*
I want to buy batteries for my camera.	*Quiero comprar pilas para mi cámara de fotos.*
At what time do you close?	*¿A qué hora cierran?*

WHEN YOU WANT TO WRITE HOME

Where can I buy a postcard and a stamp?	*¿Dónde puedo comprar una postal y un sello / una estampilla?*
Where can I drop off these letters?	*¿Dónde hay un buzón de cartas?*

AT THE DOCTOR'S OFFICE

Where does it hurt?	*¿Dónde le duele?*
I have a headache / stomachache.	*Me duele la cabeza / el estómago.*
We'll have to check you into the hospital.	*Le tendremos que ingresar en el hospital.*
You'll have to stay in bed.	*Tendrá que guardar cama.*
I need a prescription for . . .	*Necesito que me recete . . .*
I'm going to take your blood pressure / your pulse.	*Voy a tomarle la presión / el pulso.*
I have sprained my ankle.	*Me he torcido el tobillo.*
You'll need stitches.	*Va a necesitar puntos.*
I think I'm going to faint.	*Creo que me voy a desmayar.*

JUST IN CASE

Is it dangerous to swim at this beach?	*¿Es peligroso bañarse en esta playa?*
Is this water drinkable?	*¿Se puede beber este agua? / ¿Este agua es potable?*

APPENDIX D

HOW TO SOUND LIKE A NATIVE SPEAKER

Wow!	*¡Qué barbaridad!*
No way! / Amazing!	*¡No me digas!*
It's incredible!	*¡Es increíble!*
I can't believe it!	*¡No lo puedo creer!*
It looks like it might rain.	*Parece que va a llover.*
What a nice day!	*¡Qué buen día hace hoy! / ¡Qué día tan lindo!*
It's so darn cold!	*Hace un frío de mil demonios. / Hace un frío que pela.*
I'm so glad to run into you!	*¡Qué alegría verte!*
We haven't seen each other in so long!	*¡Cuánto tiempo sin vernos!*
How's your family doing?	*¿Qué tal está la familia?*
Would you like to go out with me?	*¿Quieres salir conmigo?*
You look so handsome! / You look so pretty!	*¡Qué guapo estás! / ¡Qué guapa estás!*
How wonderful!	*¡Qué maravilla!*
How embarrassing!	*¡Qué corte! / ¡Qué vergüenza! / ¡Qué pena!*
I just don't get it.	*No me entero de nada. / No entiendo nada.*
I cannot stand him / her.	*Me cae fatal. / Me cae como un tiro.*

APPENDIX E

GREAT WEB SITES TO PRACTICE AND LEARN SPANISH

WWW.TERRA.ES	The number-one portal to Spanish on the Web.
WWW.CVC.CERVANTES.ES	The URL for Instituto Cervantes, where one can find out about Spanish courses offered in the United States.
WWW.CLARIN.COM	The online edition of the most important newspaper in Argentina.
WWW.ELPAIS.ES	The online edition of the most important newspaper in Spain.
WWW.ELTIEMPO.COM	The online edition of the most important newspaper in Colombia.
WWW.REFORMA.ES	The online edition of the most important newspaper in Mexico.
WWW.MUNDOYERBA.COM	All the humor you can find in Spanish.
WWW.CNNENESPANOL.COM	If you like to read online news, this is CNN's Spanish Web site.
WWW.RAE.ES	This is the URL for Real Academia de la Lengua Española, the institution that has the last word on everything regarding the Spanish language.

WHAT DO ALL THOSE
GRAMMAR TERMS REALLY MEAN?

ADJECTIVE	a word that describes a noun, e.g., *good, red, nice*. Don't forget that in Spanish, adjectives usually come **after** the noun and they always agree with it in gender and number, e.g., *un hombre alto* but *una mujer alta*.
ADVERB	a word that describes an action (a verb), a quality (an adjective) or another adverb, e.g., *quickly*, *very*, and *often*. Adverbs never change for agreement.
AGREEMENT	changing a word to match the grammatical features of another word. In Spanish, adjectives and articles agree with the gender and number of the nouns they describe, e.g., *un hombre alto, una mujer alta, dos hombres altos, dos mujeres altas*.
ARTICLE	"a / an" or "the." Definite articles mean "the" and indefinite articles mean "a / an." In Spanish, articles match the gender and number of the noun, e.g., *un / el hombre* but *una / la mujer*.
COMPARATIVE	"more" or "less." An expression comparing two people or things or two qualities. In Spanish, the comparative is expressed with *más que*, "more than," and *menos que*, "less than," e.g., *Luis es más alto que Juan*, "Luis is taller than Juan."
CONJUGATION	changing a verb to show who the subject is and when the action takes place (i.e., tense—past, present, future). For example, *yo hablo*, but *tu hablas, ella habla, nosotros hablamos,* etc.
CONJUNCTION	a word that connects other words or phrase. The most common conjunctions are: *y*, "and," *pero*, "but," and *o*, "or."
DEMONSTRATIVE	"this" and "that." In Spanish, demonstratives match the gender and number of the nouns they describe or replace, e.g., *este hombre* but *esta mujer*.
DIRECT OBJECT	in the sentence *Le escribo una carta a Marcos*, "I'm writing a postcard to Marcos," the direct object is *una carta*, "a letter."
GENDER	strictly a grammatical category. In Spanish, nouns, adjectives, and articles have gender: they can be masculine or feminine.
IMPERSONAL CONSTRUCTION	a construction that is used to make a general statement, where the subject is a general "you, one," or "they," as in *Aquí se habla inglés*, "English is spoken here."

INDIRECT OBJECT	in the sentence *Le escribo una carta a Marcos*, "I'm writing a letter to Marcos," the indirect object is *a Marcos*, "to Marcos." Indirect objects receive the action of the verb, usually with the "help" of a preposition, like a, "to," or *por / para*, "for." In Spanish, the indirect object pronoun *le / les* is also always present in this type of sentence.
INFINITIVE	the basic form of a verb (the one you'll find in a dictionary), before it's been changed (or conjugated) to show who the subject is or when the action takes place; the infinitive endings in Spanish are *–ar,—er,* and *–ir.*
NOUN	a person, place, thing, or idea, e.g., *mujer, sopa, amor.*
NUMBER	There are two numbers: "one" or "more than one," also called "singular" and "plural."
PARTITIVE	words expressing a partial quantity of an item that can not be counted, like "water," "rice," or "pie," i.e. "some / a little / any of." In Spanish, the partitive is expressed with the expressions *algo de*, "some of," *nada de*, "any of," or the expressions *un poco de*, "a little bit of" or *mucho de*, "a lot of."
PAST PARTICIPLE	the form of a verb (usually ending in *–ado* and *–ido*) used to form the present perfect or used as an adjective, e.g., *He hablado*, "I spoke," or *Está dormido*, "He's asleep."
POSSESSIVE	"my / mine, your / yours," etc. A word that shows ownership. In Spanish, possessives agree in gender and number with the object or person **possessed**, not the owner, e.g., *mi coche*, "my car," *mis coches*, "my cars."
PREPOSITION	"to, from, on, in," etc. A connective word that shows spatial, temporal, or other relationships between other words.
PRONOUN	"I, him, mine, this one," etc. A word that takes the place of a noun.
REFLEXIVE VERB	a verb conjugated with a reflexive pronoun: *me*, "myself," *te*, "yourself," *se*, "him / herself, themselves," *nos*, "ourselves," *os*, "yourselves."
SUBJECT	a person, place, or thing performing the action of the verb or being in the state described by it, e.g., in *Marcos is jogging* or *This vase is beautiful*, "Marcos" and "the vase" are subjects.
SUFFIX	an ending that is attached to a word to change its meaning, e.g., *-ito / ita*, meaning "small," or *–mente*, the equivalent of English "–ly," which changes an adjective to an adverb.
SUPERLATIVE	"most, least," etc. An expression indicating the highest degree and used when comparing three or more things, people, or qualities, e.g., *Ella es la chica más bella del mundo*, "She's the most beautiful girl in the world."
TENSE	the time of an action or state of being, i.e. past, present, future, etc.
VERB	a word showing an action or a state of being, e.g., *hablar*, "to speak," or ser, "to be."

GLOSSARY

Abbreviations

adjective	*adj.*	masculine	*m.*
adverb	*adv.*	Mexico	*Mex.*
Argentina	*Arg.*	noun	*n.*
article	*art.*	object	*obj.*
colloquial	*coll.*	pejorative	*pej.*
Caribbean	*Carib.*	preposition	*prep.*
Colombia	*Col.*	plural	*pl.*
definite	*def.*	pronoun	*pr.*
dimunitive	*dim.*	relative	*rel.*
direct	*dir.*	singular	*sg.*
feminine	*f.*	verb	*v.*
formal	*fml.*	Spain	*Sp.*
indirect	*ind.*	slang	*slng.*
informal	*infml.*		

SPANISH–ENGLISH

A

a (ah) *to, at, in, on, by, for*
  a todos lados (ah TOH-dohs LAH-dohs) *everywhere*
  a veces (ah BEH-sehs) *sometimes*
  a ver... (ah BEHR) *let's see*
abajo (ah-BAH-hoh) *under; down; below*
abierto (ah-BYEHR-toh) *open*
el abogado, –a (ah-boh-GAH-doh) *lawyer*
abonar (ah-boh-NAHR) *to pay*
el abrigo (ah-BREE-goh) *coat*
abril (ah-BREEL) *April*
abrir (ah-BREER) *to open*
la abuela (ah-BWEH-lah) *grandmother*
el abuelo (ah-BWEH-loh) *grandfather*
aburrido, –a (ah-boo-RREE-doh) *boring; bored*
acá (ah-KAH) *here*
acabar de (ah-kah-BAHR deh) *just finished*
acampar (ah-kahm-PAHR) *to camp*
acaso (ah-KAH-soh) *in case; maybe*
acceder (ahk-seh-DEHR) *to access*
aceptar (ah-sehp-TAHR) *to accept*
acercarse (ah-sehr-KAR-seh) *to get closer; to approach*
acondicionado (ah-kohn-dee-syoh-NAH-doh) *conditioned; air-conditioned*

aconsejar (ah-kohn-seh-HAHR) *to give advice*
acostumbrarse (ah-kohs-toom-BRAHR-seh) *to get used / accustomed to*
la actividad (ahk-tee-bee-DAHD) *activity*
el actor / la actriz (ahk-TOHR / ahk-TREES) *actor, actress*
la actuación (ahk-twah-SYOHN) *performance*
acuerdo, de (deh-ah-KWEHR-doh) *all right*
adelantar (ah-deh-lahn-TAHR) *to pass*
además (ah-deh-MAHS) *also; besides*
adentrarse (ah-dehn-TRAHR-seh) *to go in*
adiós (ah-DYOHS) *good-bye*
adjuntar (ahd-hoon-TAHR) *to enclose*
el admirador, –a (ahd-mee-rah-DOHR) *admirer*
el adulto, –a (ah-DOOL-toh) *adult*
aéreo, –a (ah-EH-reh-oh) *aerial*
el aeropuerto (ah-eh-roh-PWEHR-toh) *airport*
afortunadamente (ah-fohr-too-nah-dah-MEHN-teh) *fortunately*
la agencia (ah-HEHN-syah) *agency*
la agenda (ah-HEHN-dah) *agenda*
el / la agente (ah-HEHN-teh) *agent*

agosto (ah-GOHS-toh) *August*
agradable (ah-grah-DAH-bleh) *nice, friendly*
agregar (ah-greh-GAHR) *to add*
el agua (AH-gwah) *water*
el aguacate (ah-gwah-KAH-teh) *avocado*
el aguardiente (ah-gwahr-DYEHN-teh) *Colombian liquor*
ahí (ah-HEE) *there*
ahora (ah-OH-rah) *now*
  ahorita mismo (ah-oh-REE-tah MEES-moh) *right now* (Mex.)
ahorrar (ah-oh-RRAHR) *to save (money)*
el aire (AHY-reh) *air*
  al aire libre (ahl AHY-reh LEE-breh) *outdoors*
alborotarse (ahl-boh-roh-TAHR-seh) *to get agitated*
el alboroto (ahl-boh-ROH-toh) *fuss, noise*
alejarse (ah-leh-HAHR-seh) *to go farther*
algo (AHL-goh) *something*
alguien (AHL-gyehn) *somebody*
algún, alguno, –a (ahl-GOON, ahl-GOO-noh) *some, any*
  alguna vez (ahl-GOO-nah behs) *some time*
el alias (AH-lyahs) *nickname; a.k.a.*
allá (ah-YAH) *there*

allí (ah-YEE) *there*

almorzar (ahl-mohr-SAHR) *to have lunch*

el almuerzo (ahl-MWEHR-soh) *lunch*

alojarse (ah-loh-HAHR-seh) *to stay, to lodge*

alquilar (ahl-kee-LAHR) *to rent*

el alquiler (ahl-kee-LEHR) *rent*

alrededores (ahl-rreh-deh-DOH-rehs) *surroundings*

la altitud (ahl-tee-TOOD) *altitude*

alto, –a (AHL-toh) *tall, high*

amanecer (ah-mah-neh-SEHR) *to dawn; to wake up*

amar (ah-MAHR) *to love*

amarillo, –a (ah-mah-REE-yoh) *yellow*

el ambiente (ahm-BYEHN-teh) *atmosphere*

americano, –a (ah-meh-ree-KAH-noh) *American*

el amigo, –a (ah-MEE-goh) *friend*

el amor (ah-MOHR) *love*

añadir (ah-nyah-DEER) *to add*

anaranjado, –a (ah-nah-rahn-HAH-doh) *orange*

ancho, –a (AHN-choh) *wide*

andar (ahn-DAHR) *to walk*

la anécdota (ah-NEHK-doh-tah) *anecdote*

animar (ah-nee-MAHR) *to cheer*

el año (AH-nyoh) *year*

anoche (ah-NOH-cheh) *last night*

antes (AHN-tehs) *before*

anticipación (ahn-tee-see-pah-SYOHN) *in advance; anticipation*

anticipado (ahn-tee-see-PAH-doh) *advanced*

antiguo, –a (ahn-TEE-gwoh) *antique, old, former*

antipático, –a (ahn-tee-PAH-tee-koh) *unfriendly*

la antropología (ahn-troh-poh-loh-HEE-ah) *anthropology*

aparecer (ah-pah-reh-SEHR) *to appear, to show up*

el apartamento (ah-pahr-tah-MEHN-toh) *apartment*

el apellido (ah-peh-YEE-doh) *last name*

el aperitivo (ah-peh-ree-TEE-boh) *appetizer*

aprender (ah-prehn-DEHR) *to learn*

apropiado (ah-proh-PYAH-doh) *appropriate*

aprovechar (ah-proh-beh-CHAHR) *to take advantage of*

apurarse (ah-poo-RAHR-seh) *to hurry up*

aquí (ah-KEE) *here*

el árbol (AHR-bohl) *tree*

el archivo (ahr-CHEE-boh) *file*

arder (ahr-DEHR) *to burn*

el área (AH-reh-ah) *area*

la arepa (ah-REH-pah) *Colombian corn tortilla*

el arquitecto, –a (ahr-kee-TEHK-toh) *architect*

la arquitectura (ahr-kee-tehk-TOO-rah) *architecture*

arriba (ah-RREE-bah) *up*

el arte (AHR-teh) *art*

el artículo (ahr-TEE-koo-loh) *article*

el / la artista (ahr-TEES-tah) *artist*

el asado (ah-SAH-doh) *roast*

asado, –a (ah-SAH-doh) *roasted*

así (ah-SEE) *that way, so, this way*

así de bien (ah-SEE deh byehn) *that good*

así es (ah-SEE ehs) *that's it*

el aseo (ah-SEH-oh) *toilet*

el asiento (ah-SYEHN-toh) *seat*

asistir (ah-sees-TEER) *to attend*

el aspecto (ahs-PEHK-toh) *appearance*

el asunto (ah-SOON-toh) *issue, affair*

asustar (ah-soos-TAHR) *to scare*

atentamente (ah-tehn-tah-MEHN-teh) *respectfully*

aterrizar (ah-teh-rree-SAHR) *to land*

atractivo, –a (ah-trahk-TEE-boh) *attractive*

atrás (ah-TRAHS) *behind*

aún (ah-OON) *still*

aunque (OWN-keh) *even though*

Australia (ows-TRAH-lyah) *Australia*

auténtico / a (ow-TEHN-tee-koh) *authentic*

el auto (OW-toh) *car*

el autobús (ow-toh-BOOS) *bus*

el autógrafo (ow-TOH-grah-foh) *autograph*

el automóvil (ow-toh-MOH-beel) *car*

autónomo, –a (ow-TOH-noh-moh) *autonomous, self-governed*

la aventura (ah-behn-TOO-rah) *adventure*

el avión (ah-BYOHN) *plane*

¡Ay! (ahy) *ouch!*

ayer (ah-YEHR) *yesterday*

el / la ayudante (ah-yoo-DAHN-teh) *helper*

ayudar (ah-yoo-DAHR) *to help*

el azúcar (ah-SOO-kahr) *sugar*

azul (ah-SOOL) *blue*

B

bailar (bahy-LAHR) *to dance*

el baile (BAHY-leh) *dance*

bajar (bah-HAHR) *to go down; to get off a vehicle*

bajo, –a (BAH-hoh) *short*

el baloncesto (bah-lohn-SEHS-toh) *basketball*

la banana (bah-NAH-nah) *banana*

bañarse (bah-NYAHR-seh) *to swim; take a bath, to bathe*

la bandera (bahn-DEH-rah) *flag*

el bandoneón (bahn-doh-neh-OHN) *musical instrument, used to play a tango*

el baño (BAH-nyoh) *swim, bath*

el bar (bahr) *bar*

barato, –a (bah-RAH-toh) *cheap*

barbaridad (bahr-bah-ree-DAHD) *atrocity*

¡Qué barbaridad! (keh bahr-bah-ree-DAHD) *Wow!; My goodness!*

el barco (BAHR-koh) *boat*

basta (BAHS-tah) *enough*

la basura (bah-SOO-rah) *garbage*

la batería (bah-teh-REE-ah) *battery*

batir (bah-TEER) *to beat*

el / la bebé (beh-BEH) *baby*

beber (beh-BEHR) *to drink*

la bebida (beh-BEE-dah) *drink*

bello, –a (BEH-yoh) *pretty, beautiful*

el bembé (behm-BEH) *noise (Carib.)*

bendito, –a (behn-DEE-toh) *blessed*

besar (beh-SAHR) *to kiss*

la bicicleta (bee-see-KLEH-tah) *bicycle*

bien (byehn) *good (adj.); very (adv.)*

bienvenido, –a (byen-beh-NEE-doh) *welcome*

el bife (BEE-feh) *beef (Arg.)*

el billete (bee-YEH-teh) *ticket*

el banco (BAHN-koh) *bank; bench*

blanco, –a (BLAHN-koh) *white*

la blusa (BLOO-sah) *blouse*

bobo, –a (BOH-boh) *dumb, stupid*

el bocadillo (boh-kah-DEE-yoh) *sandwich (Sp.)*

bola de tacaños (BOH-lah deh tah-KAH-nyohs) *bunch of cheap people*

el boleto (boh-LEH-toh) *ticket*

el bollo (BOH-yoh) *pastry, bread (Sp.)*

el bombón (bohm-BOHN) *chocolate*

bonito, –a (boh-NEE-toh) *pretty*

boricua (boh-REE-kwa) *person from Puerto Rico*

el bosque (BOHS-keh) *forest*

la botella (boh-TEH-yah) *bottle*

el botón (boh-TOHN) *button*

el botones (boh-TOH-nehs) *bellboy*

el boxeo (bohk-SEH-oh) *boxing*

boyacense (boh-yah-SEHN-seh) *person from the Boyacá, region in Colombia*

la brocheta (broh-CHEH-tah) *skewer*

la broma (BROH-mah) *joke, prank*

bruto, –a (BROO-toh) *ignorant* (Col.)

bucear (boo-seh-AHR) *to scuba dive*

budista (boo-DEES-tah) *Buddhist*

buen (bwehn) *good*

buen provecho (bwehn proh-BEH-choh) *enjoy your meal*

buen tipo (bwehn TEE-poh) *good guy*

buenísimo, –a (bweh-NEE-see-moh) *very good*

bueno, –a (BWEH-noh) *good; well*

buenos días (BWEH-nohs DEE-ahs) *good morning*

buenas tardes (BWEH-nahs TAHR-dehs) *good afternoon*

buenas noches (BWEH-nahs NOH-chehs) *good evening; good night*

bueno, –a (estar) (BWEH-noh ehs-TAHR) *to be healthy*

el buscador (boos-kah-DOHR) *search engine*

buscar (boos-KAHR) *to look for, to search*

C

el caballo (kah-BAH-yoh) *horse*

la cabecera (kah-beh-SEH-rah) *headboard*

cachaco, –a (kah-CHAH-koh) *person from the Bogotá area in Colombia*

el cactus (KAHK-toos) *cactus*

cada (KAH-dah) *each; every*

caer (kah-EHR) *to fall*

el café (kah-FEH) *coffee*

café con leche (kah-FEH kohn LEH-cheh) *coffee with milk*

la caja (KAH-hah) *box; cash register*

el / la cajera (kah-HEH-rah) *cashier*

la calaverita (kah-lah-beh-REE-tah) *little skull* (Mex.)

la calefacción (kah-leh-fahk-SYOHN) *heat, heater*

calentar (kah-lehn-TAHR) *to heat up*

caliente (kah-LYEHN-teh) *hot*

callar (kah-YAHR) *to be silent, to shut up*

la calle (KAH-yeh) *street*

la calma (KAHL-mah) *calm*

el calor (kah-LOHR) *heat*

la cama (KAH-mah) *bed*

la cámara (KAH-mah-rah) *camera*

el cambio (KAHM-byoh) *change*

en cambio (ehn KAHM-byoh) *on the other hand*

el camerino (kah-meh-REE-noh) *dressing room*

caminar (kah-mee-NAHR) *to walk*

el camino (kah-MEE-noh) *way*

la camisa (kah-MEE-sah) *shirt*

la camiseta (kah-mee-SEH-tah) *T-shirt*

el campeón, –a (kahm-peh-OHN) *champion*

el canal (kah-NAHL) *channel*

la canción (kahn-SYOHN) *song*

la cancelación (kahn-seh-lah-SYOHN) *cancellation*

el canguro (kahn-GOO-roh) *kangaroo*

cansado, –a (kahn-SAH-doh) *tired*

el cansancio (kahn-SAHN-syoh) *fatigue, weariness*

cansar (kahn-SAHR) *to tire*

el / la cantante (kahn-TAHN-teh) *singer*

cantar (kahn-TAHR) *to sing*

la cantidad (kahn-tee-DAHD) *quantity*

el canto (KAHN-toh) *singing* (n.)

el Cañón del Colorado (kah-NYOHN dehl koh-loh-RAH-doh) *Grand Canyon*

el capital (kah-pee-TAHL) *capital*

el capítulo (kah-PEE-too-loh) *chapter*

la cara (KAH-rah) *face*

caramba (kah-RAHM-bah) *Wow!* (coll.)

el caramelo (kah-rah-MEH-loh) *caramel sauce; candy*

cargar (kahr-GAHR) *to load*

caribeño, –a (kah-ree-BEH-nyoh) *Caribbean*

cariñoso, –a (kah-ree-NYOH-soh) *affectionate*

la carne (KAHR-neh) *meat*

la carnicería (kahr-nee-seh-REE-ah) *meat market*

caro, –a (KAH-roh) *expensive*

la carretera (kah-rreh-TEH-rah) *road*

el carro (KAH-rroh) *car*

la carta (KAHR-tah) *letter; menu*

la casa (KAH-sah) *house*

casado, –a (kah-SAH-doh) *married*

casi (KAH-see) *almost*

el caso (KAH-soh) *case*

castaño, –a (kahs-TAH-nyoh) *brown-haired*

la casualidad (kah-swah-lee-DAHD) *coincidence*

la catedral (kah-teh-DRAHL) *cathedral*

católico, –a (kah-TOH-lee-koh) *Catholic*

catorce (kah-TOHR-seh) *fourteen*

la causa (KAW-sah) *cause*

la cebolla (seh-BOH-yah) *onion*

celebrar (seh-leh-BRAHR) *to celebrate*

los celos (SEH-lohs) *jealousy*

celoso, –a (seh-LOH-soh) *jealous*

el celular (seh-loo-LAHR) *cellular telephone*

la cena (SEH-nah) *dinner*

cenar (seh-NAHR) *to eat dinner, to have dinner*

la ceniza (seh-NEE-sah) *ash*

el cenote (seh-NOH-the) *cenote, natural underground reservoir*

central (sehn-TRAHL) *central*

el centro (SEHN-troh) *center*

la cerámica (seh-RAH-mee-kah) *ceramics, pottery*

cerca (SEHR-kah) *near*

cerca de (SEHR-kah deh) *close to*

cerquita (sehr-KEE-tah) *really close*

el cerdo (SEHR-doh) *pork*

el cereal (seh-reh-AHL) *cereal*

cerrado, –a (seh-RRAH-doh) *closed*

cerrar (seh-RRAHR) *to close*

el cerro (SEH-rroh) *hill*

la cerveza (sehr-BEH-sah) *beer*

el chamaquito (chah-mah-KEE-toh) *kid* (Mex.)

el champán (chahm-PAHN) *champagne*

la chaqueta (chah-KEH-tah) *jacket*

la charla (CHAHR-lah) *chat*

charlar (chahr-LAHR) *to chat*

el chat (chaht) *chat room* (slng.)

chatear (chah-teh-AHR) *to chat via the Internet*

el chavo (CHAH-boh) *pal, friend* (Mex.)

che (cheh) *Hey!* (Arg.)

chévere (CHEH-beh-reh) *cool* (slng. Col.)

la chica (CHEE-kah) *girl, female teenager*

el chico (CHEE-koh) *boy, male teenager*

el chile (CHEE-leh) *hot pepper*

chillar (chee-YAHR) *to scream, to cry out*

el chocolate (choh-koh-LAH-teh) *chocolate*

el chorizo (choh-REE-soh) *type of sausage*

chulo, –a (CHOO-loh) *cocky; lovely* (Mex.) (Sp.)

el ciclismo (see-KLEES-moh) *cycling*

ciego, –a (SYEH-goh) *blind*

cielito (syeh-LEE-toh) *sweetheart* (coll.)

el cielo (SYEH-loh) *sky; heaven*

cien (syehn) *one hundred*

cierto, –a (SYEHR-toh) *real, true, certain*

el cigarrillo (see-gah-RREE-yoh) *cigarette*

cinco (SEEN-koh) *five*

el cine (SEE-neh) *cinema*

circular (seer-koo-LAHR) *to circulate*

la ciudad (syoo-DAHD) *city*
claro, –a (KLAH-roh) *clear*
  claro (KLAH-roh) *of course* (expression)
la clase (KLAH-seh) *class*
clásico, –a (KLAH-see-koh) *classic*
el club (kloob) *club, team*
cocer (koh-SEHR) *to boil*
el coche (KOH-cheh) *car*
la cocina (koh-SEE-nah) *kitchen*
cocinar (koh-see-NAHR) *to cook*
la coincidencia (koyhn-see-DEHN-syah) *coincidence*
la cola (KOH-lah) *line (Sp.)*
la colección (koh-lehk-SYOHN) *collection*
el colegio (koh-LEH-hyoh) *school*
Colombia (koh-LOHM-byah) *Colombia*
colombiano, –a (koh-lohm-BYAH-noh) *Colombian*
la colonia (koh-LOH-nyah) *neighborhood (in Mexico City)*
colonial (koh-loh-NYAHL) *colonial*
coloquial (koh-loh-KYAHL) *colloquial*
el coloquio (koh-loh-KYOH) *discussion*
el color (koh-LOHR) *color*
el comedor (koh-meh-DOHR) *dining room*
comentar (koh-mehn-TAHR) *to talk about, to comment*
comenzar (koh-mehn-SAHR) *to begin*
comer (koh-MEHR) *to eat*
la comida (koh-MEE-dah) *food; meal*
la comisaría (koh-mee-sah-REE-ah) *police station*
como (KOH-moh) *like, as*
cómo (KOH-moh) *how?*
cómodo, –a (KOH-moh-doh) *comfortable*
el compadre (kohm-PAH-dreh) *godfather*
la compañía (kohm-pah-NYEE-ah) *company*
el / la compañero, –a (kohm-pah-NYEH-roh) *colleague; companion*
comparar (kohm-pah-RAHR) *to compare*
la competición (kohm-peh-tee-SYOHN) *competition*
complementar (kohm-pleh-mehn-TAHR) *to complement*
completamente (kohm-pleh-tah-MEHN-teh) *absolutely*
completo, –a (kohm-PLEH-toh) *complete*
complicado, –a (kohm-plee-KAH-doh) *complicated*

componer (kohm-poh-NEHR) *to compose*
la composición (kohm-poh-see-SYOHN) *composition*
la compra (KOHM-prah) *purchase*
compras (KOHM-prahs) *shopping*
comprender (kohm-prehn-DEHR) *to understand*
comprensivo, –a (kohm-prehn-SEE-boh) *understanding*
comprimir (kohm-pree-MEER) *to compress*
la computadora (kohm-poo-tah-DOH-rah) *computer*
con (kohn) *with*
  con mucho gusto (kohn MOO-choh GOOS-toh) *with pleasure*
el concierto (kohn-SYEHR-toh) *concert*
condensado, –a (kohn-dehn-SAH-doh) *condensed*
conectado, –a (koh-nehk-TAH-doh) *connected*
la conferencia (kohn-feh-REHN-syah) *conference, lecture*
confundido, –a (kohn-foon-DEE-doh) *confused*
el congreso (kohn-GREH-soh) *congress, conference*
conmigo (kohn-MEE-goh) *with me*
conocer (koh-noh-SEHR) *to meet; to know*
conquistar (kohn-kees-TAHR) *to conquer*
el consejo (kohn-SEH-hoh) *piece of advice*
la contaminación (kohn-tah-mee-nah-SYOHN) *pollution*
contar (kohn-TAHR) *to count; to tell*
contemplar (kohn-tehm-PLAHR) *to contemplate; to consider*
contenido (kohn-teh-NEE-doh) *content*
contento, –a (kohn-TEHN-toh) *happy*
contestar (kohn-tehs-TAHR) *to answer*
contigo (kohn-TEE-goh) *with you*
continuar (kohn-tee-NWAHR) *to continue*
contratar (kohn-trah-TAHR) *to hire*
el control (kohn-TROHL) *control*
convincente (kohn-been-SEHN-teh) *convincing*
cooperativo, –a (koh-oh-peh-ra-TEE-boh) *cooperative*
La Copa del Mundo (lah KOH-pah dehl MOON-doh) *World Cup (soccer)*
el corazón (koh-rah-SOHN) *heart, sweetie*
el cordero (kohr-DEH-roh) *lamb*
  cordero del diablo (kohr-DEH-roh dehl DYAH-bloh) *devil's lamb*
Corea (koh-REH-ah) *Korea*

correcto (koh-RREHK-toh) *correct*
el correoelectrónico (koh-RREH-oh eh-lehk-TROH-nee-koh) *electronic mail (email)*
correr (koh-RREHR) *to run*
la corriente eléctrica (koh-RRYEHN-teh eh-LEHK-tree-kah) *electrical power*
cortar (kohr-TAHR) *to cut*
la cosa (KOH-sah) *thing*
costar (kohs-TAHR) *to cost*
costeño, –a (kohs-TEH-nyoh) *person from the Atlantic or the Pacific coastal regions of Colombia*
el cráter (KRAH-tehr) *crater*
el crédito (KREH-dee-toh) *credit*
creer (kreh-EHR) *to believe, to think*
cruel (krwehl) *cruel*
cruzar (kroo-SAHR) *to cross*
el cuadro (KWAH-droh) *picture, painting*
cuál (kwahl) *what?, which one?*
cuándo (KWAHN-doh) *when?*
cuando (KWAHN-doh) *while*
cuánto, –a, –os, –as (KWAHN-toh) *how many?, how much?*
cuarenta (kwah-REHN-tah) *forty*
el cuarto (KWAHR-toh) *room*
  el cuarto de estar (KWAHR-toh deh ehs-TAHR) *living room (Sp.)*
cuarto, –a (KWAHR-toh) *fourth*
el cuate (KWAH-teh) *pal, buddy (Mex.)*
cuatro (KWAH-troh) *four*
cubano, –a (koo-BAH-noh) *Cuban*
cubrir (koo-BREER) *to cover*
el cuento (KWEHN-toh) *short story, tale*
la cuerda (KWEHR-dah) *rope*
el cuerpo (KWEHR-poh) *body*
la cuestión (kwehs-TYOHN) *matter, issue*
cuidado (kwee-DAH-doh) *careful, care*
la culpa (KOOL-pah) *fault*
cultural (kool-too-RAHL) *cultural*
el cumbe (KOOM-beh) *African dance*
la cumbia (KOOM-byah) *Colombian dance*
el cumpleaños (koom-pleh-AH-nyohs) *birthday*
el curador, –a (koo-rah-DOHR) *curator*
curioso, –a (koo-RYOH-so) *curious*

D

dar (dahr) *to give*
de (deh) *from; of; for; by; on*
  de memoria (deh meh-MOH-ryah) *by heart*
  de moda (deh MOH-dah) *fashionable*

de nada (deh NAH-dah) *you're welcome*

de repente (deh rreh-PEHN-teh) *suddenly*

deber (deh-BEHR) *to have to, must; to owe*

decenas (deh-SEH-nahs) *tenths*

decidir (deh-see-DEER) *to decide*

decir (deh-SEER) *to say, to tell*

la decisión (deh-see-SYOHN) *decision*

definitivamente (deh-fee-nee-tee-bah-MEHN-teh) *definitely; permanently*

dejar (deh-HAHR) *to leave; to let; to allow*

del (dehl) **de** *and* **el** *together*

delgado, –a (dehl-GAH-doh) *thin, slim*

demasiado, –a, –os, –as (deh-mah-SYAH-doh) *too much, too many*

dentro (DEHN-troh) *inside*

el dependiente, –a (deh-pehn-DYEHN-teh) *salesperson*

el deporte (deh-POHR-teh) *sport*

deportivo, –a (deh-pohr-TEE-boh) *sporty; athletic*

deprimido, –a (deh-pree-MEE-doh) *depressed*

la desaparición (deh-sah-pah-ree-SYOHN) *disappearance*

el desastre (deh-SAHS-treh) *disaster*

desayunar (deh-sah-yoo-NAHR) *to eat breakfast*

el desayuno (deh-sah-YOO-noh) *breakfast*

descansar (dehs-kahn-SAHR) *to rest*

descargar (dehs-kahr-GAHR) *to download; to unload*

desconocido, –a (dehs-koh-noh-SEE-doh) *stranger; unkown*

descubrir (dehs-koo-BREER) *to discover*

desde (DEHS-deh) *from; since*

desde luego (DEHS-deh LWEH-goh) *of course*

desear (deh-seh-AHR) *to desire; to want*

desesperado, –a (deh-sehs-peh-RAH-doh) *desperate*

deshelar (deh-seh-LAHR) *to defrost*

desinfectar (deh-seen-fehk-TAHR) *to disinfect*

desintoxicar (deh-seen-tohk-see-KAHR) *to detoxify*

desmayarse (dehs-mah-YAHR-seh) *to pass out, to faint*

despegar (dehs-peh-GAHR) *(for an airplane) to take off*

despejado, –a (dehs-peh-HAH-doh) *clear*

despertarse (dehs-pehr-TAHR-seh) *to wake up*

después (dehs-PWEHS) *later, after*

destino (dehs-TEE-noh) *destination; destiny*

detrás (deh-TRAHS) *behind*

el día (DEE-ah) *day*

día libre (DEE-ah LEE-breh) *day off*

el diablo (DYAH-bloh) *devil*

diario (DYAH-ryoh) *daily*

diciembre (dee-CYEHM-breh) *December*

diecinueve (dyeh-see-NWEH-beh) *nineteen*

dieciocho (dyeh-see-OH-choh) *eighteen*

dieciséis (dyeh-see-SAYS) *sixteen*

diecisiete (dyeh-see-SYEH-teh) *seventeen*

la dieta (DYEH-tah) *diet*

diez (dyehs) *ten*

diferente (dee-feh-REHN-teh) *different*

difícil (dee-FEE-seel) *hard, difficult*

el dinero (dee-NEH-roh) *money*

Dios (dyohs) *God*

la dirección (dee-rehk-SYOHN) *address*

directo, –a (dee-REHK-toh) *straight*

incapacitado, –a (dees-kah-pah-see-TAH-doh) *handicapped; disabled*

la discoteca (dees-koh-TEH-kah) *disco*

discoteca de moda (dees-koh-TEH-kah deh MOH-dah) *fashionable disco*

disculparse (dees-KOOL-pahr) *to apologize*

la discusión (dees-koo-SYOHN) *discussion, argument*

la disquera (dees-KEH-rah) *record company*

la distancia (dees-TAHN-syah) *distance*

la diversión (dee-behr-SYOHN) *fun activity*

divertido, –a (dee-behr-TEE-doh) *fun, amusing*

divertirse (dee-behr-TEER-seh) *to have fun*

divorciado, –a (dee-bohr-SYAH-doh) *divorced*

doble (DOH-bleh) *double*

doble techo (DOH-bleh TEH-choh) *double ceiling*

doce (DOH-seh) *twelve*

el documento (doh-koo-MEHN-toh) *document*

doler (doh-LEHR) *to hurt*

domingo (doh-MEEN-goh) *Sunday*

dominicano, –a (doh-mee-nee-KAH-noh) *Dominican*

Don (dohn) *Mr., sir*

Doña (DOH-nyah) *Mrs., Madam*

dónde (DOHN-deh) *where?*

dormir (dohr-MEER) *to sleep*

dormirse (dohr-MEER-seh) *to fall asleep*

el dormitorio (dohr-mee-TOH-ryoh) *bedroom*

dos (dohs) *two*

ducharse (doo-CHAHR-seh) *to take a shower*

el dueño, –a (DWEH-nyoh) *owner*

durante (doo-RAHN-teh) *during*

durar (doo-RAHR) *to last*

duro, –a (DOO-roh) *hard*

la edad (eh-DAHD) *age*

efectivo, –a (eh-fehk-TEE-boh) *effective, cash*

el ejército (eh-HEHR-see-toh) *army*

el (ehl) *the (m.)*

él (ehl) *he*

la electricidad (eh-lehk-tree-see-DAH) *electricity*

electrónico, –a (eh-lehk-TROH-nee-koh) *electronic*

elegante (eh-leh-GAHN-teh) *elegant*

elevado, –a (eh-leh-BAH-doh) *elevated*

ella (EH-yah) *she*

ellas (EH-yahs) *they, them (f.)*

ellos (EH-yohs) *they, them (m.)*

embarazada (ehm-bah-rah-SAH-dah) *pregnant*

embarcar (ehm-bahr-KAHR) *to board a boat or a plane*

el embarque (ehm-BAHR-keh) *loading, boarding*

el emilio (eh-MEE-lyoh) *e-mail (slng. Sp.)*

la emisión (eh-mee-SYOHN) *emission*

emitir (eh-mee-TEER) *to issue*

empapado, –a (ehm-pah-PAH-doh) *soaked*

empatar (ehm-pah-TAHR) *to tie*

el / la emperador, –triz (ehm-peh-rah-DOHR), (ehm-peh-rah-TREES) *emperor, empress*

empezar (ehm-peh-SAHR) *to start*

el empleado, –a (ehm-pleh-AH-doh) *employee*

en (ehn) *in*

en cambio (ehn KAHM-byoh) *in exchange; on the other hand*

enamorarse (eh-nah-moh-RAHR-seh) *to fall in love*

encantado, –a (ehn-kahn-TAH-doh) *pleased, charmed*

encantar (ehn-kahn-TAHR) *to love (something), to enjoy*

encestar (ehn-sehs-TAHR) *to score a basket*

enchilada (ehn-chee-LAH-dah) *enchilada*

el encierro (ehn-SYEH-rroh) *running of the bulls*

encontrar (ehn-kohn-TRAHR) *to find*

enero (eh-NEH-roh) *January*

el enfermo, –a (ehn-FEHR-moh) *ill person*

engañar (ehn-gah-NYAHR) *to fool*

enloquecido, –a (ehn-loh-keh-SEE-doh) *insane*

enojado, –a (eh-noh-HAH-doh) *angry*

enojarse (eh-noh-HAHR-seh) *to get angry*

enorme (eh-NOHR-meh) *huge*

la ensalada (ehn-sah-LAH-dah) *salad*

enseñar (ehn-seh-NYAHR) *to teach*

entender (enh-tehn-DEHR) *to understand*

enterarse (ehn-teh-RAHR-seh) *to inform, to become aware of; to understand* (coll. Sp.)

entonces (ehn-TOHN-sehs) *then*

la entrada (ehn-TRAH-dah) *entrance; tickets*

entrar (ehn-TRAHR) *to enter*

entre (EHN-treh) *between*

entretenido, –a (ehn-treh-teh-NEE-doh) *amusing* (with *ser*); *occupied* (with *estar*)

la entrevista (ehn-treh-BEES-tah) *interview*

enviar (ehn-BYAHR) *to send*

el equipaje (eh-kee-PAH-heh) *luggage*

el equipo (eh-KEE-poh) *team; equipment*

equivocarse (eh-kee-boh-KAHR-seh) *to be wrong*

la era (EH-rah) *age*

era (EH-rah) *was, used to be*

el escándalo (ehs-KAHN-dah-loh) *scandal*

el escarabajo (ehs-kah-rah-BAH-hoh) *beetle*

escribir (ehs-kree-BEER) *to write*

el escritorio (ehs-kree-TOH-ryoh) *desk*

escuchar (ehs-koo-CHAHR) *to listen*

la escuela (ehs-KWEH-lah) *school*
　escuela secundaria (ehs-KWEH-lah seh-koon-DAH-ryah) *secondary school*

el escultor, –a (ehs-kool-TOHR) *sculptor*

la escultura (ehs-kool-TOO-rah) *sculpture*

ese, –a (EH-seh) *that* (adj.)

el esfuerzo (ehs-FWEHR-soh) *effort*

eso, –a, (EH-soh) *that one* (pr.)

España (ehs-PAH-nyah) *Spain*

español, –a (ehs-pah-NYOHL) *Spanish; Spaniard*

espantoso, –a (ehs-pahn-TOH-soh) *horrific*

especial (ehs-peh-SYAHL) *special*

la especialidad (ehs-peh-syah-lee-DAH) *specialty*

especialmente (ehs-peh-syahl-MEHN-teh) *specially*

específico, –a (ehs-peh-SEE-fee-koh) *specific*

el espectáculo (ehs-pehk-TAH-koo-loh) *show*
　espectáculo de tango (ehs-pehk-TAH-koo-loh deh TAHN-goh) *tango show*

esperar (ehs-peh-RAHR) *to wait; to hope; to expect*

la espina (ehs-PEE-nah) *thorn*

el esposo, –a (ehs-POH-soh) *spouse*

el esquí (ehs-KEE) *ski*

el / la esquimal (ehs-KEE-mahl) *Eskimo*

la estación (ehs-tah-SYOHN) *station; season*

el estacionamiento (ehs-tah-syoh-nah-MYEHN-toh) *parking lot*

el estadio (ehs-TAH-dyoh) *stadium*

el estado (ehs-TAH-doh) *state*

Estados Unidos (ehs-TAH-dohs oo-NEE-dohs) *United States*

estadounidense (ehs-tah-doh-oo-nee-DEHN-seh) *from the United States*

estallar (ehs-tah-YAHR) *to explode*

estar (ehs-TAHR) *to be*

la estatua (ehs-tah-TOO-rah) *statue*

este, –a (EHS-teh) *this* (adj.)

estilazo (ehs-tee-LAH-soh) *good style*

estimado, –a (ehs-tee-MAH-doh) *dear*

esto (EHS-toh) *this*

el estómago (ehs-TOH-mah-goh) *stomach*

estos, –as (EHS-tohs) *these*

estrechito, –a (ehs-treh-CHEE-toh) *tight, narrow*

la estrella (ehs-TREH-yah) *star*
　estrella latina (ehs-TREH-yah lah-TEE-nah) *Latin star*

estresado, –a (ehs-treh-SAH-doh) *stressed*

el / la estudiante (ehs-too-DYAHN-teh) *student*

estudiar (ehs-too-DYAHR) *to study*

el estudio (ehs-TOO-dyoh) *study, study room, studio*

estupendo (ehs-too-PEHN-doh) *wonderful*

estúpido, –a (ehs-TOO-pee-doh) *stupid*

eternos (eh-TEHR-noh) *eternal*

exacto, –a (ehk-SAHK-toh) *exact*

exagerar (ehk-sah-heh-RAHR) *to exaggerate*

el examen (ehk-SAH-mehn) *exam*

excelente (ehk-seh-LEHN-teh) *excellent*

excéntrico, –a (ehk-SEHN-tree-koh) *eccentric*

exclamar (ehks-klah-MAHR) *to exclaim*

exclusivamente (ehks-kloo-see-bah-MEHN-teh) *exclusively*

la excursión (ehks-koor-SYOHN) *field trip*

la exhibición (ehk-see-bee-SYOHN) *exhibition*

el éxito (EHK-see-toh) *success*

la experiencia (ehks-peh-RYEHN-syah) *experience*

el experto, –a (ehks-PEHR-toh) *expert*

la explicación (ehks-plee-kah-SYOHN) *explanation*

explicar (ehks-plee-KAHR) *explain*

la exposición (ehks-poh-see-SYOHN) *exhibition*

exterior (ehks-teh-RYOHR) *exterior; abroad*

extrañar (ehks-trah-NYAHR) *to miss*

el extranjero, –a (ehks-trahn-HEH-roh) *foreigner*

extraño, –a (ehks-TRAH-nyoh) *strange*

F

fácil (FAH-seel) *easy*

facturar (fahk-too-RAHR) *to invoice, to check luggage*

la falda (FAHL-dah) *skirt*

falso, –a (FAHL-soh) *false*

faltar (fahl-TAHR) *to lack, left to do, still needed*

la familia (fah-MEE-lyah) *family*

famoso, –a (fah-MOH-soh) *famous*

el / la fan (fahn) *fan*

fantástico, –a (fahn-TAHS-tee-koh) *fantastic*

fascinar (fah-see-NAHR) *to love*

favor (fah-BOHR) *favor*

favorito, –a (fah-boh-REE-toh) *favorite*

febrero (feh-BREH-roh) *February*

la fecha (FEH-chah) *date*

la federación (feh-deh-rah-SYOHN) *federation*

fenomenal (feh-noh-meh-NAHL) *fantastic*

feo, –a (FEH-oh) *ugly*

la fiebre (FYEH-breh) *fever, temperature*

la fiesta (FYEHS-tah) *party*

la FIFA (FEE-fah) *International Federation of Soccer Associations*

la fila (FEE-lah) *line*
el final (fee-NAHL) *final, end*
finalmente (fee-nahl-MEHN-teh) *finally*
fino, –a (FEE-noh) *fine*
la firma (FEER-mah) *signature; brand name*
físicamente (FEE-see-kah-mehn-teh) *physically*
el flan (flahn) *type of dessert*
flaquito, –a (flah-KEE-toh) *skinny*
flechazo (fleh-CHAH-soh) *love at first sight (figuratively)*
el foro (FOH-roh) *forum*
la foto (FOH-toh) *photograph*
fotografiar (foh-toh-grah-FYAHR) *to take a picture*
el fotógrafo, –a (foh-TOH-grah-foh) *photographer*
el fracaso (frah-KAH-soh) *failure*
francés, –a (frahn-SEHS) *French*
la frazada (frah-SAH-dah) *blanket*
la frecuencia (freh-KWEHN-syah) *frequency*
frecuente (freh-KWEHN-teh) *frequent*
frecuentemente (freh-kwehn-teh-MEHN-teh) *frequently*
fresco, –a (FREHS-koh) *fresh; fresco*
frijoles (free-HOH-lehs) *beans; Holy Cow! (slng. Mex.)*
frío, –a (FREE-oh) *cold*
frito, –a (FREE-toh) *fried*
la fruta (FROO-tah) *fruit*
la frutería (froo-teh-REE-ah) *fruit store*
fuera (FWEH-rah) *outside*
fuerte (FWEHR-teh) *strong*
la fuerza (FWEHR-sah) *strength*
fumador, –a (foo-mah-DOHR) *smoker*
fumar (foo-MAHR) *to smoke*
funcionar (foon-syoh-NAHR) *to function, to work*
furioso, –a (foo-RYOH-soh) *furious*
el fútbol (FOOT-bohl) *soccer*

G

la galería (gah-leh-REE-ah) *gallery*
ganar (gah-NAHR) *to win; to earn*
gastar (gahs-TAHR) *to spend*
el gaucho (GAHOO-choh) *Argentinean cowboy*
general (heh-neh-RAHL) *general*
el género (HEH-neh-roh) *type*
generoso, –a (heh-neh-ROH-soh) *generous*
genial (heh-NYAHL) *brilliant*
la gente (HEHN-teh) *people*
la geografía (heh-oh-grah-FEE-ah) *geography*

el geólogo, –a (heh-OH-loh-goh) *geologist*
gigante (hee-GAHN-teh) *gigantic*
el gimnasio (heem-NAH-syoh) *gym*
la gira (HEE-rah) *tour*
el gol (gohl) *goal*
el golazo (goh-LAH-soh) *good goal*
gordo, –a (GOHR-doh) *fat*
la gota (goh-TEE-tah) *drop*
gracias (GRAH-syahs) *thank you*
  gracias a Dios (GRAH-syahs ah dyohs) *thank God*
la gramática (grah-MAH-tee-kah) *grammar*
gran (grahn) *big; great*
el granadero, –a (grah-nah-DEH-roh) *riot police (Mex.)*
grande (GRAHN-deh) *big*
el gringo, –a (GREEN-goh) *foreigner (usually from the United States) (pej. or infml.)*
gritar (gree-TAHR) *to scream, to shout*
el grito (GREE-toh) *scream*
el grupo (GROO-poh) *group*
el guacamole (gwah-kah-MOH-leh) *Mexican avocado sauce*
la guagua (GWAH-gwah) *bus*
guapo, –a (GWAH-poh) *good-looking*
guardar (gwahr-DAHR) *to keep, to put away*
el / la guía (GEE-ah) *guide*
gustar (goos-TAHR) *to like*
el gusto (GOOS-toh) *taste*

H

haber (ah-BEHR) (see also **hay**) *to be; to have (helping v.)*
la habitación (ah-bee-tah-SYOHN) *room*
hablar (ah-BLAHR) *to talk*
hace (AH-seh) *does; ago*
hacer (ah-SEHR) *to do*
  hacer caso (ah-SEHR KAH-soh) *to pay attention*
  hacerse (ah-SEHR-seh) *to become*
  hacerse daño (ah-SEHR-seh DAH-nyoh) *to get hurt*
hacia (AH-syah) *toward*
el hambre (AHM-breh) *hunger*
hasta (AHS-tah) *until*
  hasta en la sopa (AHS-tah ehn lah SOH-pah) *everywhere*
  hasta la camisa (AHS-tah lah kah-MEE-sah) *everything*
  hasta luego (AHS-tah LWEH-goh) *see you later*
  hasta pronto (AHS-tah PROHN-toh) *see you soon*
hay (ahy) *there is, there are*

la heladería (eh-lah-deh-REE-ah) *ice cream shop*
el helado (eh-LAH-doh) *ice cream*
el hermano, –a (ehr-MAH-noh) *brother; sister*
la hijita (ee-HEE-tah) *daughter (dim.)*
el hijo (EE-hoh) *son*
el / la hincha (EEN-chah) *sports fan; supporter*
hispano, –a (ees-PAH-noh) *Hispanic*
la historia (ees-TOH-ryah) *history, story*
la hoja (OH-hah) *sheet; leaf*
hola (OH-lah) *hello*
el hombre (OHM-breh) *man*
honesto, –a (oh-NEHS-toh) *honest*
la hora (OH-rah) *hour, time*
el horario (oh-RAH-ryoh) *schedule*
el horno (OHR-noh) *oven*
horrible (oh-RREE-bleh) *horrible*
horror (oh-RROHR) *horror*
el hospital (ohs-pee-TAHL) *hospital*
el hotel (OH-tehl) *hotel*
hoy (oy) *today*
  hoy en día (oy ehn DEE-ah) *nowadays*
hs. *times, abbreviation for the word horas*
el hueso (WEH-soh) *bone*
el huevo (WEH-boh) *egg*
la humedad (oo-meh-DAHD) *humidity*
el huracán (oo-rah-KAHN) *hurricane*

I

la idea (ee-DEH-ah) *idea*
el / la idealista (ee-deh-ah-LEES-tah) *idealist*
la identificación (ee-dehn-tee-fee-kah-SYOHN) *identification*
el idioma (ee-DYOH-mah) *language*
el ídolo (EE-doh-loh) *idol*
la iglesia (ee-GLEH-syah) *church*
la ignorancia (eeg-noh-RAHN-syah) *ignorance*
ignorante (eeg-noh-RAHN-teh) *ignorant*
igual (ee-GWAHL) *equal, the same*
igualmente (ee-gwahl-MEHN-teh) *equally*
ilustrar (ee-loos-TRAHR) *illustrate*
la imaginación (ee-mah-hee-nah-SYOHN) *imagination*
imaginar (ee-mah-hee-NAHR) *to imagine*
la importancia (eem-pohr-TAHN-syah) *importance*
importante (eem-pohr-TAHN-teh) *important*
importar (eem-pohr-TAHR) *to be important to, to matter*

imposible (eem-poh-SEE-bleh) impossible

imprescindible (eem-preh-seen-DEE-bleh) essential

impresionado, –a (eem-preh-syoh-NAH-doh) impressed

impresionante (eem-preh-syoh-NAHN-teh) amazing

la impresora (eem-preh-SOH-rah) printer

la inauguración (ee-nah-goo-rah-SYOHN) opening

incluir (een-KLWEER) include

incluso (een-KLOO-soh) plus

la incógnita (een-KOHG-nee-tah) unknown

increíble (een-kreh-EE-bleh) incredible

independiente (een-deh-pehn-DYEHN-teh) independent

indicar (een-dee-KAHR) to show; to indicate

indiscreto, –a (een-dees-KREH-toh) indiscreet

individual (een-dee-bee-DWAHL) individual

la infancia (een-FAHN-syah) childhood

la información (een-fohr-mah-SYOHN) information

la informática (een-fohr-MAH-tee-kah) computer science

el informe (een-FOHR-meh) report

la ingeniería (een-heh-nyeh-REE-ah) engineering

inglés, –a (een-GLEHS) English

el ingrediente (een-greh-DYEHN-teh) ingredient

el ingreso (een-GREH-soh) entrance, entry

inmediatamente (een-meh-dyah-tah-MEHN-teh) immediately

inmediato, –a (een-meh-DYAH-toh) immediate

inteligente (een-teh-lee-HEHN-teh) intelligent

intentar (een-TEHN-tahr) to try

el interés (een-teh-REHS) interest

interesado, –a (een-teh-reh-SAH-doh) interested

interesante (een-teh-reh-SAHN-teh) interesting

interesar (een-teh-reh-SAHR) to interest

interior (een-teh-RYOHR) interior

intermedio (een-tehr-MEH-dyoh) half time

el internet (een-tehr-NEHT) Internet

interrumpir (een-teh-rroom-PEER) to interrupt

introducir (een-troh-doo-SEER) to introduce

la investigación (een-behs-tee-gah-SYOHN) investigation; research

investigar (een-behs-tee-GAHR) to investigate; to research

el invierno (een-BYEHR-noh) winter

la invitación (een-bee-tah-SYOHN) invitation

el invitado, –a (een-bee-TAH-doh) guest

invitar (een-bee-TAHR) to invite

ir (eer) to go
ir de camping (eer deh KAHM-peeng) to go camping
ir de compras (eer deh KOHM-prahs) to go shopping

irregular (ee-rreh-goo-LAHR) irregular

el istmo (EEST-moh) isthmus

italiano, –a (ee-tah-LYAH-noh) Italian

J

jamás (hah-MAHS) never

Japón (hah-POHN) Japan

japonés, –a (hah-poh-NEHS) Japanese

el jardín (hahr-DEEN) garden; yard

el jefe, –a (HEH-feh) boss

la jornada (hohr-NAH-dah) day

joven (HOH-behn) young

el judo (YOO-doh) judo

el juego (HWEH-goh) game

jueves (HWEH-behs) Thursday

jugar (hoo-GAHR) to play; to gamble

el juguete (hoo-GEH-teh) toy
juguetito (hoo-geh-TEE-toh) little toy (dim.)

juguetón, –a (hoo-geh-TOHN) playful

julio (HOO-lyoh) July

junio (HOO-nyoh) June

juntos (HOON-tohs) together

la juventud (hoo-behn-TOOD) youth

K

el kilómetro (kee-LOH-meh-troh) kilometer

L

la (lah) her, you (fml.); it (f.); the

el laburo (lah-BOO-roh) work (Arg.)

lado, al (LAH-doh) next to

el lago (LAH-goh) lake

el lápiz (LAH-pees) pencil

largo, –a (LAHR-goh) long

las (lahs) them (people and things; you (fml. pl. and f.); the (pl.)

la lata (LAH-tah) can (n.); pain (slng.)

laterales (lah-teh-RAH-lehs) lateral

Latinoamérica (lah-tee-noh-ah-MEH-ree-kah) Latin America

le (leh) to / for him, her, you (fml. ind. obj. pr.)

la lección (lehk-SYOHN) lesson

la leche (LEH-cheh) milk

leer (leh-EHR) to read

el legado (leh-GAH-doh) legacy

lejos (LEH-hohs) far

el lenguaje (lehn-GWAH-heh) language

levantarse (leh-bahn-TAHR-seh) to get up

liado, –a (LYAH-doh) tied up

libre (LEE-breh) free

la librería (lee-breh-REE-ah) book store

libremente (lee-breh-MEHN-teh) freely

el libro (LEE-broh) book

ligar (lee-GAHR) to bind; to flirt (Sp.)

limitado, –a (lee-mee-TAH-doh) limited

el limón (lee-MOHN) lemon

la limonada (lee-moh-NAH-dah) lemonade

limpiar (leem-PYAHR) to clean

limpio, –a (LEEM-pyoh) clean

lindo, –a (LEEN-doh) nice, pretty

la línea (LEE-neh-ah) line

la linterna (leen-TEHR-nah) flashlight

líquido, –a (LEE-kee-doh) liquid

la lista (LEES-tah) list

el living (LEE-been) living room (Arg.)

llamar (yah-MAHR) to call

llanero, –a (yah-NEH-roh) cowboy

llegar (yeh-GAHR) to arrive

lleno, –a (YEH-noh) full

llevar (yeh-BAHR) to take; to carry

llorar (yoh-RAHR) to cry

llover (yoh-BEHR) to rain

la lluvia (YOO-byah) rain

lo (loh) him, you (fml.); it (m. dir. obj. pr.)
lo mejor (loh meh-HOHR) the best
lo siento (loh SYEHN-toh) I'm sorry

la localidad (loh-kah-lee-DAH) seat in a stadium

loco, –a (LOH-koh) crazy

lógico, –a (LOH-hee-koh) logic

lomito (loh-MEE-toh) cut of meat (usually beef)

los (lohs) them (people and things, m. pl. and m. and f. pl.); you (fml. pl.); the (m. pl. def. art.)

la lotería (loh-teh-REE-ah) lottery

lucir (loo-SEER) to show

luego (LWEH-goh) *later, then*
el lugar (loo-GAHR) *place*
el lujo (LOO-hoh) *luxury*
la luna (LOO-nah) *moon*
lunes (LOO-nehs) *Monday*
la luz (loos) *light*

M

la madre (MAH-dreh) *mother*
madrileño, –a (mah-dree-LEH-nyoh) *person from Madrid*
la madrugada (mah-droo-GAH-dah) *early morning*
el maestro, –a (mah-EHS-troh) *teacher*
magnífico, –a (mahg-NEE-fee-koh) *magnificent, great*
mal (mahl) *bad, evil, wrong*
la maleta (mah-LEH-tah) *suitcase*
malísimo, –a (mah-LEE-see-moh) *really bad*
malo, –a (MAH-loh) *bad; sick*
mamá (mah-MAH) *mommy*
Mañana (mah-NYAH-nah) *tomorrow; morning*
manejar (mah-neh-HAHR) *to drive*
la mano (MAH-noh) *hand*
mano (MAH-noh) *(short for) bro, brother (slng. Mex.)*
mantener (mahn-teh-NEHR) *to maintain, to keep*
maquillar (mah-kee-YAHR) *to put on make up*
maravillado, –a (mah-rah-bee-YAH-doh) *amazed*
maravilloso, –a (mah-rah-bee-YOH-soh) *marvelous*
las margaritas (mahr-gah-REE-tahs) *daisies*
los mariachis (mah-ree-AH-chees) *Mexican music band*
la marina (mah-REE-nah) *Marines*
marrón (mah-RROHN) *brown*
martes (MAHR-tehs) *Tuesday*
marzo (MAHR-soh) *March*
más (mahs) *more*
  más tarde (mahs TAHR-deh) *later*
matar (mah-TAHR) *to kill*
las matemáticas (mah-teh-MAH-tee-kahs) *mathematics*
el matrimonio (mah-tree-MOH-nyoh) *marriage*
mayo (MAH-yoh) *May*
mayor (mah-YOHR) *older*
la mayoría (mah-yoh-REE-ah) *majority*
máximo, –a (MAHK-see-moh) *the most; maximum*
me (meh) *me; to me; myself*
medio, –a (MEH-dyoh) *half*
medio (en) (MEH-dyoh) *in the middle*

mejor (meh-HOHR) *better, best*
la memoria (meh-MOH-ryah) *memory*
  (de) memoria (deh meh-MOH-ryah) *by heart*
menor (meh-NOHR) *younger*
menos (MEH-nohs) *less; minus*
  menos mal (MEH-nohs MAHL) *thank God*
el mensaje (mehn-SAH-heh) *message*
  mensaje electrónico (mehn-SAH-heh eh-lehk-TROH-nee-koh) *e-mail*
el menú (meh-NOO) *menu*
merendar (meh-rehn-DAHR) *to have a snack at teatime*
el merengue (meh-REHN-geh) *merengue; type of music*
la merienda (meh-RYEHN-dah) *snack*
el mes (mehs) *month*
la mesa (MEH-sah) *table*
el mesero, –a (meh-SEH-roh) *waiter, waitress*
el metro (MEH-troh) *subway*
el metro (MEH-troh) *meter*
mexicano, –a (meh-hee-KAH-noh) *Mexican*
mezclar (mehs-KLAHR) *to mix*
mi (mee) *my*
mí (mee) *(to) me*
el miedo (MYEH-doh) *fear*
  tener miedo (teh-NEHR MYEH-doh) *to be scared*
el / la miembro (MYEHM-broh) *member*
mientras (MYEHN-trahs) *while*
miércoles (MYEHR-koh-lehs) *Wednesday*
mijo, –a *dear, darling (coll. Mex.)*
mil (meel) *thousand*
el milagro (mee-LAH-groh) *miracle*
milagroso, –a (mee-lah-GROH-soh) *miraculous*
miles (MEE-lehs) *thousands*
la milla (MEE-yah) *mile*
millonario, –a (mee-yoh-NAH-ryoh) *millionaire*
la milonga (mee-LOHN-gah) *type of music typical of Argentina*
mínimo, –a (MEE-nee-moh) *minimum*
mío, –a (MEE-oh) *mine*
mirar (mee-RAHR) *to look, to see*
mis (mees) *my*
el misterio (mees-TEH-ryoh) *mystery*
misterioso, –a (mees-teh-RYOH-soh) *mysterious*
la mitad (mee-TAHD) *half*
la mochila (moh-CHEE-lah) *backpack*
el mochilazo (moh-chee-LAH-soh) *big backpack*
el modelo (moh-DEH-loh) *model*

moderno , –a (moh-DEHR-noh) *modern*
moler (moh-LEHR) *to grind*
el momento (moh-MEHN-toh) *moment*
la montaña (mohn-TAH-nyah) *mountain*
el monumento (moh-noo-MEHN-toh) *monument*
moreno, –a (moh-REH-noh) *dark-haired (Sp.), dark-skinned*
morir (moh-REER) *to die*
la motocicleta (moh-toh-see-KLEH-tah) *motorcycle*
el motor (moh-TOHR) *motor*
el móvil / celular (MOH-beel) (seh-loo-LAHR) *mobile / cellular telephone*
el mozo, –a (MOH-soh) *conscript, waiter (Mex.)*
la muchacha (moo-CHAH-chah) *girl*
mucho, –a, –os, –as (MOO-choh) *a lot, much, many*
  muchas gracias (MOO-chahs GRAH-syahs) *thanks a lot*
  mucho gusto (MOO-choh GOOS-toh) *pleased to meet you*
el mueble (MWEH-bleh) *piece of furniture*
muerto, –a (MWEHR-toh) *dead*
la mujer (moo-HEHR) *woman*
mundial (moon-DYAHL) *worldwide*
  mundiales de fútbol (moon-DYAHL-ehs deh FOOT-bohl) *World Cup soccer*
el mundo (MOON-doh) *world*
la muñeca (moo-NYEH-kah) *doll*
la muñequita (moo-nyeh-KEE-tah) *little doll*
el mural (moo-RAHL) *mural*
el museo (moo-SEH-oh) *museum*
la música (MOO-see-kah) *music*
musical (moo-see-KAHL) *musical*
la mutua (MOO-twah) *type of business (Sp.)*
muy (mwee) *very*

N

la nación (nah-SYOHN) *nation*
nacional (nah-syon-NAHL) *national*
nada (NAH-dah) *nothing*
nada más (NAH-dah MAHS) *nothing else*
nadar (nah-DAHR) *to swim*
nadie (NAH-dyeh) *no one, nobody*
la narración (nah-rrah-SYOHN) *story*
el narrador, –a (nah-rrah-DOHR) *narrator*
navegar (nah-beh-GAHR) *to sail*
la Navidad (nah-bee-DAHD) *Christmas*

necesario, -a (neh-seh-SAH-ryoh) *necessary*

necesitar (neh-seh-see-TAHR) *to need*

necio, -a (NEH-syoh) *stupid, foolish*

negativo, -a (neh-gah-TEE-boh) *negative*

el negocio (neh-GOH-syoh) *business*

negro / a (NEH-groh) *black*

el nene (NEH-neh) *boy; guy* (slng.)

nervioso, -a (nehr-BYOH-soh) *nervous*

nevar (neh-BAHR) *to snow*

ni (nee) *neither*

ni siquiera (nee see-KYEH-rah) *not even*

la nieve (NYEH-beh) *snow*

ningún (neen-GOON) *none*

ningún lado (neen-GOON LAH-doh) *nowhere*

ninguno, -a (neen-GOO-noh) *none, no one*

el niño (NEE-nyoh) *little boy; child*

no (noh) *no*

la noche (NOH-cheh) *night*

la Nocilla (noh-SEE-yah) *brand name of a chocolate spread* (Sp.)

el nombre (NOHM-breh) *name*

el nopal (noh-PAHL) *nopal; prickly pear*

nopalitos (noh-pah-LEE-tohs) *little nopals*

normal (nohr-MAHL) *normal*

normalmente (nohr-mahl-MEHN-teh) *usually*

el norte (NOHR-teh) *north*

nos (nohs) *us; to us; ourselves*

nosotros, -as (noh-SOH-trohs) *we*

las noticias (noh-TEE-syahs) *news*

el noticiero (noh-tee-SYEH-roh) *newsreel*

la novela (noh-BEH-lah) *novel*

la novia (NOH-byah) *girlfriend; bride; fiancee*

noviembre (noh-BYEHM-breh) *November*

el novio (NOH-byoh) *boyfriend; groom; fiance*

la nube (NOO-beh) *cloud*

nublado, -a (noo-BLAH-doh) *cloudy*

nuestro, -a (NWEHS-troh) *our*

nueve (NWEH-beh) *nine*

nuevo, -a (NWEH-boh) *new*

numerar (noo-meh-RAHR) *to number*

el número (NOO-meh-roh) *number, shoe size*

numeroso, -a (noo-meh-ROH-soh) *numerous*

nunca (NOON-kah) *never*

O

o (oh) *or*

o sea (oh SEH-ah) *so, that is, in other words*

la obra (OH-brah) *construction; work (of art)*

obra de teatro (OH-brah deh the-AH-troh) *theatrical play*

obtener (ohb-teh-NEHR) *to obtain*

la ocasión (oh-kah-SYOHN) *occasion*

el océano (oh-SEH-ah-noh) *ocean*

ocho (OH-choh) *eight*

octubre (ohk-TOO-breh) *October*

ocupado, -a (oh-koo-PAH-doh) *busy*

la ocurrencia (oh-koo-RREHN-syah) *idea* (coll.)

ocurrir (oh-koo-RREER) *to occur*

odiar (oh-DYAHR) *to hate*

ofender (oh-fehn-DEHR) *to offend*

el oficial (oh-fee-SYAHL) *officer*

la oficina (oh-fee-SEE-nah) *office*

ofrecer (oh-freh-SEHR) *to offer*

oír (oh-EER) *to hear*

el ojo (OH-hoh) *eye*

las olimpiadas (oh-leem-PYAH-dahs) *Olympics*

olvidar (ohl-bee-DAHR) *to forget*

once (OHN-seh) *eleven*

la ópera (OH-peh-rah) *opera*

la oportunidad (oh-pohr-too-nee-DAHD) *opportunity*

ordenado, -a (ohr-deh-NAH-doh) *organized*

el ordenador (ohr-deh-nah-DOHR) *computer* (Sp.)

ordenar (ohr-deh-NAHR) *to order; to arrange* (Sp.)

organizar (ohr-gah-nee-SAHR) *to organize*

orgulloso, -a (ohr-goo-YOH-soh) *proud*

el origen (oh-REE-hehn) *origin*

el oro (OH-roh) *gold*

oscuro, -a (ohs-KOO-roh) *dark*

el otoño (oh-TOH-nyoh) *autumn*

otra vez (OH-trah BEHS) *again*

otro, -a (OH-troh) *another*

oye (OY-eh) *listen* (command form)

P

el padre (PAH-dreh) *father*

los padres (PAH-drehs) *parents*

padrísimo (pah-DREE-see-moh) *great, super* (Mex.)

la paella (pah-EH-yah) *Spanish rice dish*

pagar (pah-GAHR) *to pay*

la página (PAH-gee-nah) *page*

el pago (PAH-goh) *payment*

el país (pah-EES) *country*

paisa (PAHY-sah) *person from the Medellin region* (Col.)

el paisaje (pahy-SAH-heh) *landscape*

la palabra (pah-LAH-brah) *word*

el palacio (pah-LAH-syoh) *palace*

pálido, -a (PAH-lee-doh) *pale*

el pan (pahn) *bread*

la panadería (pah-nah-deh-REE-ah) *bakery; bread shop*

pánico (PAH-nee-koh) *panic*

el pantalón (pahn-tah-LOHN) *pants*

la pantalla (pahn-TAH-yah) *screen*

el Papa (PAH-pah) *pope*

papá (pah-PAH) *daddy*

las papas fritas (PAH-pahs FREE-tahs) *french fries*

para (PAH-rah) *for*

la parada (pah-RAH-dah) *stop (bus)*

parar (pah-RAHR) *to stop*

parcialmente (pahr-syahl-MEHN-teh) *partially*

parecer (pah-reh-SEHR) *to seem like; look like*

la pareja (pah-REH-hah) *couple*

el parking (PAHR-keen) *parking* (Sp.)

la parrilla (pah-RREE-yah) *grill restaurant* (Arg.)

la parte (PAHR-teh) *part*

el / la participante (pahr-tee-see-PAHN-teh) *participant*

participar (pahr-tee-see-PAHR) *to take part; to participate*

particular (pahr-tee-koo-LAHR) *particular*

el partido (pahr-TEE-doh) *game; political party*

partir (pahr-TEER) *to leave; to break*

pasado / a (pah-SAH-doh) *past*

el pasaje (pah-SAH-he) *passage; ticket* (Sp.)

el pasajero, -a (pah-sah-HEH-roh) *passenger*

el pasaporte (pah-sah-POHR-teh) *passport*

pasar (pah-SAHR) *to pass; to spend (time)*

pasar por (pah-SAHR pohr) *to stop by*

¿Qué pasa? (keh PAH-sah) *What's up?*

pasear (pah-seh-AHR) *to stroll*

el paseo (pah-SEH-oh) *stroll, walk*

el pasillo (pah-SEE-yoh) *hallway, corridor*

la pasión (pah-SYOHN) *passion*

pasito (pah-SEE-toh) *slowly; carefully* (Col.)

el paso (PAH-soh) *step*

la pastelería (pas-teh-leh-REE-ah) *bakery*

el pastel (pahs-TEHL) *cake*
patriota (pah-TRYOH- tah) *patriot*
patrullar (pah-troo-YAHR) *to patrol*
el PC (PEH-SEH) *personal computer*
pedir (peh-DEER) *to ask for*
peinar (pay-NAHR) *to brush one's hair*
el pelao (peh-LAH-oh) *guy* (Col., Mex.) (slng.) (pej.)
pelear (peh-leh-AHR) *to fight*
la película (peh-LEE-koo-lah) *movie*
la pelota (peh-LOH-tah) *ball*
pelotudo, –a (peh-loh-TOO-doh) *jerk; stupid* (Arg.)
penal (peh-NAHL) *fault, penalty (in soccer)* (Arg.)
pensar (pehn-SAHR) *to think*
la pensión (pehn-SYOHN) *inn; retirement pension*
peor (peh-OHR) *worse*
pequeño, –a (peh-KEH-nyoh) *small*
perder (pehr-DEHR) *to lose*
perderse (pehr-DEHR-seh) *to get lost*
perdido, –a (pehr-DEE-doh) *lost*
el perdón (pehr-DOHN) *forgiveness*
perdonar (pehr-doh-NAHR) *to forgive*
perfectamente (pehr-fehk-tah-MEHN-teh) *perfectly*
perfecto, –a (pehr-FEHK-toh) *perfect*
el perico (peh-REE-koh) *coffee with milk* (Col.)
el periódico (peh-RYOH-dee-koh) *newspaper*
el periodismo (peh-ryoh-DEES-moh) *journalism*
el / la periodista (peh-ryoh-DEES-tah) *journalist*
pero (PEH-roh) *but*
el perro (PEH-rroh) *dog*
la persona (pehr-SOH-nah) *person*
personal (pehr-soh-NAHL) *personal*
pesado, –a (peh-SAH-doh) *heavy; annoying*
la pescadería (pehs-kah-deh-REE-ah) *fish market*
el pescado (pehs-KAH-doh) *fish*
la peseta (peh-SEH-tah) *peseta*
el peso (PEH-soh) *peso*
la petición (peh-tee-SYOHN) *petition*
el pibe (PEE-beh) *guy, kid* (Arg.)
el pie (pyeh) *foot*
la pieza (PYEH-sah) *room* (Arg.)
el pilar (pee-LAHR) *pillar*
el / la piloto (pee-LOH-toh) *pilot*
la pimienta (pee-MYEHN-tah) *pepper*
la piñata (pee-NYAH-tah) *hollow figure filled with candy for parties*
pintado (peen-TAH-doh) *coffee with milk* (Col.)

el pintor, –a (peen-TOHR) *painter*
el plan (plahn) *plan*
la planta (PLAHN-tah) *plant; floor* (Sp.)
plata (PLAH-tah) *silver*
la plata (PLAH-tah) *money*
la platea (plah-TEH-ah) *orchestra section in theater*
la plática (PLAH-tee-kah) *conversation*
platicar (plah-tee-KAHR) *to talk* (Mex.)
el platillo (plah-TEE-yoh) *saucer; dish*
el plato (PLAH-toh) *plate, dish*
la playa (PLAH-yah) *beach*
la plaza (PLAH-sah) *square*
  plaza de toros (PLAH-sah deh TOH-rohs) *bullfighting ring*
pobre (POH-breh) *poor*
poco (POH-koh) *little*
poder (poh-DEHR) *to be able to, can; power*
la poesía (poh-eh-SEE-ah) *poetry*
la policía (poh-lee-SEE-ah) *police*
el pollo (POH-yoh) *chicken*
poner (poh-NEHR) *to put*
ponerse (poh-NEHR-seh) *to put clothes on; to become*
popular (poh-poo-LAHR) *popular*
por (pohr) *by; through; for*
  por acá (pohr ah-KAH) *around here*
  por ahora (pohr ah-OH-rah) *for now*
  por cierto (pohr SYEHR-toh) *by the way*
  por desgracia (pohr dehs-GRAH-syah) *unfortunately*
  por eso (pohr EH-soh) *because of that*
  por favor (pohr fah-BOHR) *please*
  por fin (pohr FEEN) *finally*
  por qué (pohr KEH) *why?*
  por supuesto (pohr soo-PWEHS-toh) *of course*
porque (POHR-keh) *because*
el portátil (pohr-TAH-teel) *laptop computer* (Sp.)
porteño, –a (pohr-TEH-nyoh) *person from Buenos Aires*
portorriqueño, –a (pohr-toh-rree-KEH-nyoh) *Puerto Rican*
la posada (poh-SAH-dah) *inn*
posible (poh-SEE-bleh) *possible*
la posición (poh-see-SYOHN) *position*
el postre (POHS-treh) *dessert*
practicar (prahk-tee-KAHR) *to practice*
práctico, –a (PRAHK-tee-koh) *useful, practical*
el precio (PREH-syoh) *price*

precioso, –a (preh-SYOH-soh) *beautiful*
precisamente (preh-see-sah-MEHN-teh) *precisely*
preferir (preh-feh-REER) *to prefer*
la pregunta (preh-GOON-tah) *question*
preguntar (preh-goon-TAHR) *to ask*
preliminar (preh-lee-mee-NAHR) *preliminary*
la prensa (PREHN-sah) *press*
preocupado, –a (preh-oh-koo-PAH-doh) *worried*
preocuparse (preh-oh-koo-PAHR-seh) *to be worried*
la preparación (preh-pah-rah-SYOHN) *preparation*
preparado, –a (preh-pah-RAH-doh) *prepared*
preparar (preh-pah-RAHR) *to prepare*
presentar (preh-sehn-TAHR) *to introduce*
el presidente, –a (preh-see-DEHN-teh) *president*
prestar (prehs-TAHR) *to loan*
el pretendiente (preh-tehn-DYEHN-teh) *suitor*
pretérito (preh-TEH-ree-toh) *preterite (tense)*
previo, –a (PREH-byoh) *previous*
la primavera (pree-mah-BEH-rah) *spring*
primer, –o, –a (pree-MEH-roh) *first*
el primo, –a (PREE-moh) *cousin*
la princesa (preen-SEH-sah) *princess*
principal (preen-see-PAHL) *main*
la prisa (PREE-sah) *hurry; speed; haste*
probable (proh-BAH-bleh) *probable*
probablemente (proh-bah-bleh-MEHN-teh) *probably*
probar (proh-BAHR) *to try; to prove; to taste*
el problema (proh-BLEH-mah) *problem*
problemático, –a (proh-bleh-MAH-tee-koh) *problematic*
procesamiento (proh-seh-sah-MYEHN-toh) *prosecution*
producir (proh-doo-SEER) *to produce*
el profe (PROH-feh) *teacher; professor* (coll.)
profesional (proh-feh-syoh-NAHL) *professional*
el profesor, –a (proh-feh-SOHR) *teacher*
el programa (proh-GRAH-mah) *program*
pronto (PROHN-toh) *soon*
propio, –a (PROH-pyoh) *proper; own*

el protagonista (proh-tah-goh-NEES-tah) *protagonist*

protestar (proh-tehs-TAHR) *to protest*

el próximo, –a (PROHK-see-moh) *next*

provecho (proh-BEH-choh) *benefit*

el público (POO-blee-koh) *public, audience*

el pueblo (PWEH-bloh) *town, village*

la puerta (PWEHR-tah) *door*

el puerto (PWEHR-toh) *harbor*

pues (pwehs) *so*

el punto (POON-toh) *point; period*

puro, –a (POO-roh) *pure*

Q

que (keh) *that, which, who, whom; than*

qué (keh) *what? how?*

  ¡Qué aproveche! (keh ah-proh-BEH-che) *Enjoy (your meal)!*

  ¡Qué va! (keh bah) *Not at all!, No way!*

quedar (keh-DAHR) *to be left; to meet (with en)*

quedarse (keh-DAHR-seh) *to stay*

la queja (KEH-hah) *complaint*

querer (keh-REHR) *to want*

  querer decir (keh-REHR deh-SEER) *to want to say, to mean*

querido, –a (keh-REE-doh) *loved, dear*

la quesadilla (keh-sah-DEE-yah) *Mexican pizza*

el queso (KEH-soh) *cheese*

quién (kyehn) *who?*

quince (KEEN-seh) *fifteen*

quinto, –a (KEEN-toh) *fifth*

quitar (kee-TAHR) *to take away*

quizá (kee-SAH) *maybe*

R

el radio–taxi (RRAH-dyoh TAHK-see) *taxi by phone*

rápidamente (RRAH-pee-dah-mehn-teh) *quickly*

rápido, –a (RRAH-pee-doh) *fast*

raro, –a (RRAH-roh) *strange*

rato (RRAH-toh) *while*

la razón (rrah-SOHN) *reason*

la récamara (rreh-KAH-mah-rah) *bedroom* (Mex.)

el recambio (rreh-KAHM-byoh) *spare part*

el / la recepcionista (rreh-sehp-syoh-NEES-tah) *receptionist*

la receta (rreh-SEH-tah) *recipe; prescription*

reciclar (rreh-see-KLAHR) *to recycle*

recién (rreh-SYEHN) *just*

recién llegado, –a (rreh-SYEHN yeh-GAH-doh) *just arrived*

recientemente (rreh-syehn-teh-MEHN-teh) *recently*

el recipiente (rreh-see-PYEHN-teh) *container*

el recital (rreh-SEE-tahl) *recital*

la recomendación (rreh-koh-mehn-dah-SYOHN) *recommendation*

recordar (rreh-kohr-DAHR) *to remember*

la red (rrehd) *net; Web (Internet)*

la redacciòn (rreh-dah-SYON) *central office*

el referí (rreh-feh-REE) *referee* (Arg.)

reformar (rreh-fohr-MAHR) *to reform*

refrescar (rreh-frehs-KAHR) *to refresh*

el refresco (rreh-FREHS-koh) *soda*

la región (rreh-HYOHN) *region*

regresarlo, –a (rreh-greh-SAHR-loh) *to return it*

regular (rreh-goo-LAHR) *regular, not so great*

el relámpago (rreh-LAHM-pah-goh) *lightning*

religioso, –a (rreh-lee-HYOH-soh) *religious*

el relleno (rreh-YEH-noh) *stuffing, filling*

reparar (rreh-pah-RAHR) *to repair*

repetir (rreh-peh-TEER) *to repeat*

repicar (rreh-pee-KAHR) *to ring*

el reportaje (rreh-pohr-TAH-heh) *news article*

el reporte (rreh-POHR-teh) *report*

el reportero, –a (rreh-pohr-TEH-roh) *reporter*

  reportero deportivo (rreh-pohr-TEH-roh deh-pohr-TEE-boh) *sports reporter*

règuete (rreh-KEH-teh) *very* (Mex.)

règuetebueno, –a (rreh-keh-teh-BWEH-noh) *very good* (Mex.)

la resaca (rreh-SAH-kah) *hangover*

la reserva (rreh-SEHR-bah) *reservation* (Sp.)

la reservación (rre-sehr-bah-SYOHN) *reservation*

reservar (rreh-sehr-BAHR) *to reserve*

responsable (rrehs-pohn-SAH-bleh) *responsible*

el restaurante (rrehs-tow-RAHN-teh) *restaurant*

el resultado (rreh-sool-TAH-doh) *result*

retirar (rreh-tee-RAHR) *to pick up; to retire; to withdraw*

el reventón (rreh-behn-TOHN) *blowout; party* (Mex.)

la revista (rreh-BEE-sta) *magazine*

la revolución (rreh-boh-loo-SYOHN) *revolution*

el rey (rrehy) *king*

los reyes (RREH-yehs) *kings*

rezar (rreh-SAHR) *to pray*

rico, –a (RREE-koh) *rich; good*

el río (RREE-oh) *river*

el ritmo (RREET-moh) *rhythm*

River Plate *soccer team from Argentina*

rodeado, –a (rroh-deh-AH-doh) *surrounded*

rojo, –a (RROH-hoh) *red*

el rollo (RROH-yoh) *roll; pain* (slng.)

romántico, –a (rroh-MAHN-tee-koh) *romantic*

romper (rrohm-PEHR) *to break*

el ron (rrohn) *rum*

la ropa (RROH-pah) *clothes*

roquero, –a (rroh-KEH-roh) *rock 'n' roll singer*

rosa (RROH-sah) *pink*

rosado, –a (rroh-SAH-doh) *pink*

roto, –a (RROH-toh) *broken*

rubio, –a (RROO-byoh) *blond*

ruborizarse (rroo-boh-ree-SAHR-seh) *to blush*

la rueda de prensa (RRWEH-dah deh PREHN-sah) *press conference*

el ruido (RRWEE-doh) *noise*

la rumba (RROOM-bah) *type of music* (Sp.)*; party time* (Col.)

rumbear (RROOM-beh-ahr) *to go out, to party* (Col.)

Rusia (RROO-syah) *Russia*

ruso, –a (RROO-sah) *Russian*

S

sábado (SAH-bah-doh) *Saturday*

saber (sah-BEHR) *to know*

sabroso, –a (sah-BROH-soh) *delicious*

sacar (sah-KAHR) *to take out*

el saco (SAH-koh) *sack, sweater* (Col.)*, jacket* (Arg.)

la sal (sahl) *salt*

la sala (SAH-lah) *living room; chat room*

  sala de baño (SAH-lah deh BAH-nyoh) *bathroom*

  sala de espera (SAH-lah deh ehs-PEH-rah) *waiting room*

la salida (sah-LEE-dah) *exit; departure*

salir (sah-LEER) *to go out; to leave*

  salir en televisión (sah-LEER ehn teh-leh-bee-SYOHN) *to appear on TV*

salirse (sah-LEER-seh) *to get out*

el salón (sah-LOHN) *living room*

la salsa (SAHL-sah) *sauce; type of music*
saltar (sahl-TAHR) *to jump*
la salud (sah-LOOD) *health*
saludar (sah-loo-DAHR) *to greet*
se (seh) *to him, her, it, you; oneself, himself, herself, itself; impersonal one, you, they (used to form passive obj. pr.)*
la secciòn (sehk-SYON) *section*
el secreto (sehk-KREH-toh) *secret*
el sector (sehk-TOHR) *sector*
la sed (sehd) *thirst*
seguir (seh-GEER) *to follow; to continue*
según (seh-GOON) *according to*
segundo, –a (seh-GOON-doh) *second*
seguro, –a (seh-GOO-roh) *sure, certain; safe*
seis (says) *six*
la selección (seh-lehk-SYOHN) *selection, team*
seleccionar (seh-lehk-syoh-NAHR) *to select*
la selva (SEHL-bah) *jungle*
la semana (seh-MAH-nah) *week*
sencillo, –a (sehn-SEE-yoh) *simple*
el señor (seh-NYOHR) *Mr.; gentleman*
  Señor Caido (seh-NYOHR kah-EE-doh) *image of the Lord fallen on the cross*
la señora (seh-NYOH-rah) *Mrs.; lady*
la sensibilidad (sehn-see-bee-lee-DAHD) *sensitivity*
sentarse (sehn-TAHR-seh) *to sit down*
sentir (sehn-TEER) *to feel; to be sorry*
separado, –a (seh-pah-RAH-doh) *separated*
septiembre (sehp-TYEHM-breh) *September*
séptimo, –a (SEHP-tee-moh) *seventh*
ser (sehr) *to be*
serie (SEH-ryeh) *series*
serio, –a (SEH-ryoh) *serious*
el servicio (sehr-BEE-syoh) *service; restroom*
servir (sehr-BEER) *to serve*
sesenta (seh-SEHN-tah) *sixty*
sexto, –a (SEHKS-toh) *sixth*
si (see) *if*
sí (see) *yes*
el / la sicoanalista (see-koo-ah-nah-LEES-tah) *psychoanalyst*
siempre (SYEHM-preh) *always*
siete (SYEH-teh) *seven*
significar (seeg-nee-fee-KAHR) *to mean*
siguiente (see-GYEHN-teh) *next*
el silencio (see-LEHN-syoh) *silence*

la silla (SEE-yah) *chair*
simpático, –a (seem-PAH-tee-koh) *nice, friendly*
sin (seen) *without*
el sitio (SEE-tyoh) *place*
  sitio de moda (SEE-tyoh deh MOH-dah) *the "in" place*
sobre (SOH-breh) *about; on, over, above*
la sociedad (soh-syeh-DAH) *society*
el sofá (soh-FAH) *sofa*
el sol (sohl) *sun*
solamente (soh-lah-MEHN-teh) *only*
solas (a) (ah SOH-lahs) *by ourselves, by themselves*
soleado, –a (soh-leh-AH-doh) *sunny*
sólo (SOH-loh) *only*
solo, –a (SOH-loh) *alone*
soltero, –a (sohl-TEH-roh) *single*
sonar (soh-NAHR) *to sound*
soñar (soh-NYAHR) *to dream*
la sopa (SOH-pah) *soup*
sorprender (sohr-prehn-DEHR) *to surprise*
la sorpresa (sohr-PREH-sah) *surprise*
sos (sohs) *you are (Arg.)*
su (soo) *his; her; your*
subir (soo-BEER) *to go up; get on (a vehicle)*
sublime (soo-BLEE-meh) *sublime*
el subte (SOOB-teh) *subway (Arg.)*
sucio, –a (SOO-syoh) *dirty*
el sueño (SWEH-nyoh) *dream*
la suerte (SWEHR-teh) *luck*
el sueter (SWEH-tehr) *sweater*
sufrir (soo-FREER) *to suffer*
la sugerencia (soo-heh-REHN-syah) *suggestion*
la suite (SWEET) *suite*
el superior (soo-peh-RYOHR) *superior*
el supermercado (soo-pehr-mehr-KAH-doh) *supermarket*
supersticioso, –a (soo-pehrs-tee-SYOH-soh) *superstitious*
supletorio, –a (soo-pleh-TOH-ryoh) *extra, additional*
el sur (soor) *south*
sus (soos) *his, her, its, their, your*
suyo, –a (SOO-yoh) *his, hers, theirs, yours*

T

la tabla (TAH-blah) *board*
el taco (TAH-koh) *taco; (Mexican food)*
tal (tahl) *such*
¿Qué tal? (keh tahl) *What's up?*
el taller (tah-YEHR) *workshop*
el talón (tah-LOHN) *ticket*
el tamal (tah-MAHL) *tamal (a kind of food)*

también (tahm-BYEHN) *also*
tampoco (tahm-POH-koh) *neither*
tan (tahn) *so*
  tan . . . . como (tahn KOH-moh) *as . . . as*
el tango (TAHN-goh) *tango*
tanto, –a, –os, –as (TAHN-toh) *so much, so many*
la tapa (TAH-pah) *Spanish appetizer*
tarde (TAHR-deh) *late*
la tarde (TAHR-deh) *afternoon*
la tarifa (tah-REE-fah) *tariff, tax*
la tarjeta (tahr-HEH-tah) *card*
  tarjeta de crédito (tahr-HEH-tah de KREH-dee-toh) *credit card*
  tarjeta de identificación de prensa (tahr-HEH-tah de ee-dehn-tee-fee-kah-SYOHN) *press credentials*
el taxi (TAK-see) *taxi*
el / la taxista (tak-SEES-tah) *taxi driver*
la taza (TAH-sah) *cup*
te (teh) *you; to you (fam.); yourself (infml. obj. pr.)*
el teatro (teh-AH-troh) *theater*
el techo (TEH-choh) *ceiling*
el técnico, –a (TEHK-nee-koh) *technician*
la tecnología (tehk-noh-loh-HEE-ah) *technology*
tecnológico, –a (tehk-noh-LOH-hee-koh) *technological*
telefonear (teh-leh-foh-neh-AHR) *to phone*
el teléfono (teh-LEH-foh-noh) *telephone*
la telenovela (teh-leh-noh-BEH-lah) *soap opera*
la televisión (teh-leh-bee-SYOHN) *television*
el tema (TEH-mah) *theme, topic*
temer (teh-MEHR) *to fear*
tener (teh-NEHR) *to have*
  tener que (teh-NEHR keh) *to have to*
  tener razón (teh-NEHR rrah-SOHN) *to be right*
el tenis (TEH-nees) *tennis*
tequila (teh-KEE-lah) *Mexican liquor*
tercero, –a (tehr-SEH-roh) *third*
terminado (tehr-mee-NAH-doh) *finished*
terminar (tehr-MEE-nahr) *to finish*
la ternura (TEHR-noo-rah) *tenderness*
la terraza (teh-RRAH-sah) *terrace*
ti (tee) *you (infml. prep. pr.)*
el tiempo (TYEHM-poh) *time, weather*

la tienda (TYEHN-dah) *store*
  tienda de campaña (TYEHN-dah deh kahm-PAH-nyah) *camping tent*
tímido, –a (TEE-mee-dah) *timid, shy*
el tinto (TEEN-toh) *red wine; dark coffee* (Col.)
el tío, –a (TEE-oh) *uncle; aunt; guy* (slng.)
típico, –a (TEE-pee-koh) *typical*
el tipo, –a (TEE-poh) *guy*
el tiro (TEE-roh) *throw, shot*
el tobillo (toh-BEE-yoh) *ankle*
tocar (toh-KAHR) *to touch, to play*
todavía (toh-dah-BEE-ah) *still; yet*
todo, –a, –os, –as (TOH-doh) *all*
  todo el mundo (TOH-doh ehl MOON-doh) *everybody*
tomar (toh-MAHR) *to take, to drink*
  tomar el sol (toh-MAHR ehl sohl) *to sunbathe*
el tomate (toh-MAH-teh) *tomato*
la tormenta (tohr-MEHN-tah) *storm*
el toro (TOH-roh) *bull*
la torre (TOH-rreh) *tower*
la tostada (tohs-TAH-dah) *toast*
el total (toh-TAHL) *total*
totalmente (toh-tahl-MEHN-teh) *totally*
trabajador, –a (trah-bah-hah-DOHR) *hardworking*
trabajar (trah-bah-HAHR) *to work*
el trabajo (trah-BAH-hoh) *work*
traducir (trah-doo-SEER) *to translate*
el traductor, –a (trah-dook-TOHR) *translator*
traer (trah-EHR) *to bring*
el traje de chaqueta (TRAH-heh deh chah-KEH-tah) *suit*
tranquilo, –a (trahn-KEE-loh) *calm*
el tránsito (TRAHN-see-toh) *traffic*
transversal (trahns-behr-SAHL) *type of street* (Col.)
tras (trahs) *after*
tratar (trah-TAHR) *to try*
trece (TREH-seh) *thirteen*
treinta (TRAYN-tah) *thirty*
tres (trehs) *three*
trescientos, –as (treh-SYEHN-tohs) *three hundred*
la tribuna (tree-BOO-nah) *platform*
triple (TREE-pleh) *triple*
triste (TREES-teh) *sad*
el trueno (TRWEH-noh) *thunder*
tú (too) *you*
tu (too) *your*
el turismo (too-REES-moh) *tourism*
el / la turista (too-REES-tah) *tourist*
turístico, –a (too-REES-tee-koh) *tourist*

U

la última vez (OOL-tee-mah behs) *last time*
últimamente (OOL-tee-mah-mehn-teh) *lately*
un, uno, –a (oon) (OO-noh) *one, a*
  una vez (OO-nah behs) *one time, once*
único, –a (OO-nee-koh) *unique; only*
la unidad (oo-nee-DAHD) *unity; unit*
unido, –a (oo-NEE-dohs) *together, united*
unir (oo-NEER) *to unite; to join*
la universidad (oo-nee-behr-see-DAHD) *university*
usar (oo-SAHR) *to use*
usted (oos-TEHD) *you* (formal)
usualmente (oo-swahl-MEHN-teh) *usually*
útil (OO-teel) *useful*
utilizar (oo-tee-lee-SAHR) *to use*

V

la vaca (BAH-kah) *cow, beef*
las vacaciones (bah-kah-SYOH-nehs) *vacation*
vale (BAH-leh) *okay* (Sp.)
válido, –a (BAH-lee-doh) *valid*
valiente (bah-LYEHN-teh) *brave*
el valle (BAH-yeh) *valley*
el vallenato (bah-yeh-NAH-toh) *type of music from Colombia*
valluno, –a (bah-YOO-noh) *person from the Cauca Valley in Colombia*
varias veces (BAH-ryahs BEH-sehs) *several times*
varios, –as (bah-RYOHS) *several*
veces (BEH-sehs) *times*
el vecino / a (beh-SEE-noh) *neighbor*
vegetariano, –a (beh-geh-tah-RYAH-noh) *vegetarian*
veinte (BAYN-teh) *twenty*
la velada (beh-LAH-dah) *evening*
vender (behn-DEHR) *to sell*
venir (beh-NEER) *to come*
la venta (BEHN-tah) *sale*
la ventanilla de venta (behn-tah-NEE-yah deh BEHN-tah) *ticket window*
ver (behr) *to see*
el verano (beh-RAH-noh) *summer*
el verbo (BEHR-boh) *verb*
la verdad (behr-DAHD) *truth*
verdadero, –a (behr-dah-DEH-roh) *truthful*

la vergüenza (behr-GWEHN-sah) *embarrassment; shame*
el vestíbulo (behs-TEE-boo-loh) *hall, lobby*
el vestido (behs-TEE-doh) *dress*
vestir (behs-TEER) *to dress*
vez (behs) *time*
  a la vez (ah lah behs) *at the same time*
viajar (byah-HAHR) *to travel*
el viaje (BYAH-heh) *trip*
la vida (BEE-dah) *life*
el vídeo (BEE-deh-oh) *video*
los viejitos (byeh-HEE-tohs) *parents* (Arg.)
viejo, –a (BYEH-hoh) *old*
el viento (BYEHN-toh) *wind*
viernes (BYEHR-nehs) *Friday*
el vino (BEE-noh) *wine*
la visita (bee-SEE-tah) *visit*
visitar (bee-see-TAHR) *to visit*
viudo, –a (BYOO-doh) *widower, widow*
vivir (bee-BEER) *to live*
el vocabulario (boh-kah-boo-LAH-ryoh) *vocabulary*
volar (boh-LAHR) *to fly*
el volcán (bohl-KAHN) *volcano*
volver (bohl-BEHR) *to return, to come or go back*
volverse (bohl-BEHR-seh) *to become*
volver loco, –a (boh-BEHR LOH-koh) *to drive crazy*
vos (bohs) *you* (sg.) (Arg.)
vosotros (boh-SOH-trohs) *you* (pl.) (Sp.)
la voz (bohs) *voice*
el vuelo (BWEH-loh) *flight*
vueltas (BWEHL-tahs) *rounds*

Y

y (ee) *and*
ya (yah) *already, now, finally; no longer*
  ya veo (yah BEH-oh) *I see*
yo (yoh) *I*

Z

la zapatería (sah-pah-teh-REE-ah) *shoe store*
el zapato (sah-PAH-toh) *shoe*
el Zócalo (SOH-kah-loh) *market; main square* (Mex.)
la zona (SOH-nah) *zone, area*

ENGLISH–SPANISH

A

a (an) *un, uno, una*
a lot *mucho, -a, -os, -as*
able to (to be): *poder*
above *sobre*
abroad *exterior*
about *sobre; acerca de*
absolutely *completamente, absolutamente*
accept (to) *aceptar*
access *acceder*
activity *la actividad*
actor *el actor*
actress *la actriz*
add (to) *añadir, agregar*
additional *supletorio*
address *la dirección*
admirer *el admirador*
adult *el adulto, -a*
advanced *anticipado / a, avanzado / a*
adventure *la aventura*
adverb *el adverbio*
advice *el consejo*
aerial *aéreo, -a*
affectionate *cariñoso, -a*
after *después; tras; luego*
afternoon *la tarde*
again *otra vez*
age *la edad; la era*
agency *la agencia*
agenda *la agenda*
agent *el / la agente*
ago *hace*
air *el aire*
air-conditioned *acondicionado, -a*
airport *el aeropuerto*
all *todo, -a, -os, -as*
allow (to) *dejar*
almost *casi*
alone *solo, -a*
already *ya*
also *además, también*
altitude *la altitud*
always *siempre*
amazed *marvillado, -a*
amazing *impresionante*
American *americano, -a*
Amusing *divertido, -a, entretenido, -a (with ser)*
and *y*
anecdote *la anécdota*
angry *enojado, -a*
ankle *el tobillo*
annoying *pesado, -a (coll.)*
another *otro, -a, -os, -as*
answer (to) *contestar, responder*
anthropology *la antropología*

anticipation *anticipación*
antique *antiguo*
apartment *el apartamento*
apologize (to) *disculpar*
appear (to) *aparecer*
appear on TV (to) *salir en televisión*
appearance *el aspecto*
appetizer *el aperitivo*
April *abril*
approach (to) *acercarse*
appropriate *apropiado*
architect *arquitecto*
architecture *la arquitectura*
area *el area, la zona*
argument *la discusión*
army *el ejército*
around *alrededor*
around here *por acá*
arrange (to) *ordenar*
arrive (to) *llegar*
art *el arte*
article *el artículo*
artist *el / la artista*
as *coma*
as as; *tanto, como*
ash *la ceniza*
ask (to) *preguntar*
ask for (to) *pedir*
at the same time *a la vez*
athletic *deportivo, -a*
atmosphere *el ambiente*
atrocity *la barbaridad*
attend (to) *asistir*
attentively *atentamente*
attractive *atractivo, -a,*
audience *el público, la audiencia*
August *agosto*
Australia *Australia*
authentic *auténtico, -a*
autograph *el autógrafo*
autonomous, self-governed *autónomo, -a*
Autumn *el otoño*
avocado *el aguacate*

B

baby *el / la bebé*
backpack *la mochila*
bad *malo, -a, -os, -as, mal*
backpack *la mochila*
bakery *la pastelería, la panadería*
ball *la pelota*
banana *la banana*
bank *el banco*
bar *el bar*
basketball *el baloncesto*

bath *el baño*
bathe (to) *bañarse*
bathroom *el aseo, el baño, el cuarto de baño*
battery *la batería*
be (to) *estar, ser, haber*
  be able to (to) *poder*
  be afraid of (to) *temer*
  be angry (to) *enojarse*
  be healthy (to) *sano, -a estar*
  be important to (to) *importar*
  be interesting to (to) *interesar*
  be right (to) *tener razón*
  be silent (to) *callar*
  be worried (to) *preocuparse*
beach *la playa*
bean *el frijol*
beat (to) *batir*
beautiful *precioso, -a; bello, -a*
because *porque*
  because of that *por eso*
become *hacerse, volverse*
become aware of *enterarse*
bed *la cama*
bedroom *dormitorio, recámara (Mex.)*
beef *la carne de res*
beer *la cerveza*
beetle *el escarabajo*
before *antes*
begin (to) *comenzar, empezar*
behind *atrás, detrás de*
believe (to) *creer*
bellboy *el botones*
below *abajo*
bench *el banco*
benefit *provecho*
besides *además*
better *mejor*
between *entre*
bicycle *la bicicleta*
big *grande, gran*
bind *unir; atar, ligar*
birthday *el cumpleaños*
black *negro, -a*
blanket *la frazada*
blessed *bendito, -a*
blind *ciego, -a*
blond *rubio, -a*
blouse *la blusa*
blowout *el reventón*
blue *azul*
blush *ruborizarse*
board *la tabla*
board (to) *embarcar (to a boat or plane)*
boarding *el embarque*
boat *el barco*
body *el cuerpo*

boil (to) *cocer, hervir*
bone *el hueso*
book *el libro*
board *aburrido / a*
boring *aburrido*
boss *el jefe, -a*
bottle *la botella*
box *la caja*
boxing *el boxeo*
boy *el chico, el nene, el niño*
boyfriend *el novio*
brave *valiente*
bread *el pan*
break (to) *romper, partir*
breakfast *desayuno*
bride *la novia*
brilliant *genial*
bring (to) *traer*
broken *roto, -a*
brother *hermano, mano (Mex.)*
brown *marrón*
brown–haired *castaño, -a*
brush (to) *cepillar*
brush one's hair *peinarse*
Buddhist *budista*
bull *el toro*
bullfighting ring *plaza de toros*
burn (to) *arder*
bus *el autobús, el camión (Mex.), la guagua (Puerto Rico)*
business *el negocio*
busy *ocupado, -a*
but *pero*
button *el botón*
by *por, de*
by heart *de memoria*
by ourselves *solas (a.)*
by the way *por cierto*
by themselves *solas (a.)*

C

cactus *el cactus*
cake *el pastel*
call (to) *llamar*
calm *la calma, tranquilo, -a*
camera *la cámara*
camp (to) *acampar*
camping tent *tienda de campaña*
can *la lata*
cancel (to) *cancelar*
cancellation *la cancelación*
candy *el caramelo*
capital *el capital (money)*
capital *la capital (city)*
car *el automóvil, el auto, el coche (Sp.), el carro (Latin America)*
caramel *el caramelo*
card *la tarjeta*
Caribbean *caribeño*
careful *cuidadoso, -a*
carry (to) *llevar*

case *el caso*
cash register *la caja*
cashier *el cajero, -a*
cathedral *la catedral*
Catholic *católico, -a*
cause *la causa*
ceiling *el techo*
celebrate (to) *celebrar*
cellular telephone *celular, móvil (Sp.)*
center *el centro*
central *central*
Central office (of a newspaper) *redacción*
ceramic *cerámica*
cereal *el cereal*
certain *cierto, -a*
chair *la silla*
champagne *el champán*
champion *el campeón, -a*
change *el cambio*
channel *el canal*
chapter *el capítulo*
charmed *encantado*
chat *la charla*
chat room *el chat, la sala*
chat via Internet *chatear*
cheap *barato, -a*
cheer (to) *animar*
cheese *el queso*
chicken *el pollo*
child *el niño, -a*
childhood *la infancia*
chocolate *el bombón (de chocolate), el chocolate*
Christmas *la Navidad*
church *la iglesia*
cigar *el puro*
cigarette *el cigarrillo*
cinema *el cine*
circular *circular*
circulate (to) *circular*
city *la ciudad*
class *la clase*
classic *clásico, -a*
clean (to) *limpiar*
clean *limpio, -a*
clear *claro, -a; despejado (weather)*
close (to) *cerrar*
close *cerca (de)*
close (to) *cerca de*
closed *cerrado, -a*
clothes *ropa*
cloud *la nube*
cloudy *nublado*
club *el club*
coat *el abrigo*
coffee *el café*
    coffee with milk *café con leche (Sp.), perico (Col.), pintado (Col.)*
coincidence *la casualidad*

cocky *chulo, -a (Sp.)*
cold *frío, -a*
colleague *el / la compañero, -a*
collection *la colección*
colloquial *coloquial*
Colombia *Colombia*
Colombian *colombiano, -a*
colonial *colonial*
color *el color*
come (to) *venir*
comfortable *cómodo*
comment (to) *comentar*
communism *el comunismo*
company *la compañía*
compare (to) *comparar*
competition *la competición*
complaint *la queja*
complement (to) *complementar*
complete *completo, -a*
complicated *complicado, -a*
compose (to) *componer*
composition *la composición*
compress (to) *comprimir*
computer *la computadora; el computador; el ordenador (Sp.)*
computer science *la informática*
concert *el concierto*
condensed *condensado, -a*
conference *la conferencia, el congreso*
confused *confundido, -a*
congress *el congreso*
connected *conectado, -a*
conquer (to) *conquistar*
construction *obras*
container *el recipiente*
contemplate (to) *contemplar*
content *el contenido*
continue (to) *continuar*
control *el control*
conversation *la conversación, la plática (Mex.)*
convincing *convincente*
cook (to) *cocinar*
cool *chévere (sing. Col.)*
cooperative *cooperativo*
correct *correcto, -a*
cost (to) *costar*
count (to) *contar*
country *el país*
couple *la pareja, el par*
cousin *el primo, -a*
cover (to) *cubrir*
cow *la vaca*
cowboy *llanero, -a*
crater *el cráter*
crazy *loco, -a*
credit *el crédito*
    credit card *la tarjeta de crédito*
cross (to) *cruzar*
cruel *cruel*
cry (to) *llorar*

Cuban *cubano, -a*
cultural *cultural*
curator *curador, -a*
cup *la taza*
curious *curioso, -a*
cut (to) *cortar*
cycling *el ciclismo*

D

daisies *las margaritas*
daddy *papá, papi*
daily *diario*
daisy *la margarita*
dance *el baile*
dance (to) *bailar*
dark *oscuro, -a*
dark–skinned *moreno, -a (Latin America)*
date *la fecha*
daughter *la hija*
dawn (to) *amanecer*
day *el día, la jornada*
day off *día libre*
dead *muerto, -a*
dear *estimado, -a (in a letter); mijo (coll. Mex.)*
December *diciembre*
decide (to) *decidir*
decision *la decisión*
definitely *definitivamente*
defrost *deshelar*
delicious *sabroso, -a*
departure *la salida*
depressed *deprimido, -a*
desire (to) *desear*
desk *escritorio*
desperate *desesperado, -a*
dessert *el postre*
destination *el destino*
destiny *el destino*
detoxify (to) *desintoxicar*
devil *el diablo*
   devil's lamb cordero del diablo (Arg.)
die (to) *morir*
diet *la dieta*
different *diferente*
difficult *difícil*
dining room *el comedor*
dinner *la cena*
dirty *sucio, -a*
disappearance *la desaparición*
disaster *el desastre*
disco *la discoteca*
discover (to) *descubrir*
discussion *el coloquio, la discusión*
dish *el plato, el platillo*
disinfect (to) *desinfectar*
distance *la distancia*
divorced *divorciado, -a*
do (to) *hacer*

document *el documento*
does *hace*
dog *el perro*
doll *la muñeca*
Dominican *dominicano*
door *la puerta*
double *doble*
double ceiling *doble techo*
download (to) *descargar*
dream *el sueño*
dream (to) *soñar*
dress *el vestido*
dress (to) *vestir*
dressing room *camerino*
drink *la bebida*
drink (to) *beber*
drive (to) *manejar, conducir (Sp.)*
   drive crazy (to) volver loco, -a
drop *la gota*
down *abajo*
dumb *bobo, -a*
during *durante*

E

each *cada*
early morning *la madrugada*
earn (to) *ganar*
easy *fácil*
eat (to) *comer*
eccentric *excéntrico, -a*
effective *efectivo, -a*
effort *el esfuerzo*
egg *el huevo*
eight *ocho*
eighteen *dieciocho*
either *tampoco*
electrical power *corriente eléctrica*
electricity *la electricidad*
electronic *electrónico, -a*
electronic mail *correo electrónico*
elegant *elegante*
elevated *elevado, -a*
eleven *once*
e–mail *mensaje electrónico, el emilio (Sp.)*
embarrassment *la vergüenza*
emission *la emisión*
emperor *el emperador*
empress *la emperadora*
employee *el empleado, -a*
enclose (to) *adjuntar*
engineering *la ingeniería*
English *inglés*
enjoy (to) *disfrutar, gozar, encantar*
   enjoy your meal buen provecho; ¡qué aproveche!
enough *basta, suficiente*
enter (to) *entrar*
entrance *el ingreso; la entrada*
equal *igual*

equally *igualmente*
equipment *el equipo*
Eskimo *el esquimal*
essential *imprescindible*
eternal *eterno, -a*
even though *aunque*
evening *la velada*
everything *todo, hasta la camisa (slng.)*
everywhere *en todos lados; hasta en la sopa (slng.)*
exact *exacto, -a*
exaggerate (to) *exagerar*
exam *el examen*
excellent *excelente*
exclaim (to) *exclamar*
exclusively *exclusivamente*
exhibition *la exposición*
exit *la salida*
expect (to) *esperar*
expensive *caro, -a*
experience *la experiencia*
expert *el experto, -a*
explain (to) *explicar*
explanation *la explicación*
explode (to) *estallar*
exterior *exterior*
extra *supletorio*
eye *el ojo*

F

face *la cara*
failure *el fracaso*
faint *desmayarse*
fall *el otoño*
fall (to) *caer*
fall asleep (to) *dormirse*
fall in love (to) *enamorarse*
false *falso, -a*
family *la familia*
famous *famoso, -a*
fan *admirador, -a, el / la fan*
fantastic *fantástico, -a; fenomenal*
far *lejos*
fashionable *de moda*
fast *rápido, -a*
fat *gordo, -a*
father *padre*
fault *la culpa*
favor *el favor*
favorite *favorito, -a*
fear *el miedo*
fear (to) *temer*
February *febrero*
federation *la federación*
feel (to) *sentir*
fever *la fiebre*
field trip *la excursión*
fifteen *quince*
fifth *quinto, -a*
fight (to) *pelear*
file *el archivo*

final *el final*
  finally *finalmente, por fin*
fine *fino, -a; bien*
find (to) *encontrar*
finish (to) *terminar*
finished *terminado*
first *primero, -a*
fish *pescado (if dead), pez (if alive)*
fish market *la pescadería*
five *cinco*
flag *la bandera*
flashlight *la linterna*
flirt (to) *ligar (Sp.)*
floor *la planta (Sp.)*
follow (to) *seguir*
food *la comida*
fool (to) *engañar*
foot *el pie*
for *por, para; de*
  for now *por ahora*
foreigner *extranjero, -a, el / la gringo, -a (usually from the United States)*
forget (to) *olvidar*
forgive (to) *perdonar*
forgiveness *el perdón*
forest *el bosque*
fortunately *afortunadamente*
forty *cuarenta*
four *cuatro*
fourteen *catorce*
fourth *cuarto, -a*
free *libre*
freely *libremente*
French *francés, a*
french fries *las papas fritas*
frequency *la frecuencia*
frequent *frecuente*
frequently *frecuentemente*
fresh *fresco, -a*
Friday *viernes*
fried *frito, -a*
friend *el amigo, -a*
friendly *agradable, simpático, -a*
from *de, desde*
from the United States *estadounidense*
fruit *la fruta*
fruit store *la frutería*
full *lleno, -a*
fun *divertido, -a*
function (to) *funcionar*
furious *furioso*
furniture *el mueble*
fuss *el alboroto*

G

gallery *la galería*
game *el partido, el juego*
garbage *la basura*

garden *el jardín*
gamble (to) *jugar*
general *general*
generous *generoso, -a*
geography *la geografía*
geologist *geólogo, -a*
get (to) *obtener*
  get agitated (to) *alborotarse*
  get angry (to) *enojarse*
  get closer (to) *acercarse*
  get hurt (to) *hacerse daño*
  get lost (to) *perderse*
  get on (a vehicle) (to) *subir*
  get out (to) *salirse*
  get up (to) *levantarse*
  get used to (to) *acostumbrarse*
giant *el / la gigante*
gigantic *gigante*
girl *la niña, la chica, la muchacha*
girlfriend *la novia*
give (to) *dar*
  give advice (to) *aconsejar*
go down (to) *bajar*
go (to) *ir*
  go farther *alejarse*
  go in (to) *adentrarse*
  go camping (to) *ir de camping*
  go shopping (to) *ir de compas*
  go out (to) *salir*
  go out (to) *rumbear*
  go up (to) *subir*
goal *el gol*
God *Dios*
gold *el oro*
good *bien, buen, bueno, -a, rico, -a*
  good afternoon *buenas tardes*
  good-bye *adiós*
  good evening *buenas noches*
  good guy *buen tipo*
  good looking *guapo, -a*
  good morning *buenas días*
  good night *buenas nochas*
  good style *estilazo*
grammar *la gramática*
grammar school *colegio, escuela primaria*
Grand Canyon *el Cañón del Colorado*
grandfather *el abuelo*
grandmother *abuela*
great *gran, magnífico; padrísimo (Mex.)*
greet (to) *saludar*
grill *la parrilla*
grind (to) *moler*
groom *el novio*
group *el grupo*
guest *el invitado*
guide *el / la guía*
guy *tipo, pibe (Arg.), tío (Sp.)*
gym *el gimnasio*

H

half *mitad, medio, -a*
halftime *intermedio*
hall *el vestíbulo*
hallway *el pasillo*
hand *la mano*
handicapped *incapacitado, -a*
hangover *resaca (coll. Sp.)*
happy *contento, -a*
harbor *el puerto*
hard *difícil, duro, -a*
hard–working *trabajador, -a*
hate (to) *odiar*
have (to) *tener; haber (helping V.)*
  have fun (to) *divertirse*
  have breakfast (to) *desayunar*
  have dinner (to) *cenar*
  have lunch (to) *almorzar*
  have to (to) *tener que*
he *él*
headboard *la cabecera*
health *la salud*
healthy *bueno, -a (estar), sano, -a (estar)*
hear (to) *oír*
heart *el corazón*
heat *el calor*
heater *la calefacción*
heat up (to) *calentar*
heavy *pesado*
hello *hola*
help (to) *ayudar*
helper *el / la ayudante*
her *su, la (obj. pr.),*
hers *suyo*
here *aquí, acá*
high *alto, -a*
hill *el cerro*
him *se, lo (obj. pr.)*
himself / herself *su*
hire (to) *contratar*
his *su, sus; suyo, -a, -os, -as*
hispanic *hispano, -a*
history *la historia*
honest *honesto, -a*
hope (to) *esperar*
horrible *horrible*
horrific *espantoso / a*
horror *el horror*
horse *el caballo*
hospital *el hospital*
hot *caliente*
hot pepper *el chile picante*
hotel *el hotel*
hour *la hora*
house *la casa*
how? *cómo*
how many? *cuántos, -as*
how much? *cuánto, -a*
huge *enorme*
humidity *la humedad*

hunger *el hambre*
hurricane *el huracán*
hurry *prisa*
hurry up (to) *apurarse; darse prisa*
hurt (to) *doler; lastimar*
husband *el esposo*

I

I *yo*
  I see *ya veo*
ice cream *el helado*
ice cream shop *la heladería*
idea *la idea, la ocurrencia (coll.)*
idealist *idealista*
identification *la identificación*
idol *el ídolo*
if *si*
ignorance *la ignorancia*
ignorant *ignorante, bruto (Col.)*
ill *enfermo, -a*
ill person *el / la enfermo, -a*
illustrate (to) *ilustrar*
imagination *la imaginación*
imagine (to) *imaginar*
immediate *inmediato, -a*
immediately *inmediatamente*
importance *la importancia*
important *importante*
important to (to be) *importar*
impossible *imposible*
impressed *impresionado, -a*
impressing *impresionante*
in *en*
in advance *por anticipado*
in case *acaso*
in exchange *en cambio*
include (to) *incluir*
incredible *increíble*
independent *independiente*
indicate *indicar*
indiscreet *indiscreto, -a*
individual *individual*
inform (to) *informar, enterarse*
information *la información*
ingredient *el ingrediente*
inn *la posada, la pensión*
insane *enloquecido, -a*
inside *dentro*
intelligent *inteligente*
interest *el interés*
interest (to) *interesar*
interested *interesado, -a*
interesting *interesante*
interior *el interior*
Internet *el internet*
Interrupt *interrumpir*
interview *la entrevista*
introduce (to) *presentar (socially); introducir (physically)*
investigate (to) *investigar*
investigation *la investigación*

invitation *la invitación*
invite (to) *invitar*
invoice *la factura*
invoice (to) *facturar*
irregular *irregular*
issue *el asunto, la cuestión*
issue (to) *emitir*
isthmus *el istmo*
it *la, lo*
Italian *italiano, -a*
it's true *es cierto*

J

jacket *la chaqueta, el saco (Arg.)*
January *enero*
Japan *Japón*
Japanese *japonés, -a*
jealous *celoso, -a*
jealousy *los celos*
jerk *imbécil, pelotudo, -a (Arg.)*
join *unir*
joke *la broma*
journalist *el / la periodista*
journalism *el periodismo*
judo *el judo*
June *junio*
jump (to) *saltar*
July *julio*
jungle *la selva*
just *recién; justo, -a*
just arrived *recién llegado, -a*
just finished . . . *acabar de (+ inf.)*

K

kangaroo *el canguro*
keep (to) *guardar; mantener*
kid *el chamaquito (Mex.)*
kill (to) *matar*
kilometer *el kilómetro*
king *el rey*
kings *los reyes*
kitchen *la cocina*
kiss (to) *besar*
know (to) *saber; conocer*
Korea *Corea*

L

lack *falta*
lack (to) *faltar*
lady *la señora*
lake *el lago*
lamb *el cordero*
land (to) *aterrizar*
landscape *el paisaje*
language *el idioma, el lenguaje*
laptop *portátil*
last (to) *durar*
last name *apellido*
last night *anoche*

last time *última vez*
late *tarde*
lately *últimamente*
later *después, luego, más tarde*
lateral *laterales*
Latin *latino, -a*
Latin American *Latinoamérica*
Lawyer *el / la abogado, -a*
Leaf *la hoja*
learn (to) *aprender*
leave (to) *dejar, partir, salir*
left (to be) *quedar*
legacy *el legado*
lemon *el limón*
lemonade *la limonada*
lend (to) *prestar*
less *menos*
lesson *la lección*
let *dejar*
let's see *a ver . . .*
letter *la carta*
life *la vida*
light *la luz*
lightning *el relámpago*
like *como*
like (to) *gustar*
limited *limitado, -a*
line *la fila, la línea, la cola (Sp.)*
liquid *líquido, -a*
list *la lista*
listen (to) *escuchar, oir*
listen *oye (command form)*
little *poco*
live (to) *vivir*
living room *la sala, el cuarto de estar*
load (to) *cargar*
loading *el embarque*
lodge (to) *alojarse*
logic *lógico, -a*
long *largo, -a*
look (to) *mirar*
  look for (to) *buscar*
  look like (to) *parecer*
lose (to) *perder*
lost *perdido*
lottery *la lotería*
love *el amor*
love (to) *amar, querer; encantar; fascinar*
lovely *chulo, -a (Mex.) (Sp.)*
loved *querido, -a*
luck *la suerte*
luggage *el equipaje*
lunch *el almuerzo*
luxury *el lujo*

M

magazine *la revista*
magnificent *magnífico, -a*
main *principal*
maintain (to) *mantener*

majority la mayoría
make up (to apply) maquillar
man el hombre
many mucho, -a
March marzo
Marines los marines
market el mercado, el zócalo
marriage el matrimonio
married casado, -a
marvelous maravilloso, -a
mathematics las matemáticas
maximum máximo
May mayo
maybe quizá
me me, mí
meal la comida
mean (to) significar, querer decir
meat la carne
meat market la carnicería
meet (to) reunirse; conocer (for
    the first time); quedar (Sp.)
member el miembro
memory la memoria
menu el menú, la carta
message el mensaje
meter el metro
Mexican mexicano, -a
middle medio (en)
mile la milla
milk la leche
millionaire millonario, -a
mine mío, -a, -os, -as
minimum mínimo, -a
minus menos
miracle el milagro
miraculous milagroso, -a
miss (to) extrañar, echar de
    menos
mix (to) mezclar
model el / la modelo
modern moderno, -a
moment el momento
mommy mamá, mami
Monday el lunes
money dinero, plata (slng.) (Arg.)
month el mes
monument el monumento
moon la luna
more más
morning la mañana
mother la madre
motor el motor
motorcycle la motocicleta, la moto
mountain la montaña
movie la película
Mr. señor, Don
Mrs. señora, Doña
much mucho, -a, -os, -as
mural el mural
museum el museo
music la música
must deber
musical musical

my mi, mis
myself me, yo mismo, -a
mysterious misterioso, -a
mystery el misterio

N

name el nombre
narrator el narrador, -a
narrow estrechito
nation la nación
national nacional
near cerca (de)
necessary necesario, -a
need (to) necesitar
negative negativo, -a
neighborhood la colonia (in
    Mexico City)
neither tampoco; ni
nervous nervioso, -a
net la red
never nunca
new nuevo, -a
news las noticias
    news article el reportaje
newspaper el periódico
newsreel el noticiero
next próximo, -a, siguiente
    next to al lado
nice lindo, -a; bonito, -a; sim-
    pático, -a; agradable
nickname el alias
night la noche
nine nueve
nineteen diecinueve
no no
no one nadie
no more nomás (Mex.) (Col.)
noise el ruido, el bembé (Carib.)
none nadie, nigún, ninguno, -a
normal normal
north el norte
nosy curioso, -a
not at all ¡qué va!
not even ni siquiera
nothing nada
    nothing else nada más
novel la novela
November noviembre
now ahora
nowadays hoy en día
nowhere ningún lado
number el número
numerous numeroso, -a

O

obtain (to) obtener
occasion la ocasión
occupied ocupado, -a,
    entretenido (with estar)
occur (to) ocurrir
ocean el océano

October octubre
of de
of course claro, por supuesto,
    desde luego
offend (to) ofender
offer (to) ofrecer
office oficina
officer el oficial
okay vale (Sp.); de acuerdo
old viejo, -a
older mayor
Olympics las olimpiadas
on de, sobre
on the other hand en cambio
once una vez
one un, uno, -a
one hundred cien
one time una vez
onion la cebolla
only solamente, sólo, único, -a
open abierto, -a
open (to) abrir
opening la inauguración
opera la ópera
opportunity la oportunidad
or o
orange anaranjado (adj.);
    naranja (n.)
origin el origen
organize (to) organizar
organized ordenado, -a
oven el horno
over sobre
ouch! ¡Ay!
our nuestro, -a
ourselves nos
outside fuera
outdoors el aire libre
owe (to) deber
own propio, -a
owner el dueño, -a

P

page la página
pain dolor, la lata
painter el pintor, -a
pal cuate (Mex.), tío, -a (Sp.),
    chavo (Mex.)
palace el palacio
pale pálido, -a
panic el pánico
pants el pantalón
parents los padres; los viejos (Arg.)
parking lot el estacionamiento,
    parking (Sp.)
part la parte
partially parcialmente
participant el / la participante
participate (to) participar
particular particular
party la fiesta; el partido (political), el reventón (Mex.)

party (to) *rumbear* (Col.)
pass *el pase*
passage *el pasaje*
pass (to) *adelantar, pasar*
pass out (to) *desmayarse*
passenger *el pasajero, -a*
passion *la pasión*
passport *el pasaporte*
past *el pasado, -a, -os, -as*
pastry *el bollo*
patriot *patriota*
patrol (to) *patrullar*
pay (to) *pagar*
pay attention (to) *hacer caso*
payment *el pago*
pencil *el lápiz*
people *la gente*
pepper *la pimienta*
perfect *perfecto, -a*
perfectly *perfectamente*
performance *la actuación*
period *el punto*
permanently *definitivamente*
person *la persona*
personal *personal*
personal computer *el pc*
peso *el peso*
petition *la petición*
phone *el teléfono*
phone (to) *telefonear*
photo *la foto*
photographer *el fotógrafo, -a*
physically *físicamente*
pick up (to) *recoger, retirar*
picture *el cuadro, la foto*
pillar *el pilar*
pilot *el / la piloto*
pink *rosado, -a*
place *el lugar, el sitio*
plan *el plan*
plane *el avión*
plant *la planta*
plate *el plato*
platform *la plataforma, la tribuna*
play theatrical *obra de teatro*
play (to) *jugar* (a sport, a game); *tocar* (an instrument)
playful *juguetón, -a*
please *por favor*
pleased *encantado, -a*
   pleased to meet you *mucho gusto*
plus *incluso, además*
poetry *la poesía*
point *el punto*
police *la policía*
   police station *la comisaría*
political party *el partido*
pollution *la contaminación*
poor *pobre*
Pope *el Papa*
popular *popular*

pork *el cerdo*
position *la posición*
possible *posible*
pottery *la cerámica*
power *el poder*
practice (to) *practicar*
pray (to) *rezar*
precisely *precisamente*
prefer (to) *preferir*
pregnant *embarazada*
preliminary *preliminar*
preparation *la preparación*
prepare (to) *preparar*
prepared *preparado, -a*
prescription *la receta*
president *el presidente, -a*
press *la prensa*
press conference *la rueda de prensa*
preterit *el pretérito*
pretty *bello, -a; bonito, -a; lindo, -a*
previous *previo, -a*
price *el precio*
princess *la princesa*
printer *la impresora*
probable *probable*
probably *probablemente*
problem *el problema*
problematic *problemático*
produce (to) *producir*
professional *profesional*
professor *profesor, el profe* (Coll.)
program *el programa*
proper *propio, -a; correcto, -a; educado, -a*
prosecution *el procesamiento*
protaganist *protaganista*
protest (to) *protestar*
prove (to) *probar*
proud *orgulloso, -a*
psychoanalist *el / la sicoanalista*
public *el público*
pure *puro, -a*
Puerto Rican *portorriqueño, -a*
purchase *la compra*
put (to) *poner*
put on (to) *ponerse*
put on make up (to) *maquillar*

Q

quantity *la cantidad*
question *la pregunta, la cuestión*
quickly *rápidamente*

R

rain *la lluvia*
rain (to) *llover*
raining *lloviendo*

read (to) *leer*
real *cierto, -a; real*
reason *la razón*
receipt *el recibo*
recepcionist *el / la recepcionista*
recipe *la receta*
recital *el recital*
recommendation *la recomendación*
recently *recientemente*
record *el disco*
   record company *la compañía discográfica*
recycle (to) *reciclar*
red *rojo, -a*
referee *el árbitro, el referí* (Arg.)
reform (to) *reformar*
refresh (to) *refrescar*
region *la región*
regular *regular*
religious *religioso, -a*
remain (to) *quedar*
remember (to) *recordar*
rent (to) *alquilar*
rent *el alquiler*
repair (to) *reparar*
repeat (to) *repetir*
report *el informe, el reportaje, el reporte*
reporter *el reportero, -a; el / la periodista*
research *la investigación*
research (to) *investigar*
reserve (to) *reservar*
reservation *la reservación*
respectfully *atentamente*
responsible *responsable*
rest (to) *descansar*
restaurant *el restaurante*
result *el resultado*
retire (to) *retirar*
retirement *la jubilación*
return (to) *volver, devolver, regresar*
return it *regresarlo*
revolution *la revolución*
rhythm *el ritmo*
rich *rico, -a*
right *correcto, -a*
right (to be) *tener razón*
   right now *ahora mismo*
ring (to) *repicar*
river *el río*
road *la carretera*
roast *el asado*
roasted *asado, -a*
rock and roll singer *roquero, -a*
roll *el rollo*
romantic *romántico, -a*
room *el cuarto, la habitación, la pieza* (Col.) (Arg.)
rope *la cuerda*
round *la vuelta*

rum *el ron*
run (to) *correr*
Russia *Rusia*
Russian *ruso, -a*

S

sack *el saco*
sad *triste*
safe *seguro, -a*
sail (to) *navegar*
salad *la ensalada*
sale *la venta; la rebaja (Sp.)*
salesperson *el dependiente, -a*
salt *la sal*
same *igual*
sandwich *el bocadillo (Sp.)*
Saturday *el sábado*
sauce *la salsa*
saucer *el platillo*
sausage *el chorizo, la salchicha*
save (to) *ahorrar (money, energy); salvar*
say (to) *decir*
scandal *el escándalo*
scare (to) *asustar*
schedule *el horario*
school *la escuela, el colegio*
score (to) *marcar*
score a basket (to) *encestar*
scream *el grito*
scream (to) *chillar, gritar*
screen *la pantalla*
scuba dive (to) *bucear*
sculptor *el escultor, -a*
sculpture *la escultura*
sea *el mar*
search *buscar*
search engine *el buscador*
season *la estación, la temporada*
seat *el asiento, la localidad*
second *segundo, -a*
secondary school *escuela secundaria*
secret *el secreto*
section *la sección*
sector *el sector*
see (to) *ver*
see you later *hasta luego*
see you soon *hasta pronto*
seem (to) *parecer*
select (to) *seleccionar*
selection *la selección*
sell (to) *vender*
send (to) *enviar*
sensibility *sensatez*
separado *separado, -a*
September *septiembre*
series *la serie*
serious *serio, -a*
serve (to) *servir*
service *el servicio*
seven *siete*

seventeen *diecisiete*
seventh *séptimo, -a*
several *varios, -as*
several times *varias veces*
she *ella*
sheet *la hoja*
shirt *la camisa*
shoe *el zapato*
shoe store *la zapatería*
shopping *compras*
short *bajo, -a*
short story *el cuento*
shot *el tiro*
show *el espectáculo*
show (to) *indicar; enseñar*
shy *tímido*
signature *la firma*
silence *el silencio*
silent (to be) *callar*
silver *la plata*
simple *sencillo, -a; simple*
since *desde*
sing (to) *cantar*
singer *el / la cantante*
singing *el canto*
single *soltero, -a*
sister *la hermana*
sit down (to) *sentarse*
six *seis*
sixteen *dieciséis*
sixth *sexto, -a*
sixty *sesenta*
skewer *la brocheta, el pinchito*
ski (to) *esquiar*
skinny *delgado, -a, flaco, -a (coll.)*
skirt *la falda*
sky *el cielo*
sleep (to) *dormir*
slowly *pasito (Col.)*
small *pequeño, -a*
smoke (to) *fumar*
smoker *fumador, -a*
snack *la merienda*
snow *nieve*
snow (to) *nevar*
so *o sea, pues, tan, así*
so many *tantos, -as*
so much *tanto, -a*
soaked *empapado, -a*
soap opera *la telenovela*
soccer *fútbol*
society *la sociedad*
soda *el refresco*
sofa *el sofá*
some *algún, alguno, -a, los, las*
some time *alguna vez*
somebody *alguien, alguno, -a*
someone *alguien, alguno, -a*
something *algo*
son *el hijo*
song *la canción*
soon *pronto*

sorry *perdón, lo siento (I'm sorry)*
sound (to) *sonar*
soup *la sopa*
south *el sur*
Spain *España*
Spaniard *español, -a*
Spanish *español, -a*
spare part *el recambio*
special *especial*
specially *especialmente*
specialty *la especialidad*
specific *específico, -a*
spend (to) *gastar (money); pasar (time)*
sport *el deporte*
sports fan *el / la hincha*
sporty *deportivo*
spouse *el esposo, -a*
spring *la primavera*
square *la plaza; el cuadrado*
stadium *el estadio*
star *la estrella*
start (to) *empezar, comenzar*
state *el estado*
station *la estación*
statue *la estatua*
stay (to) *quedarse, permanecer; (as guest) alojarse*
step *el paso*
still *aún, todavía*
stomach *el estómago*
stop (to) *parar*
stop by (to) *pasar por*
store *la tienda*
storm *la tormenta*
story *la historia, la narración*
straight *directo, -a*
strange *extraño, -a, raro, -a*
stranger *desconocido, -a, forastero, -a*
street *la calle*
strength *la fuerza*
stressed *estresado, -a*
stroll (to) *pasear*
strong *fuerte*
student *el / la estudiante*
studies *los estudios*
studio *el estudio*
study *el estudio*
study (to) *estudiar*
stuffed *relleno, -a; lleno, -a*
stupid *estúpido, -a; necio, -a, pelotudo (Arg.)*
sublime *sublime*
subway *el metro, el subte (Arg.)*
such *tal*
success *el éxito*
suddenly *de repente*
suffer (to) *sufrir*
sugar *el azúcar*
suggestion *la sugerencia*
suit *el traje de chaqueta*
suitor *pretendiente*

suitcase *la maleta*
suite *la suite*
summer *el verano*
sun *el sol*
sunbathe (to) *tomar el sol*
Sunday *el domingo*
sunny *soleado, -a*
superior *superior*
supermarket *el supermercado*
superstitious *supersticioso, -a*
sure *seguro, -a*
surprise *la sorpresa*
surprise (to) *sorprender*
surrounded *rodeado, -a*
surroundings *los alrededores*
sweater *el saco* (Col.), *el suéter*
sweetheart *cielito*
swim (to) *nadar, bañarse*

T

T–shirt *la camiseta, la playera*
table *la mesa*
take (to) *llevar, tomar*
  take a bath (to) *bañarse*
  take advantage (of) *aprovechar*
  take a picture (to) *fotografiar*
  take a shower (to) *ducharse*
  take a walk (to) *pasear, dar un paseo*
  take away (to) *quitar*
  take off (to) *despegar* (for an airplane)
  take out (to) *sacar*
  take part (to) *participar*
talk (to) *hablar, platicar* (Mex.)
tall *alto, -a*
tariff *la tarifa*
taste *el sabor, el gusto*
taste (to) *degustar, probar*
taxi *taxi*
taxi driver *el / la taxista*
teach (to) *enseñar*
teacher *el maestro, -a; el profesor, -a*
team *el equipo*
technician *el técnico, -a*
technological *tecnológico, -a*
technology *tecnología*
television *la televisión, la tele* (coll.)
tell (to) *contar*
ten *diez*
tenderness *la ternura*
tennis *tenis*
tenths *decenas*
terrace *la terraza*
than *que*
thank God *gracias a Dios, menos mal*
thank you *gracias*
that *ese, -a, eso; que* (rel.)
that good *así de bien*

that way *así*
that's it *así es*
the *el* (m.), *la* (f.), *los* (m. pl.), *las* (f. pl.)
the best *lo (la, el) mejor*
the most *máximo*
theatre *el teatro*
them *los, las* (obj. pr.'s.); *ellos, ellas* (prep. pr.'s)
theme *el tema*
then *entonces*
there *ahí, allí, allá*
there is / there are *hay*
these *estos, estas*
they *ellos, ellas*
thin *delgado*
thing *la cosa*
think (to) *pensar, creer*
third *tercero, -a*
thirst *la sed*
thirteen *trece*
thirty *treinta*
this *este, esta, esto*
thorn *la espina*
thousand *mil*
thousands *miles*
three *tres*
three hundred *trescientos, -as*
through *por, a través*
throw (to) *tirar, lanzar*
thunder *el trueno*
Thursday *el jueves*
ticket *billete, entrada, boleto* (Mex.), *pasaje* (Sp.), *el talón*
  ticket window *ventanilla de venta*
tie (to) *empatar; atar*
tied up *liado, -a* (Sp.)
tight *estrechito, -a*
time *el tiempo, la vez*
times *veces*
timid *tímido, -a*
tire (to) *cansar*
tired *cansado, -a*
tiredness *el cansancio*
to *a; hasta*
to us *nos; a nosotros*
to you *te; a ti; a ustedes*
toast *la tostada*
today *hoy*
together *juntos, -as*
toilet *el aseo*
tomato *el tomate*
tomorrow *mañana*
too much *demasiado*
total *el total*
totally *totalmente*
touch (to) *tocar*
tour *la gira*
tourist *el / la turista*
tourism *el turismo*
touristic *turístico, -a*
toward *hacia*

tower *la torre*
town *el pueblo*
toy *el juguete*
traffic *el tránsito, el tráfico*
translate (to) *traducir*
translator *el traductor, -a*
travel (to) *viajar*
tree *el árbol*
trip *el viaje*
triple *triple*
try (to) *intentar*
true *cierto*
truth *la verdad*
truthful *verdadero, -a*
try (to) *probar, intentar, tratar de* (+ inf.)
Tuesday *el martes*
twelve *doce*
twenty *veinte*
twenty thousand *veinte mil*
two *dos*
type *tipo, el género*
typical *típico, -a*

U

ugly *feo, -a*
uncle *el tío*
under *abajo, debajo de*
understand (to) *comprender, entender, enterarse* (coll. Sp.)
understanding *comprensivo, -a*
unfortunately *por desgracia*
unfriendly *antipático*
unique *único, -a*
unite (to) *unir*
United States *Estados Unidos*
unity *la unidad*
university *la universidad*
unknown *desconocido, -a, la incógnita*
until *hasta*
up *arriba*
us *nos, nosotros, -as*
use (to) *usar, utilizar*
used to be *era, solía*
useful *práctico, -a, útil*
usually *normalmente, usualmente*

V

vacation *las vacaciones*
valid *válido, -a*
valley *el valle*
vegetarian *vegetariano, -a*
verb *el verbo*
very *muy, réquete*
very good *buenísimo, réquete-bueno*
video *el vídeo*
village *el pueblo*
visit (to) *visitar*
vocabulary *el vocabulario*

voice *la voz*
volcano *el volcán*

W

wait (to) *esperar*
waiter *el mesero, -a; camarero, -a*
  (Sp.), *mozo* (Mex.)
waiting room *la sala de espera*
wake up (to) *despertarse,*
  amanecer
walk (to) *andar, caminar, pasear*
want (to) *querer, desear*
want to say (to) *querer decir*
was *era*
water *el agua*
way *el camino*
we *nosotros, -as*
weather *el tiempo*
web *la red* (Internet)
Wednesday *el miércoles*
week *la semana*
welcome *bienvenido, -a*
what? *qué; cuál*
what's up? *¿Qué pasa?*
when? *cuándo*
where? *dónde*
which? *cuál*

which *que*
while *mientras* (adv.), *rato* (n.)
white *blanco, -a*
who? *quién, que*
whom *que*
why? *por qué?*
wide *ancho, -a*
widower *viudo*
win (to) *ganar*
wind *el viento*
wine *el vino,* (red wine) *tinto*
winter *el invierno*
with *con*
with me *conmigo*
with pleasure *con mucho gusto*
with you *contigo; con usted*
withdraw (to) *retirar*
without *sin*
woman *la mujer*
wonderful *estupendo*
word *la palabra*
work *el trabajo, el laburo* (Arg.)
work (to) *trabajar; funcionar*
work (of art) *la obra*
workshop *el taller*
world *el mundo*
World Cup *la Copa del Mundo*
worldwide *mundial*

worried *preocupado, -a*
worried (to be) *preocuparse*
worse *peor*
wow! *caramba* (coll.)
write (to) *escribir*
wrong (to be) *equivocarse*
wrong *mal*

Y

yard *el jardín*
year *el año*
yellow *amarillo*
yes *sí*
yesterday *ayer*
yet *todavía, ya; aún*
you *tú, vosotros, usted, ustedes, vos*
  (Arg.); *ti* (prep. pr.)
young *joven*
younger *menor*
you're welcome *de nada*
your *tuyo, suyo* (fml.)
yours *suyo* (fml.)
youth *la juventud*

Z

zone *la zona*

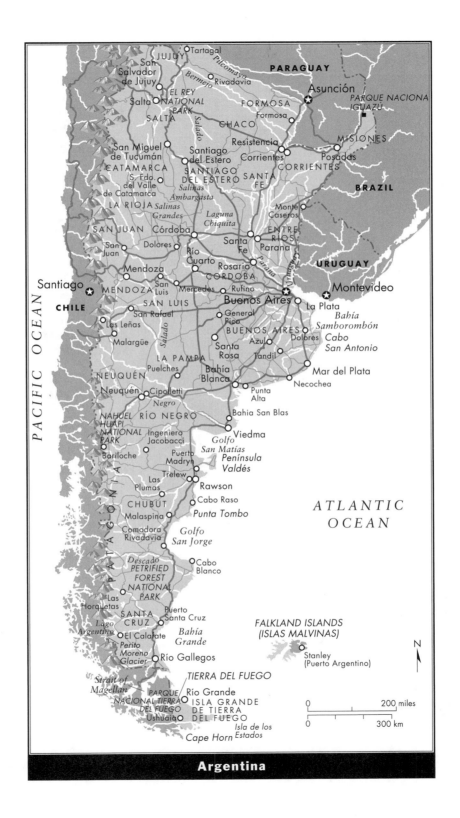

Argentina

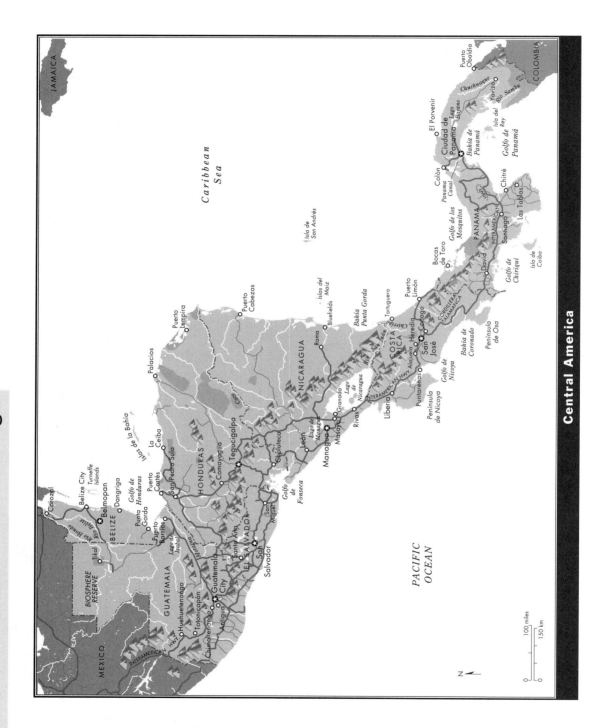

Central America

Colombia

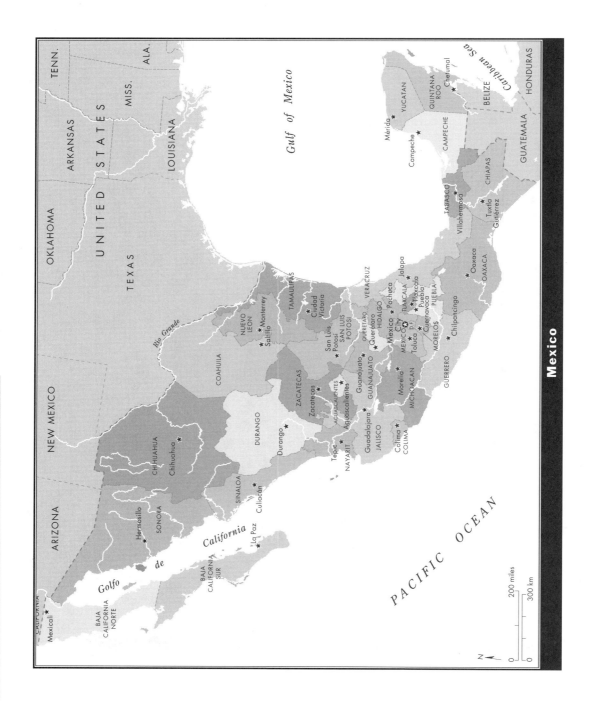

Mexico

Caribbean Sea

Barranquilla
Cartagena
La Guaira
Caracas
TRINIDAD & TOBAGO
ATLANTIC OCEAN

Maracaibo
Mérida
Orinoco R.
VENEZUELA
GUYANA
Georgetown
Paramaribo

Medellín
Bogotá
COLOMBIA
Cali
SURINAM
Cayenne
FRENCH GUIANA
Guiana Highlands

EQUATOR
Quito
ECUADOR
Macapá
EQUATOR

Guayaquil
Cuenca
Amazon R.
Belém
Fortaleza

Iquitos
Manáus
Tapajós R.
Xingu R.
Tocantins R.

ANDES
Madeira R.
BRAZIL
São Francisco R.
Recife

PERU
Lima
Cuzco
Lake Titicaca
Puno
BOLIVIA
La Paz
Sucre
Potosí
BRAZILIAN HIGHLANDS
Brasília
Salvador
Porto Seguro

Arequipa
Iquique
PARAGUAY
EL CHACO
Asunción
Iguazú Falls
Belo Horizonte
Rio de Janeiro
São Paulo

San Félix (Chile)
PACIFIC OCEAN
CHILE
Paraná R.
Uruguay R.

Viña del Mar
Valparaíso
Santiago
Rosario
URUGUAY
Punta del Este
Montevideo

Islas de Juan Fernandez (Chile)
Buenos Aires
ARGENTINA
Rio de la Plata
Mar del Plata

N
1000 miles
1500 km

PATAGONIA
ANDES

Stanley
Falkland Islands
(UK; Las Malvinas)
South Georgia (UK)

Punta Arenas
Tierra del Fuego
Cape Horn

South America

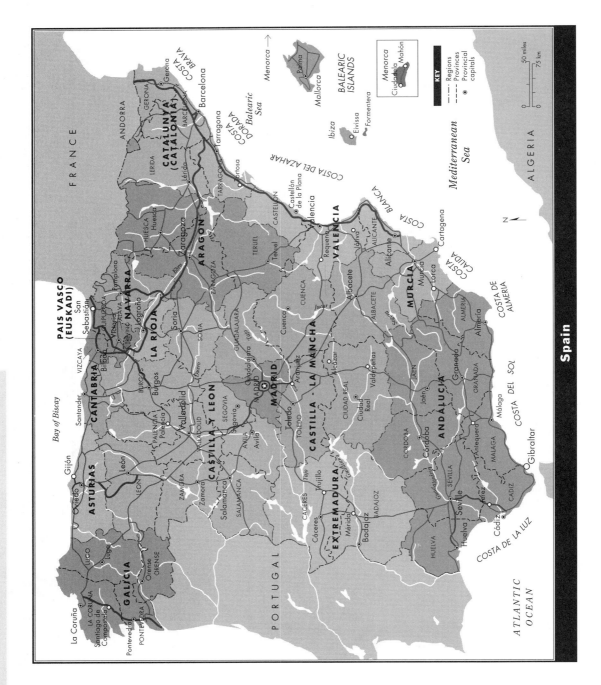

Spain

FRANCE

ANDORRA

PORTUGAL

ALGERIA

ATLANTIC OCEAN

Mediterranean Sea

Bay of Biscay

Balearic Sea

BALEARIC ISLANDS

Menorca

Mallorca

Ibiza

Eivissa

Formentera

GALICIA
La Coruña
LA CORUÑA
Santiago de Compostela
Pontevedra
PONTEVEDRA
Orense
ORENSE
Lugo
LUGO

ASTURIAS
Gijón
Oviedo

CANTABRIA
Santander

PAIS VASCO (EUSKADI)
San Sebastián
VIZCAYA
Bilbao
GUIPUZCOA
Vitoria
ALAVA

NAVARRA
Pamplona

LA RIOJA
Logroño

CASTILLA Y LEON
León
LEÓN
ZAMORA
Zamora
Salamanca
SALAMANCA
Valladolid
VALLADOLID
PALENCIA
Palencia
BURGOS
Burgos
SEGOVIA
Segovia
ÁVILA
Ávila
SORIA
Soria

ARAGON
Huesca
HUESCA
Zaragoza
ZARAGOZA
TERUEL
Teruel

CATALUNYA (CATALONIA)
LERIDA
Lérida
GERONA
Gerona
Barcelona
BARCELONA
Tarragona
TARRAGONA
Tortosa

COSTA BRAVA
COSTA DORADA
COSTA DEL AZAHAR

CASTELLON
Castellón de la Plana

VALENCIA
Valencia
Requena
ALICANTE
Alicante

COSTA BLANCA

MADRID

GUADALAJARA
Guadalajara

CASTILLA - LA MANCHA
Aranjuez
Toledo
TOLEDO
CUENCA
Cuenca
ALBACETE
Albacete
CIUDAD REAL
Ciudad Real
Valdepeñas
Alcázar

EXTREMADURA
CÁCERES
Cáceres
Trujillo
Mérida
Badajoz
BADAJOZ

MURCIA
Murcia
Lorca
Cartagena

COSTA CALIDA
COSTA DE ALMERÍA

ANDALUCÍA
HUELVA
Huelva
SEVILLA
Seville
CÁDIZ
Cádiz
CÓRDOBA
Córdoba
JAÉN
Jaén
GRANADA
Granada
Antequera
MÁLAGA
Málaga
ALMERÍA
Almería
Gibraltar

COSTA DE LA LUZ
COSTA DEL SOL

Menorca
Ciudadela
Mahón

KEY
— — — Regions
- - - - Provinces
● Provincial capitals

50 miles
75 km

INDEX